Dogma in
Medieval Jewish Thought

THE LITTMAN LIBRARY OF
JEWISH CIVILIZATION

FOUNDER

L. T. S. Littman

EDITORS

David Goldstein
Louis Jacobs
Vivian D. Lipman

For the love of God
and in memory of

JOSEPH AARON LITTMAN

'Get wisdom, get understanding:
Forsake her not and she shall preserve thee.'

DOGMA IN MEDIEVAL JEWISH THOUGHT

From Maimonides to Abravanel

MENACHEM KELLNER

Published for
THE LITTMAN LIBRARY
by
OXFORD UNIVERSITY PRESS
1986

Oxford University Press, Walton Street, Oxford OX2 6DP

Oxford New York Toronto
Delhi Bombay Calcutta Madras Karachi
Petaling Jaya Singapore Hong Kong Tokyo
Nairobi Dar es Salaam Cape Town
Melbourne Auckland

and associated companies in
Beirut Berlin Ibadan Nicosia

Oxford is a trade mark of Oxford University Press

Published in the United States
by Oxford University Press, New York

© Menachem Kellner 1986

British Library Cataloguing in Publication Data
Kellner, Menachem Marc
Dogma in medieval Jewish thought: from Maimonides
to Abravanel.—(The Littman library of Jewish
civilization)
1. Judaism—Doctrines—History
I. Title II. Series
296.3'09'02   BM601
ISBN 0-19-710044-9

Library of Congress Cataloging in Publication Data
Kellner, Menachem Marc, 1946–
Dogma in medieval Jewish thought.
(The Littman library of Jewish civilization)
Bibliography: p.
Includes index.
1. Judaism—Doctrines—History. 2. Philosophy,
Jewish-History. 3. Philosophy, Medieval-History.
4. Thirteen articles of faith (Judaism) 5. Maimonides,
Moses, 1135-1204—Teachings. I. Title. II. Series.
BM603.K44 1986   296.3'09'02   85-31074
ISBN 0-19-710044-9

Printed in Great Britain by
The Alden Press, Oxford

To the memory of
my brother
Harold N. Kellner
1936–1983

2 Samuel 1: 26

Preface

This work is a study of dogma in medieval Jewish thought. It is the first study of its kind, concentrating on thinkers largely ignored by David Neumark in his *Toledot ha-Ikkarim be-Yisrael* and treated only briefly by Louis Jacobs in his magisterial *Principles of the Jewish Faith*. That the subject has received such little modern critical attention is surprising in that many of the major figures of late medieval Jewish thought devoted considerable reflection to the issue. It is my hope to throw fresh light on this matter.

A good portion of this book is devoted to Maimonides. I wish to point out here that in my approach to Maimonides I make two important assumptions: (*a*) Maimonides saw no radical discontinuity between his philosophic and halakhic commitments (that is to say, I find Isadore Twersky and David Hartman, *et al.*, closer to the mark in their understanding of Maimonides than Leo Strauss and Shlomo Pines, *et al.*); and (*b*) Maimonides' writings, despite their having been written over a span of more than half a century, are marked by essential continuity of intention and outlook. I therefore allow myself a measure of freedom in building arguments based on texts written in different periods of Maimonides' life.

My general approach to the subject at hand may be characterized as that of the history of ideas (as brilliantly realized in Lovejoy's *Great Chain of Being*) as opposed to intellectual history. I have set as my basic goal the examination of a set of related texts in the hope that I will be able to clarify and follow the development of certain central ideas found in these texts. This may be contrasted with an approach which focuses on the connections between ideas and societies and which produces a history of intellectuals as opposed to a history of ideas.

I have included in this volume translations of texts not otherwise available in English. These translations are my own and, where appropriate, are based upon texts which I have critically edited. I have also included the text of Maimonides' thirteen principles from *Perek Ḥelek* (in the translation of David R. Blumenthal). Even though this text is available in several English translations, its central place in the discussion justifies the space given over to it here. Note should be taken of the fact that I use the word 'dogmatic' in two senses in this book: in its general sense, meaning 'pertaining to creed or dogma', and in a specific sense referring to a particular understanding of the term 'dogma'. In each case, the sense I have in mind is clear from the context.

My work on this study has been facilitated by the help of many kind friends and colleagues who have given generously of their time and expertise. I would particularly like to thank Harvey Chisick, Seymour Feldman, Zev Harvey, Raphael Jospe, Barry Kogan, Daniel Lasker, Abraham Nuriel, Chava Rembrand, Norbert Samuelson, Steven Schwarzschild, Rafi Talmon, and Chaim Vidal. For their constant support and encouragement I wish also to thank Abe and Rose Shoulson, Avinoam and Rivka Kellner, and, beyond all others, my wife Jolene Kellner.

Research for this book was supported by a grant from the Israel Ministry of Immigrant Absorption and facilitated by the services of the Haifa University Research Authority. I express here my thanks to the Ministry and to the Secretary of the Haifa University Research Authority, Mr David Bukai.

Publication of this book was made possible by grants from the Faculty of Humanities of the University of Haifa, the Publications Committee of the University of Haifa, and the Louis and Minna Epstein Fund of the American Academy for Jewish Research. I here record my gratitude to them all.

Portions of this study have already appeared in print. I would like to thank the editors and publishers concerned for their kindness in granting me permission to reprint material from the following:

'Maimonides' "Thirteen Principles" and the Structure of the *Guide of the Perplexed*', *Journal of the History of Philosophy*, xx, no. 1 (Jan. 1982), pp. 76–84.

'Rabbi Shimon ben Ẓemaḥ Duran on the Principles of Judaism', *PAAJR*, xlviii (1981), pp. 231–65.

'Jewish Dogmatics After the Spanish Expulsion: Rabbis Isaac Abravanel and Joseph Yaʻbeṣ on Belief in Creation as an Article of Faith', *JQR*, lxxii (1982), pp. 178–87.

Isaac Abravanel, *Principles of Faith (Rosh Amanah)*, translated with introduction and notes by M. M. Kellner (East Brunswick, NJ, Associated University Presses for Littman Library of Jewish Civilization, 1982).

'What is Heresy?' *Studies in Jewish Philosophy*, iii (1983), pp. 55–70.

'Kefirah be-Shogeg be-Hagut Yehudit biymei ha-Benayim: ha-Rambam ve-Abravanel Mul Rashbaẓ ve-Raḥak?' *Meḥkarei Yerushalayim be-Maḥshevet Yisrael*, iii (1984), pp. 393–403.

I further record here my gratitude to David R. Blumenthal for his kindness in allowing me to quote from David R. Blumenthal, *The Commentary of R. Ḥoter ben Shelomoh to the Thirteen Principles of Maimonides* (Leiden, E. J. Brill, 1974).

Haifa   M. K.
September 1985

Acknowledgements

We gratefully acknowledge assistance in the
publication of this volume from:
The Faculty of Humanities of the University of Haifa,
The Publications Committee of the University of Haifa,
The Louis and Minna Epstein Fund of the American
Academy for Jewish Research.

Contents

Abbreviations   xiv

Introduction   1

1   Maimonides

     I. The Text of Maimonides' Thirteen Principles   10
     II. What is a 'Foundation of the Torah'?   17
     III. Maimonides' Statement of the Principles in the *Mishneh Torah*   21
     IV. Divisions into which the Principles Fall   24
     V. Why Maimonides Posited his Principles   34
     VI. The Thirteen Principles and the *Guide of the Perplexed*   49
     VII. Missing Principles   53
     VIII. Maimonides' Principles and Other Torah Beliefs   61
     IX. The Special Status of the Twelfth Principle (Messiah)   63
     X. Summary   65

2   From Maimonides to Duran

     I. Introduction   66
     II. Abba Mari   69
     III. Falaquera   74
     IV. David ben Samuel Kokhavi d'Estella   75
     V. David ben Yom Tov ibn Bilia   77
     VI. Shemariah ben Elijah ben Ya'akov ha-Ikriti of Negropont   79
     VII. Transition to the Fifteenth Century   80

3   Duran

     I. The Texts   83
     II. Duran's Principles   95
     III. Was Duran Decisively Influenced by Averroës?   103
     IV. Duran's Influence   105

4   Ḥasdai Crescas
    I.   Introduction   108
    II. The Texts   110
    III. Crescas's System of Principles   116
    IV. Crescas's Use of the Concept 'Principle of Faith'   125
    V.   Does the Torah Command Belief?   127
    VI. Crescas on Inadvertent Heresy   129
    VII. Crescas, Rabbenu Nissim, and Duran   137

5   Joseph Albo
    I.   Albo's System of Principles   140
    II. *Ikkarim*, *Shorashim*, and *Anafim*   146
    III. Judaism as a Science   149
    IV. Heresy   151
    V.   Duran, Crescas, and Albo   155

6   Shalom, Arama, and Yaveẓ
    I.   Abraham Shalom   157
    II. Isaac Arama   159
    III. Joseph Yaveẓ   161

7   Abraham Bibago
    I.   Bibago's System of Principles   165
    II. Bibago's Analysis of Maimonides' Principles   170
    III. Bibago, Maimonides, and Abravanel   175

8   Isaac Abravanel
    I.   Abravanel's Analysis of Maimonides   179
    II. Does Abravanel Truly Reject the Claim that Judaism has
         Principles of Faith?   184

9   Four Minor Figures
    I.   Muehlhausen   196
    II. Delmedigo   197
    III. David ben Judah Messer Leon   197
    IV. Mabit   198

10 Summary and Conclusions

    i. Statements of the Creed   200

    ii. Dogma, Heresy, and Schisms   207

    iii. Creation and Messiah   213

Appendix: Texts and Translations of Maimonides'
                Commentary on *Perek Ḥelek*   218

Notes   220

Bibliography   287

General Index   303

Index of Biblical Citations   309

Abbreviations

CCAR Yearbook	*Central Conference of American Rabbis Year-book*
HUCA	Hebrew Union College Annual
JNUL	Jewish National and University Library (Jerusalem)
JQR	Jewish Quarterly Review
MGWJ	*Monatsschrift für Geschichte und Wissenschaft des Judentums*
PAAJR	*Proceedings of the American Academy for Jewish Research*
REJ	*Revue des Études Juives*

Introduction

Attempts formally to expound the theology of rabbinic Judaism are found for the first time in the gaonic period. Philo had listed principles of biblical faith but his discussion does not fall within our purview here for two reasons: he did not operate within the context of rabbinic Judaism as it had developed to his day and he certainly made no direct contributions to its further development.[1]

Once Sa'adia Gaon had for the first time methodically expounded the beliefs of Judaism in the tenth century, systematic theology became a standard and widely accepted branch of Jewish intellectual endeavour.[2] It was not until the twelfth century, however, that we find the first comprehensive account of the dogmas of Judaism.[3] Maimonides (1135–1204) was the first non-Karaite Jewish author systematically, self-consciously, and explicitly to posit specific beliefs which all Jews *qua* Jews had to accept. In the two centuries following the publication of Maimonides' principles the question of the dogmas of Judaism received almost no attention. The fifteenth century saw intensive interest in the subject; with the close of that century, however, the subject disappeared almost entirely from the agenda of Jewish intellectuals, to resurface only in the late eighteenth and early nineteenth centuries.

This study will examine the dogmatic systems of Maimonides and of those post-Maimonidean medieval Jewish thinkers who wrote on the subject in a sustained and orderly fashion; it will compare and contrast those systems; it will demonstrate Maimonides' all-pervasive influence; it will argue that the plethora of competing systems reflects not conflicting views of the nature of Judaism, but a dispute concerning the nature of dogmas or principles of faith; it will seek to explain why the subject was dropped after Maimonides and only picked up again after two centuries had elapsed; finally, it will suggest that the whole project of creed formulation is basically alien to biblical-rabbinic Judaism.

Maimonides' innovation did not occur in a vacuum.[4] In this introduction I wish to describe briefly and generally the Muslim, Jewish, and Karaite background against which Maimonides elaborated his principles. But first it is necessary to explain, if only briefly, why systematic theology was not attempted by Jews until after the talmudic period.

Why are there no orderly attempts in the Talmud to expound the beliefs of Judaism? In a certain sense, the question is anachronistic. We raise the question, I think, more because Islam and Christianity are characterized by repeated attempts to expound their theologies systematically than because such an approach to theology is intrinsic to monotheistic faith. Talmudic Judaism was a faith which neither lent itself easily to the theological systematization nor needed such a theology. Let me explain the second point first.

Now, why might a religion need to expound its beliefs in an organized fashion? One reason might be that it held that adherence to those beliefs was a criterion for being accepted as an adherent of that religion or was a criterion for salvation however that religion understood the term.[5] Talmudic Judaism, however, did not define a Jew in terms of his beliefs: a Jew was a person born of a Jewish mother or a person converted to Judaism (which in effect meant that he was adopted by the Jewish people as one of its own). The laws of conversion, as enunciated in the Talmud, concern themselves with the observance of the commandments to the almost total exclusion of questions relating to the affirmation of beliefs.[6] Personal salvation, too, did not depend upon orthodoxy in the strict sense of the term (*orthos*=straight; *doxos*=thinking) but upon submission to the will of God as expressed in the commandments of the Torah. Thus, talmudic Judaism did not need systematic theology either to define what a Jew was or how a Jew earned a share in the world to come.

Another reason why a religion might be compelled to expound its beliefs in an orderly fashion would be to attract outsiders to the fold. In such a case it would have to put its house in order, so to speak, so as to make it comprehensible to others. Talmudic Judaism, however, was not a proselytizing faith and was thus spared the need to present itself in this way to facilitate the conversion of Gentiles.

If a religion felt itself to be attacked on a theological plane by a competing faith it might feel constrained to formulate its doctrines more systematically the better to repulse the attack. But what faiths challenged rabbinic Judaism? Paganism in various forms, Zoroastrianism, and Christianity. All three were conceived by the rabbis as polytheistic and so were hardly perceived as serious threats to Judaism on a theological plane. While individual Jews might be attracted to one or another of these faiths, it was not because they were perceived as presenting a more coherent religious picture of the universe than did the Judaism of the rabbis. These competing faiths might have challenged rabbinic Judaism, but it was not because they were more attractive theologically than was Judaism. That, at least, was surely the opinion of the rabbis of the Talmud.[7]

Why then, do we suddenly find systematic theology among the Jews of Babylonia in the tenth century? The answer to this question, it seems to me, is related to the rise of Islam and of Karaism.[8] Following the Muslim victories the Jews found themselves in a new situation. Suddenly they were confronted with an enthusiastically expansionist rival religion every bit as monotheistic as Judaism. Many Muslim theologians utilized the tools of Greek philosophy.[9] Judaism had to defend itself against this external threat. One aspect of that defence took the form of an attempt to show that Jewish beliefs were in no way inferior to those of other religions; i.e. the orderly exposition of Jewish beliefs.

At roughly the same time Judaism was sharply confronted from within by the Karaite heresy. The Karaites used Greek philosophical concepts in their arguments and forced the Rabbanites to do likewise.[10] Here, too, in order to defend itself, rabbinic Judaism was forced to define itself in conceptual terms. This was all the more so with the Karaites, who claimed to be Jews and whose practices did not diverge dramatically from those of contemporary Rabbanite Judaism. If practice did not sufficiently distinguish the Rabbanite from the Karaite then theology would have to.

We might even say that by the tenth century, confronted as it was without and within by rival faiths which it could not ignore, both of which chose to explain themselves in a theologically systematic fashion, rabbinic Judaism was literally forced to engage in the project of systematic theology. Sa'adia Gaon, the doughty opponent of Karaism and the first Jew methodically and rationally to expound the central beliefs of Judaism, was thus very much a product of his time and place.

The considerations adduced thus far, brief and impressionistic as they are, help to explain why we find no systematic theology in talmudic Judaism.[11] They are surely true enough so far as they go, but in an important sense they all share a certain secondary, external nature. This is so because not only did talmudic Judaism not need an organized theology for the various sorts of fundamen-

tally extrinsic, historical reasons presented above, but, more
importantly, it was a faith which by its very nature did not lend
itself to systematic theological exposition.

Judaism, for the rabbis of the Talmud, was not a series of
propositions which could be either affirmed or denied. Rabbinic
Judaism does not demand belief that certain propositions are true
or false; it does demand belief in (*emunah*) or trust in (*bitaḥon*) God.
The Talmud does not conceive of Judaism as a science affirming
propositions which could be true or false. Rabbinic faith is not a
matter of conviction, but of loyalty; not assent, but consent.[12]

We may express this in other terms. The Bible and Talmud
present God as primarily free, undetermined will and as the source
of moral imperatives. This God is mysterious and transcendent; He
can be encountered, but He cannot be described. A religion
conceived of in these terms has little place for theology at all. It
does, however, have place for faith, so long as that faith is defined
more in terms of dispositions and states of mind than in terms of
statements which can be proven.[13]

Speaking generally, in Greek thought the term 'belief' (*pistis*)
was ordinarily conceived more in propositional terms (i.e. that one
accepts or rejects certain propositions) than in terms of trust or
faith. This is, perhaps, a reflection of or related to the fact that in
Greek thought by and large God is conceived of as the source or
guarantor of order (cosmological order for the pre-Socratics, moral
order for Plato, and physical and metaphysical order for Aristotle).
Christianity from its inception and Islam from at least the time of
the Kalam onward both seem to define faith in Greek rather than in
biblical and rabbinic terms: that is, in terms of the specific
propositional content of faith.[14] Formal systems of dogma are a
logical outgrowth of such a conception of faith. In laying down his
principles Maimonides gave expression to the fact that by his day
Jews, too, had begun to understand their religion in propositional
terms.

The rabbis, who understood faith in terms of trust in God, i.e. in
terms of the way in which the believer related to God and not in the
way in which he thought about Him, had no need systematically to
present the specific beliefs of the Torah, since their main concern
was not the niceties of theological formulations but to see to it 'that
man does justice, loves mercy, and walks humbly with the Lord'.

A religion conceived of in these terms has no place for theological systematization, has no place even for theology (in the sense of 'providing a *logos* of the divine'[15]). It does, however, have plenty of room for faith, so long as the content of that faith is defined in terms of dispositions and states of mind rather than in terms of statements which can be proven.[16] Aristotelian philosophy certainly defined 'belief' in terms of 'belief *that*', as opposed to 'belief *in*'.[17] When Jewish thinkers began working in that context (for the reasons outlined above) it is not surprising that they began to define Judaism in similar terms.

A number of texts may be adduced by way of evidence to indicate that Jewish thinkers in the early Middle Ages did indeed begin to understand 'belief' in terms of 'belief that' as opposed to 'belief in'. Sa'adia Gaon sought to convert the *amānāt* of Judaism ('doctrines accepted as an act of religious faith') into *i'tiqādāt* (doctrines subject to 'an attitude of firm belief as the result of a process of speculation').[18] This latter term (ordinarily rendered into Hebrew as *emunah* and into English as 'belief') Sa'adia defines as follows:

> . . . it behooves us to explain what is meant by *i'tiqād*. We say that it is a notion that arises in the soul in regard to the actual character of anything that is apprehended. When the cream of investigation emerges, [and] is embraced and enfolded by the minds and, through them acquired and digested by the souls, then the person becomes convinced of the truth of the notions he has thus acquired. He then deposits it in his soul for a future occasion or future occasions . . .[19]

The subject of *i'tiqādāt* then, are propositions which are either true or false. Judaism for Sa'adia, it must be emphasized, is a matter of both *amānāt* and *i'tiqādāt*, specific discrete propositions.

Maimonides presents a similar definition for the term: 'Know, thou who studiest this my Treatise that *i'tiqād* is not the notion that is uttered, but the notion that is represented in the soul when it is has been averred of it that it is in fact just as it has been represented.'[20] Furthermore, Maimonides uses this term, and its Hebrew cognate *da'at*, consistently in the context of religious beliefs.[21] For Sa'adia and Maimonides, then, religious belief was more than a matter of trust, loyalty, and faith; it was also a matter of the affirmation or denial of certain propositions.

But, this being the case, it was only a matter of time before someone would seek to introduce into Judaism a formal set of dogmas. 'If faith is a conviction that something is as we conceive it to be,' Kenneth Seeskin notes, 'then a religion without articles of faith is a contradiction in terms.'[22] From this perspective, it is not surprising that Maimonides posited a creed; it is, rather, surprising that he was the first Rabbanite author to have done so.

In these few pages I have suggested that systematic theology in general, and the laying down of formal creeds in particular, do not occur in rabbinic Judaism both because they are foreign to its intrinsic nature and because, historically, rabbinic Judaism had no need for them. Once the circumstances had changed and there was a need to present Jewish belief in a systematic form, and, concomitantly, once Jewish authorities began to understand their religion in propositional terms, the development of formal creeds was only a matter of time. That it took so long (slightly more than 200 years elapsed between the publication of Sa'adia's *Emunot ve-Deot* and the publication of Maimonides' creed) is probably a tribute to the conservative nature of religious traditions.

The project of creed formulation in Judaism, then, represents not only an innovation, but a whole new way of looking at Judaism. It was not immediately recognized as such, however, and very quickly achieved respectability. But despite its respectability tensions remained and there were important Jewish thinkers who, perhaps not exactly understanding why, resisted the enterprise altogether or at least sought to modify it.

Laying down dogmas for Judaism for the first time, therefore, is seen from this perspective as being clearly innovative. It would take a bold person to do such a thing. Maimonides had the requisite boldness; but even he, as will be shown below, exercised caution in laying down his principles. Maimonides' undertaking was made easier by the fact that his principles, even though they were the first systematic, self-conscious attempt by a Rabbanite Jew to posit dogmas for Judaism, did not appear in a vacuum. Developments in Muslim and Karaite theology, as well as elements in the writings of certain Jewish authors, provided the background against which Maimonides posited his principles and facilitated his attempt to lay down articles of faith for Judaism in a way in which it might appear that he was not innovating at all.

It is not my intent to provide even a brief account of Muslim dogmatics. Rather, I merely want to indicate how important and pervasive discussions of dogmatics were in Muslim contexts and note some points about the Muslim discussion which are particularly relevant to a full understanding of Maimonides' account of the dogmas of Judaism.

The question of creed arose in early Islam in response to the need to answer two related questions: (*a*) Who is a Muslim and who is an unbeliever? (*b*) Who will achieve salvation and who will be condemned to damnation?[23] These questions, in turn, resolved themselves into the further question, what sort of sins, if any, cut off a person from the community (*ummah*) of Islam and, consequently, from salvation? The answer which orthodox Islam developed to this question was that no matter what one did one remained a Muslim so long as one's beliefs were correct.[24] This being so, it became essential to define precisely those beliefs the acceptance of which was a necessary condition for being a Muslim and for gaining access to paradise. Many creeds were formulated in answer to this need.[25] Not surprisingly, a large number of these creedal discussions took place in strictly legal contexts.[26]

Not only was dogma an important issue in Muslim theology and law, but it was an issue addressed by many of those Muslim thinkers who are identified as central figures in the history of Muslim philosophy.[27]

We may summarize this information in the following list of points, all of which will turn out to be relevant for our discussion of Maimonides.

(*a*) right belief defines who a Muslim is;
(*b*) right belief is a necessary condition for access to paradise in Islam;
(*c*) sin (which does not compromise right belief) does not cause one to cease being a Muslim nor does it cut one off from paradise;
(*d*) creed was an issue deemed important enough to be worthy of the attention of philosophers;
(*e*) creed was dealt with in legal contexts.

In the non-Karaite Jewish world there was no comparable attention paid to the question of dogmatics till the publication of Maimonides' 'thirteen principles'. There were, however, other Jewish authors prior to Maimonides who spoke of certain beliefs as being in some sense prior to others. Sa'adia, for example, structures his *Emunot ve-Deot* around a discussion of some of the beliefs of Judaism which he apparently understands in some sense to be more important than those beliefs he does not discuss.

Bahya (eleventh century) speaks of belief in the unity of God as the 'most important cornerstone' (*'uwakkid 'arkān*) of Judaism, as its priniciple (*'asl*) and 'foundation' (*ussa*).[28] In general, he says that his book is devoted to an examination of the 'principles' (*'usul*) of the duties of the heart.[29] He thus uses terminology which, as we shall see, is typical of later medieval Jewish discussions of dogmatics.

At the end of the *Kuzari* Judah Halevi (*c.*1074–1140) lists six 'presuppositions' (*al-maqaddima*) upon which Judaism is based.[30]

Abraham ibn Daud (1110–80), explicitly following in Sa'adia's footsteps, devotes the second volume of his *Emunah Ramah* to a discussion of six 'principles' (*ikkarim* — Arabic original of the text lost) of the faith of Judaism.

In a distinctly non-theological context we find that Rabbenu Hananel ben Hushiel of Kairouan (*c.*975–1057), commenting on Exod. 14: 31 ('. . . and they believed in the Lord and His servant Moses), states that belief (*emunah*) is divided into four 'parts': (*a*) belief in god; (*b*) belief in the prophets whom we have been obligated to obey; (*c*) belief in the world to come; (*d*) belief in the Messiah, 'a great corner-stone of the Torah'. According to Rabbenu Hananel the believer merits a place in the garden of Eden and a share in the life of the world to come; the non-believer does not merit redemption and life in the world to come.[31] Rabbenu Hananel is the only pre-Maimonidean Rabbanite thinker to specify certain beliefs as prerequisites for salvation. In so doing he anticipates an important element in Maimonides' own formulation of the principles of Judaism. But whereas it appears that Rabbenu Hananel viewed these beliefs as necessary prerequisites for salvation we have no evidence that he considered them to be also sufficient conditions for salvation. It was Maimonides who first explicitly took that step.

Although the four thinkers other than Rabbenu Hananel all distinguish certain beliefs from among all the teachings of Judaism for special attention, none of them suggests that these beliefs have special status, either dogmatic or structural,[32] within Judaism. They do not posit these beliefs as defining Judaism, as being especially required by the Torah, as being in themselves uniquely necessary or sufficient for attaining salvation, or as underlying in some sense or other the rest of the teachings of the Torah.

Note also ought to be taken here of a pre-Maimonidean Karaite author who explicitly, and apparently following Muslim models, posited a creed for (Karaite) Judaism. Yehudah Hadassi (twelfth century) was a Byzantine Karaite who wrote a dogmatic work called *Eshkol ha-Kofer*.[33]

From this brief survey it should be evident that had Maimonides posited his 'thirteen principles' in a purely talmudic context, the work would have been seen clearly as an innovation. Given the development of systematic theology within Judaism, the example provided by Islam and Karaism,[34] and the writings of some of Maimonides' Jewish philosophical predecessors, Maimonides was able to posit his creed without appearing to innovate at all.

I

Maimonides

1. The Text of Maimonides' Thirteen Principles

Tractate Sanhedrin of the Mishnah deals with the power, authority, and responsibility of courts in Jewish law. One of the major subjects discussed in the tractate is capital punishment. It is in that context that we find the tenth[1] chapter of Sanhedrin, *Perek Ḥelek*, which teaches that even those condemned to death by a court have a portion in the world to come.[2] The chapter opens with the following mishnah:

All Israelites have a share in the world to come, as it states, *Thy people are all righteous, they shall inherit the land forever* [Isa. 60: 21].[3] But the following have no share in the world to come: he who says there is no resurrection,[4] that the Torah is not from heaven,[5] and the *epikoros*.[6] Rabbi Akiba says: 'Even he who reads in the external books[7] and he who whispers over a wound, saying, *I will put none of the diseases upon thee, which I have put upon the Egyptians; for I am the Lord that healeth thee* [Exod. 15: 26]'.[8] Abba Saul says: 'Even he who pronounces the name according to its letters'.[9]

This mishnah is the only explicit instance in rabbinic literature of a systematic attempt to spell out those beliefs which a Jew must hold in order to merit salvation.[10] It is hardly surprising, therefore, that this text served as the springboard for attempts to define the principles of Judaism.[11] The first, and to this day the most influential of all these attempts, may be found in Maimonides' commentary to this mishnah.[12] This commentary is actually an extended essay dealing, in the main, with two subjects: the world to come and the definition of the various terms occurring in the mishnah. It is by way of defining the term 'Israelite', as Arthur Hyman points out,[13] that Maimonides lays down thirteen beliefs which must be held by every Jew in order to earn a place in the world to come.

Maimonides opens his commentary as a whole with the following words: 'I have seen fit to speak here about many principles[14] concerning very important doctrines.'[15] After completing his discussion of the world to come and the other terms in the mishnah which need definition, Maimonides introduces his thirteen principles themselves with the following statement: 'What is appropriate for me to record now — and this is the most appropriate place to record them — is that the principles of our pure Torah and its foundations[16] are thirteen foundations.'[17] He then proceeds to list and explain the principles:

The first foundation is the existence of the Creator,[18] may He be praised; to wit, that there exists a being in the most perfect type of existence and that it is the cause of the existence of all other beings. In this being is the source of their existence, and from it derives [their] continued existence. If we were able to eliminate its existence, then the existence of all other beings would be nullified and nothing would remain. However, if we were able to eliminate the existence of all beings other than it, His existence, may He be exalted, would not be nullified nor be lacking for He is self-sufficient, dependent upon no other for His existence. Everything other than He of the Intelligences, meaning the angels, the matter [lit., bodies] of the spheres, etc., is dependent upon Him for its existence. This first foundation is attested to by the verse: *I am the Lord, thy God* [Exod. 20: 2; Deut. 5: 6].[19]

The second foundation is God's unity, may he be exalted; to wit, that this One, Who is the cause of [the existence of] everything, is one. His oneness is unlike the oneness of a genus, or of a species. Nor is it like the oneness of a single composed individual, which can be divided into many units. Nor is His oneness like that of the simple body which is one in number but infinitely divisible. Rather He, may He be exalted, is one with a oneness for which there is no comparison at all. This second foundation is attested to by the verse: *Hear, O Israel, the Lord thy God, the Lord is One* [Deut. 6: 4].

The third foundation is the denial of corporeality to Him; to wit, that this One is neither a body nor a force within a body. None of the characteristics of a body appertains to Him, either by His essence or as an accident thereof, as for example, movement and rest. It is for this reason that they, may they rest in peace, denied to Him division and continuity in saying: 'There is no sitting, nor standing, nor *oref*, or *ippui* in heaven'.[20] They meant that there is no 'division' which is *oref*, nor is there any continuity, for *ippui* means 'continuity' as it is said: *ve-afu be khatef pelishtim* [Isa. 11: 14] meaning, 'they shall push them with their shoulders [to form a continuous mass] because they are closely packed together', as the Targum says, 'they shall put their shoulders together'.[21] The prophet has said: *To whom then will you compare Me so that I be similar?* [Isa. 40: 25]. Were God a body, He would then resemble bodies.[22] Everything mentioned in the Scriptures which describes Him, may He be exalted, as having the attributes of a body, such as moving from place to place, or standing, or sitting, or speaking, and so on, is all metaphors, allegories, and riddles, as they have said, 'The Torah speaks in the language of man'.[23] And men have philosophized a great deal about this matter. This third foundation is attested to by the verse *You saw no image* [Deut. 4: 15] meaning, 'you did not perceive Him, may He be exalted, as having an image' for He is, as we have said, neither a body nor a force within a body.

The fourth foundation is God's precedence;[24] to wit, that this one who has just been described is He Who precedes (everything) absolutely. No other being has precedence with respect to Him. There are many verses attesting to this in Scripture. The verse attesting to it [best] is: *the God of eternity is a dwelling place* [Deut. 33: 27].[25]

The fifth foundation is that He, may He be exalted, is He Whom it is proper to worship and to praise; and [that it is also proper] to promulgate praise of Him and obedience to Him. This may not be done for any being other than Him in reality, from among the angels, the spheres, the elements, and that which is composed of them for all these have their activities imprinted upon them. They have no destiny [of their own] and no rootedness [of their own in reality] other than His love, may He be exalted, [of them]. Do not, furthermore, seize upon intermediaries in order to reach Him but direct your thoughts toward Him, may He be exalted, and turn away from that which is other than He. This fifth foundation is the prohibition against idolatry and there are many verses in the Torah prohibiting it.

The sixth foundation is prophecy; to wit, it should be known that, within the species of humanity, there are individuals who have a greatly superior disposition and a great measure of perfection. And, if their souls are prepared so that they receive the form of the intellect, then that human intellect will unite with the Agent Intelligence which will cause a great emanation to flow to it. These people are prophets, this [process] is prophecy; and this is its content. The explanation of this principle to its fullest, however, would be very long and it is not our intention to demonstrate each of its basic premises, or to explain the ways by which it is perceived for that is the epitome of all the sciences. Here we shall mention it only in the form of a statement. The verses of the Torah testifying to the prophecy of the prophets are many.

The seventh foundation is the prophecy of Moses, our Teacher; to wit, it should be known[26] that: Moses was the father of all the prophets — of those who came before him and of those who came after him; all were beneath him in rank and that he was the chosen of God from among the entire species of humanity and that he comprehended more of God, may He be exalted, than any man who ever existed or will exist, ever comprehended or will comprehend and, that he, peace be upon him, reached a state of exaltedness beyond humanity such that he perceived the level of sovereignty and became included in the levels of angels. There remained no veil which he did not pierce, no material hindrance burdened him, and no defect whether small or great mingled itself with him. The imaginative and sensible faculties in his perceptions were stripped from him, his desiderative faculty was still, and he remained pure intellect only. For this reason, they remarked of him that he discoursed with God without the intermediacy of an angel. I would have been obligated to explain this strange subject, to unlock the secrets firmly enclosed in the verses of the Torah, and to expound the meaning of *mouth to mouth* [Num. 12: 8] together with the whole of this verse and other verses belonging to the same theme had I not seen that this theme is very subtle and that it would need abundant statement, introductions and illustrations. The existence of angels would, first, have to be made clear and, then, the distinction between their ranks and that of the Creator. The soul would have to be explained and all its faculties. The circle would then grow wider until we should have to say a word about the images which the prophets attribute to the Creator and the angels. The *Shiur Komah*[27] and its meaning would have to enter [into our survey]. And, even if I were to be as brief as possible, this purpose alone could not be attained even in a hundred pages. For this reason, I shall leave it to its place, whether in 'the book of the interpretation of the discourses' which I have promised, or in 'the book of prophecy' which I have begun, or in a book which I shall compose as a commentary to these foundations. I shall now return to the purpose of this seventh foundation and say that the prophecy of Moses is separated from the prophecy of all other prophets by four differences:

The first difference: To every other prophet that ever was, God did not speak except by an intermediary. But Moses had no intermediary, as it is said *mouth to mouth did I speak with him* [Num. 12: 8].

The second difference: Every other prophet received inspiration only when in a state of sleep, as He said in various places: *in a dream of the night* [Gen. 20: 3], *he dreamed and he saw a ladder* [Gen. 28: 12], *in a dream of a vision of the night* [Job 33: 15], and in many other places with similar intent; or during the day, after a deep sleep had fallen upon the prophet and his condition had become one in which his sense-perceptions were rendered inactive and in which his thoughts were empty as in sleep. This condition is called *maḥazeh* and *mar'eh* and it is referred to in the phrase *in visions of God* [Ezek. 8: 3, 40: 2]. But to Moses, peace be upon him, discourse came in the day when he was *standing between the two cherubim*, as God had promised him, *And, there, I will meet with you and I will speak with you* [Exod. 25: 22]. And He, may He be exalted, also said, *If there be a prophet among you, I, the Lord, will make Myself known to him in a vision and will speak with him in a dream. Not so my servant Moses. He, in all my house, is faithful* [Num. 12: 6–8].

The third difference: Every other prophet receives inspiration only in a vision and by means of an angel (and) indeed his strength becomes enfeebled, his body becomes deranged, and a very great terror falls upon him so that he is almost broken by it, as is illustrated when Gabriel spoke to Daniel in a vision and Daniel said, *And there remained no strength in me and my dignity became destructive for me* [Dan. 10: 8]. He also said *I was in a deep sleep on my face and my face was towards the ground* [Dan. 10: 16]. But not so with Moses. Rather, discourse came to him and no confusion of any kind overtook him as He, may he be exalted, has said, *And the Lord spoke to Moses face to face as a man speaks to his neighbor* [Exod. 33: 11]. This means that just as no man feels disquieted when his neighbor talks with him, so he, peace be upon him, had no fright at the discourse of God, although it was face to face. This was so because of the strength of his union with the [Agent] Intelligence, as we have said.

The fourth difference: Every other prophet did not receive inspiration by his own choice but by the will of God. The prophet could remain a number of years without inspiration, or an inspiration could be communicated to the prophet but he could be required to wait some days or months before prophesying, or not to make it known at all. We have seen that there are those among them who prepared themselves by simplifying their soul and by purifying their minds as did Elisha when he declared *Bring me, now, a minstrel* [2 Kgs 3: 15] and then inspiration came to him. It was not, however, necessarily that he received inspiration after he was prepared for it. But Moses, our Teacher, was able to say whenever he wished, *Stand, and I shall hear what God shall command concerning you* [Num. 9: 8]. And He also said, *Speak to Aaron, your brother, that he not come at any time into the sanctuary* [Lev. 16: 2]. (To this), they said, 'Aaron was bound by the prohibition "that he not come at any time" but Moses was not bound by that prohibition'.[28]

The eighth foundation is that the Torah is from heaven; to wit, it [must] be believed[29] that the whole of this Torah which is in our hand today is the Torah that was brought down to Moses, our Teacher; that all of it is from God [by] the transmission which is called metaphorically 'speech'; that no one knows the quality of that transmission except he to whom it was transmitted, peace be upon him; and, that it was dictated to him while he was of the rank of a scribe; and, that he wrote down all of its dates, its narratives, and its laws — and, for this, he is called the legislator[30] [Num. 21: 18]. There is no difference between *the sons of Ham were Cush, Miṣrayim, Fut, and Canaan* [Gen. 10: 6] and *the name of his wife was Mehetabel, the daughter of Matred* [Gen. 36: 39] on the one hand, and *I am the Lord your God* [Exod. 20: 2] and *Hear, O Israel, the Lord, our God, the*

Lord is One [Deut. 6: 4] on the other hand. Everything is from the mouth of the Mighty One; everything is the Torah of God: whole, pure, holy [and] true.[31] Indeed, Menasseh became, in the eyes of the Sages, the person strongest in heresy and hypocrisy for he thought that the Torah was composed of kernels and husks and that these dates and these narratives had no value and that they were composed by Moses. This is the issue of 'the Torah is not from heaven'.[32] And the Sages have said that he who believes that 'the Torah is entirely from the mouth of the Almighty except for this (i.e., any given) verse which was not said by the Holy One, blessed be He, but Moses said it on his own authority' is one to whom the following verse applies, *He disdains the word of God* [Num. 15: 31].[33] May God be exalted above that which the heretics say! Rather, every letter of the Torah contains wisdom and wonders for him whom God has given to understand it. Its ultimate wisdom cannot be perceived as it is said, *Its measure is greater than the earth and broader than the sea* [Job 11: 9]. A man can only follow in the steps of David, the anointed of the God of Jacob, the most pleasant singer of the hymns of Israel, who prayed singing, *Unmask my eyes that I may see wonders from Your Torah* [Ps. 119: 18]. Similarly, its interpretation as it has been handed down is also 'from the mouth of the Almighty'. That which we observe today, such as the form of Sukkah, the Lulav, the Shofar, the Ẓiẓit, the Tefilin, and other such forms are the actual forms which God told to Moses and which he told to us. He is the transmitter of the Message, faithful in its transmission. The verse on the basis of which this eighth foundation is attested is his [i.e., Moses'] saying, *By this shall you know that the Lord has sent me to do all these things* [Num. 16: 28].

The ninth foundation is the [denial of the] Abrogation [of the Torah]; to wit, that this Torah of Moses, our Teacher, shall not be abrogated or transmuted; nor shall any other law come from God. It may not be added to, nor subtracted from — not from its text nor from its explanation — as it is said, *You shall not add to it, nor subtract from it* [Deut. 13: 1]. We have already explained that which it is necessary to explain concerning this foundation in the Introduction to this book.[34]

The tenth foundation is that He, may He be exalted, has knowledge of the acts of men and is not neglectful of them. It is not as the opinion of someone who says, *God has abandoned the earth* [Ezek. 8: 12, 9: 9] but as the opinion of him who says, *[God is] great in counsel, and mighty in work; whose eyes are open upon all the ways of the sons of men* [Jer. 32: 19]. It is also said, *God saw that the evil of man was great* [Gen. 6: 15], and *the cry of Sodom and Gemorrah was great* [Gen. 18: 20]. This attests to this tenth foundation.

The eleventh foundation is that He, may He be exalted, rewards him who obeys the commands of the Torah and punishes him who violates its prohibitions; and, that the greatest of His rewards is the World to Come while the severest of His punishments is 'being cut off'. We have already expounded sufficiently on this in this chapter. The verse which attests to this foundation is . . . *if You forgive their sin, and if not, erase me then, from Your book which You have written* [Exod. 32: 32] taken together with His answer, may He be exalted, *Him who has sinned against Me, shall I erase from My book* [Exod. 32: 33]. These verses are attestations to [the fact that] the obedient person and the rebellious person will reach [a point] with Him, may He be exalted, where He will reward the one and punish the other.

The twelfth foundation is the days of the Messiah; to wit, the belief in,[35] and the assertion of,[36] the truth of his coming. He shall not be a long time *and if he tarries, wait for him* [Hab. 2: 3]. No time for his coming may be set nor may the verses of Scripture be interpreted to reveal the time of his coming, as our Sages have said, 'May the wits of those who calculate the date of the end [of the present period of time] be added'.[37] One must believe in[38] him by praising him, loving him, and praying for his coming according to that which has been revealed by all the prophets from Moses to Malachi. He who doubts, or who treats his command lightly, says that the Torah, which promised his coming specifically in the readings of *Balaam* and *Atem Niṣavim*, is lying. One of the general ideas of this foundation is that Israel will have no king except from David, and that he will be descended especially from the seed of Solomon. Whoever disobeys the command of this dynasty denies God and the verses of the prophets.

The thirteenth foundation is the resurrection and we have already explained it.[39]

When all these foundations are perfectly understood and believed in by a person he enters the community of Israel and one is obligated to love and pity him and to act towards him in all ways in which the Creator has commanded that one should act towards his brother, with love and fraternity. Even were he to commit every possible transgression, because of lust and because of being overpowered by the evil inclination, he will be punished according to his rebelliousness, but he has a portion [of the world to come]; he is one of the sinners of Israel. But if a man doubts any of these foundations, he leaves the community [of Israel], denies the fundamental,[40] and is called a sectarian,[41] *epikoros*, and one who 'cuts among the plantings'.[42] One is required to hate him and destroy him. About such a person it was said, *Do I not hate them, O Lord, who hate Thee?* [Ps. 139: 21]. But I have discussed these issues too much and have digressed from the intended aim of my composition. I did this, however, because of the great benefit it bestows with respect to [the strengthening of] faith for I have collected for you valuable things which are scattered in many important books. Attain felicity through them. Review these things many times and study them well. If your soul leads you astray so that you think that you understand them after one or [even] ten readings, God knows that it has misled you. Therefore, do not read it hastily, because I did not compose it in a haphazard fashion but [only] after extended study, careful consideration, investigation of true and false beliefs, the summarization of which among them must be believed, and its clarification with arguments and proofs for each issue. I pray that God may lead me on the proper path.

Maimonides' statements here cry out for comment and explanation. Indeed they received much of both — and plenty of criticism besides — in the centuries which followed their publication. In many ways it is the purpose of this book to follow the various paths taken by the discussion of dogma in medieval Judaism and to demonstrate the centrality of Maimonides in that discussion. But we cannot follow these different paths without first understanding their origin, and they all originate, in one way or another, in Maimonides' commentary on Sanhedrin x. 1.

11. What is a 'Foundation of the Torah'?

Maimonides nowhere tells us precisely what a 'foundation of the Torah' is. He uses two Arabic terms — *qa'ida* and *aṣl* — interchangeably. While each principle is introduced as a *qa'ida* the principles as a group are introduced with both terms. In his other writings, especially the *Guide of the Perplexed*, Maimonides uses these terms for a wide variety of beliefs and doctrines.[43] It does not seem, therefore, that there is much to learn about Maimonides' understanding of the nature of his principles from a purely terminological perspective.

From Maimonides' peroration at the end of the principles, however, we can learn a number of important facts concerning his public attitude towards them. In the first place, it is acceptance of these principles which defines a person as a Jew: 'When all these foundations are perfectly understood and believed in by a person he enters the community of Israel.' Maimonides apparently took this theological definition of what it means to be a Jew seriously since he deduces from it the following two consequences: first, the halakhic rights which Jews may demand of their fellows — to be treated with love, pity, and fraternity[44] — are derived from the acceptance of these principles and, second, one's portion in the world to come — i.e. one's personal salvation — is dependent upon the acceptance of these principles. We further learn that denial of any of these principles (or, if we take Maimonides literally, and there is no reason not to, the *doubting* of any one of these principles) causes one to be excluded from the community of Israel with the two consequences that the halakhah requires that the Jew hate and destroy such a one[45] and that he loses his portion in the world to come. Maimonides, it is evident, denies the possibility of what we may call inadvertent or accidental heresy (*kefirah be-shogeg*). Even if a person denies a Torah teaching (or affirms a teaching denied by the Torah) because he thinks that is what the Torah demands of him he is still a heretic, cut off from the Jewish people and denied a portion in the world to come. This position is a direct consequence of the new, propositional understanding of the concept 'belief' that we find reflected in Maimonides' writings. If one's faith is defined by the specific beliefs one holds then if one holds incorrect beliefs — for whatever reason — one is a heretic.

Lest it be thought that I am reading too much into Maimonides' statement here, it ought to be noted that he is consistent in all his major writings on his insistence upon doctrinal orthodoxy as a prerequisite for salvation. He repeats the thirteen principles with almost no change in the *Mishneh Torah*,[46] there also threatening with extinction all who deny any one of them. At the end of the *Guide of the Perplexed* (iii. 51), in the 'parable of the palace' he makes clear that doctrinal error leads to the loss of salvation.

Perhaps more to the point, Maimonides emphasizes the seriousness of his characterization of the principles as what I call dogmas in the strict sense of the term in his commentary on Mishnah Sanhedrin. Sanhedrin x. 2 states: 'Three kings and four commoners have no portion in the world to come . . .' Maimonides comments:

Those are mentioned because of their great degree of wisdom. One might think that because of their great wisdom and by virtue of the Torah of which they know much that they would have a portion [in the World to come]. There [the Mishnah] made it known to us that the foundations of faith[47] were corrupted by them and they had doubts concerning some of them. They were therefore excluded from life in the world to come.[48]

Maimonides continues in the same vein in his commentary to Mishnah Sanhedrin xi. 3: 'Anyone who destroys one of these foundations[49] which I explained to you has left the community of Torah adherents.'[50]

On the basis of this evidence we may safely conclude that Maimonides' principles in the commentary to *Perek Ḥelek* are laid down as dogmas; i.e. as beliefs laid down by religious authority (in this case the Torah as interpreted by Maimonides), the holding of which both defines adherence to a particular religion (in this case Judaism) and is a necessary condition for salvation (having a portion in the world to come).

Whereas from a modern perspective it may not be noteworthy that Maimonides postulated dogmas for the Jewish faith, there are a number of good reasons for noting this fact. In the first place, Maimonides' definition of a Jew by virtue of his beliefs is an absolute innovation in Judaism. This fact was appreciated by his contemporaries and successors, many of whom accepted as authoritative his list of principles but almost none of whom accepted his definition of the principles as dogmas. It should further be noted that Maimonides' insistence on defining a Jew in terms of his or her beliefs had direct halakhic consequences: in 'Laws of Forbidden Intercourse', xiv. 2 Maimonides, describing the procedure of conversion, maintains that we are to inform the prospective convert 'of the principles of the religion[51] viz., God's unity and the prohibition of idolatry.[52] One expatiates upon this at length.' With respect to the commandments, on the other hand, Maimonides maintains that we inform the prospective convert concerning 'some of the light commandments and some of the graver commandments, but we do not expatiate upon this issue at length'.[53] Thus Maimonides' definition of a Jew as a person who adheres to certain beliefs finds concrete halakhic expression. Those beliefs, then, which define the Jew and which enable him to earn a portion in the world to come are dogmas in the strict sense of the term.

This situation is further reflected in the terminology which Maimonides uses in the *Mishneh Torah* for heresy and in the sanctions which he imposes upon the heretic. In 'Laws of Repentance', iii. 7 Maimonides defines a *min* (sectarian) as one who denies any one of the first five of his thirteen principles. At 'Laws of Idolatry', ii. 5 he says that sectarians are not Israelites at all,[54] and that one may neither converse with them nor even respond to their greetings. He equates them with idolaters and calls them 'wanton disbelievers'. Furthermore, he says that even if they repent their repentance is not accepted. In his responsa he characterizes sectarians as those 'whose faith in the foundations of the Torah has been destroyed, including those who say "there is no Torah from Heaven" '.[55] Maimonides received a query concerning his statement in 'Laws of Idolatry', ii. 5 that the repentance of the sectarian is not accepted. His correspondent asked how that was possible in light of Maimonides' statement ('Laws of Repentance', iii. 14) that 'nothing stands in the way of repentance . . .'.[56] Maimonides responds by saying that we (i.e. the community of Israel) do not accept the repentance of a sectarian since we can never be sure that it is sincere. God, however, does accept the repentance of the sincerely repentant sectarian. But from the point of view of the community once a person has excluded himself from it through sectarianism there is no way he can return to the fold.

At 'Laws of Repentance', iii. 8 Maimonides defines an *epikoros* as one who denies prophecy, Mosaic prophecy, and God's knowledge. The *epikoros* is said to be guilty of 'wanton disobedience' at 'Laws of the Murderer', iv. 10 and 'Laws of Mourning', i. 10. In the latter context Maimonides lays down that at their deaths *epikorsim* are not to be mourned; rather, one is to rejoice at their death. At 'Laws of Idolatry', x. 1 they are equated with 'informers' (*mosrim*) and we are instructed that it is a positive commandment to destroy them. At 'Laws of Testimony', xi. 10 Maimonides informs us that *epikorsim* have no portion in the world to come and that there is no need to state that they are ineligible to serve as witnesses, since they are not Israelites at all. At 'Laws of Ritual Slaughtering', iv. 14 *epikorsim* are characterized as those who deny the Torah and Moses, and it is stated that animals which they slaughter are unfit for consumption (*nevelah*).[57] At 'Laws of Phylacteries', i. 13 we find that Torah scrolls, *mezuzot*, and phylacteries prepared by an *epikoros* are to be burned. At 'Laws of Robbery', xi. 2 Maimonides says that one is not obligated to return lost objects to the *epikoros*. In a number of places ('Testimony', xi. 10 — compare 'Laws of the Murderer', iv. 10 and 'Idolatry', x. 1) Maimonides goes so far as to say that the *epikoros* is to be killed outright.[58]

At 'Laws of Repentance', iii. 8 Maimonides characterizes as deniers (*kofrim*) those who deny the Torah, resurrection, and the coming of the Messiah. At 'Laws of Rebels', iii. 2 those who deny the oral Torah are equated with sectarians and *epikorsim*. They are further equated with those who deny Torah from heaven altogether and are called 'informers' and 'apostates'. Maimonides goes on to codify as law that deniers are to be killed without recourse to legal procedure.[59]

Maimonides' comments in the *Mishneh Torah* on the various types of heretic as summarized here lead to the following conclusion: Maimonides does not carefully distinguish among the terms sectarian, *epikoros*, and denier. He identifies the *epikoros* with the denier at 'Testimony', xi. 10, 'Ritual Slaughtering', iv. 14, and 'Rebels', iii. 2. The sectarian is identified with the denier in *Responsa*, 263. Furthermore all three are said to be equivalent to idolaters, all three are said not to be Israelites at all, and all three are denied a portion in the world to come. Maimonides' dogmatic conception of his principles of faith, therefore, clearly informs his discussions of heresy and heretics in the *Mishneh Torah*.

It should be emphasized that one can accept the idea that Judaism has principles of faith without understanding them to be dogmas in the sense in which Maimonides quite clearly used the term. One can follow Crescas in seeing them as those beliefs which are analytical to the concept, 'Torah from heaven'; one can follow Albo in seeing them as only those beliefs which must be common to all true religions; one can follow Abravanel in seeing them as nothing more than pedagogical devices; one can follow other thinkers, such as Bibago and Arama, in defining them yet differently. This point will become clear in what follows.

III. Maimonides' Statement of the Principles in the *Mishneh Torah*

Maimonides presents his principles a second time in his great code of Jewish law, the *Mishneh Torah*. This book opens with a section called 'Laws of the Foundations of the Torah'. Surprisingly, although most of the principles are referred to here, some are not.[60] This is surprising since, as Isaac Abravanel intimated,[61] the thirteen beliefs listed in *Perek Ḥelek* are introduced as 'foundations of the Torah'; one would expect to find them repeated in a text devoted to the 'Laws of the Foundations of the Torah'. One might simply reply that Maimonides had changed his mind about which beliefs were 'foundations of the Torah'. The problem with this, however, is that in the same book of the *Mishneh Torah* in which we find the 'Laws of the Foundations of the Torah', the *Book of Knowledge*, we also find a section entitled 'Laws of Repentance' in which the original thirteen principles are repeated with almost no change. One can only surmise that in the *Mishneh Torah* Maimonides used the term 'foundations of the Torah' in a more general, less technical sense than the way he used it in his commentary on *Ḥelek*.

The third chapter of 'Laws of Repentance', as Nachum Rabinovitch has pointed out,[62] is devoted to defining the terms 'wicked person', 'intermediate person', and 'righteous person'. Through the medium of repentance one can improve one's state, rising from wicked to intermediate and from intermediate to righteous. There are varying degrees of wickedness and righteousness. The most wicked of the wicked are those who have forfeited their share in the world to come. It is in this context that Maimonides presents us with a list of those who have no share in the world to come. He writes:

> The following have no portion in the world to come, but are cut off and perish, and for their great wickedness and sinfulness are condemned for ever and ever. Sectarians[63] and *epikorsim*; those who deny the Torah, the resurrection of the dead or the coming of the Redeemer; apostates;[64] those who cause a multitude to sin, and those who secede from the way of the community; anyone who commits transgressions like Jehoiakim, in high-handed fashion and openly; informers; those who terrorize a community not for a religious purpose; murderers and slanderers, and one who obliterates the physical mark of his Jewish origin.
>
> Five classes are termed sectarians: he who says that there is no God and the world has no Ruler; he who says that there is a ruling power but that it is vested in two or more persons; he who says there is one ruler, but that He is a body and has form; he who denies that He alone is the First Cause and Rock[65] of the Universe; likewise he who renders worship to anyone beside Him, to serve as a mediator between the human being and the Lord of the Universe. Whoever belongs to any of these five classes is termed a sectarian.
>
> Three classes are called *epikorsim*; he who denies the reality of prophecy and maintains that there is no knowledge which emanates from the Creator and directly reaches the human mind; he who denies the prophecy of Moses, our teacher; and he who asserts that the Creator has no cognizance of the deeds of the children of men. Each of these classes consists of *epikorsim*.
>
> Three classes are deniers of the Torah: he who says that the Torah is not of divine origin — even if he says of one verse, or of a single word, that Moses said it by himself — is a denier of the Torah; likewise, he who

denies its interpretation, that is the Oral Torah and repudiates its
reporters as Zadok and Boethus did; he who says that the Creator changed
one commandment for another, and that this Torah, although of divine
origin, is now obsolete, as the Nazarenes and Moslems assert. Everyone
belonging to any of these classes is a denier of the Torah.[66]

It is immediately evident that this list of twenty-four[67]
categories of persons who have forfeited their share of the world to
come falls into two groups: the first five categories deal with beliefs;
all the others deal with actions.[68] Since our central concern here is
to compare this text to the thirteen principles listed in *Perek Ḥelek*,
we will ignore the various actions which cost one his share in the
world to come and examine the forbidden beliefs. We may then take
note of the following interesting facts. First, all but the eleventh of
Maimonides' thirteen principles — retribution — appear in this
list. Second, the list contains exactly thirteen beliefs (the eighth
principle listed in the commentary to *Ḥelek* — Torah from
heaven — is here divided into two parts, one relating to the written
Torah and the second relating to the oral Torah).[69] Third, the
principles are here divided into five groups.[70] Fourth, resurrection
precedes Messiah in this list while it follows Messiah in the
commentary to *Ḥelek*.[71] Fifth, the principles here follow almost
exactly the order of the original formulation. Aside from the
reversal of Messiah and resurrection the only other difference is
that here the tenth principle from the commentary on *Ḥelek* —
God's knowledge — appears eighth in the list. Sixth, Maimonides
was as careful here as he was in the original listing to avoid including
belief in creation in his list of principles.[72] Seventh, the original list
was phrased in positive terms while this one is framed negatively.[73]
Eighth, the original list dealt exclusively with beliefs; this list deals
exclusively with people who hold certain beliefs.[74]

In short we find here a list which is remarkably consistent with
the original formulation in the commentary to *Ḥelek*. Differences of
order aside (and these may be a function of the grouping introduced
here by Maimonides), there is only one substantial difference: the
replacement of the eleventh principle from *Ḥelek* with a bifurcated
eighth principle. It may be that we have here a bit of anti-Karaite
polemic: after his arrival in Egypt, where he wrote the *Mishneh
Torah*, Maimonides may have been more aware of the Karaite
threat than he had been either in his native Spain or in the countries

through which he wandered before he reached Egypt (and during which wanderings he composed his commentary on the Mishnah) and sought, therefore, to emphasize the doctrinal importance of belief in the oral Torah. Still he wished to retain the number thirteen (for whatever reason)[75] and thus had to sacrifice one of the beliefs. He chose one — retribution — which was at least implied by two of the others (Messiah and resurrection). This, it seems to me, shows how strongly attached Maimonides was to his original formulation.

IV. Divisions into which the Principles Fall

I noted just above that Maimonides groups the principles in 'Laws of Repentance' in a particular fashion. A great deal of attention has been paid to the question of whether or not the principles fall into any groups and it is rather surprising that no one, to the best of my knowledge, has paid any attention to Maimonides' own grouping as presented in 'Laws of Repentance'. I will return to this point after summarizing and analysing the explanations offered by others.

R. Shimon ben Ẓemaḥ Duran (1361–1444) was the first author — whose works are known to us today — explicitly to treat the question of the divisions into which the principles fall. It is well known that Duran reduced Maimonides' thirteen principles to three: God's existence, Torah from heaven, and retribution.[76] As I will show below, Duran did not introduce his three principles to replace those of Maimonides but to clarify them. He saw his three principles as the fundamental principles from which all the thirteen could be derived. He summarizes his position in the beginning of the introduction to his *Magen Avot*:

I have divided this book into four parts. I have called the first part *Ḥelek Eloha mi-Ma'al*;[77] [in it] I refute the opinions of the *epikorsim*. I have divided it into five chapters: (1) God's existence, (2) His unity, (3) [His] incorporeality, (4) that He is eternal *a parte ante* — to this I added that He ought to be worshipped. These five principles, according to my opinion, are included [under the rubric] '*epikoros*' mentioned in the mishnah for he who denies them is an *epikoros* as I wrote in my book, *Ohev Mishpat*[78] — (5) concerning attributes.

The second part relates to the statement, 'the Torah was not divinely revealed'. I called it *Ḥelek Shoseinu*[79] and have divided it into four chapters: (1) prophecy, (2) Mosaic prophecy, (3) revelation, (4) the eternity of the Torah.

The third part relates to the one who says 'that resurrection is not taught in the Torah'.[80] I called it *Ḥelek Ya'akov*[81] for Jacob our father did not die.[82] I divided it into four chapters: (1) God's knowledge, (2) providence, reward, and punishment, (3) the days of the Messiah, (4) resurrection of the dead.

These are the three principles which earlier scholars[83] summarized in the verse, 'And that the land be not desolate' [Gen. 47: 19]:[84] revelation, reward and punishment, God's existence.[85] [These are] the foundations of the Torah for it is a foundation of the faith to believe in God, in His existence, unity, eternity *a parte ante*, incorporeality, and that He ought to be worshipped. This is included [under the rubric] *'epikoros'* as mentioned above. After this [it is a foundation of the Torah] to believe in the prophecy of the prophets, in the prophecy of Moses, in the Torah, and in its eternity. This is included [under the rubric] 'the Torah is . . . from heaven'. After this [it is a foundation of the Torah] to believe in reward and punishment and its branches. This is included [under the rubric] 'resurrection'.[86]

We see here how Duran presents his principles as a commentary on Sanhedrin x. 1 and how he links them to all of Maimonides' principles. He renounces any claim to originality, alleging that the idea was formulated before his time. There is no way of knowing if this is a sincere disclaimer or simply an attempt to gain greater authority for an innovation of his own. He further links each of his three principles (and, through them, all thirteen of Maimonides') to a different term in the mishnah, showing in effect how Maimonides' formulation of the principles can be construed as a commentary directly on the mishnah's text. He thus indirectly explains why Maimonides chose to promulgate his principles in this place precisely and, by construing them more as commentary than as theological innovation, strengthens the claim of the principles to authority and secures Maimonides against the claim that he was tampering with the tradition by introducing innovations into it.

Duran's division of the principles is very persuasive. So much so that Joseph Albo took it over whole, failing, however, to credit his source.[87] Through Albo it passed on to late medieval Jewry as a whole. In our own day the position has been urged again by Arthur Hyman.[88] Not only do the thirteen principles seem to fall quite naturally into the categories posited by Duran, but if we examine both the relationship between the categories and the relationship between the principles within the categories, we find further reason to be persuaded that Maimonides did intend to divide his principles in the fashion suggested by Duran.

In the first place, we must remember that Maimonides introduced his principles as foundations of the Torah. We may then see that the first five principles relate to God, the Commander (*mezaveh*) of the Torah; principles 6–9 deal with the Torah itself; the last principles deal with the rewards for obedience to the Torah. Thus all three categories are important for our full understanding of the Torah. Isaac Abravanel phrased substantially the same idea in the following terms: we can obey the Torah either because of the excellence of its Commander (principles 1–5), or because of its own excellence (principles 6–9), or because of the rewards of such obedience (principles 10–13).[89]

When we turn to look at the relationship which obtains between the various principles themselves, when arranged in the way suggested by Duran, we further see that a case can be made for stating that the principles proceed in a particular order: from general to particular, or from logically prior to logically posterior. In the first group, we begin with God's existence; that belief is both logically prior to and more general than the other beliefs listed in the principles. Unity and incorporeality (principles 2 and 3) imply each other according to Maimonides. Unity precedes incorporeality, however, since it more clearly opposes idolatry (the aim of the entire Torah, according to Maimonides)[90] and, possibly since it is explicitly taught in the Torah.[91] God's ontic priority (principle 4) is a more particular belief than the first three while that God alone is worthy of worship (principle 5) is a consequence of the first four principles.[92]

The second group — prophecy, Mosaic prophecy, Torah from heaven (the content of Moses' prophecy), and the non-abrogability of the Torah — clearly move from the general to the particular.[93]

The third group opens with principle 10, God's knowledge of particulars, a belief logically necessary for any belief in divine reward and punishment,[94] proceeds to the statement of reward and punishment itself (principle 11), and concludes with the two classic examples of that reward and punishment (Messiah and resurrection).

It seems very hard to claim that all this — the fact that the principles fall so naturally into three different groups, that the three groups themselves each deal with another aspect of acceptance of the Torah, and that within the groups themselves the principles seem to proceed from general to particular or from logically prior to logically consequent — was all an accident and that Maimonides did not indeed intend the principles to be divided much as Duran divided them. This conclusion will receive further support below when we come to examine the relationship between the principles and the *Guide of the Perplexed*.

In his discussion of the dogmas of Judaism, Joseph Albo (fifteenth century) was strongly influenced by Duran. Like Duran, he reduces the principles of the Torah to three (God's existence, revelation, and reward and punishment[95]) and similarly shows how all of Maimonides' principles can be derived from them:

> It may be that Maimonides has the same idea concerning the number of fundamental principles as the one we have just indicated, and that his list consists of the three chief principles that we mentioned, plus the derivative dogmas issuing from them, all being called by him principles. Thus he lays down the existence of God, a fundamental doctrine, as the first principle. Then he enumerates along with it as principles four other dogmas which are derived from it, viz., unity, incorporeality, eternity, and exclusive worship. Then he lists as principles revelation, another fundamental doctrine, together with three other dogmas derived from it, viz., prophecy, superiority of Moses, and immutability of the law. Then comes divine omniscience and providence in reward and punishment, the third fundamental doctrine, together with three other dogmas implied in it and derived therefrom, viz., spiritual retribution, Messiah, and resurrection.[96]

Through Albo, Duran's ideas received wide attention and exerted considerable influence on subsequent Jewish thought. As will be seen below, many commentators on Maimonides' principles adopt Duran's division, but always with reference to Albo, not Duran.

Albo's contemporary, Abraham ben Shem Tov Bibago (fifteenth century)[97] devoted considerable space in his *Derekh Emunah* to an analysis of the principles of Judaism in general and of Maimonides' formulation of them in particular. In the course of his discussion Bibago is led to consider the structure of the thirteen principles and proposes dividing them into two groups: those which deal with God's negative attributes and those which deal with His attributes of action. Bibago's analysis, then, is predicated upon the assumption that Maimonides' theory of negative attributes, which he adumbrated in his last major work, the *Guide of the Perplexed*, may be read into his first major work, the *Commentary on the Mishnah*.

Bibago divides the principles into two groups: those relating to God and those relating to His works. The first group is divided into four negations: negation of non-existence (principle 1), negation of multiplicity (principle 2), negation of composition (principle 3), negation of coming to be (principle 4). The second group of principles deals with God's actions. This group is divided again into two subgroups. The first subgroup contains one principle (the fifth) dealing with the appropriate behaviour of one type of entity created by God's actions (human beings). The second subgroup is divided in the following way:

(A) Continuing actions
    1. on the living (providence; principle 10)
    2. on the dead (retribution; principle 11)

(B) completed actions
    1. affecting part of the world
        a. affecting part of all the world (prophecy; principle 6)
        b. affecting part of part of the world (Mosaic prophecy; principle 7)
    2. affecting all of the world
        a. single, specific action (revelation; principle 8)
        b. preserving an action (eternity of the Torah; principle 9)

(C) future actions
    1. upon the living (Messiah; principle 12)
    2. upon the dead (resurrection; principle 13).[98]

Perhaps realizing that this hopelessly cumbersome and wholly inelegant account of the structure of Maimonides' principles was not likely to arouse enthusiastic approbation, Bibago proposed a second way of analysing the structure of the principles. There are, he says, four signs of the divinity of a *nomos* or system of laws: (*a*) the perfection of the promulgator, (*b*) the perfection of the *nomos* itself; (*c*) that there are provisions in the *nomos* to make those led by it recognize its perfection; (*d*) that the *nomos* leads its adherents to perfection and felicity. Maimonides' principles may be divided according to these four categories and as such they are signs of the divinity of the Torah:

(*a*) perfection of the promulgator: principles 1–4
(*b*) perfection of the *nomos*: principles 6–9
(*c*) 'self advertisement' of the *nomos*: principle 5

(*d*) *nomos* leads adherents to perfection and felicity: principles 10–13.[99]

A simplified version of this schema was proposed by Isaac Abravanel. In the tenth chapter of his *Rosh Amanah* Abravanel proposes three separate explanations for the structure of Maimonides' principles. The first explanation may have been suggested to Abravanel by Bibago's second account, presented above, but Abravanel divides the principles as did Duran and Albo. On this understanding the first five principles describe God, the Commander; the next four relate to the content of His commands, the Torah; the last four relate to those whom God commands, the Israelites. The emphasis here, however, is on how the principles lead to obedience to the Torah. We observe the Torah either because of the exalted nature and 'perfect rank' of its Commander, because of its own perfection, or because of the 'hope for reward and the fear of punishment'; the latter is the subject of the last four principles.

The second of the three explanations relates to the cognitive status of the principles. Here Abravanel seems to be breaking new ground entirely. He divides the principles into four groups. The first (principles 1–3) consists of those which are philosophically acceptable without reservation. These are principles which Maimonides, according to Abravanel, thought were rationally demonstrable. The next three principles, while not being entirely acceptable philosophically, are rationally demonstrable to one degree or another. The third group (principles 7–9) consists of principles about which Aristotelian philosophy must remain agnostic since they relate to claims (about the Torah) which may be true or false but which are not necessarily so, one way or the other. According to this analysis the last four principles must be rejected by Aristotelian philosophy since they all deal with ramifications of God's knowledge of particulars, which Aristotle denies.

Abravanel's first explanation clearly builds upon that of Duran, but adds a new dimension to it, enhancing its importance and explanatory power. The second explanation appears to be original with Abravanel. It should be noted that he includes the fourth principle in the second group as opposed to the first, since he understands it to teach belief in creation.[100] It may very well be that Maimonides did indeed list his principles roughly in order of declining philosophical acceptability and that Abravanel thus draws our attention to another facet of the order and structure of the principles.

Abravanel's third explanation is directly derived, at least in part, from Bibago. He divides the principles into two groups: those relating to God and those relating to His works. The first group is comprised of principles 1–4. The principles of unity, incorporeality, and eternity (priority) are shown to be related to Maimonides' doctrine of negative attributes. The second group, principles 4–13 (principle four falling into both groups) is itself divided into four parts. The first subdivision consists of principles relating to those actions of God which are general and occasional (creation, miracles, prophecy). The principles in the second subdivision relate to those of God's actions which are particular and transitory and which relate to the Jewish people specifically. In this group Abravanel includes the superiority of Mosaic prophecy, divine revelation, and the immutability of the Torah. The third subdivision consists of those principles which relate to the actions of God which are both general and permanent. This category includes God's knowledge and providence, and retribution. Those particular actions of God which will occur in the future (Messiah and resurrection) define the last of the four subdivisions. On this account, the thirteen principles are shown to follow Maimonides' discussion of divine attributes.[101] They all express either attributes of negation or attributes of action. These are the only kind of attributes which, according to Maimonides, may be predicted of God.

Not only is this analysis cumbersome and inelegant (a sure sign in and of itself that it is not true to Maimonides), but it also suffers from specific weaknesses as well. It assumes that in his fourth principle Maimonides meant to teach creation and in his fifth, miracles; and it assumes that prophecy is an occasional action of God, contradicting the position expressed in the *Guide*.[102] We may safely conclude that this discussion does not significantly advance our understanding of the structure of Maimonides' principles.

Abravanel was the last medieval scholar to address the question of the structure of Maimonides' principles. In our day a number of scholars have taken up the issue. These include David Neumark, Mordecai Waxman, Arthur Hyman, Ya'akov Stieglitz, Naḥum Arieli, Nachum Rabinovitch, and Scholom Ben-Chorin. Neumark's analysis need not detain us long. It is based upon his tendentious division of all Jewish dogmas into the essential and the historical.[103] Waxman,[104] Stieglitz,[105] and Rabinovitch[106] all accept the threefold division first proposed by Duran as pretty much a given. Waxman echoes Abravanel's first account of the structure of the principles by calling the third group of principles 'man' as opposed to 'reward and punishment'. Ben-Chorin[107] follows in their footsteps, but he further subdivides the last four principles into two divisions: principles 10 and 11, he says, deal with man while principles 12 and 13 deal with eschatology. This approach is open to question since Maimonides clearly includes in the eleventh principle a reference to the world to come, an eschatological category.[108]

Naḥum Arieli proposes an original and intriguing account of the structure of Maimonides' principles in his master's thesis, 'Torat ha-Ikkarim shel ha-Rambam'. Arieli also divides the principles into three groups. The first four are what he calls 'philosophical' principles. Principles 5 to 10 are 'theological' while principles 11 to 13 are 'eschatological'. We see here an approach similar in some degree to Abravanel's second account of the structure of the principles. Arieli's account differs from Duran's not only in its nomenclature, but in that he separates the fifth principle from the first four and the tenth principle from the last four.[109] I think that his account, intriguing and clever as it is, is ultimately less convincing than Duran's. Worship of God, especially as Maimonides describes it towards the end of the *Guide*,[110] and the exclusion of all worship of intermediaries,[111] is no more 'theological' than 'philosophical'. The categories themselves — philosophical, theological, and eschatological — bespeak, it seems to me, more modern than Maimonidean ways of looking at the world. Arieli's account also violates the integrity of principles 6–9 which clearly all deal with one subject — revelation. Further, why is God's knowledge (principle 10) a theological as opposed to a philosophical claim? This hardly accords with Maimonides' own position as stated in the *Guide*.[112]

Arthur Hyman's seminal essay on the principles of Maimonides contains a valuable and acute analysis of many of the issues raised by them. Hyman first introduces the question of the structure of the principles by taking it as a given that Maimonides divided them into three groups and related each group to a different term in Sanhedrin x. 1.[113] In this Hyman follows Duran's analysis.

Towards the end of his article, however, he discusses why
Maimonides chose to posit the principles at all and, building upon
Duran's division, goes significantly beyond it. He argues that the
first five principles teach true conceptual knowledge about God; the
second group of principles (6–9) are designed to guarantee the
validity of a divine Law in general and of the Torah in particular;
and the last group of principles are required for instilling obedience
to the Torah, dealing as they do with reward and punishment.[114]
We find here an echo of Abravanel's first account of the structure of
the principles.

Hyman refers to the structure of the principles in a third passage
in his article. There he maintains that in *Guide*, i. 35 Maimonides
discussed his principles. On the basis of that alleged discussion of
the principles Hyman proposes dividing the principles according to
their philosophical status. The first principles are to be accepted by
the masses and the philosophers alike.[115] Principles 6 (prophecy),
10 (God's knowledge), and 11 (reward and punishment) are called
'secrets of the Torah' by Maimonides in *Guide*, i. 35. They are to be
understood one way by the philosopher and another by the masses.
Principles 7–9 and 12–13 are not mentioned in *Guide*, i. 35. Being
non-philosophical in nature, Hyman maintains, they fall outside
the subject-matter of the *Guide* and are thus not discussed in it.[116]

Although I think that *Guide*, i. 35 is very important for our
understanding of why Maimonides posited his principles, I do not
find Hyman's use of it in order to analyse the structure of the
principles particularly helpful. For one thing Maimonides does not
give any hint to the effect that he considered his discussion at i. 35 to
have anything at all to do with the thirteen principles. That in itself
proves nothing, of course. But what is more significant is that
Maimonides discusses several beliefs here — concerning God's
attributes, how they should be negated, creation, divine will, divine
names, etc. — that do not appear in the thirteen principles. Hyman
ignores these altogether in his discussion.

It is noteworthy that of all the various accounts of the structure of
the principles we have analysed here, there is not one of them which
relates seriously to Maimonides' own division of the principles in
'Laws of Repentance'.[117] We noted above that Maimonides
divided his thirteen principles in 'Laws of Repentance' according to
the following five categories of individuals: (*a*) sectarians, who deny
principles 1–5; (*b*) *epikorsim*, who deny principles 6, 7, and 10; (*c*)

deniers of the Torah, who deny principles 8 and 9; (*d*) deniers of the resurrection, who deny principle 13; and (*e*) deniers of the Messiah, who deny principle 12. Even if we follow Stieglitz in merging categories (*c*), (*d*), and (*e*) — all of which refer to 'deniers' — we still have a division very different from that of Duran and one which does violence to the original order of the principles, since it groups them as follows: 1–5; 6, 7, and 10; and 8, 9, 13, and 12.

It may be that Maimonides changed his mind about the proper order and grouping of the principles and that the listing and grouping of the principles in 'Laws of Repentance' represents a revision of his earlier views in that regard. Given, however, that Maimonides constantly revised the actual texts of his various works, seeking ever more precise and elegant formulations,[118] and even revised the text of the thirteen principles themselves,[119] but did not change their order at all, and given further that in some of his last works he refers to the principles as laid down in *Ḥelek*, and does not indicate that they need any revisions, it is not likely that the change of order and grouping in 'Laws of Repentance' represents a fundamental revision of Maimonides' views on the subject.

Ya'akov Stieglitz[120] and Nachum Rabinovitch[121] both suggest that the various differences which obtain between the two listings of the principles can best be explained in terms of the different aims of the works in which they are found. Stieglitz in particular points out the educational as opposed to halakhic orientation of the commentary on *Ḥelek*. The latter lists and groups the principles according to categories of doctrines; the 'Laws of Repentance' according to categories of sinners.

The simplest answer to the question of why Maimonides organized the principles in 'Repentance' as he did is based upon an examination of the talmudic texts on which he apparently based his halakhic codification there. These texts (Tosefta Sanhedrin xiii[122] and Rosh ha-Shanah 17a[123]) divide those who are condemned to Gehinnom into the following classes: sectarians, apostates, informers, *epikorsim*, deniers of the Torah, those who abandon the ways of the community, deniers of resurrection, those who sin and cause the masses to sin, those who cast their fear upon the land of the living, and those who stretch forth their hands upon the Temple.[124] What arises from this is that Maimonides, while remaining faithful to the textual sources on which the halakhot he codifies in 'Repentance' iii are based, manages to reproduce his original thirteen principles with only slight changes. First, he interprets all but sectarians, *epikorsim*, deniers of the Torah, and deniers of resurrection in purely actional terms, removing them from the purview of the thirteen principles. Then, he takes these remaining terms and interprets them so that, with the addition of deniers of the Messiah (which he adds even though there is no textual basis for it in the sources), they reproduce his thirteen principles. His fivefold division here follows the textual sources precisely (with the addition of Messiah): sectarians, *epikorsim*, deniers of the Torah, deniers of resurrection, and deniers of the Messiah. This, more than anything else, shows that his listing of the principles in 'Laws of Repentance' demonstrates Maimonides' fidelity and commitment to his original formulation.

In sum, we may say that Maimonides' fivefold division of the principles in 'Laws of Repentance' in no way refutes the claim that Duran's threefold division of the principles is, of all the proposals here examined, the most acceptable.

v. Why Maimonides Posited his Principles

Several theories have been proposed to explain why Maimonides posited his thirteen principles. In his *Rosh Amanah* Abravanel proposes two separate theories. He defends Maimonides to the extent that the latter's principles were only pedagogical devices, designed

correctly to guide those men who neither studied nor served their teachers enough. Since they could not comprehend or conceive of all the beliefs and opinions which are included in the divine Torah, Maimonides chose the thirteen most general beliefs to teach them briefly . . . in such a way that all men, even the ignorant, could become perfected through their acceptance . . .[125]

Abravanel goes on to say that Maimonides called these beliefs 'principles and foundations' only so that he would be understood by the masses, while he himself did not consider them to be anything more than summaries of all the beliefs of the Torah. Since Abravanel denied that Judaism had any beliefs which could be labelled principles or dogmas[126] this account of Maimonides' reasons for laying down the principles is clearly meant to exculpate Maimonides from the charge of elevating some beliefs of Judaism to the level of principles or dogmas.

In another context, however, Abravanel proposes what might be called a historical explanation for the principles, maintaining that Maimonides, along with Crescas and Albo, was

brought to postulate principles in the divine Torah only because they were drawn after the custom of gentile scholars as described in their books. For they saw in every science, whether natural or mathematical, roots and principles which ought not to be denied or argued against.[127]

In other words, Abravanel proposed that Maimonides and the others had been influenced by the example of the sciences and sought to propose axioms for the science of Judaism. This represents, I believe, an accurate analysis of the position of Albo but wholly misses the mark with Maimonides. In the first place, Maimonides presented his principles as those beliefs which must be held by a person in order to assure him a place in the world to come. By his own evidence, his interest was purely dogmatic and not axiomatic.[128] Second, if Maimonides were proposing axioms of the Torah, then there are some beliefs notably absent from his list; creation and human choice. In other contexts Maimonides emphasizes the axiomatic importance of both these beliefs. If he proposed his principles as axioms, these two beliefs should certainly have appeared in the list.[129]

Solomon Schechter and David Neumark followed Abravanel in appealing to influence outside Judaism in order to account for Maimonides' principles. In his essay, 'The Dogmas of Judaism', Schechter writes as follows:

But living among followers of the 'imitating creeds' (as he calls Christianity and Mohamedism), who claimed that their religion had superseded the Law of Moses, Maimonides, consciously or unconsciously, felt himself compelled to assert the superiority of the prophecy of Moses. And so we may guess that every article of Maimonides which seems to offer difficulties to us contains an assertion of some related belief, or a protest against the pretensions of other creeds, though we are not always able to discover the exact necessity for them.[130]

Neumark takes a similar position, insisting that Maimonides definitely posited his creed in response to Islam.[131]

Arthur Hyman has pointed out the weakness of this approach in explaining why Maimonides laid down articles of faith. First, the principles themselves give no indication of having been written for polemical reasons or under the influence of contemporary events;

second, Maimonides evinces little interest in historical matters anywhere in his writings; third, he pays little attention to Christianity and Islam in his speculative works.[132]

Arthur Hyman derives what he calls a 'political' interpretation of Maimonides' principles from Lawrence V. Berman's dissertation, 'Ibn Bajjah ve-ha-Rambam'.[133] In a discussion of al-Farabi's views on different levels of knowledge (views with which, Berman holds, Maimonides was in substantial agreement[134]) Berman distinguishes among '(1) knowledge of the parables (2) knowledge of the results of philosophic investigation *per se* without independent understanding (3) the knowledge of the philosopher, who knows reality as it is and who can demonstrate the truth of his convictions'.[135] Berman contends that for al-Farabi (and, by extension, for Maimonides) the first two grades of knowledge have no intrinsic intellectual value. They do, however, have ethical and political value. 'There are three reasons for this,' Berman writes,

One reason is that the belief that there is a God and that there is a certain order in the world would influence them[136] to mold their actions in accordance with the cosmic order so that the city may remain stable. Secondly, if the opinions of the people in the virtuous city are close to the opinions of the philosophers, the philosophers will be able to live in society and guide it with less friction. Thirdly, if the opinions of the masses are closer to philosophic truth it will be easier for individuals of a philosophic nature to achieve true philosophic knowledge without having to free themselves from the habits of faith which may oppose philosophic truth.[137]

While Berman does not himself directly apply this analysis to the thirteen principles, Hyman does.[138] On this analysis the principles represent knowledge of the first two classes (myths and philosophic conclusions); Maimonides posited them for the three 'political' reasons just cited.[139]

Although there is no doubt merit in this account, I do not find it completely satisfactory. For one thing, it is premised upon the assumption that Maimonides' principles are nothing other than window-dressing, a group of myths designed for the consumption of the masses and which differ in important ways from Maimonides' true beliefs.[140] Second, Berman's account in no way explains why Maimonides chose to ignore certain beliefs — most importantly creation[141] — which one might very plausibly consider to be excellent candidates for inclusion in the principles. But even if Berman's analysis is correct, it represents at best part of the story.

Hyman himself proposes what he calls a 'metaphysical' interpretation of the principles. According to Hyman the first five principles are designed to make immortality available to all Jews by guaranteeing them true conceptual knowledge of God. Principles 6–9 are 'historical principles', designed to guarantee the validity of Divine Law in general and the Torah of Moses in particular. Principles 10–13 are 'required for instilling obedience to the Law' since the masses will obey it only 'out of fear of punishment or expectation of reward'.[142]

While Hyman's thesis is certainly novel and suggestive, and — especially in the detailed way in which he works it out and defends it — draws attention to some important aspects of Maimonides' principles, I do not think that it is, ultimately, correct. There are two problems with his account of the 'metaphysical' character of the first five principles. On the one hand, as David Hartman pointed out, it makes gaining immortality a purely mechanical act without religious or philosophical significance: the parrot-like affirmation of certain beliefs is all that is required for admission to the world to come.[143] On the other hand, it is inconceivable that Maimonides would actually hold that affirmation of beliefs, as opposed to demonstrative knowledge of conceptually significant facts, represents intellectual perfection. Indeed, Hyman cites Berman (without comment!) to the effect that 'the knowledge required by Maimonides of the masses possesses no intrinsic intellectual value'.[144] In this Berman is certainly right.

Hyman's account of the importance of principles 5–9 is also dubious. If Hyman is correct then Maimonides is arguing in circular fashion. As justification for his principles he appeals to biblical verses. Now when he does this in the first five principles it makes excellent sense according to Hyman. He is simply presenting what the Torah teaches about God. But if the second group of principles is meant to guarantee the validity of the Torah, how can he appeal to that very Torah in support of its own validity?

Hyman's claims concerning the third group of principles are also ultimately unconvincing. In the body of his Introduction to *Helek*, as Hyman himself notes,[145] Maimonides goes to a great deal of trouble to argue that we ought to obey God out of love for Him and not out of fear of punishment or in expectation of reward. If we are to accept Hyman's thesis then we must assume that Maimonides was of the opinion that his readers would have wholly forgotten that argument by the time they reached his last few principles which encourage them to obey the Torah, according to Hyman, 'out of fear of punishment or expectation of reward'.

I would like to propose another explanation of why Maimonides laid down his principles. As will become evident as my account develops, my thoughts here have been stimulated by comments and suggestions made by Arthur Hyman, Shlomo Pines, David Hartman, and, especially, Isadore Twersky.

In the *Guide* Maimonides himself tells us that the masses ought not to be allowed to persist in false opinions concerning, above all, God's incorporeality:

> For just as it behooves to bring up children in the belief, and to proclaim to the multitude, that God, may he be magnified and honoured, is one and that none but He ought to be worshipped, so it behooves that they should be made to accept on traditional authority the belief that God is not a body . . .[146]

Maimonides explains that the doctrine of divine incorporeality is of central importance. 'For there is no profession of unity unless the doctrine of God's corporeality is denied'.[147] In these passages Maimonides explains simply and straightforwardly why he would want to lay down at least the first five principles: to make the masses accept on traditional authority true beliefs about God.

We may now ask, why should the masses not be allowed to persist in incorrect opinions? There are a number of reasons. In *Guide*, iii. 27 Maimonides writes that 'The Law as a whole aims at two things: the welfare of the soul and the welfare of the body. As for the welfare of the soul, it consists in the multitude's acquiring correct opinions corresponding to their respective capacity'.[148] That the Torah does seek to inculcate true opinions is a sign of its divinity:

> If, on the other hand, you find a Law all of whose ordinances are due to attention being paid, as was stated before, to the soundness of the circumstances pertaining to the body and also to the soundness of belief — a Law that takes pains to inculcate correct opinions with regard to God, may He be exalted, in the first place, and with regard to the angels, and that desires to make man wise, to give him understanding, and to awaken his attention, so that he should know the whole of that which exists in its true form — you must know that this guidance comes from Him, may He be exalted, and that this Law is divine.[149]

We have here an excellent explanation — based upon Maimonides' own statements — of why Maimonides may have laid down his principles. He posited them, I submit, so that the masses would not persist in false opinions concerning God and so that they would acquire other correct opinions. In doing so he was both fulfilling the mandate of the Torah and making its divine character clear to all.

It is this last point which clarifies where Berman and I differ. He, too, holds that Maimonides posited the principles so that the masses would not persist in false opinions concerning God. But, for Berman, Maimonides' aim was purely political: the need to ensure stability so that the philosopher could live and work in peace. On my account Maimonides' aim was to realize an important goal of the Torah. He was of the opinion, stated at least twice in the *Guide*, that perfected halakhic obedience was dependent upon holding correct opinions. 'Do you not see the following fact', he asks in the introduction to the *Guide*,

That God, may His mention be exalted, wished us to be perfected and the state of our societies to be improved by His laws regarding actions. Now this can come about only after the adoption of intellectual beliefs, the first of which being His apprehension, may He be exalted, according to our capacity. This, in its turn, cannot come about except through divine science, and this divine science cannot become actual except after a study of natural science.[150]

We see here that in order perfectly to obey the halakhah ('laws regarding actions') the Jew must hold certain correct beliefs. These beliefs deal with metaphysics and physics (the subjects taken up, it should be noted, in the opening sections of Maimonides' book concerning 'laws regarding actions', the *Mishneh Torah*). Maimonides reiterates this position in the very last chapter of the *Guide*, arguing that 'wisdom' must precede knowledge concerning 'the legal science of the Law'.[151] Thus, for Maimonides there is a concretely halakhic reason for laying down the principles: correct beliefs (as summarized in the principles) are a prerequisite for its proper observance.[152]

We may illustrate Maimonides' contentions concerning the relationship between correct beliefs and halakhic observance, at least with respect to the first five principles, by noting the following facts. We saw above that in the third chapter of 'Laws of Repentance' Maimonides defined as a *min* (sectarian) one who denies any of the first five principles. In 'Laws of Idolatry', ii. 5, we find that Maimonides defines a *min* as a person who violates *gufei Torah* (literally: 'the bodies of the Torah'). Mishnah Ḥagiga i. 8 defines *gufei Torah* as the specific halakhot of the Torah. In 'Laws of the Sabbath', xii. 8 Maimonides uses the term, it seems, in the same way. Assuming that Maimonides was as careful in his use of words as he claimed to be[153] and further assuming, therefore, that his use of the term *min* in these various contexts was no accident, we see that Maimonides held either that one who denied any of the first five principles (a *min*) would be led to violate the halakhah (*gufei Torah*) or that violation of the halakhah was a sign that one had denied one or more of the first five principles.

We find further support for this approach in a point to which Isadore Twersky has lately drawn attention.[154] In explaining why the Sages bring up the issue of *Ma'aseh Bereshit* ('account of creation') and *Ma'aseh Merkavah* ('account of [Ezekiel's vision of the] chariot') in Mishnah Ḥagiga ii. 1, Maimonides writes that first they spoke of *gufei Torah* and then of *ikkarei* (the principles of) *gufei Torah*.[155] In the Maimonidean scheme, *Ma'aseh Bereshit* refers to physics and *Ma'aseh Merkavah* refers to metaphysics.[156] We thus see that for Maimonides in his earliest major work, the foundations of the halakhah are physics and metaphysics: correct beliefs concerning physics and metaphysics are a prerequisite (*ikkar-aṣl* — principle) for proper observance of the halakhah (*gufei Torah*).

Our point concerning the relationship between the first five principles at least, and halakhic observance may be illustrated in yet another way. Maimonides repeatedly emphasizes the centrality of belief in God's unity. In 'Laws of the Foundations of the Torah', i. 6 he asserts that one who denies God's unity — even if only in thought, and not in word — 'denies the *ikkar* since this is the great *ikkar* upon which everything depends'. He repeats this claim in 'Laws of the Reading of the Shema', i. 2. Why is God's unity 'the great *ikkar* upon which everything depends'? The answer is straightforward: denial of God's unity means the affirmation of idolatry and it was 'the intent of the whole Law and the pole around which it revolves to put an end to idolatry [and] to efface its traces'.[157] Thus, whatever other purposes they may have had, one of the fundamental purposes of all the halakhot of Judaism is the rooting out of idolatry. The first five principles come to do exactly that. They teach God's existence, His unity, His incorporeality (without acceptance of which there can be no acceptance of His unity as Maimonides makes clear in *Guide*, i. 35), that He alone is ontically prior to the world, and that no other being may be worshipped. If the entire Torah comes to root out idolatry, the first five principles provide a theoretical underpinning for the project.[158]

It may be useful now to summarize the analysis to this point. I contend that Maimonides posited his principles because he thought that the masses ought not to be permitted to persist in false beliefs, especially false beliefs concerning God. Maimonides held this position for a number of reasons. First, the Torah as a whole sought to inculcate true doctrines; in laying such doctrines down for the masses Maimonides was furthering the aims of the Torah. Second, that the Torah inculcates true doctrines is a mark of its divinity; in laying down his principles as 'foundations of the Torah' Maimonides emphasized its divine character. Third, Maimonides held that perfected halakhic observance depends upon the holding of true doctrines concerning God since holding false doctrines about God is idolatry; thus it is impossible to observe the halakhah, Maimonides held, without accepting the first five principles at least. I think that it is fair to restate this point in stronger terms: one who conscientiously observes the halakhah while believing in the corporeality of God is, in effect, performing idolatry. Such a person is literally worshipping 'a strange God'.[159]

In maintaining this position concerning the principles I am not suggesting that Maimonides laid down his first five principles in order to guarantee every Jew a minimum measure of intellectual perfection (as Hyman proposed); nor am I adopting a position on the question of whether or not Maimonides wanted the masses of the Jews to accept his principles as matters of *belief* or demonstrated *knowledge*.[160] I am, rather, suggesting that Maimonides truly believed that proper observance of the halakhot commanded by the Torah is impossible without an underpinning of correct belief. If a Jew has incorrect beliefs about God then every commandment which he fulfils is actually an act of idolatry. On this basis we may say that the first five principles are dogmas in the sense that if one denies them one loses one's share in the world to come. Whether they (and the other principles) are also dogmas in the sense that their affirmation is a sufficient condition for enjoying a share in the world to come is a question which will be raised below.

The analysis put forward here stands or falls independently of the question whether or not Maimonides truly insists that some measure of intellectual perfection (attained through the acquisition — as opposed to simple affirmation — of demonstrated metaphysical truths) is a necessary condition for achieving a portion in the world to come. If that is indeed Maimonides' position, and I have no doubt that it is, then acceptance of the principles could not truly be both necessary and sufficient conditions for entry into the world to come since one can affirm them without understanding them. But they would still be beliefs which must be accepted in order properly to observe the halakhah, even if such observance alone does not guarantee one a portion in the world to come.

One might ask if this is the case why Maimonides would bother to lay down principles for the masses if their acceptance does not guarantee a portion in paradise. This question is not hard to answer. Obedience to the Torah is commanded by God and, as Maimonides never tires of reminding his readers, ought to be performed without reference to possible rewards. In laying down the principles Maimonides was making true obedience to the Torah possible. It might be further asked why Maimonides would care whether or not the masses of the Jews properly obeyed the Torah. To ask this question, however, is to ignore the fact that even if Maimonides was a philosopher, he was also certainly a rabbi, dedicated to the strengthening of Torah observance and to the well-being of the Jewish community.[161]

Our discussion so far has concentrated on the first five principles. What about the others? If it is correct to say that Maimonides sought in the principles to lay down beliefs which would inculcate in the masses true opinions (as opposed to demonstrative knowledge of conceptual truths) both because the Torah seeks to inculcate such opinions and in order to provide a theoretical underpinning for halakhic observance, then we should expect to find among the principles beliefs which can be given both philosophical and popular expositions and which are conducive towards halakhic observance. Given the fact that the principles are repeated in 'Laws of Repentance', we should also expect that the principles will have some textual basis in halakhic literature.[162]

Even a cursory reading of the principles highlights the fact that the exposition of principles 6–13 differs considerably from the exposition of the first five principles. In the first group Maimonides makes use of highly abstract, one is tempted to say austere, philosophical terminology;[163] this is consistent with his claim that the masses ought to be made to accept conceptually true claims about God to the greatest extent possible.[164] The exposition of principles 6–13, on the other hand, is more popular, more relaxed, and, in some cases, more prolix. With the exception of the sixth principle (which may be seen as a kind of bridge between the two groups[165]), Maimonides uses almost no technical philosophical terminology in the last eight principles. Maimonides' intention here is to teach beliefs which have a philosophically true kernel but which may and ought to be taught to the masses in a popular fashion.

In *Guide*, i. 35, as Hyman notes,[166] Maimonides distinguishes the doctrines of God's existence, unity, incorporeality, ontic priority, and unique worship, on the one hand, from the doctrines of His attributes, creation, governance and providence, will, apprehension, knowledge, prophecy, and names on the other hand. These latter, according to Maimonides, are

Truly the mysteries of the Torah and the secrets constantly mentioned in the books of the prophets and in the dicta of the Sages, may their memory be blessed. They are matters that ought not to be spoken of except in chapter headings, as we have mentioned, and only with an individual as has been described.[167]

In choosing among these latter beliefs those which ought to be included in a list of 'foundations of the Torah' we could expect Maimonides to include only those which he felt were absolutely necessary to provide a theoretical underpinning for proper observance of the halakhah. We might also expect the exposition of these beliefs to be more popular than philosophical. Turning to the principles themselves, this is exactly what we find. Maimonides included among the latter principles beliefs concerning God's prophecy, knowledge, and governance of the world couched in a popular fashion, along with other beliefs meant to illustrate and exemplify these basic beliefs in such a fashion as to grip the imagination of the masses.[168]

Proper observance of the halakhah, according to Maimonides, depended upon a proper conception of God (to the greatest extent possible to the masses), some understanding of how the Torah came to be, and some understanding of God's relationship with the world. This explains why he chose to posit his principles and, to a large extent, explains the particular principles he included in his list.

Now we are faced with an important question. Can we really believe that Maimonides maintained that the Torah intended all along, as it were, to inculcate correct opinions in the masses providing them thus with a theoretical underpinning for their halakhic observance, but that it was only with the rise of Moses Maimonides that this was done in a fashion accessible to the masses? Of course not! It is Maimonides' contention that the Torah originally taught metaphysical truths as part of the oral revelation.[169] But 'knowledge of this matter has ceased to exist in the entire religious community'[170] for three reasons: the long period of time which has elapsed since the revelation, the domination of Jews by idolaters (i.e. the exile), and the fact that the teaching was originally meant to be esoteric and not clearly divulged to all.[171]

Thus, in laying down correct beliefs for the masses (clearly where they could and should be divulged clearly, and guardedly where they were not meant for clear exposition to the masses), Maimonides was not innovating anything; he was, rather, compensating for a long period of intellectual decline among the Jews. This in itself was certainly a bold and audacious move, but wholly in keeping with the character of the author of the *Mishneh Torah*. By including his principles in his commentary on the Mishnah he implies that the Mishnah meant to teach these principles and that they are, therefore, part of the oral Torah.

Maimonides obliquely refers to this doctrine of a lost metaphysical tradition in *Guide*, i. 31. There he seeks to explain how disagreement over conceptual matters could arise. He quotes three reasons advanced by Alexander of Aphrodisias (love of domination and strife, difficulty of the subject-matter, and the ignorance and inability of most people with respect to these matters) and adds one of his own: habit and upbringing. People naturally defend opinions to which they have become habituated. 'This happened', Maimonides tells us,

to the multitude with regard to the belief in His corporeality and many other metaphysical subjects as we shall make clear. All this is due to people being habituated to, and brought up with, texts that it is an established usage to think highly of and to regard as true and whose external meaning is indicative of the corporeality of God and of other imaginings with no truth in them, for these have been set forth as parables and riddles.[172]

The Jews, then, once possessors of a tradition of metaphysical truths, part of it (dealing with God) exoteric and part of it (dealing with other beliefs) esoteric, have become habituated to false beliefs. What is Maimonides' response to this situation? He takes the first opportunity afforded him[173] to lay down for the masses[174] a series of correct beliefs (and beliefs which exemplify, illustrate, and concretize the correct beliefs) in didactic fashion, and then insists that his reader study these beliefs over and over again[175] and threatens the reader with dire punishment for failure to accept the beliefs: loss of the world to come. In effect Maimonides is seeking to inculcate in the masses new habits of thought to replace the incorrect habits with which they had been brought up.

We now have a theory which explains why Maimonides chose to posit certain beliefs as 'foundations of the Torah', which explains how he chose the beliefs he included in his list, and why he listed these beliefs in a didactic fashion. What we don't have yet, however, is an adequate explanation of why Maimonides chose to list these beliefs in the form of principles of faith. As noted above, Maimonides introduces these beliefs as dogmas in the strict sense of the term, an act for which there is no precedent in rabbinic theology. We must furthermore ask if Maimonides was truly serious in his claim that doubting even one of the principles would cost a Jew his share in the world to come. After all, if one had perfected one's intellect, and had accepted all the principles, say, but the thirteenth, why ought one therefore to lose one's share in the world to come?

Solutions to these questions suggest themselves if we consider the milieu in which Maimonides wrote. Just as today many Jews, even those learned to one degree or another in Judaism, use essentially alien categories in their own understanding of Judaism (a good example is my own use of the term 'salvation' in this book), so Maimonides' audience lived in a culture suffused with elements of Greek and Muslim thought and very likely understood at least portions of their own faith in terms of categories borrowed from the host society.

In the introduction I have described briefly how the category 'principle of faith' had become central to Islam by Maimonides' day. Maimonides, it is plausible to suggest, adopted this category knowing that it would be familiar to contemporary Jews and that it was not likely to arouse in them surprise or opposition.[176] This is not to say that Abravanel, Schechter, and Neumark were right and that Maimonides simply copied an idea earlier adopted by Islam. Rather, Maimonides thought it important for the Jewish masses to believe that Judaism had a creed.

Why was this so important? Maimonides sincerely believed that proper halakhic observance depended upon (at least some) correct beliefs. Jews had fallen into mistaken habits of thought; Maimonides sought to replace those mistaken habits with correct ones. Given the times in which he lived, and the state of the Jewish people in the lands in which he lived, the laying down of a creed in just the way in which it was done in Muslim contexts was the most efficient way for Maimonides to achieve his goal.[177] There is a further point to be noted here. Although it might be thought that, by laying down principles of faith and excluding from the community of Israel all those who fail to accept them, Maimonides was trying to narrow the class of Israelites, the reverse might actually be the case. Remembering Maimonides' apparently secret Jewish life in North Africa, and his family's concern for forced converts,[178] it is entirely possible that Maimonides was seeking to define as good Jews those who remained faithful 'in their hearts' even if in their outward practice they were forced to deviate from halakhic norms. Thus, the principles might be seen as a method not of excluding many Jews from the fold, but of including as many Jews as possible in the community of Israel.[179]

We are now in a position to respond to the second question raised above. Did Maimonides actually believe that if one had doubts about the literal veracity of even one of the principles then one was cut off from the Jewish people and condemned to extinction? I think not (at least with respect to principles 6–13). After all, if those beliefs were dogmas in the strict sense of the term then we would hardly expect to find Maimonides taking the sorts of liberties with their formulation and number that we do find in 'Laws of Repentance'. But if Maimonides wanted the masses to adopt correct beliefs he could not afford publicly to adopt a *laissez-faire* attitude about what the masses believed. He had to lay down a set of beliefs for them in strict, no-nonsense terms, demand their total and unswerving acceptance, and threaten the recalcitrant with dire punishment.

I do not mean to imply here that Maimonides viewed his principles merely as window-dressing and did not himself accept them. Rather, I mean to assert that Maimonides did not himself believe that these thirteen beliefs (or, more accurately, beliefs 6–13) had a salvific status higher than the other teachings of the Torah. Maimonides, I think, felt that in order to accomplish his ends he had to adopt the claim that Judaism had dogmas in the same sense as Islam.[180]

Although Maimonides mentions his principles in a number of places in his later writings,[181] there is only one place in which he gives some indication for the reasons which led him to posit the principles. Examination of that text supports the interpretation of the principles advanced here. At the beginning of one of his last works, the *Treatise on Resurrection*, Maimonides notes that when he discovered that the masses of Jews (including those who imagine themselves to be Sages of Israel) were not pure in their belief in God's incorporeality, and that their brains were filled with wonders, foolishness, and baseless imaginings, 'like children and women' (*sic*), he saw that it was appropriate

to explain in our legal compositions the principles of religion didactically, not demonstratively, since the teaching of those foundations demands familiarity with many sciences[182] about which the scholars of the Torah know nothing, as we explained in the *Guide*.[183] We therefore desired at the very least that these truths be accepted [as such] by everyone.[184] Therefore, we mentioned in the Introduction to the composition on the Mishnah principles which ought to be accepted concerning prophecy and also the foundations of the Oral Torah and what every Rabbanite must accept concerning it. We explained in *Perek Ḥelek* principles connected with the beginning and the end; i.e., that which is related to [God's] unity and the world to come, along with the rest of the foundations of the Torah. We did this also in the great composition called the *Mishneh Torah* . . . All this built on religious principles so that they might not despise the knowledge of God,[185] but rather place as their greatest ambition and devote their greatest effort to that which would bring them to perfection and bring them closer to their Creator rather than what would make them appear perfect in the eyes of the masses.[186]

It is not unreasonable to interpret this passage in the following way. There are certain beliefs which both the masses and 'scholars of the Torah' as such[187] ought to accept. Maimonides discovered that these beliefs were held imperfectly or not at all by both the masses and the legal scholars. In two legal compositions, therefore, Maimonides sought to supply the lack by listing, didactically, those beliefs which the masses and the 'scholars of the Torah' ought to accept. Since it is the obligation of the masses to obey the halakhah, and the obligation of the 'scholars of the Torah' as such to interpret it, we may safely assume that the beliefs Maimonides wished to teach in his legal compositions were those which underlay the correct observance and interpretation of the halakhah; otherwise there would be no reason for insisting that the masses and the 'scholars of the Torah' as such accept these doctrines.

It is worthy of note, additionally, that in this reference to the principles in the commentary on *Ḥelek* Maimonides mentions one from the first group of principles — God's unity — and one from principles 6–13 — the world to come (as an example of reward and punishment). He calls these 'the beginning and the end'. God's unity is 'the beginning', since it is the most concrete denial of idolatry, upon which denial the entire Torah, as we have seen, is based. The world to come is 'the end', for it is the end towards which the Torah directs us. Between them are 'the rest of the foundations of the Torah'.

Maimonides' statements here in the *Treatise on Resurrection* do not prove that my interpretation of his principles — that they were posited to provide a theoretical underpinning for halakhic observance and took their form from the need to counter established ways of thinking and engender new habits of thought — is correct, but they certainly do tend to support it.

I have examined here the following theories concerning why Maimonides posited his principles: (*a*) that they are simply pedagogical devices (Abravanel); (*b*) that Maimonides was copying contemporary sciences (Abravanel) or religions (Schechter and Neumark); (*c*) that Maimonides was trying to guarantee to even the simplest Jew a portion in the world to come (Hyman); and (*d*) that Maimonides was seeking to guarantee political stability among the Jews (Berman). I have also put forward my own explanation which may be summarized as follows: seeking to make possible more perfect halakhic observance among the Jews — which depended upon the holding of correct beliefs at least about God — Maimonides sought to replace incorrect habits of thought. In order to achieve his aims while arousing the least possible amount of hostility, Maimonides, patterning his discussion after a common Muslim practice, laid down his thirteen principles as dogmas without committing himself on the question of whether he himself actually thought they were dogmas in the sense of being both necessary and sufficient conditions for enjoying a portion in the world to come.

My explanation, while suffering from none of the faults shown to afflict the other explanations, has the advantages of (*a*) taking seriously Maimonides' commitment to Torah and the Jewish people; (*b*) being consistent with interpretations of Maimonides which affirm that intellectual perfection is the *sine qua non* for salvation and interpretations which deny that; and (*c*) being based firmly on Maimonides' texts (as demonstrated above).

VI. The Thirteen Principles
and the *Guide of the Perplexed*

The *Guide of the Perplexed*, Maimonides' major work of philosophical theology, contains no explicit reference to the thirteen principles. A number of scholars have argued that the *Guide* is actually meant to explicate the principles as such. That, according to Isaac Abravanel, for example, is the 'secret' of the *Guide*.[188] I do not find these attempts to read the *Guide* as a commentary on the principles convincing.[189] I do think, however, that there is a relationship between the *Guide* and the principles, a relationship which throws light upon them both.

Maimonides himself divided the *Guide* into three parts.[190] Although a number of modern scholars have dealt with the issue of the tripartite division of the *Guide*[191] I think that there is room for further comment on the question. We noted above that Duran divided Maimonides' thirteen principles into three groups. It is my contention that an important parallelism obtains between the subject-matter of each part of the *Guide* and the subject-matter of each group of principles as divided (if not necessarily as named) by Duran. The subject-matter of the first group of principles is God; this is clearly the subject-matter of the first part of the *Guide*. The subject-matter of the second group of principles is prophecy in general and Mosaic (revelatory) prophecy in particular. This, I will argue below, is the subject-matter of the second part of the *Guide*.

The subject-matter of the third group of principles is reward and punishment, and in particular the reward and punishment attendant upon the Torah of Moses, and, like the third part of the *Guide*, deals with the questions of God's knowledge and providence, both of which are intimately connected with the question of reward and punishment.

The first part of the *Guide* is devoted to the following subjects: interpretations of biblical terms which seem to impute corporeality to God (i. 1–50), divine attributes (i. 51–60), the divine names (i. 61–70), and Kalam proofs for the existence, unity, and incorporeality of God (i. 71–6). The first three principles, God's existence, unity, and incorporeality, are explicitly and exhaustively taken up here. The fourth principle, God's eternity (i.e. His ontic priority) is discussed explicitly in i. 35, where all the first five principles are discussed and where their interrelated character is made clear, and in chapters 57, 68, 70, and 72. The fifth principle, that God alone may be worshipped, is in addition discussed and its importance emphasized in i. 36.

While no one is likely to contest the claim that the first part of the *Guide* deals almost exclusively with the subject of God, the truth of my thesis concerning the parallelism between groups two and three of the principles and parts ii and iii of the *Guide* is less immediately obvious and will have to be shown in greater detail.

With respect to the second part of the *Guide*, we find the following major subjects: Aristotelian premises necessary for the proof of God's existence, unity, and incorporeality (introduction), Aristotelian proofs of God's existence, unity, and incorporeality (ii. 1), the Separate Intellects (ii. 2–12), creation (ii. 13–31), and prophecy (ii. 32–48).

According to the scheme proposed here the introduction and the first chapter of part ii would seem to belong in the first part of the *Guide*, dealing as they do with God, while the discussions of the Separate Intellects and creation would seem to be out of place as well, and perhaps better off in part i.

The connection between these last two discussions and prophecy, however, is not difficult to discover. Maimonides, as he himself points out in ii. 25, had to posit creation in order to make Mosaic prophecy (the revelation of the Torah) possible. Furthermore, he explicitly linked prophecy and creation at the beginning of

ii. 32, saying that 'the opinions of people concerning prophecy are like their opinions concerning the eternity of the world or its creation in time' (p. 360). Maimonides' discussion of the Separate Intellects is, moreover, basically an analysis of the divine 'overflow' (emanation) which is the basis for prophecy (and other phenomena).[192] But what of Maimonides' Aristotelian proofs of God's existence, unity, and incorporeality with which he opens part ii? In the first instance it ought to be pointed out that these proofs serve as the beginning and basis for the analysis of the divine 'overflow' which itself is a prerequisite for the discussion of prophecy. They are thus entirely germane to the subjects of prophecy and revelation. Furthermore, without God, prophecy as anything more than a psychological phenomenon becomes impossible. It might further be suggested that Maimonides included this material here in order to demonstrate to the philosophic Jew that accepting the basic premisses of Aristotelianism, even to the extent of being able to prove God's existence, unity, and incorporeality thereby, does not commit one to believe in the eternity of the world. Belief in eternity, in turn, would involve belief in the necessary existence of the world, making it impossible to interpret revelation and prophecy in any other than a wholly naturalistic fashion.[193] Be this last as it may, there can be little doubt that the focus of part ii is the epistemology of the phenomenon of prophecy in general (corresponding to principle 6), and of the unique legislative prophecy of Moses in particular (corresponding to principles 7–9).

There are five major subjects dealt with in part iii of the *Guide*. They are: explanation of Ezekiel's vision [*Ma'aseh Merkavah*] (iii. 1–7), evil (iii. 8–12), providence and God's knowledge (iii. 13–24), rational explanation of the commandments (iii. 25–50), and the end of man (iii. 51–4).

Certain correspondences between the third group of principles and this part of the *Guide* are immediately obvious. Principle 10 asserts that God knows the deeds of men and principle 11 asserts that God rewards the righteous and punishes the wicked. These principles clearly correspond to the discussions in the *Guide* of God's knowledge and providence. The discussion of evil is a necessary prerequisite for Maimonides' analyses of both providence and God's knowledge. The explanation of Ezekiel's vision (*Ma'aseh Merkavah*) — which Maimonides construes as 'divine science' or metaphysics[194] — concerns God's control of the world, just as the driver controls the chariot. This clearly relates to the issues of God's knowledge and reward and punishment.

We may further express the correspondence between the third group of principles and the third part of the *Guide* by noting the following. Both the third group of principles and the third part of the *Guide* are meant to lead society[195] (as expressed in principle 12 concerning the Messiah) and the individual (as expressed in principle 13 concerning resurrection) to perfection and excellence. Principles 12 and 13 spell out in detail the claim of principle 11 (divine reward and punishment) which in turn is based upon principle 10 (God's knowledge).

We have shown the essential congruence between the third group of principles and the third part of the *Guide*; both deal with the rewards and punishments attendant upon obedience or disobedience to the Torah. They deal with them, however, it ought to be noted, in different ways. The third group of principles is aimed at the simple Jew. It encourages his obedience to the Torah by positing that God knows of his activities and by holding out the hope of a reward (resurrection) that the simple Jew can understand. The third part of the *Guide* is intended to do the same thing with respect to the philosophic Jew. It justifies belief in God's providence and knowledge of individuals, it explains that the seemingly irrational laws of the Torah are susceptible of rational explanation (and hence worthy of obedience) and holds out the hope of a reward attractive to the philosophic Jew, *olam ha-ba* (the world to come). This latter is the subject-matter of *Guide*, iii. 51–4, both in terms of a future life and in terms of how the commitment to the love of God and *olam ha-ba* are manifested in the philosophic Jew's life in this world.[196]

In sum, the first group of principles and the first part of the *Guide* deal with God, the second group of principles and the second part of the *Guide* deal with Torah and prophecy, while the third group of principles and the third part of the *Guide* both concern God's knowledge of the world, the goal of His Torah, and the reward and punishment attendant upon its observance or non-observance.

I do not mean to imply here that the *Guide* is only a philosophical commentary upon and explication of the thirteen principles; nor do I mean to imply that the *Guide* is an exoteric work, containing nothing more startling than an exposition of the thirteen principles.

I do not further, mean to imply that Maimonides accepted the beliefs included in the thirteen principles at their face value, the way he wanted the masses to accept them. I want to show here rather that Duran's tripartite division of the principles is supported by the fact that the *Guide* is divided in a parallel fashion. On the basis of the parallelism here demonstrated I think it is further plausible to suggest that one of Maimonides' aims in writing the *Guide* was to explain in philosophic terms the truths taught in popular terms in his thirteen principles and that the overall structure of the *Guide* was determined by and reflects that aim.[197]

VII. Missing Principles

There are, of course, many beliefs having the sanction of Torah and tradition which Maimonides might have included in his statement of the dogmas of Judaism but which do not appear there.[198] There are even beliefs which Maimonides himself, in works other than the *Commentary on the Mishnah*, characterizes as 'principles' or 'foundations'. In the *Mishneh Torah* Maimonides says of human choice: 'This thing is a great principle; it is the pillar of the Torah and commandment[s].'[199]

In the *Guide of the Perplexed* Maimonides characterizes a number of beliefs as 'principles'[200] and 'foundations'.[201] There are also five beliefs, not included in the list of thirteen principles, which he calls 'foundations of the Torah', just as he called his principles: creation *ex nihilo*,[202] that God's knowledge of future contingent events does not destroy their contingent nature,[203] the limits of the love and fear of God,[204] that prophets consider their prophecies to be true,[205] and what the Torah teaches concerning the existence of angels.[206]

In Maimonides' 'Letter on Astrology' we find that human choice and creation *ex nihilo* are both called 'principles of the Torah'.[207]

We might dismiss all this by saying that Maimonides may have simply changed his mind about what he considered to be principles and foundations of the Torah; we are, after all, dealing with a body of work written over nearly half a century.[208] We might also say that even if Maimonides did not change his mind about what constituted the principles and foundations of the Torah he may have been using his terminology differently and meant different things by the same term when used in contexts as different, say, as the Mishnah commentary and the *Guide of the Perplexed*. These two considerations render rather less pressing than might otherwise be thought an inquiry into why Maimonides did not include among his thirteen principles beliefs which in other contexts he also called principles or foundations of the Torah. There is, however, one exception to this general conclusion. Toward the end of his life Maimonides revised the original version of the thirteen principles so as explicitly to include creation *ex nihilo* as one of the principles. Thus, of the various beliefs which, on the basis of Maimonides' own usage, we might have considered candidates for inclusion in the thirteen principles, only one was actually later included: creation *ex nihilo*.

We find the following added to the original formulation of the fourth principle (God's ontic priority):

Know that a foundation of the great Torah of Moses[209] is that the world is created: God formed it and created it after its absolute non-existence. That you see me circling around the idea of the eternity of the world is [only] so that the proof of His existence will be absolute as I explained and made clear in the *Guide*.[210]

This statement is found in a marginal note written by Maimonides himself in what many scholars consider to be an autograph manuscript of the Mishnah commentary.[211] This text was, apparently, unknown to Maimonides' contemporaries and successors.[212] That in itself is not surprising. Solomon ben Joseph ibn Ya'akov and the other translators of Maimonides' commentary on *Helek* were working with a text which had become famous already in Maimonides' lifetime. They would have had no reason to suspect that its author had altered it towards the end of his life. All the later medievals (Falaquera excepted) used the various Hebrew translations and were thus unaware of Maimonides' revision.

We must now ask whether this addition to the fourth principle represents an elucidation of a position which Maimonides had always held (namely that the fourth principle implied belief in creation) or represents a revision of his original position (namely that he did not originally hold creation to be a principle of Judaism). There are several different reasons for assuming that this addition to the fourth principle represents a revision of Maimonides' original position rather than merely an elucidation of it. First, if we are dealing with an elucidation and not a revision we must ask why

Maimonides did not make this point explicit in his original statement of the principles. After all, he himself insists that he laid down the principles very carefully. He wrote, concerning them:

Therefore, do not read it hastily, because I did not compose it in a haphazard fashion but [only] after extended study, careful consideration, investigation of true and false beliefs, the summarization of which among them must be believed, and its clarification with arguments and proofs for each issue.[213]

If the addition to the fourth principle is an elucidation and not a revision, then, we would have to assume a certain amount of carelessness in Maimonides' original formulation, despite his insistence that he wrote the foundations with scrupulous care.

Second, if Maimonides always held creation to be a principle of the Torah, why did he wait till the very end of his life to make the point explicit? Why did he not take the opportunity afforded by the texts which postdate the Mishnah commentary and in which he either lists or mentions the principles?[214] It would have made excellent sense for him to have mentioned creation in his summary listing of the principles in 'Laws of Repentance'; he introduced other variations into the principles there[215] and, as Joel Kraemer notes, it is very curious that nowhere in 'Laws of Repentance' does he mention belief in creation.[216]

Third, if this addition represents nothing other than an elucidation of Maimonides' long-held views, we must ask why he did not take the opportunity at the same time to revise any of the other principles. After all, he was bitterly attacked over his alleged rejection of belief in resurrection. These late additions would have been an excellent opportunity to expand upon his statement concerning resurrection in the thirteenth principle. It was during this period of his life that he composed his *Treatise on Resurrection* to combat the claim that he did not believe in bodily resurrection. That he did not add anything to the thirteenth principle indicates that he only made additions to the principles where he had something new to say, and not simply to expand upon what he had already said.

Fourth, we find that in the first four principles, and in their parallel texts,[217] Maimonides is careful in every place but one not to refer to God as 'Creator'. He uses, rather, philosophic expressions which lend themselves to the interpretation that God is ontologically but not temporally prior to the universe.[218] The only exception to this is the first principle where God is called 'Creator' (*al-bari*). It is not likely that by this term Maimonides meant 'Creator after absolute non-existence', since the term is immediately defined in the rest of the principle in terms of causation, not creation.[219] Thus, if Maimonides originally meant the fourth principle to teach creation, why was he so careful in the original statement of that principle, in the surrounding principles, in all the parallel texts, to avoid usages which might have led the reader to understand that creation *ex nihilo* was originally meant to be taught by the principles?

Similarly, if Maimonides' original intent was to teach creation in the fourth principle, why was he so careful to avoid the term and the idea in his restatement of the principle in 'Laws of Repentance'?[220]

It is clear, therefore, that Maimonides' addition to the fourth principle represents a revision of his views and not an elucidation of them. That being the case, we ought to address ourselves to two different questions: Why did Maimonides not include creation among the principles in their original formulation, and why did he revise his opinions on the matter?

The second question, it seems to me, may be answered rather simply. Maimonides provides the answer himself by his reference in the addition to the *Guide of the Perplexed*.[221] We ought to note that when Maimonides wrote the Mishnah commentary he was to all intents and purposes an unknown figure, with no special responsibilities to the Jewish community.[222] By the end of his life he had already become 'the Rambam' perhaps the single most widely respected Jewish leader of his day. After his reputation was established he may very well have felt duty bound to rewrite parts of his popular works which might have confused the masses to whom they were addressed. Thus, if Maimonides' true position in the *Guide* involved a denial of creation *ex nihilo*,[223] and if he wanted to keep that position a secret (whether to protect himself or to protect the masses from confusion), it would make excellent sense for him to 'cover his tracks', so to speak, in his earlier works and emphasize his belief in creation in contexts where the question might come up, as in the fourth principle. If, on the other hand, Maimonides in the final analysis did accept creation *ex nihilo*, and wanted to be sure that readers understood that — despite the ambiguities of the *Guide* — then it would make sense for him to emphasize his belief in creation in contexts where the question might come up, as in the fourth principle. We know that Maimonides was not entirely insensitive to public criticism or misunderstanding of his views — witness his *Treatise on Resurrection*. Especially after the publication of the *Guide*, with all its ambiguities, Maimonides might have wanted to forestall the sort of furore that arose around the question of resurrection.

We may now revert to the first question we asked above. We have seen that Maimonides attached sufficient importance to belief in creation to add it to his principles in his final revision of them; why did he exclude belief in creation from the original formulation?[224] A number of medieval and modern authors have assumed that Maimonides' fourth principle included within it belief in creation. We find this position held — explicitly or implicitly — by Rabad of Posquières,[225] Shem Tov Falaquera,[226] Hoter ben Shelomoh,[227] Shem Tov ben Yizhak ibn Shaprut,[228] the author of the synagogue hymn 'Yigdal',[229] Abraham Bibago,[230] Isaac Abravanel,[231] David Neumark,[232] Louis Jacobs,[233] Shlomo Pines,[234] Joseph Kafih,[235] and Colette Sirat.[236] We have shown above, however, why this position is dubious.

There have also been a number of medieval and modern authors who have sought to explain why Maimonides did not (originally) include belief in creation in his thirteen principles. For example, in the eighth chapter of the introduction to his *Ohev Mishpat* Duran raises the problem as part of a critique levelled against Maimonides by another, unnamed writer:

I have seen a short treatise by one of the intellectuals of our people[237] in which he wrote that Maimonides wanted to follow the Torah which wrote that God had thirteen attributes, this being their correct number according to what has become widely accepted among our people. Since this number forced him neither to add to nor subtract [from his list of principles] he eliminated other principles which he ought to have counted, such as belief that the world was created.[238]

This unknown author in effect accuses Maimonides of arbitrariness: choosing the principles of Judaism to make their number accord with the traditionally accepted number of God's attributes. Duran himself raises the related question of why Maimonides did not include belief in human choice among the principles of Judaism.[239] He answers both questions in the following way:

But the answer [to the questions] concerning creation and choice [is as follows]: it is clear and well known that belief in both of them is necessary for us because of their derivative principles. The derivative principle of creation is miracles and the derivative principle of choice is reward and punishment. Were it not for these derivative principles, which every adherent of the Torah must believe, then there would be no harm in believing in the eternity *a parte ante* of the world. The verses can be interpreted so as to render this unproblematic. There would also be no harm in believing that man is determined in his actions. But since it is only necessary to believe in these two principles because of the derivative principles, one ought not to count among the principles any except the derivative principles by virtue of which we are forced to believe in the fundamental principles. By believing in the derivative principles we thereby believe in the fundamental principles. Maimonides, therefore, did not include in these principles belief in creation and belief in [human] choice [having included] their derivative principles — the derivative principle of creation being resurrection of the dead, for one who believes in resurrection of the dead must believe in the creation of the world and derivative principle of choice being reward and punishment, as was stated above.[240]

On the face of it, Duran's answer seems absurd. He suggests that Maimonides failed to include creation in his list of principles since he included resurrection, a belief logically dependent upon belief in creation. It would seem that it would have made more sense, and also have been simpler and more straightforward, if Maimonides had included creation in his list of principles and had omitted resurrection, rather than the other way around.

Duran's answer, however, makes more sense in the light of a further claim which he made. In answering the question, by what criterion did Maimonides choose his principles, Duran writes:

What appears to be correct here is that Maimonides only included among the principles those which were taught by explicit verses; these he made fundamental principles, even though they could be considered derivative principles. [Those principles] which were not taught by explicit verses he made dependent upon the fundamental principles, even though one who denies them is like one who denies the fundamental principles.[241]

Duran interprets Maimonides as using the term 'principle' in the strict sense of being a belief laid down by divine authority, the holding of which is necessary for salvation. As such, it made excellent sense for him to maintain that Maimonides chose his principles according to teachings laid down explicitly in the Torah. On this basis Duran can argue that the Torah explicitly demands belief in resurrection — thus raising it to the status of a principle — while not explicitly demanding belief in creation which belief is therefore relegated to the status of a derivative principle, even though logically it precedes resurrection.

The difficulty with this is that it does not fit the facts. There may or may not be verses explicitly teaching resurrection in the Torah but there can be no doubt that the verses teaching belief in creation are both more numerous and less equivocal. Duran's solution to the problem, it seems to me, fails.

Abraham Shalom argues that Maimonides did not count creation among the principles 'because it is their foundation. There is a great difference between a foundation [*yesod*] and a principle [*ikkar*]: every foundation is a principle, but not every principle is a foundation . . .'[242] Shalom's ingenious argument claims that belief in creation is a foundation of faith while the beliefs listed by Maimonides are principles of faith logically posterior to belief in creation. His argument rests upon the distinction between *yesod* and *ikkar*. The principles in Maimonides' commentary on *Helek* were called in the Hebrew version used by Shalom *ikkarim*. But Maimonides, as we saw above,[243] used both the terms *qa'ida* (*yesod*, foundation) and *asl* (*ikkar*, principle) with reference to his principles. Shalom's solution, in the terms in which he presents it, depends upon a distinction without a difference and fails.

Arthur Hyman has taken note of the question of Maimonides' failure to count creation as a principle. Following a line of reasoning initiated by Duran, Hyman explains that the principles 'contain Maimonides' account of basic Jewish beliefs *set down according to the structure of the mishnah on which he comments*'.[244] Thus, since Sanhedrin x. 1 provided Maimonides with no excuse, as it were, for discussing creation, it does not appear in the list of principles which Maimonides composed as part of his *commentary* on that mishnah.

Hyman's suggestion rests upon the assumption that Maimonides' reasoning went something like the following: 'Our mishnah excludes from the world to come persons who deny one or both of two beliefs: revelation and resurrection. Now, are these two beliefs themselves based on any other belief? Clearly, they are both based upon belief in God, so we may add that to our list of protodogmas adumbrated in the mishnah. Resurrection, we may note, is a form of reward and punishment. What beliefs are significantly connected with belief in reward and punishment? Obviously, God's knowledge of particulars, Messiah, and, of course, resurrection. Thus, our last four principles. The first five are derived from belief in God's existence and the next four from belief in revelation.'

I find this understanding of Maimonides unconvincing for a number of reasons. In the first place, if we are looking for beliefs significantly connected with reward and punishment, then what happened to the belief in human choice? After all, of all the beliefs 'missing' from the thirteen principles Maimonides emphasizes this one in his other writings more than any other except creation. Secondly, this whole approach works only if we assume that Maimonides actually thought that this mishnah determined the principles and foundations of the Torah once and for all time. But if he did feel this way, why did he allow himself the liberty of adding belief in creation at the end of his life? In doing so, on this analysis, he was taking serious liberties with the dogmas of Judaism, as established, not by himself, but by mishnaic authority. On the other hand, if we argue that Maimonides did not believe that this mishnah established the principles and foundations of the Torah for all time, but excluded creation from his principles because to a commentator the mishnah offered no excuse for including this belief, why then did he not include it in his summary list of principles as found in 'Laws of Repentance'? In that context he was not constrained by Sanhedrin x. 1 and he certainly could have introduced belief in creation as a principle of the Torah there did he consider it to be such. Finally, if, as on Hyman's analysis, Maimonides' listing of the principles was constrained by his commentarial stance, where in the principles does some reference to the *epikoros* find expression? In the commentary on *Ḥelek* Maimonides defines *epikoros* as an Aramaic word meaning 'making light of a despising of the Torah or the scholars of the Torah; therefore they use the word generally with reference to one who does not believe[245] the foundation of the Torah, or denigrates the scholars, or any student of the scholars, or his master'.[246] There is no reference in the principles to losing one's portion in the world to come for despising a scholar.[247] In short, I don't think that Hyman's explanation of why Maimonides did not include creation in his original list of principles is any more convincing than that of Duran or Shalom.

Why, then, did Maimonides not include creation in his original formulation of the thirteen principles? We argued above that Maimonides posited his principles so that the masses would not persist in incorrect beliefs, especially beliefs concerning God, so that their halakhic observance might be perfected. He included beliefs not having to do with a correct understanding of God cautiously, since many of them are 'mysteries of the Torah' and included only those which he felt were absolutely necessary to provide a theoretical underpinning for proper observance of the Torah or to illustrate and exemplify those principles necessary for proper halakhic observance. Creation is explicitly listed as a mystery of the Torah in the *Guide* (i. 30; p. 80); as such, it ought not to be taught to the masses unless it is absolutely necessary. Since, however, especially in the eyes of the masses, halakhic observance in no way depends upon one's understanding of creation, Maimonides did not include it in his thirteen principles. As we noted above, towards the end of his life Maimonides may have thought he had compelling reasons for amending his original formulation of the principles and including creation, even though it was a 'mystery of the Torah'. We will return to this point later in the book when we take up the question of why so many of the post-Maimonideans who dealt with the principles of the Torah emphasized the central importance of belief in creation in their dogmatic schemes.

VIII. Maimonides' Principles and Other Torah Beliefs

There are a number of different ways in which one can understand the relationship which Maimonides thought obtained between his principles on the one hand and the other teachings of Judaism on the other hand. Isaac Abravanel presented two different models of the relationship, one of which he accepted and one of which he rejected.[248] According to the model which Abravanel rejected the principles stand apart from the other beliefs of Judaism for one of two reasons: either they are logically prior to the rest of the teachings of the Torah or they are unique in that adherence to them — and specifically to them — is a necessary and sufficient condition for attaining a portion in the world to come. In the first case, the principles are axioms (viewing Judaism as a kind of geometric system) while in the second they are dogmas. Abravanel rejects the idea that Judaism has either dogmas or axioms.

Abravanel proposes another model whereby we may understand the relationship between Maimonides' principles and other teachings of the Torah. On this account the principles are seen as general beliefs which, by virtue of the way in which they summarize much of Jewish teachings, are of substantial pedagogical value for those 'who did not delve deeply in the Torah'.[249] They have no special dogmatic or logical importance and as such are acceptable to Abravanel.

Isadore Twersky has proposed a third way of looking at the relationship between the principles and the other beliefs of Judaism. Criticizing Abravanel's contention 'that all laws are equal in worth and that it is impossible to single out thirteen basic principles',[250] Twersky maintains that '*Yesodot* [foundations] are synchronically related to all commandments; they permeate the entire law'. Speaking of the *yesodot* of the *Mishneh Torah* ('Laws of the Foundations of the Torah'), but with reference to the thirteen principles as well, Twersky says that their relationship to the other laws is 'horizontal and synchronic rather than vertical and diachronic'.[251]

According to Twersky Maimonides held that 'law is two dimensional: legal (in the restricted, positive sense) and meta-legal or philosophical, two related components of the Oral Law that must not be dissociated'.[252] Philosophical foundations and positive law ought to be intertwined: 'steady, smooth, rhythmic movement from one to the other should sustain the fusion of action and contemplation'.[253] Thus, the thirteen principles are not specific beliefs chosen from among all the beliefs of Judaism for their special status; rather, they relate to all the beliefs and practices of Judaism, demonstrating the inseparability of 'details of positive law and principles of religion'.[254]

Abravanel and Twersky are certainly correct in rejecting the idea that Maimonides posited all his principles as either axioms or dogmas of Judaism. If Maimonides were indeed trying to present all of Judaism *more geometrico*, or was laying down a list of dogmas, then why does he maintain that we teach only two of the thirteen principles to converts?[255] Why does Maimonides refer to all sorts of beliefs not included among the thirteen principles as *foundations* of the Torah?[256] Why are beliefs which are by no stretch of the imagination axiomatic to Judaism included in the 'Laws of the *Foundations* of the Torah'?[257]

Abravanel and Twersky, however, are both mistaken in their insistence that none of the principles enjoys a special status. Twersky's general analysis of Maimonides' conception of the relationship between law and philosophy is certainly correct and the principles may indeed be an example of that conception. But even so there are certain Jewish teachings which Maimonides did indeed understand as being more important, more general, and more basic than (if not axiomatically prior to) all other Jewish beliefs; namely, teachings concerning the correct understanding of God. As I argued above in section v Maimonides posited his first five principles because all of Judaism — most emphatically including proper halakhic observance — is impossible without a proper conception of God. This is, indeed, the 'great *ikkar* upon which everything depends'.[258]

To the extent, then, that proper halakhic observance is impossible without a proper conception of the beliefs taught in the first five principles, these principles have a special status. They may not be axioms or dogmas in the strict sense of either term but they are withal truly foundations of the Torah.

ix. The Special Status of the Twelfth Principle (Messiah)

It is well-known that the doctrine of the Messiah played an important role in Maimonides' theological writings.[259] He deals directly with the Messiah in his commentary on *Helek*, in 'Laws of Repentance', in 'Laws of Kings', and in his 'Letter to Yemen'.[260] There are messianic references and overtones in the *Guide*.[261] There are even those who claim that Maimonides saw the *Mishneh Torah* as the constitution of a messianic state, the imminent establishment of which he expected and for which he ardently hoped.[262] Thus, Maimonides' interest in the Messiah is well established.

To the best of my knowledge, however, it has never been noted before that this emphasis on the Messiah finds expression in the thirteen principles. There are a number of ways in which Maimonides emphasizes the twelfth principle. First, instead of citing specific verses in support of the principle, as is his custom with most of the principles, he says that the coming of the Messiah has been 'revealed by all the prophets from Moses to Malachi'.[263] He further says that one who even just doubts this principle 'says that the Torah . . . is lying'.[264] Maimonides is more emphatic, then, in establishing Messiah as a centrally important teaching of the Torah than he appears to be in the other principles.

Second, it has been noted that Maimonides presented his principles didactically, without reference to their cognitive status:[265] in most cases he does not say if the principles are supposed to be objects of knowledge, belief, or something else altogether. In the text of the thirteen principles three Arabic roots with cognitive import appear: *i'tiqād* ('firm belief'),[266] *'īmān* ('faith'),[267] and *taṣdīq* ('sincere affirmation').[268] The first root appears in the seventh, eighth, and twelfth principles. The latter two appear only in the twelfth. Thus, with respect to the Messiah, and unlike all the other principles, Maimonides demands firm belief, faith, and sincere affirmation. Maimonides chose his language very carefully. His usages in the twelfth principle demonstrate the special importance he attached to the Messiah even at this early stage in his career.

It might be objected that if Maimonides wanted to emphasize the importance of the Messiah, he should not have placed the principle dealing with the Messiah at the end of this list; if it was so important to him, why did he not place it higher? This objection is easily met. If we accept Duran's division of the principles into three groups, and further accept my claim that the order of the groups is determined by their subject-matter and that the order of the principles within the groups is one of general to particular or logically prior to logically posterior,[269] then it is evident that the twelfth principle could not have appeared anywhere earlier than it does in the thirteen principles. Those principles dealing with retribution (the last group) cannot appear before those dealing with revelation (the second group) and these in turn cannot appear before those dealing with God (the first group). Within the last group, Messiah and resurrection are forms of retribution (the eleventh principle); retribution is dependent upon God's knowledge (the tenth principle). Thus, although the principle dealing with the Messiah appears near the end of the thirteen principles, it could not have appeared any earlier.

Maimonides' emphasis on the dogmatic importance of belief in the Messiah is unique in the literature of medieval Jewish dogmatics. We will examine this issue below.[270]

x. Summary

The main points which arise from the preceding discussion may be summarized as follows. In order to counteract perverted habits of thought and in order to perfect halakhic observance among the Jewish people of his age, Maimonides, consciously adapting Muslim religious categories to Jewish uses, laid down thirteen principles of faith which he wanted his readers to understand as dogmas in the strict sense of the term. Maimonides was consistent in his approach to these principles and, despite apparent deviations in the second text in which they occur, he was actually very faithful to his original formulation. The only exception to this is his addition of belief in creation to the fourth principle.

Maimonides arranged the thirteen principles in such a way that they fall into three groups, and arranged both the groupings and the principles themselves in a logical order. These groupings are reflected in the structure of the *Guide of the Perplexed*.

2

From Maimonides to Duran

I. Introduction

In the two hundred and fifty years following the publication of Maimonides' thirteen principles, the text itself in particular and the question of dogma in general received very little attention. Jewish philosophical and theological writing was, to be sure, dominated by Maimonides but the important thinkers of the period dealt with other aspects of the Master's thought.

During this period we find three basic ways of relating to Maimonides the philosopher, theologian, and halakhist: his work was commented upon, it was subjected to criticism, and it was invoked as an authority. But, with the exception of the work of the Yemenite Ḥoter ben Shelomoh (fifteenth century), no commentary is known to have been written on the text of the thirteen principles.[1] During the two centuries after Maimonides' death no critiques of the principles were put forward. They were not even used as a source of authority: none of the thinkers during this period who even mentioned the project of creed formulation explicitly invoked the authority of Maimonides in this connection.[2]

During the thirteenth and fourteenth centuries only five thinkers explicitly contributed to the discussion of creed formulation in Judaism: Abba Mari Astruc of Lunel, Shem Tov ibn Falaquera, David ben Samuel Kokhavi, David ibn Bilia, and Shemariah ben Elijah ha-Ikriti of Negropont.[3] Of these five, only Falaquera can be said to occupy a place in even the second rank of contemporary Jewish thinkers and only Kokhavi presents a carefully worked out system of principles.

With the beginning of the fifteenth century we find a startling change. The following fifteenth-century figures all dealt with the question of the principles of Judaism: Duran, Crescas, Albo, Bibago, Abraham Shalom, Arama, Abravanel, Yavez, Delmedigo, and David ben Judah Messer Leon. Of these, Crescas, Albo, and Abravanel devoted entire books to the subject while Bibago devoted the last part of *Derekh Emunah* to the question. The other thinkers devoted systematic — and in the cases of Duran, Arama, and Yavez — fairly extensive attention to the question. While in the thirteenth and fourteenth centuries the question of creed formulation was, at best, of peripheral concern to Jewish intellectuals, in the fifteenth century it moved much closer to the centre of the stage. The point may be rephrased even more dramatically: with the glaring exception of Maimonides no Jewish thinker before the beginning of the fifteenth century devoted systematic, self-conscious, and sustained attention to the question of the dogmas of Judaism.

The reasons for this lack of interest in the period before Maimonides were explained above in the introduction. But given that Maimonides had raised the issue, given his stature, and given that in the fifteenth century Maimonides' system of principles was subjected to serious study and analysis, it is reasonable to ask why similar attention was not devoted to the principles in the thirteenth and fourteenth centuries.[4]

In order to answer this question it will be instructive to glance at the persons known actually to have engaged in the composition of philosophical and theological treatises in the Jewish Middle Ages:

Tenth century: Sa'adia, Isaac Israeli, Dunash ibn Tamim, Shabbetai Donnolo.

Eleventh century: Gabirol, Bahya, Moses ibn Ezra.

Twelfth century: Bar Hiyya, Halevi, Abraham ibn Ezra, Netanel ben Fayyumi, Joseph ibn Zaddik, ibn Daud, Maimonides, ibn Aknin.

Thirteenth century: Samuel ibn Tibbon, Moses ibn Tibbon, Falaquera, Gershom ben Shlomo of Arles, Zerahiah Hen, Hillel of Verona, Anatoli, Albalag, Levi ben Abraham of Villefranche, Nissim of Marseilles.

Fourteenth century: Yedaiyah ha-Penini, ibn Kaspi, Gersonides, Narboni, Isaac Polgar, Yehudah ben Nissim Malka, Yehudah Romano.

This is hardly an exhaustive list but it does include almost all Jews known to have composed serious philosophical and theological treatises before the fifteenth century. Turning to that century we find the following authors: Ephodi, Duran, Crescas, Albo, the Shem Tovs, Bibago, Arama, Abraham Shalom, Isaac Abravanel, Yavez, Judah Messer Leon, David ben Judah Messer Leon, and Elijah Delmedigo.

Looking at the pre-fifteenth-century figures we find something truly remarkable. We are dealing with over thirty figures who lived over a period of half a millennium, and who were scattered over the face of the world from Baghdad to Spain. These authors are all known for the contributions they made to the development of Jewish thought. But only a few of them served as communal leaders, and even fewer bequeathed serious halakhic works to posterity. Only two of them — Sa'adia and Maimonides — stand out for the ways in which they combined important philosophic contributions with communal leadership and halakhic authority.

If we divide pre-fifteenth-century Jewish philosophy and theology into pre- and post-Maimonidean periods the point becomes even clearer. While Sa'adia was an important link in the chain of halakhic transmission and a spiritual and communal leader of the first rank, and Rabbenu Baḥya apparently served as a Dayyan, and Abraham bar Ḥiyya was known as 'the Prince', in the two hundred years following Maimonides (i.e. in the thirteenth and fourteenth centuries) we find that among the thinkers listed above there is not one who — so far as is known to us today — served as a communal leader, rabbi, or head of a Yeshiva, or made any important contribution to halakhah.[5]

Turning to the fifteenth century, however, we find another remarkable phenomenon. Of the dozen writers listed above, at least half of them — Duran, Crescas, Albo, Bibago, Arama, and Yavez — were significant rabbinic leaders. Duran, Crescas, Albo, and Abravanel also played roles in communal leadership. All of them devoted systematic attention to the project of creed formulation.

By way of explaining this state of affairs it may be pointed out that creed formulation is a parochial, narrowly religious affair, of interest to apologists and theologians and not to philosophers *qua* philosophers. What do I mean by this? In general, it may be said that the Jewish philosophers active in the thirteenth and fourteenth centuries saw themselves first and foremost as intellectuals (*maskilei muskalot* — 'cognizers of intelligibilia') interested primarily in intellectual problems. That they happened to be Jewish and, given the realities of the Middle Ages, approached intellectual problems from the perspective of their religious tradition in no way detracts from the fundamentally universal character of their quest. Their interest in Judaism was that of the pure philosopher, not that of the apologist or expositor of received religious tenets.[6] I am not suggesting that these figures did not see themselves as good Jews — on the contrary, they saw themselves as the best and most pious of Jews[7] — but their interest was not so much in Judaism *per se* as in Judaism as a route to intellectual perfection.[8]

This point may be further refined by taking note of the following: Maimonides' spiritual legacy was divided in two after his death and his followers ranged themselves into two opposed camps.[9] One may speak of 'halakhic Maimonideans' and 'philosophic Maimonideans'. The halakhists — as was always their wont — basically ignored general philosophical and even narrowly theological issues in their writing,[10] while the philosophers paid precious little attention to parochially Jewish and specifically halakhic questions in their quest for intellectual perfection. Maimonides, at least on his own testimony, sought to unite two routes to human felicity: the way of commandments and the way of intellectual perfection. His spiritual heirs emphasized one or the other of these two paths but not both. His halakhic heirs concentrated on technical questions of halakhah and thus largely ignored — as halakhists had always done — more broadly theological issues such as the formulation of creed. Maimonides' philosophic heirs concentrated their attention on philosophy and thus largely ignored — as philosophers had almost always done — more narrowly theological issues such as the formulation of creed. It may be said that after Maimonides the Jewish intellectual world divided into 'two cultures' each opposed to the other and each, for its own reasons, uninterested in so clearly a theological issue as the formulation of creed.[11]

Nevertheless, the subject of creed formulation was not wholly neglected in the thirteenth and fourteenth centuries. A number of authors raised the issue; none of them, however, made significant contributions to the question and none of them appears to have influenced either their contemporaries or posterity. I will, therefore, survey their work only briefly here.

II. Abba Mari

One of the first writers to deal at all self-consciously with the principles of Judaism after Maimonides appears to have been Abba Mari Astruc of Lunel (thirteenth century). Abba Mari took an active role in the Maimonidean debate which raged in his day.[12] He collected many of the documents relevant to the debate and published them under the title *Minḥat Kena'ot*.[13] In the fourth chapter of the introduction which he wrote to the collection, Abba Mari posits three principles: God's existence, creation, and providence. In subsequent chapters he discusses and analyses these principles.

Here follows a translation of those portions of the introduction to the *Minḥat Kena'ot* in which Abba Mari directly discusses the principles:

Chapter One.

Before I begin transcribing the letters, I will preface [the collection] with an introduction and say: that the Torah dealt at such length with its narratives shows that they are true without doubt. They were not brought for naught, but to teach some principles which are the roots of the Torah and the foundations of the faith . . .

Chapter Four.

The great principles, which are the fundamentals[14] of all the roots, and which we, the community of monotheists who believe in creation, must hold with all our heart and all our soul, are three. The first is the foundation upon which everything depends, namely, knowledge of God; the second is the Torah of Moses [which is equivalent to] belief in creation; the third is the eternal foundation,[15] belief in providence. When a person holds these three foundations with a steadfast heart, it is certain that he will neither question nor doubt the narratives of the Torah, the commandments, or the great demonstrations mentioned in the Torah and prophetic narratives; nor will he endanger himself by introducing new interpretations as many contemporary preachers have done, who have written in their compositions things which it is forbidden to hear and have expounded at length with slanderous myths . . .[16]

Chapter Five.

The first principle, knowledge of God, was made the first commandment.[17] The first utterance made to Moses at Sinai was, 'I am the Lord your God' [Exod. 20: 2]. Included in this knowledge is [the obligation] to know that God is eternal *a parte ante*, without beginning, and eternal *a parte post*, without end. He has no cause prior to Himself for He alone is the cause of all and from Him and His will descend and are created all the causes . . .

Included in this conception are [belief in God's] incorporeality, belief in [God's] absolute simplicity, and [belief in God's] unity which [latter belief] is the pillar of truth. It is [both] accepted on the basis of the Torah and known to all scholars engaged in scientific inquiry according to the well-known proof.[18]

Chapter Ten.

Up to this point we have been concerned with the first principle. Now I will begin to discuss the second principle, belief in the creation of the world, viz., to know that the world was created after its non-existence and that God created it from complete nothingness and absolute privation and brought it forth from nothingness to existence by His eternal will which will not change and which is not susceptible of change, as it is written, 'For I the Lord change not' [Mal. 3: 6]. This is the great principle through the verification of which are verified all of the wonders.[19] It is the axis and foundation upon which rests the pillar of the Torah.[20] This is the reason that the Torah began with the creation narrative: in order to establish this belief in our hearts like a tent post which will not give way. For this reason [also] the Torah was very strict concerning the Sabbath commandments, multiplying punishments and admonitions, since it serves as a demonstration and sign of creation.[21] It explained the reason for [the Sabbath], 'For in six days the Lord made the heaven and earth' [Exod. 21: 11], to drive out of the hearts of the heretics who believe in [the] eternity *a parte ante* [of the world] the belief that the world was necessarily created by God. These people do not believe in the miracles at all. For them it is absolutely impossible for a thing to change its nature; it does not fall under [the category of] the possible [at all] . . .

One who does not believe this principle, i.e., belief in creation, and follows in the footsteps of Aristotle and his companions, denies the entire Torah . . .

Chapter Twelve.

. . . But according to our opinion, we being the community of believers in creation, just as the world was created by His will at the time decreed by His wisdom, from nothingness to complete existence, without any cause forcing Him, so was the Torah created by His eternal will through true prophecy at the hands of Moses . . .[22]

Chapter Fifteen.

Having completed the discussion of the second principle, belief in creation, we will speak about the third principle, belief in providence. This is to know that God knows and comprehends particulars . . . with one [act of] knowing God knows the multiplicity of [existing] things; there is no change in God's knowledge as the objects of that knowledge change . . . the nature of the contingent remains intact; God's knowledge does not force a person to do one of two possible things — rather, the choice is in his hands . . . this issue is subject to difficulties and doubts but that is only because of the insufficiency of our intellects. But the true principle and the foundation upon which everything depends is that which was made known to us 'from the mouth of the Almighty'[23] through true prophecy which revealed to us things beyond the power of the mind to grasp; for God knows all and extends providence over all; [yet] the choice is [still] in the hands of man to be righteous or wicked . . .

Chapter Eighteen.

These are the three principles which we have posited. Isaiah hinted at all of them with one verse when he said, 'Hast thou not known? Hast thou not heard [that the everlasting God, the Lord, the Creator of the ends of the earth, fainteth not, neither is weary? His discernment is past searching out]' [Isa. 40: 28]. Its meaning is that even though you have not heard this from the prophets you should know it by scientific inquiry and [be able] to find a true demonstration to the effect that the 'everlasting God [is] the Lord'; i.e., that there is a First Existent and that everything comes from Him. But if [Isaiah] had not clarified the issue further I would have said that existence comes from Him necessarily. Therefore, he continued, saying, 'the Creator of the ends of the earth'; i.e., that He created the world after its absolute non-existence. This is the difference between 'creator' [*boré*] and 'maker' [*yozer*]. For the term *boré* is used with respect to things which are made. '[He] fainteth not, neither is weary' indicates His providence over particulars and guidance of them, [indicates] that He does not lack power, and [indicates] that He gives every thing its nature, as the Sages said, 'In the fourth [three-hour period of the day] the Holy One, blessed be He, sits and nourishes [the entire world] from the horns of the Oryx to the eggs of lice.'[24] 'His discernment is past searching out' teaches God's knowledge of particulars. He knows the needs of every one, 'not one faileth' [Isa. 40: 26].

Here you have the three great principles. All who hold them can be sure that they will neither question nor doubt the books of the Torah; nor will they deny the demonstrations recorded in the books of the prophets; nor will they interpret them so as to contradict the interpretations of the Sages. They are the scholars of truth who received the tradition from the Pairs[25] who received it from the prophets. In them are fulfilled the words of Scripture, 'The counsel of the Lord is with them that fear Him' [Ps. 25: 14].

In that I have seen that some of our people follow in the footsteps of Aristotle with respect to the issue of the eternity of the world and providence — and thus fulfil the words of Scripture, 'And they please themselves in the brood of aliens' [Isa. 2: 6], which Jonathan rendered as, 'they follow the laws of Gentiles'[26] — and deepened their corruption by interpreting Scripture as they please, therefore have I been greatly zealous and have emboldened myself before the scholars of the generation,[27] going to take counsel with the crownmaker[28] and betaking myself to Mephibosheth.[29] I said [to myself] that since my intentions were acceptable[30] and since the work was the work of heaven,[31] it would in the end endure.[32] May the words of Scripture, 'but the counsel of the Lord shall stand' [Prov. 19: 21], be fulfilled in me.

The first thing that we may note concerning this account of the principles of Judaism is that Abba Mari takes it as a given that Judaism has principles. There is no attempt to introduce the idea as something new or to justify it. It is likely that once Maimonides had explicitly introduced the idea into Jewish thought there was not felt any further need to justify a claim that the Torah had principles.

Second, it is noteworthy that Abba Mari, while introducing a system of principles distinctly at variance with that of Maimonides, did not feel need to take issue with Maimonides' account or to justify his own deviation from it. We may assume that Abba Mari was not positing his principles in order to replace those of Maimonides. He presents the principles haphazardly: the first is variously presented as our knowledge of God,[33] God's existence,[34] and God as creator;[35] the second principle is variously presented as the belief in the Torah of Moses,[36] belief in creation,[37] and belief in creation by God's free choice;[38] the third principle is consistently presented as belief in providence.[39]

This relatively informal approach to the formulation of his principles leads the reader to suspect that Abba Mari did not posit his principles as a new system of dogma, meant to replace that of Maimonides. This suspicion is strengthened when it is noted that Abba Mari twice tells us why he posited his principles: he wanted to single out for special attention those beliefs which a person must hold if he is going to maintain firm devotion to the beliefs of Judaism and remain unswerving in his obedience to the commandments of the Torah.[40] As he himself makes clear,[41] Abba Mari was opposing those Jews who had followed Aristotle in denying the creation of the world and were thereby led to allegorize all those passages in the Torah inconsistent with such a position. He therefore emphasizes the importance of belief in God's free creation and belief in God's knowledge of particulars and providence over them.

Turning to the principles themselves we find that Abba Mari lays down his three principles as *avot* (literally, 'fathers') or fundamental principles. If there are fundamental principles, however, it is reasonable for there to be derivative principles. Indeed we find that Abba Mari lists as beliefs which depend upon the first principle the following: God's eternal existence both *a parte ante* and *a parte post*, belief in God's incorporeality, belief in God's absolute simplicity, and belief in God's unity.

From the second principle, God's free creation of the world *ex nihilo*, Abba Mari derives belief in God's revelation of the Torah through Moses.

From the third principle Abba Mari derives belief in God's knowledge and belief in human choice.

It cannot be asserted unequivocally that Abba Mari intended to posit a two-tiered system of principles and that in doing so he anticipated the sort of multi-level approach to the positing of dogmas later adopted by Duran, Crescas, and Albo. His entire presentation is too informal to allow for such a conclusion. Nor can it be asserted with any certainty that his division of the principles of the Torah into three and his labelling them *avot* ('fathers') influenced later thinkers. There is no textual evidence to support such a claim, and the similarities appear to be no more than that: similarities.

In sum, Abba Mari's account of the principles of Judaism seems to have been made, not in order to replace or modify that of Maimonides, but for the needs of a specific hour as perceived by the author, and seems to have had no discernible impact on subsequent discussions of the issue.

III. Falaquera

Shem Tov ben Joseph Falaquera (*c*.1220–90) made a number of references to beliefs which may be construed as dogmas. In *Sefer ha-Mevakkesh* he writes:

The Seeker asked: 'What is the essence [*ikkar*] of the Torah?' The Believer responded: 'The essence of the Torah is to believe that the world has a creator, that He is one, that He brought all creatures into existence from nothing, and to believe that the world is created, not eternal *a parte ante*, as the deniers maintain; and that He causes His prophecy to overflow upon the prophet who is His messenger, sent to inform people of His will; and that he changes nature by his hand[42] and performs miracles; and to believe that the souls remain [in existence] after departing from the body: and punishment and reward'.[43]

In another context Falaquera lists as examples of 'true doctrines' (*de'ot amitiot*) of the Torah the following teachings: God's existence; His unity; creation *ex nihilo*; particular providence over man and general providence over all else; reward and punishment; miracles.[44]

On the basis of the meagre evidence before us it is not possible to determine how seriously Falaquera meant these lists as replacements for Maimonides' thirteen principles, with which he was well familiar. It appears to me unlikely, however, that such was his intent.

iv. David ben Samuel Kokhavi d'Estella

David ben Samuel Kokhavi (*c.* 1300) lived in Provence.[45] He is the author of a little-known theologico-halakhic work, *Migdal David* ('Tower of David').[46] The book is divided into two unequal parts. The first, and shorter section, deals with the beliefs of Judaism; the second part contains a listing of the six hundred and thirteen commandments of the Torah, patterned after Maimonides' *Book of Commandments*.[47]

The architectural motif evident in the title of the book dominates its first part. Kokhavi first erects the 'wall' around the Tower. This wall consists of a discussion of the relation between rabbinic and philosophic knowledge. Kokhavi comes to the unsurprising conclusion (for a self-confessed disciple of Maimonides) that the two must be fused together.[48]

Having built the wall of the tower, Kokhavi turns his attention to the gates in the Tower. The most important gate, *Sha'ar ha-Yesod* ('Foundation Gate') consists of the three 'foundations' of the Torah. These beliefs are conditions for knowing the truth and purpose of the Torah. They are:

(1) that one must observe the commandments of the Torah
(2) that one must accept the beliefs of the Torah
(3) that one must use philosophy so as better to understand the Torah.[49]

Kokhavi summarizes these three beliefs in the following way:

Behold, I have explained the three principles in the gatehouse of the Tower which I set out to explain. One ought to place them upon one's heart and nourish through them the life of one's spirit, i.e., the life of the body and the soul. For, by energetically fulfilling the commandments, by believing in the beliefs of our Torah, and by studying and investigating the sciences so far as one is able, one's heart will thereby be corrected with God's help, and one will comprehend the Torah in its perfection . . .[50]

Kokhavi has thus far built the wall around the tower and its gates. He now turns to the construction of the tower itself, and describes the seven *ammudim* ('pillars') on which 'rests the house of the Torah and commandments'.[51] These seven principles, as Kokhavi admits,[52] are little more than a summary of Maimonides' thirteen principles. In his rather extensive discussion of these seven principles Kokhavi discusses the biblical verses and rabbinic dicta relevant to each of them. The seven principles are:[53]

(1) belief in creation
(2) belief in choice and human will
(3) belief in providence
(4) belief in Torah from Heaven
(5) belief in reward and punishment
(6) belief in the prophecies concerning the end [of days]
(7) belief in resurrection of the dead.

The wall erected, the gates built, and the foundations laid, Kokhavi can now turn to the tower itself and, in the second part of his book, constructs the tower of the commandments. There is every reason to assume that this approach was influenced by Maimonides, who prefaced his great halakhic work, the *Mishneh Torah*, with the *Book of Knowledge* which deals with, among other things, the basic principles of the Torah.[54]

So far as I can determine, Kokhavi's listing of the principles of the Torah influenced no one; at least there is no evidence of such influence in the surviving medieval literature on the principles of Judaism. It also appears to be the case that Kokhavi listed these principles not in order to replace Maimonides' principles, but in order conveniently to summarize and organize the beliefs taught by the Torah. Kokhavi, like Abba Mari and Falaquera before him, does not seem to have any clear-cut definition of the concept 'principle of faith' and as such may be seen as having posited, not a list of dogmas, but simply a list of important Jewish beliefs.

v. David ben Yom Tov ibn Bilia

David ibn Bilia was a fourteenth-century writer who lived in Portugal.[55] He is the author of a curious little work called *Yesodot ha-Maskil* ('Foundations of the Intellectual'),[56] in which he takes as given that Maimonides' thirteen principles are normative for all Jews. To Maimonides' principles ibn Bilia adds thirteen more, appropriate for Jews of an intellectual cast of mind. Ibn Bilia prefaces his additional principles with the following statement:

Said David ben Yom Tov ben Bilia: I have seen fit to compose words advantageous to intellectuals who are constantly concerned about their intellects and who believe that there is a form of apprehension superior to speculative apprehension[57] which enables them to accept all [correct] theories,[58] distinguishing the edible from the inedible. These [individuals] cleave to the Torah and commandments, believing them to be given by the hand of God. Their belief is not caused by fear of the multitude, nor do they distance themselves from the words of the Sages of the Talmud for they hold them to be Sages in the absolute sense of the term.[59] They study the books of the philosophers in order [better] to recognize the superiority of our holy Torah over the other sciences and conventional laws[60] found in the world. They do not believe that our Torah is the work of the hands of man and are happy when they find some [philosophic] novellum consistent with our faith; but they reject any novellum which nullifies creation, prophecy, and providence.

The reason for all this is that their souls were hewn out of the same 'fountain of living waters' [Jer. 2: 13] from which were hewn the souls of the holy patriarchs and the pious men of [great] deeds.[61] Even though there are only few such men, we have [none the less] gathered words 'sweeter than honey' [Ps. 19: 11] [for them]. These are words taken from the compositions of scholars, scattered through their books and unified by my hand. Since these words are necessary for the faith of true intellectuals I have called them *Yesodot ha-Maskil*.

I did not see fit to adduce speculative proofs lest the intention for which they were gathered — that they be understood by all since they are foundations of the Torah — be nullified. I will, however, adduce proofs for them from the Torah, the prophets, and Hagiographa so as to arouse the souls of those who study them so that these foundations be not weak in their hands.

When they believe these thirteen with the thirteen foundations of the Torah then the foundations will be twenty-six [in number] like the number of the glorious name[62] and thus will be fulfilled the verse of the Scripture, 'The Lord is one and His name is one' (Zach. 14: 9).[63]

The text presented here was obviously written by a person convinced that the Sages of the Talmud were themselves philosophers and that the only way fully to understand the Torah was through the study of philosophy. This position could easily be derived from Maimonides[64] and it is likely that ibn Bilia derived his ideas from that source.

Ibn Bilia's presentation seems to be somewhat inconsistent. On the one hand, he argues that there are only very few intellectuals in his sense of the term and that his composition was intended to benefit them. On the other hand, he writes that he kept his presentation popular so that it could be understood by all. He seems actually to have wanted to accomplish two things. First, to summarize those beliefs which ought to be accepted by the 'intellectual' and second, to propagandize among the masses for the intellectualist position (hence the appeals only to Scripture).

Beyond saying that they are 'necessary for the faith of true intellectuals' ibn Bilia does not tell us what 'foundations' really are or by what criteria they are chosen. Indeed, the number thirteen seems to have been arrived at arbitrarily, on the basis of Maimonides' thirteen principles.

Ibn Bilia presents the following beliefs as 'Foundations of the Intellectual':

(1) 'The first foundation: belief in the existence of the Separate Intellects . . .'

(2) 'The second foundation: belief in creation of the world. This foundation was not recorded among the foundations of the Torah for some reason but I think that it ought to be a foundation . . .'[65]

(3) 'The third foundation: belief in the world to come . . .'

(4) 'The fourth foundation: belief that human souls are emanated from God . . .'

(5) 'The fifth foundation; belief that the apprehending souls are distinct one from another and that they are substances which exist of themselves . . .'

(6) 'The sixth foundation: belief that the soul which comes into being with the [birth of a] man who intellectually cognizes is distinct from the soul which separates [from that man] upon [his] death . . .'[66]

(7) 'The seventh foundation: belief that the perfect reward appertains only to the soul . . .'

(8) 'The eighth foundation: that the wise man who sins is brought to it by his lust and not his wisdom . . .'

(9) 'The ninth foundation is that our holy Torah is superior to philosophic theories . . .'

(10) 'The tenth foundation: that there are in our Torah internal [meanings] and external [meanings] . . .'[67]

(11) 'The eleventh foundation: that our holy Torah needs no correction . . .'

(12) 'The twelfth foundation: belief that the reward for [the performance of] a commandment is [the opportunity to perform] another commandment . . .'[68]

(13) 'The thirteenth foundation: belief that the actional commandments are not the ultimate aim of human perfection . . .'[69]

There is, it seems to me, little that needs to be said concerning this text. As evidence of the spread of rationalist ideas among religious intellectuals in the fourteenth century it may be of some interest, although one hardly needs ibn Bilia for evidence of the tendency.[70] It is also interesting to note that, for a self-confessed intellectual, it is odd that ibn Bilia speaks only of belief and not of knowledge.

Ibn Bilia's *Yesodot ha-Maskil* was rescued from oblivion[71] only by the fact that what is apparently the only surviving manuscript of the work came into the hands of Eliezer Askenasi. So far as I can determine, ibn Bilia's work on the principles of Judaism influenced no other writers on the subject and seems not even to have been known by his contemporaries and those who came after him.

VI. Shemariah ben Elijah ben Ya'akov ha-Ikriti of Negropont

Rather more is known of the interesting life of Shemariah of Crete (1275–1355) than is known of the lives of the other writers on the dogmas of Judaism whose work is surveyed in this chapter. He was the first known medieval Jew to translate Greek texts directly from Greek into Hebrew, he held a place for some time at the court of King Robert of Naples, and was imprisoned in Spain on the charge that he had declared himself to be the Messiah.[72]

In 1345 or 1346 Shemariah composed a short antiphilosophic treatise which he called *Sefer Amaziah*. On the penultimate page of the one surviving twenty-two page manuscript Shemariah lists five 'foundations of the Torah':

(1) God's existence
(2) God's incorporeality
(3) God's unity
(4) that God created the heaven and the earth
(5) that God created (the world) by His will 5106 years ago.

Shemariah's *Sefer Amaziah* was never published, was and is almost entirely unknown,[73] and seems to have little importance, whether in terms of intrinsic interest or literary influence.

The *Sefer Amaziah* was composed almost 200 years after the publication of Maimonides' commentary on the Mishnah. During that period few writers left any literary evidence of having dealt with the principles of Judaism. It is a mark of Maimonides' massive authority that none of the authors discussed in this chapter felt the need to justify the project of creed formulation at all even though it was unknown in Rabbanite Judaism before Maimonides. It was enough that Maimonides had formulated a creed to make the entire enterprise respectable. It is a further mark of his authority that three of our authors did not, it seems, seek to replace Maimonides' principles so much as to add to them or modify them.

VII. Transition to the Fifteenth Century

As noted above, the five figures whose comments on the subject of the dogmas of Judaism have been summarized here are the only thirteenth- and fourteenth-century Jewish writers to have paid anything even remotely approaching serious and sustained attention to the question of creed in Judaism. This contrasts sharply with the situation which obtained in the fifteenth century: all the important thinkers of that period devoted attention to the question, many of them approaching it in a sustained and systematic fashion. What caused this dramatic shift?

Between the years 1391 and 1418 the Iberian Jewish community was overwhelmed by a tidal wave of persecution.[74] The horrifying attacks on the body of the Jewish community were accompanied by persistent and carefully planned assaults on its spirit. These assaults had an explicitly theological character. These theological attacks on the Jewish religion took various forms, including disputations such as that of Tortosa and conversionary sermons which Jews were forced to attend in their synagogues such as those preached with such fervour by Vincente Ferrer. Not only were Christians attacking Jews, but Christianity was attacking Judaism.[75] In addition to all this, many thousands of Jews had been forced to convert to Christianity and many of these remained on the periphery of the Jewish community. Jewish communal leadership, therefore, was faced by a clearly theological challenge: how to defend Judaism in the face of the attacks of the Church, how to define who a Jew was in the face of the converso problem, and how to strengthen the faith of those Jews who stood firm in their Judaism, despite the pressure of the Church and the temptation represented by the conversos.[76] In other words, the traditional communal/halakhic leadership (the 'halakhic Maimonideans') was forced by the circumstances in which it found itself to embark upon a clearly theological endeavour despite the fact that it had little innate interest in purely theological (as over and above halakhic) questions.

The impression that rabbinic figures wrote works of theology in the fifteenth century in direct response to the challenges of the day which were addressed to them much more directly than they were addressed to the philosophers (the 'philosophic Maimonideans') is strengthened by the fact that almost every one of the fifteenth-century figures listed above functioned in some capacity of rabbinic or communal leadership and either participated in formal disputations, wrote polemical anti-Christian tracts, or otherwise recorded disputatious interchanges with Christians.[77]

Once the fifteenth-century figures discussed here were moved to write theological tracts it is hardly surprising that they included substantial attention to the project of creed formulation. This is so for a number of reasons. First, they were, after all, responding to Christian assaults on Judaism, and Christianity is nothing if not a creed orientated religion. In a very real sense Christianity determined the ground rules for this confrontation and to a great measure determined the categories in which it was carried out. Second, in light of the fact that one of the major problems confronting the Jewish leadership was the status of the conversos it was incumbent upon them to define who a Jew was; it is not at all unlikely that this played some role in the decision to formulate principles of faith. Third, given that Maimonides had formulated a set of principles for Judaism it is hardly surprising that when subsequent generations of rabbis were led to compose theological treatises they would adopt a category of theological discourse made kosher, so to speak, by Maimonides.

Thus, in leaving Abba Mari, Falaquera, Kokhavi, ibn Bilia, and Shemariah and turning to Duran and Crescas and those who followed them in fifteenth-century Iberia we are turning to figures who, by virtue of their rabbinic erudition and often rabbinic posts as well, had great religious authority in the contemporary Jewish world and who, by force of unhappy circumstance, came to write sustained theological accounts of Judaism. In every case they paid serious attention to the principles of the Torah as part of their theological expositions and defences of Judaism.

3

Duran

1. The Texts

Rabbi Shimon ben Zemaḥ Duran (1361–1444) was born on the island of Majorca. On 2 August 1391 the anti-Jewish outrages of that terrible year reached Majorca, and Duran, 30 years old, was forced to flee to North Africa, abandoning all his possessions. In 1407 he assumed the Chief Rabbinate of Tlemcen and functioned as one of the central leaders of North African Jewry until his death. Duran was one of the leading halakhists of the fifteenth century and his responsa are an important source of information concerning the social and economic history of North African Jewry and concerning the problems of the conversos in the first half of the fifteenth century.[1] He is less well known as a philosopher,[2] although his contribution to Jewish dogmatics is usually mentioned in connection with studies of Joseph Albo, whom he decisively influenced.[3] Duran did more than simply influence Albo, however; he introduced many of the ideas and motifs which were to dominate the discussion of Jewish dogma in the next two centuries, he demonstrated a tolerance unique to his age, and acted as a sort of bridge connecting two entirely different conceptions of what a principle of faith was. It has been alleged that many of his ideas concerning the dogmas of Judaism are derived from Averroës;[4] this is not so, and while his philosophy might have been eclectic and derivative, his comments on the dogmas of Judaism are original, if not always consistent.

Duran considers the dogmas of Judaism in two works, *Ohev Mishpat* and *Magen Avot*. The first, a commentary on Job, was apparently written in 1405.[5] The commentary itself is preceded by a treatise consisting of an introduction and thirty-five chapters. Duran mentions the principles of Judaism in the introduction to this treatise and in chapters 8–10.[6] *Magen Avot* is a commentary on Avot, preceded by a lengthy three-part treatise in which Duran analyses the basic beliefs of Judaism.[7] It is not clear which of these works precedes the other.[8]

I present here translations of the three texts in which Duran discusses the principles of Judaism:

(1) *Ohev Mishpat*: Introduction

It is known that the foundations [*yesodot*] of the Torah and the pillars [*ammudeha*] and pedestals [*adneha*] most particularly necessary for its continued existence are two. The first is belief in creation and the second is belief in providence. Among [all] other beliefs these two are the most particularly necessary for the continued existence of the Torah because the principle [*ikkar*] of the Torah is to believe that it is from heaven and to believe in the promises decreed for the fulfilment or negation of its commandments.[9] All this is built on the foundation of the possibility of things not acting in accordance with their natures. Were the world eternal *a parte ante* it would be impossible for things to deviate from their natures at all.[10] If God did not extend providence to individual men all of the promises [of the Torah] would thereby collapse. If the world is not created and if God does not extend providence there can be no Torah at all. It is also known that [belief in] God's providence necessarily follows from belief in creation, for one of the consequences of belief in creation is belief in providence, as will become clear to anyone who reads this, our book. . . .[11]

(2) *Ohev Mishpat*: Chapters viii–x

It is one of the principles of the Torah to believe in this providence which the Book of Job seeks to verify. Maimonides included it among[12] the great principles, such as belief in God's existence and beliefs similar to it, which are such that there is no hope[13] for him who denies them.

We ought to investigate here, following the development of the discussion, what Maimonides' intention was with respect to these principles, how their number was arrived at, and if their number forced him to divide them as he did. I have seen a short treatise by one of the intellectuals of our people[14] in which he wrote that Maimonides wanted to follow the Torah which wrote that God had thirteen attributes,[15] this being their correct number according to what has become widely accepted among our people.[16] Since this number forced him neither to add to nor to subtract [from his list of principles], he eliminated other principles which he ought to have counted, such as belief that the world was created. Similarly, concerning belief in God's existence, he eliminated some principles which we ought to believe. These are that He is eternal *a parte post*,[17] that He is true, that He is righteous, gracious, honest, living, intellect, knower and known, that He has neither accidents, form, nor matter, that His existence is nothing other than His essence, that He does not change, that He has neither genus, species, differentia, or definition, that He has no subject or opposite, that there is no other [being] with Him or like Him, that He has no cause, that He is not subject to division or composition, and many other principles like these. But Maimonides eliminated these because of the pressure of the number thirteen.[18] He relied on the fact that all these would be [considered as] consequences[19] of his principles.

It would have been possible for him to have shortened [his list] further by making God's existence, unity, incorporeality, eternity *a parte ante*, and that He alone ought to be worshipped — all five of them — consequences of [God's] existence, but the number thirteen pressured him. These are [the objections] as raised by that man.[20]

But his claim that Maimonides dropped belief in creation [from his list] because of the pressure of the number [thirteen] is not reasonable.

Further, why did not Maimonides count among the principles of the Torah that man is endowed with freedom and that there is nothing which forces one to act as one does for, in truth, this is a great principle of the Torah? Maimonides cited it in the *Book of Knowledge*,[21] in his commentary on the Mishnah to tractate Avot,[22] and in the *Guide of the Perplexed*.[23]

But the answer [to the questions] concerning creation of the world and choice [is as follows]: it is clear and well known that belief in both of them is necessary for us because of their derivative principles.[24] The derivative principle of creation is miracles and the derivative principle of choice is reward and punishment. Were it not for these derivative principles, which every adherent of the Torah must believe, then there would be no harm in believing in the eternity *a parte ante* of the world. The verses can be interpreted so as to render this unproblematic.[25] There would also be no harm in believing that man is determined in his actions. But since it is only necessary to believe in these two principles because of the derivative principles, one ought not to count among the principles any except the derivative principles by virtue of which we are forced to believe in the fundamental principles. By believing in the derivative principles we thereby believe in the fundamental principles. Maimonides, therefore, did not include in these principles belief in creation and belief in [human] choice [having included] their derivative principles — the derivative principle of creation being resurrection of the dead, for one who believes in resurrection of the dead must [p. 14a] believe in the creation of the world, and the derivative principle of choice being reward and punishment, as was stated above.

However, with respect to the principles relating to belief in God, which Maimonides presented as being five [in number] — no fewer and no more — there is room to investigate why Maimonides did this. For, had it been his intention to count only the fundamental principles and not the derivative principles, then there is only one principle: to believe that we have one God, living, powerful, willing, wise, eternal, etc. [that He is neither a body nor the power of a body, that He has no cause, that there is nothing like Him, etc.,][26] and that we ought to worship Him alone. Maimonides did indeed include these in the *Book of Knowledge* and calls him who denies them a sectarian.[27] Were it his intention to count each of the derivative principles separately [then] there are more than five and Maimonides should not have felt it necessary, by virtue of the number thirteen, to drop great principles, which are derived from faith.[28]

What appears to be correct here is that Maimonides only included among the principles those which were taught by explicit verses; these he made fundamental principles, even though they could be considered derivative principles. [Those principles] which were not taught by explicit verses he made dependent upon the fundamental principles, even though one who denies them is like one who denies the fundamental principles.

This is similar to what the Sages did in listing the [prohibited] activities of the Sabbath.[29] Those activities which, as was established by tradition, related to the [building of the] Tabernacle they established as fundamental categories[30] — for only those activities relating to the [building of the] Tabernacle were forbidden on the Sabbath. They made those activities which did not relate to the [building of the] Tabernacle derivative categories[31] even though they are punishable by stoning, just like the fundamental categories.

We have thus accurately expressed[32] Maimonides' opinion concerning this list [of principles]. It was not the case that the number pressured him in such a place which is the essence of religion. We conclude that it was the dependence upon the verses which forced Maimonides; we do not conclude that he counted every principle subject to independent proof [separately] for he counted that God is neither a body nor the power of a body as one principle even though each has an independent proof [relating to God's] existence and unity.[33]

Were it not for the dependence upon the verses, the number [of principles] would be smaller or greater [than thirteen]; for if we counted [only] the fundamental principles we would have only three principles, while if we counted the derivative principles there would be more than thirteen.[34] However, the fundamental principles are three and no more. Belief in God and what follows [from that Belief] is one principle. [The consequences of this principle are:] existence, unity, eternity *a parte ante*, incorporeality, and that one ought to worship God and no other. These five [derivative] principles all follow from one fundamental principle. Belief in the Torah and the necessary corollary beliefs constitute one principle which is that God through the intermediation of the Separate Intellects causes a divine overflow to extend to those who cleave to Him so that they become prophets of various ranks. Included in the principle are four [derivative] principles: prophecy, Mosaic prophecy, Torah from heaven, and that the Torah will never be changed or altered, for divine activity[35] is perfect, enduring, and eternal. Belief in retribution and its necessary corollary beliefs constitute one principle which is that God knows the deeds of men and rewards and punishes them according to their deeds, either in this world or in the next world, and either in the days of the Messiah or after the resurrection of the dead. Included in this principle are four [derivative] principles: God's knowledge and retribution, the coming of the Messiah, and the resurrection of the dead.[36]

Reason requires that every adherent of the Torah[37] include them[38] in these three principles for we ought to believe in God and what follows from that belief, that He commands His creations to serve Him and what follows from that belief, and that He rewards and punishes with respect to the end of man and what follows from that belief. With these three beliefs is a man perfected; without them he has no perfection.

We have already stated that there are more than thirteen derivative principles. There are principles which are derivations [of the three fundamental principles] beyond those which we mentioned but we did not wish to state them here [p. 14b] for this is not really our subject; the development of the discussion brought us to discuss these things.[39]

Were it not for the dependence upon the verses Maimonides would not have counted [God's] unity and incorporeality as two [separate] principles for incorporeality necessarily follows from unity, as anyone who has studied science [even] a little would know. But that which forced Maimonides to make the principles more than three but not more than thirteen was the dependence upon the verses, as we explained.

This is what we wanted to explain [here].

Chapter ix

In the preceding chapter we explained why Maimonides did not include creation of the world among the principles of the Torah. But one objection to what he said remains, for he wrote,

The fourth principle is eternity *a parte ante*. One must believe that this aforementioned One is eternal *a parte ante* in the absolute sense of the term, and that every existent other than He is not eternal *a parte ante* when we compare it to Him.[40]

The heart of whoever sees Maimonides' words here pounds, for this kind of precedence is accepted by those who deny creation of the world.[41] They said that even though the world is uncreated[42] God precedes it by virtue of being its cause, even though He does not precede it temporally. Maimonides should have written, 'Every existent other than He is not eternal *a parte ante* at all.' But that it[43] is not eternal *a parte ante* when we compare it to Him is a belief which would be accepted by those who deny creation of the world and assert its eternity *a parte ante*.

One ought not to suspect that Maimonides held this belief for his thirteenth principle is resurrection of the dead which necessitates [belief in] the creation of the world and in all of the miracles of the Torah and prophets. [Further,] in the *Guide of the Perplexed* he made known his opinion that the world was created from absolute nothingness.[44]

Know, O ye reader, that the great principle in all of this is that one ought to believe what is included in the Torah concerning these matters. He who denies something included in the Torah, knowing that it is the opinion of the Torah, is a denier and is not included in the community of Israel.[45] On this basis it would be correct to say that the [number of the] principles of the Torah accords with the number of letters of the Torah, or words, or verses, or accords with the number of commandments.[46] For one who fails to admit to [even] one of them is an apostate and is not included in the community of Israel. It would also be correct to say that there is only one principle in the Torah: to believe that everything included in the Torah is true. This is the point of the Talmudic dictum of R. Simlai, who said, 'Six hundred and thirteen commandments were given to Moses at Sinai . . . Habakkuk came and reduced them all to one, as it is said, "But the righteous shall live by his faith" [Hab. 2: 4].'[47] By this he meant to say that from the aspect of their particularity they[48] were many, while from the aspect of their generality they are only one principle, it being the belief explained just above.

You also ought to know that one who has properly accepted the roots of the Torah but was moved to deviate from them by the depths of his speculation and who thereby believed concerning one of the branches[49] of the faith the opposite of what has been accepted as what one ought to believe and tries to explain the verses of Scripture according to his belief, even though he errs he is no denier.[50] For he was not brought to this deviation by heresy at all and if he found a tradition from the Sages to the effect that he ought to turn from the position he had adopted, he would do so. He only holds that belief because he thinks it is the intention of the Torah. Therefore, even though he errs he is not a denier and sectarian according to what is agreed upon by our people since he accepted the roots of the Torah as he should.

Do you not find among the Sages of Israel some who believed the opposite of what we agree is taught by our faith concerning the creation of the world? One said that an order of time preceded this one.[51] There was one who said that the Lord created worlds and destroyed them.[52] Maimonides quoted a dictum of R. Eliezer the Great from which it appears at first reading [that he held] that the world [p. 15a] was created from something.[53] Heaven forfend that we say of them that they are excluded from the community of Israel because they were confused in their beliefs concerning creation!

There was also one of the Sages of Israel who said, 'There will be no days of the Messiah for Israel for they have already enjoyed them in the days of Hezekiah.'[54] Even though the Sages condemned him for his statement and revealed his error, they did not say that he was a heretic even though one who believed this today would be a heretic according to what Maimonides firmly taught. The reason for this is as we stated above: since they accept the roots we ought not to exclude them from the community of Israel if they fail to believe in one branch of the roots because of their mistaken interpretation of Scripture.

The case of Elisha ben Abuyah, [however,] involved the contradiction of all the principles in their generality: he believed in two powers, contrary to Scripture, which cries out, '[Hear, O Israel,] the Lord our God, the Lord is One' [Deut. 6: 4]. It was because of this that they said that he 'cut among the plantings'.[55] But one who preserves the plantings according to their roots, and cuts among the branches of the stalk is, even though he errs, no heretic or sectarian.

The discussion has now brought us to [the point where we can] rise to the defence of the scholars of our nation who adopted alien ideas which we are forbidden to believe. We are not permitted to denigrate them because of this and say that they belong to sects which reject the Shekhinah, heaven forfend — may there be none like that in Israel! — for they have perfect faith, they are careful to avoid violating the [commandments of the] Torah and they strengthen themselves to observe the commandments properly.

The Rabad[56] seized upon this [to criticize] Maimonides' statement to the effect that one who says that God has a body is a sectarian.[57] He wrote: '[Even though] the essence of the belief is like this,[58] if one believes that God has a body because he understood the words of the midrashim literally, one ought not [therefore] to be called a sectarian.'[59]

Do you not see that Maimonides, in one of the chapters of the *Guide of the Perplexed*, turned to an alien opinion concerning the opening of the ass's mouth[60] even though the plain meaning of Scripture teaches the opposite of his opinion as does the plain meaning of rabbinic dicta [on this subject]?[61] Is it possible to say that through this belief he contradicted the principles of the Torah? Heaven forfend!

Gersonides also, in one of the chapters of the *Milḥamot Adonai* turned to an alien opinion concerning the creation of the world.[62] This, despite that he proved philosophically that it was created. We may not say, heaven forfend, that he contradicted the principles of the Torah because of this divergence.[63]

The reason for this is that these perfect ones, and those from among our people who followed them, believed in the principles with perfect faith. It was their deep speculation, by which they sought to approximate things to the intelligible,[64] and in which they opposed the multitude of scholars, which brought them to this divergence. If they err according to conventional belief they do not [thereby] contradict the principles of religion just as the Sages of the Midrash did not contradict the principles of religion with those opinions that they held which opposed conventional belief. There is no difference between them except that the Sages of the Midrash turned to these opinions on the basis of their exegesis of the verses [of Scripture] while these scholars turned to them by the necessity of speculation. [In this speculation] they preserved the roots and forced their commentaries on the branches to accord with the roots.

You ought further to know that the Torah does not force us to believe false opinions.[65] For this reason we are permitted to interpret the verses which indicate that God is a body, with hand, foot, and other limbs, in accord with the demonstrated truth that He is incorporeal.[66] We learn this from Jonathan ben Uzziel[67] and from Onkelos the Proselyte[68] who did not translate those places in accord with the exoteric meaning of the text.[69] Were it proved by demonstration that the world was eternal *a parte ante*, we would interpret in a non-literal fashion those verses which indicate that it was created, just as we did with the verses which indicate [that God is] corporeal.[70] But since the eternity *a parte ante* of the world has not been proved by demonstration we are not [p. 15b] forced to interpret them non-literally and we believe in the creation of the world in accord with the plain sense of Scripture. We have seen that in this way the Torah and its miracles will be upheld for, according to the belief in the eternity *a parte ante* of the world, nothing at all can act except in accordance with its nature and the Torah as a whole would be abolished, since it is all of it [founded upon] supernatural miracles.

You ought further to know that the necessity of believing in the creation of the world — in order to uphold the miracles of the Torah — does not relate to absolute creation, i.e., the belief that the world was created from absolute nothingness. For you will not find any of the miracles of the Torah or prophets which involve creation *ex nihilo*.[71] All of the miracles involve [creation of] something from something: a snake from a staff,[72] manna from the air,[73] and likewise with them all. If creation as it was believed by the ancient philosophers — that the world was created from something, its creation involving a transition from chaotic to ordered motion — were proved by demonstration, all the miracles of the Torah would be upheld by this belief and we could believe it safely, without fear of heresy.[74]

After these propositions you should understand what Maimonides wrote in the fourth principle, namely that every existent other than God is not eternal *a parte ante* when we compare it to God. For now you know that one is only called a heretic if one uproots the principles from their place. But one who believes in the principles and cuts among the branches because of the necessity of [his] speculation is, because he upholds the principles of the Torah, not a heretic, even though he errs. Thus, one who believes in the temporal precedence [to the world] of something other than God, but at the same time believes in the possibility of things departing from their natures, and [believes in] resurrection and things like it, even though he errs, and even though he ought to believe that nothing precedes the world, temporally or causally, but God, he is no heretic, for this belief did not lead him to pull up the roots, nor to deny what is included in the Torah, for his speculation compelled him to extend the meaning of the verses with respect to the branches while upholding the roots.

This is what we wanted to establish.

Chapter x

It might be asked that, inasmuch as belief in providence is one of the principles of the Torah and is such that one who denies it is excluded from the community of Israel,[75] why is there no explicit commandment in the Torah in which God states, 'Believe that I extend providence over the whole world!'? Nor have we found that the Sages maintained that it was a positive commandment to believe in providence.[76]

The answer to this question is that no principle among the principles of the Torah ought to be counted as a commandment[77] since every commandment stands independently, such that if it were abolished, the Torah in its generality would not collapse.[78] But that which is a principle among the principles of the Torah ought not to be called a 'commandment' as such but a 'foundation' or 'principle'. It is not God's way, concerning foundations and principles, to write, 'I command you to believe this principle!' for the Torah in its generality constitutes a commandment concerning this principle.[79] This is the burden of R. Isaac's observation, 'There is no need for the Torah to have begun before "This month . . ."' [Exod. 12: 2],[80] [and the explanation of why] he sought a reason for the fact that the Torah opened with 'In the beginning' [Gen. 1: 1], even though it is a principle among the principles of the Torah.[81] The reason for this is that that which is a principle of the Torah without which the Torah cannot stand[82] need not be commanded in the Torah itself. This is the case with all the principles.

There are only four exceptions to this generalization: [God's] existence, [God's] unity, that He alone ought to be worshipped, and the uprooting of the Torah,[83] for these four principles are counted among the commandments.[84] We can account for this in the following fashion: each of these four principles is in one sense a principle and in one sense a branch.[85] From the perspective of its being a principle it is not counted among the commandments while from the perspective of its being a branch it is counted among the commandments.

Thus, in the belief concerning God's existence, there is a principle; this is to keep away from the belief of Epicurus [p. 16a] 'and his followers'[86] who maintained that there is no God in the World. From the perspective of its being a principle [this belief] is not included among the commandments. But, based upon this belief in divinity is the commandment [to believe] that it was this God who, by His strength and will, brought us out of Egypt.[87] From this perspective it is counted among the commandments according to the opinion of [at least] some of our scholars, for there are those among them who did not count the utterance[88] 'I am' [Exod. 20: 2] among the commandments.[89]

Thus, in the belief of [God's] unity there is a principle; this is the denial of dualism which was believed in by the dualists who say that there are two gods. From the perspective of its being a principle [this belief] is not included among the commandments. But, based upon this belief in unity is the commandment [to believe] that this One is one in every respect, and is not susceptible of division, decomposition, multiplicity, or composition, for if He were corporeal — even if He was one body — since He would be susceptible of division His unity would not be absolute; for this reason we have a commandment to believe in this unity.[90]

On this basis you will be able to understand Rabbi Abraham ben David's statement to the effect that those who believe in [God's] corporeality, even though they are mistaken, ought not to be called heretics and sectarians, for their belief [only] contradicts one of the branches of [the belief in God's] unity, and does not involve uprooting the root and cutting among the plantings.[91] According to Maimonides even such a one[92] is called a sectarian because the commandment here is to believe that He will then turn 'to the people a pure language, that they may all call upon the name of the Lord, to serve Him with one consent' [Zeph. 3: 9],[93] as it was explained by our Sages, and then 'shall the Lord be one and His name one' [Zach. 14: 9].[94]

Thus, in the belief concerning worshipping only God, there is a principle; this is not to ascribe divinity to any entity but He. This is not included in the notion of [God's] unity — we have seen that Maimonides made it a separate principle — for, coupled with belief in [God's] unity, it would be possible to believe that there existed a necessary existent other than God on a lower plane [of existence] than God. For this reason there is a [separate] principle in the Torah not to believe this, for every entity other than God exists contingently such that were we to conceive of its non-existence God would still exist. God alone is necessarily existent such that we cannot at all conceive of His non-existence and [simultaneously conceive of the continued] existence of any other thing. There is a branch of this [belief] which is properly considered a commandment; this is the admonition concerning idolatry. From this perspective it is counted as a commandment.

Thus, in the belief concerning the uprooting [of the Torah] there is a principle; this is that the Torah will never be altered nor exchanged in its entirety. There is [also] a branch, that we are not to add or subtract individual commandments on our own initiative even though the Torah as a whole continues to exist. From this perspective it is counted as a commandment.

It might be further asked why the Sages did not include in 'These are those who have no share in the world to come' he who denies God's providence. [It might be asked] further why only very few of the thirteen principles were mentioned there[95] even though in the Mishnah and Baraita the Sages recorded in exaggerated fashion many things the doing of which would cost one his share in the world to come.[96] They did this by way of admonition so that one would not do these things, even though they are not principles of the Torah.

We have already provided the answer to this above.[97] For, were it not for the necessity of the verses, we should have been satisfied with the listing of three principles, the fundamental principles of them all. These are: belief in God, belief in the Torah, and belief in retribution. This is the reason why the mishnah only mentioned three [beliefs]: he who says that there is no resurrection taught in the Torah, that there is no Torah from heaven, and the *epikoros*.

The mishnah stated 'the *epikoros*' in place of 'belief in God' since it is known from the opinions of the ancients that Epicurus was a man who believed that the world came about by chance and that it has no Guide. With respect to this the Sages said, 'Be diligent in studying Torah [. . .] how to respond to an *epikoros*.'[98] Even though the Masters of the Talmud explained that the word [*epikoros*] is derived from *hefker* ['lawlessness' or 'abandonment'], and assimilated it to one who acts [p. 16b] in a disrespectful fashion towards scholars,[99] they did this [only] because their honour is associated with that of God's as they expounded: ' "Thou shalt fear the Lord thy God" [Deut. 6: 13] — this includes the Sages.'[100] But the principle of the doctrine of the *epikoros* is the denial of God. The Baraita explained that 'the sectarians and *epikorsim* are sent to Gehinnom and judged there for generation after generation'.[101] They said further that the sectarians and the *epikorsim* are sent down but are not brought up.[102]

It is known that the sectarians are those who believe in many gods. It ought to be asked, then, why they were not mentioned in this mishnah. It appears that *epikoros* is a term used in [both] general and particular senses. In a general sense it is used of those who deny God and in a particular sense of those who denigrate the Sages. Maimonides counted among them[103] those who deny prophecy.[104] As we see it is more appropriate to include them[105] among those who deny Torah from heaven as we shall explain. Since [the meaning of the term] *epikoros* includes every evil belief concerning God the mishnah did not mention sectarians but mentioned the *epikoros* and said, in place of the belief in the Torah, 'one who says there is no Torah from heaven'. Included in this are those who deny prophecy, and the prophecy of Moses, and the uprooting of the Torah, for all of this follows from belief in the Torah.

In place of belief in retribution [the mishnah] said, 'he who says there is no resurrection from the Torah' for this is the end of retribution. Included in this are those who deny the coming of the Messiah, for by his hand will the dead live. Included in this [also] are those who deny retribution to souls, for one who believes in the resurrection of body and soul will certainly believe in the world that will come after death, which was called by some of the Sages, 'the world of souls'.[106] Included in this [also] are those who deny God's knowledge for it precedes belief in retribution as we saw above. Maimonides included this under the rubric *epikoros*.[107] But we have listed it in the most appropriate fashion as we see it.

This is what we wanted to explain.

(3) *Magen Avot*, 'introduction'

We have learned in the Mishnah: 'All Israel have a portion in the world to come, for it is written, "Thy people also shall be all righteous; they shall inherit the land forever, the branch of my planting, the work of my hands, that I may be glorified . . ." [Isa. 60: 21]. But the following have no portion therein: He who maintains that resurrection is not a biblical doctrine, the Torah was not divinely revealed, and an *epikoros*.' I now commence to explain it and tractate Avot, as I have set myself to do with God's help.[108]

I have divided this book into four parts. I have called the first part *Ḥelek Eloha mi-Ma'al*;[109] [in it] I refute the opinions of the *epikorsim*. I have divided it into five chapters: (1) God's existence, (2) His unity, (3) [His] incorporeality, (4) that He is eternal *a parte ante* — to this I added that He ought to be worshipped. These five principles, according to my opinion, are included [under the rubric] *'epikoros'* mentioned in the mishnah for he who denies them is an *epikoros* as I wrote in my book *Ohev Mishpat*[110] — (5) concerning attributes.

The second part relates to the statement, 'the Torah was not divinely revealed'. I called it *Ḥelek Shoseinu*[111] and have divided it into four chapters: (1) prophecy, (2) Mosaic prophecy, (3) revelation, (4) the eternity of the Torah.

The third part relates to the one who says 'that resurrection is not taught in the Torah'. I called it *Ḥelek Ya'akov*[112] for Jacob our father did not die.[113] I divided it into four chapters: (1) God's knowledge, (2) providence, reward, and punishment, (3) the days of the Messiah, (4) resurrection of the dead.

These are the three principles which earlier scholars summarized in the verse, 'And that the land be not desolate' [Gen. 47: 19]:[114] revelation, reward and punishment, God's existence.[115] [These are] the foundations of the Torah for it is a foundation of the faith to believe in God, in His existence, unity, eternity *a parte ante*, incorporeality, and that He ought to be worshipped. This is included [under the Rubric] '*epikoros*' as mentioned above. After this [it is a foundation of the Torah] to believe in the prophecy of the prophets, in the prophecy of Moses, in the Torah, and in its eternity. This is included [under the rubric], 'the Torah . . . is from heaven'. After this [it is a foundation of the Torah] to believe in reward and punishment and its branches. This is included [under the rubric] 'resurrection'.

The fourth part is a commentary on tractate Avot; I have called it *Ḥelek Adonai Amo*,[116] they being the Sanhedrin and the Tannaim mentioned in it. Since it is customary to begin [it] with 'All Israel have a portion in the world to come.'[117] It has the five chapters into which the tractate is divided. This section deals with the acquiring of ethical traits, they being the ladder with which to climb to the foundations of faith.

I begin now with part one concerning the opinion of the *epikoros*, even though it is the last in Mishnah. I follow the order of the Torah which began the Decalogue with belief in God. After that I will explain Torah from heaven. I will deal with resurrection at the end for it is the final reward.[118]

II. Duran's Principles

Even a cursory reading of these three texts reveals that in Duran's writings we are not confronted with a single, unified system of dogma, but with at least two different systems.

In the first text cited, the introduction to *Ohev Mishpat*, Duran, using architectural terminology (foundations, pillars, and pedestals), discusses some of the beliefs the holding of which is a prerequisite for belief in Torah from heaven. Duran's concern with isolating those beliefs which make belief in Torah from heaven possible is interestingly paralleled in Crescas, as we shall see in the next chapter.

Duran tells us here that the most important (but, by implication, not the only) beliefs necessary for belief in Torah from heaven are belief in creation and belief in providence. He immediately goes on to say, however, that belief in providence necessarily follows from belief in creation. This makes creation the single most important belief of Judaism. Duran was the first of a long series of thinkers who made this claim, as will be seen below in chapter 10. But in what sense is creation the single most important belief in Judaism? Duran's terminology here, I believe, is instructive: the 'continued existence' of the Torah depends upon this 'foundation', 'pillar', and 'pedestal'; belief in the Torah 'is built on' this belief. In this passage Duran is asking a structural question: upon what belief or beliefs is Judaism based?[119]

In order to understand the importance of this point it must be noted that Maimonides was answering a very different sort of question with his thirteen principles. Maimonides' principles were ostensibly posited to answer the question, what beliefs must a person hold in order to be considered a Jew and in order to merit a share in the world to come? The beliefs which satisfy these criteria may or may not be logically more fundamental than other beliefs; that is entirely beside the point, since what concerned Maimonides was their *dogmatic* importance, not their logical relation to the other beliefs of Judaism.

In framing the question in the way he did Duran radically shifted the universe of discourse in which medieval Jewish discussions of dogma took place. It is not hard to account for this change of emphasis and direction. Maimonides, as we saw above,[120] posited his principles against the background of earlier Muslim professions of faith in which the dogmatic conception of principles of faith appeared to predominate. Duran, on the other hand, not only had the example of Maimonides before him, but an understanding of theology which differed from that of Maimonides. Aristotle had presented a deductive model of science in his *Posterior Analytics*: each distinct science was built upon its own system of axioms which served as the basis for all statements made within that science.[121] By the late Middle Ages theology had come to be conceived as a science in this fashion as is evident, for example, from the beginning of Aquinas's *Summa Theologiae*.[122] (That Duran was familiar with at least some developments in Christian theology is evident from his anti-Christian polemic, *Keshet u-Magen*.[123])

Duran, however, was a transitional figure and did not appear to realize that he was changing the way in which the issue of dogma was to be discussed in Judaism. This may be seen when we turn to examine his statements concerning the principles of Judaism in *Ohev Mishpat*, viii–x and in the introduction to *Magen Avot*.

The treatise which Duran prefaces to his commentary on Job (i.e. the introduction and thirty-five chapters which precede the actual commentary in *Ohev Mishpat*) is devoted to an extensive and detailed discussion of the issue of divine providence.[124] It is in the context of that discussion that Duran brings up the issue of the dogmatic status of belief in providence. Taking Maimonides' thirteen principles as the classic utterance on the principles of Judaism, Duran is led to examine them. He opens his analysis of Maimonides' principles by asking why Maimonides excluded certain principles (especially creation and human freedom) and included others. Duran's intention here and throughout his discussion of the principles is not to criticize Maimonides but to explicate and defend the latter's position. Thus, he does not come to replace Maimonides' principles, only to explain them.

Duran proposes what at first sight appears to be an odd explanation of Maimonides' failure to include creation and freedom: these two beliefs are presupposed by beliefs which Maimonides does not include in the principles. This is odd since it would seem to have made more sense for Maimonides to have included the more fundamental principles (creation and freedom) rather than their derivatives (in this case resurrection and retribution).

Duran's position here, however, actually does make sense in the context of his explanation of the criterion which guided Maimonides' choice of the principles. Maimonides counted as a principle of Torah, Duran maintained, only those beliefs which were explicitly taught as such by verses of the Bible. Ignoring the question of whether or not the Torah actually does teach as obligatory beliefs those thirteen beliefs which Maimonides included in his list of dogmas, we may note that Duran's explanation of the criterion which guided Maimonides' choice makes sense only if we assume him *not* to have understood Maimonides' principles to be axiomatic or foundational to Judaism in the way in which he had posited creation and freedom to be. This is evident for a number of reasons. In the first place, axioms are not chosen by the happenstance of verses; second, Duran himself says that Maimonides had excluded from his list belief in creation, a belief which Duran maintained *was* axiomatic to Judaism; third, in a number of places Duran refers to various beliefs not included in Maimonides' list as 'principles',[125] thus showing that he did not consider Maimonides' list to be exhaustive — and an incomplete list of axioms leads to a defective science.

Duran, building upon an analogy with the laws of the Sabbath distinguishes between fundamental and derived principles (*avot* and *toladot*).[126] There are three fundamental principles among Maimonides' thirteen: belief in God, in Torah from heaven, and in retribution. In *Magen Avot* and in *Ohev Mishpat* Duran shows how each one of these beliefs is connected with a different term in Sanhedrin x. 1. This, it should be noted, expands his defence of Maimonides: Maimonides is presented, not as innovator, but as explicator of the mishnaic text.

Having raised the question in his eighth chapter of why Maimonides fails to count creation as a principle of faith, Duran develops the issue further in *Ohev Mishpat*, ix. Maimonides' fourth principle, he says, not only fails to teach creation, but can plausibly be interpreted as teaching that God precedes the world only causally, not temporally — that is, the fourth principle can be read as affirming the eternity of the world! Duran hastens to reassure the reader that Maimonides could not possibly have believed in the eternity of the world since (*a*) he accepts resurrection and other miracles and (*b*) he explicitly affirms the temporal creation of the world in the *Guide*.

Duran then goes on to say that, in any event, heresy is not the denial of a belief taught by the Torah, but the denial of a belief which one knows to be taught by the Torah. If one believes in the Torah, and accepts it as true, then even if one denies one of the beliefs taught in the Torah because one does not realize that it is a Torah belief, one is not a heretic. 'On this basis', Duran continues, 'it would be correct to say that the number of the principles of the Torah accords with the number of letters of the Torah, or words, or verses, or accords with the number of commandments.' Duran's position here depends upon the halakhically well-entrenched distinction between transgressions committed purposefully (*be-mezid*) and transgressions committed inadvertently (*be-shogeg*). Halakhah recognized ignorance of the law as an exculpating factor. Only that person who purposefully rejects a Torah teaching, Duran maintains, can be considered a heretic. A person who rejects such a teaching without meaning to rebel against the Torah (such as Rabad's corporealist) is no heretic.

It ought to be noted that, given the historical context in which Duran enunciated his position, it was remarkably tolerant.[127] He was well aware of the fact that his position conflicted with Maimonides' strict demands for doctrinal orthodoxy and approvingly quotes Rabad's strictures on Maimonides on the subject. It ought to be further noted that Duran is not here positing a position on the principles of Judaism at variance with the position sketched out in chapter viii. In that chapter he sought to explain why Maimonides had posited the principles he had: given the statements made by the mishnah on which Maimonides was commenting Maimonides' three fundamental principles were predetermined; Maimonides then chose to include those of the derivatives of those three fundamental principles which were explicitly taught by the Torah. In the present chapter he is concerned with the question of what heresy is, and enunciates his own position. But there is no contradiction; nowhere in chapter viii had he stated that Maimonides' list exhausted all the principles of Judaism. On the contrary, we noted above that Duran was quite clear in affirming that they had not. In a dogmatic sense (as opposed to a foundational, axiomatic sense) the principles of Judaism are all of its teachings.

Duran goes on to justify his position by citing examples from rabbinic literature of Sages who maintained positions — concerning creation and Messiah — at variance with accepted rabbinic doctrine. He distinguishes such Sages from the notorious apostate Elisha ben Abuyah on the grounds that while the Sages did not intend to rebel against the Torah, Elisha did. Duran's criterion for heresy is not doctrinal heterodoxy, therefore, as was the case with Maimonides, but intentional denial of (any) Torah teachings.

Duran goes on to cite heterodox statements made by Maimonides and Gersonides. Since no one could possibly accuse these two giants of the tradition of heresy, it is evident that holding opinions at variance with received opinion cannot constitute heresy. Duran makes this clear by explaining that Maimonides and Gersonides and their followers sincerely believed that their positions were those of the Torah. They were led to their positions by their philosophical speculation, he explains, and since they correctly understood that 'the Torah does not force us to believe false opinions' they believed that the positions which they held to be philosophically demonstrated must accord with the Torah. They may have been wrong, but their error was innocent and certainly did not constitute heresy.

In the tenth chapter Duran raises the following question: since providence is one of the principles of the Torah, why is there no commandment to believe in it? In answering this question he fleshes out his conception of what it takes to be a principle of the Torah in some interesting ways.

Duran begins by asserting that there is a fundamental difference between principles and commandments: the commandments stand independently, such that if one were abolished, it would have no effect on the rest of the Torah. The commandments, in effect, depend upon the Torah, and not vice versa. The principles, however, are such that if one were abolished, the whole Torah would collapse. Thus, the principles of the Torah (which we know are all of its teachings) are interrelated and basic to the existence of the Torah. Thus, if one knowingly denies any belief of the Torah, one is denying the whole Torah. In terms of its principles, the Torah is a seamless whole.

There is another difference between principles and commandments: the commandments are found explicitly in the Torah, as commands; the principles are not. The Torah does not command belief in specific principles; acceptance of the Torah implies acceptance of all its beliefs. Thus, belief in providence, a principle of the Torah, is not explicitly commanded by the Torah. This idea, concerning the distinction between principles and commandments, was picked up and expanded by Albo[128] and through him it became commonplace in fifteenth-century discussions of dogma in Judaism.[129]

Duran then deals with four possible counter-instances to his generalization that principles are not commanded, showing how in each case it is not the principle which is commanded but a 'branch' of the principle.

Having answered his first question, Duran raises a second. Granted that the Torah does not command beliefs, why did not Mishnah Sanhedrin x. 1, which does command beliefs, include providence and others of Maimonides' thirteen principles among those beliefs which must be held in order to enjoy a share in the world to come?

Duran answers this question by appealing to a point he had made already: Maimonides listed all of his thirteen principles because of 'the necessity of the verses'. Of them, there are only three which are truly fundamental (with respect to the other ten) and it is these three which are listed in the mishnah on which Maimonides was commenting when he posited his thirteen principles.

Duran closes the chapter by showing how the mishnah does indeed list those three beliefs — God, Torah, retribution — which Duran had said were the fundamental beliefs in Maimonides' list.

We may now attempt to analyse the material summarized to this point. In Duran's writings we are faced, it seems, with several accounts of the principles of the Torah. One of these, that found in the introduction to *Ohev Mishpat*, seems to construe Judaism as a deductive science, much as Aquinas construed Christianity. On this account, the Torah has two basic principles, creation and providence. Since, however, providence can be derived from creation, it is fair to say that the Torah has only one basic principle, creation.

The second account, that found in *Ohev Mishpat*, viii and x, and in the introduction to *Magen Avot*, ought not to be construed as an independent account of the principles of the Torah so much as an extended and subtle defence and explication of Maimonides' account of the principles of the Torah.

The third account, that presented in *Ohev Mishpat*, ix, makes the claim that the Torah has only one principle — to believe in what the Torah teaches — or, alternatively, that Judaism has as many principles as there are commandments in the Torah. This last account seems to be Duran's own most closely held position, since we seem to find echoes of it in the other two accounts: Duran repeatedly talks about the principles of the Torah in those contexts in ways which indicate that he has in mind a very large number of principles.[130]

In order better to understand these three accounts, it will be helpful to focus on the different questions they each seek to answer. The first account attempts to answer the question, which of the beliefs of Judaism are most fundamental or basic when we construe Judaism on the model of a deductive science? These beliefs may be logically more fundamental than others, but Duran gives us no reason to suppose that he held these beliefs to be religiously more important than others; they are principles in a logical or axiomatic sense, not in a dogmatic sense. To have asserted that they were

religiously more significant than other beliefs would have contradicted Duran's third and, to my mind, most basic account.

Duran's second account of the principles, that there are three —
God, Torah, retribution — is best understood as an answer to the
question, why did Maimonides posit just those beliefs which we
find in his thirteen principles? Duran answers the question by
showing how the thirteen beliefs found in Maimonides' statement
of the principles of the Torah are derived from three more basic or
fundamental beliefs, each of which was mentioned in Mishnah
Sanhedrin x. 1. Thus, Maimonides, in coming to comment on that
mishnah, merely amplified it, and did so in a very compelling
fashion, by listing as principles of Judaism those beliefs taught in
the mishnah, adding to the list only those beliefs which are both
derivable from the three mishnaic doctrines and are explicitly
taught in the Torah. Here too, Duran gives us no reason to suppose
that he has listed *all* the beliefs of Judaism.

Duran's third account of the principles of the Torah, in which he
in effect denies that Judaism has any principles, comes to answer
the question, what is heresy? This account of the principles, in
terms at least of the question it comes to answer, is most like that of
Maimonides. Maimonides' principles were ostensibly posited in
order to answer the question, what beliefs must a person hold in
order to be counted as a Jew and in order to merit a share in the
world to come? We may rephrase the question in another way:
Which beliefs are such that if a Jew denies them he is considered a
heretic? That is precisely the question Duran tries to answer in his
third account of the principles of Judaism. Maimonides answered
the question by positing thirteen beliefs. Duran's answer to the
question, in effect, is: either all the beliefs of Judaism (and in this he
was followed by Abravanel) or none. Let me explain this. Heresy,
for Duran, does not depend upon the affirmation or denial of
specific beliefs; it depends upon the intent with which one affirms or
denies specific beliefs. Thus if one intends to rebel, then the denial
of any belief of Judaism constitutes heresy; if one does not intend to
rebel, then, it would seem, there is no belief so special that if one
denies it one is *ipso facto* considered a heretic.[131]

In short, most historians of Judaism seem to have paid
insufficient attention to what Duran actually wrote when they assert
that his basic contribution to the discussion on the dogmas of

Judaism was the teaching that Judaism has three basic principles: God, Torah, and retribution.

III. Was Duran Decisively Influenced by Averroës?

In his important study of the sources of Albo's *Sefer ha-Ikkarim*, Julius Guttmann argued that Duran along with Albo was decisively influenced by Averroës in his claim that Judaism has three principles: '. . . there is no doubt that the source of the three principles is Averroes. But Duran and Albo took from him, not only the principles themselves, but followed him in the complete train of his thought which brought him to distinguish between one who denies the principles of a religion and one who denies other beliefs.'[132]

Guttmann summarized Averroës' position, as applied to Judaism, in the following terms:

. . . philosophic inquiry is permitted; the philosopher may interpret the Torah according to reason and if he denies a belief found in the Torah because of a mistake in his inquiry, he does not thereby become a heretic. But none of this applies to the principles of the Torah. One who deviates from one of them denies the entire Torah.

Guttmann goes on to say that 'Averroes' position does not differ from that of the Jewish philosophers from Sa'adia to Maimonides but only he expressed it in terms of a systematic teaching and Duran and Albo took that teaching from him'.[133] According to Averroës, as presented by Guttmann, there are three principles that every religionist must hold; this is as true of the philosopher as it is of the simple believer. Denial of any of these principles is heresy. These fundamental principles are belief in God, belief in prophecy, and belief in reward and punishment in the next world.[134]

Averroës himself distinguishes between two types of error concerning Scripture. The second type is

Error which is not excused to any person whatever and which is unbelief if it concerns the principles of religion. . . . This latter error is that which occurs about matters, knowledge of which is provided by all the different methods of indication so that knowledge of the matter in question is in this way possible for everyone. Examples are acknowledgment of God, Blessed and Exalted, of the prophetic missions, and happiness and misery in the next life; for these three principles are attainable by the three classes of indication, by which everyone without exception can come to assent to what he is obliged to know . . . [135]

Persons guilty of error concerning the principles of religion — God, revelation, retribution — are, then, according to Averroës, guilty of unbelief.

It is entirely possible that Albo was strongly influenced by this position of Averroës. He adopts the same principles as does Averroës,[136] and, like the latter, frames his discussion in terms of the principles of religion in general.[137] Further, again like Averroës, but, as should be clear from what we have shown above, unlike Duran, Albo condemns as guilty of unbelief and denies a share in the world to come to him who denies — whether knowingly or not — one of the basic principles of religion.[138]

The case of Duran, however, is not so simple. It would seem that Guttmann's claim for Duran's dependence upon Averroës in this context was made too hastily, perhaps on the basis of Albo's apparent dependence upon Averroës, and on his well-known dependence upon Duran. But to admit that Albo was influenced by both Averroës and Duran does not commit one to maintaining either that both Albo and Duran were influenced by Averroës or that Albo was influenced by Averroës through Duran. Albo had independent access to Averroës,[139] and careful examination shows that, despite some superficial similarities, Duran's position is actually very different from that of Averroës. It is also possible to trace some of Duran's ideas, at least, to sources other than Averroës.

In what ways does Duran differ from Averroës (and Albo)? First, he is interested not in the principles of religion generally, but in the principles of Judaism specifically. Second, as we saw above, his three 'fundamental principles' are introduced not as an independent contribution to Jewish dogmatics, but as a commentary upon and defence of Maimonides' principles; his own position is that Judaism has only one principle — to believe that all of the teachings of the Torah are true. Third, and most important, Duran, unlike Averroës and Albo, makes a sharp distinction between purposeful and accidental heresy, even with respect to his so-called 'fundamental principles'.

We may summarize the issue in the following way: Averroës' position consists of two main points: there are fundamental principles of religion and he who denies them is a heretic. Duran is at best ambiguous on the first point and denies the second one altogether.

We ought not, therefore, follow Guttmann in tracing the source of Duran's account of the principles of Judaism to Averroës. As noted above, Duran himself attributes this threefold classification of Maimonides' principles to an earlier scholar.[140] It is not known to whom he is referring if anyone. We saw in the last chapter how Abba Mari Astruc of Lunel had reduced the principles of Judaism to three and even called them *avot* ('fathers'), the same term used by Duran to denote his three fundamental principles.[141] There is no evidence, however, that Duran knew of Abba Mari's position. It seems likely to me that Duran came up with the threefold division of Maimonides' principles (which, as Guttmann failed to note, was not in any event his own system of dogmas) on his own. We saw above in the first chapter that Maimonides' thirteen principles actually do fall rather naturally into the three groups into which Duran divided them. I argued there that Maimonides himself intended this division.[142] Duran himself takes very seriously the importance of generally accepted beliefs; once Duran had introduced it, his tripartite division of Maimonides' principles was accepted by almost every subsequent scholar; there is no need to posit an Averroistic source for the idea.[143]

IV. Duran's Influence

In that Duran's contribution to the continuing discussion in medieval Judaism of the principles of faith is so little known and has so often been misrepresented, it is particularly appropriate to examine his innovations and his influence. He was the first Jewish author to posit principles of Judaism in an axiomatic sense. In this he was followed by Albo.[144] He was the first author we know of to divide Maimonides' principles into three groups (in which he was also followed by Albo)[145] and the first to show that each group could be tied to a term in Mishnah Sanhedrin x. 1, thus emphasizing Maimonides' commentarial stance, a point recently re-emphasized by Arthur Hyman.[146] Among other of Duran's ideas which we find in Albo's *Ikkarim*, there is the distinction between basic and subsidiary principles, and the term *se'if* ('branch') as applied to the subsidiary principles;[147] there is further the distinction between practical commandments and speculative teachings, and the assertion that principles of faith are not to be taken from the former;[148] finally, there is the realization that Maimonides' principles 2 to 5 are actually redundant, since they follow from principle 1.[149] It ought to be further noted that in Duran's analysis the emphasis within the principles shifts from beliefs concerning God (as was the case with Maimonides) to beliefs concerning Torah from heaven. In this Duran was followed by Albo and other fifteenth-century figures.

Duran was also the first medieval Jewish author to stress the centrality of belief in creation. In this he was not followed by Albo, although almost every other fifteenth-century Jewish author who wrote on the principles did emphasize the fundamental nature of belief in creation.[150]

There are also a number of points where Duran's discussion of dogma intersects with that of Crescas. Thus, for example, they both examine those beliefs which make acceptance of the Torah possible[151] and they both refer to the Torah as a divine *po'al* ('activity'), a remarkably neutral, non-sectarian term for something as important as the product of divine revelation, and a term which I have not seen used by other authors who dealt with the principles of Judaism.

What for a modern reader must surely be Duran's most striking innovation, his definition of heresy, did not strike a responsive chord in late medieval Jewish thought. Certainly no one followed him in explicitly declaring as a heretic only he who wilfully denied one of the teachings of the Torah or wilfully affirmed some teaching denied by the Torah.[152] Not only that, but this position (if not Duran himself) was strongly criticized by both Abraham Bibago and Isaac Abravanel. We must be careful to understand exactly what Duran was saying. He was not advocating a policy of religious tolerance; the Western world had to wait several centuries before such an idea was broached. He was, rather, drawing the boundaries of heresy very narrowly.[153] Even that is quite startling within the context of late medieval culture. In effect, Duran maintained that so long as a thinker did not purposefully contradict the Torah he was free to go wherever his thought took him.

It is possible that Duran was motivated in this regard by his great respect for Maimonides and Gersonides, the latter of whom Duran claimed as a kinsman.[154] These two thinkers, Gersonides more clearly than Maimonides, had maintained positions which were certainly heterodox with respect to commonly received Jewish opinion. By affirming that such deviations from the norm were heretical only if they were motivated by a spirit of rebelliousness (as was the case with Elisha ben Abuyah), Duran was saving Maimonides and Gersonides and their followers from the charge of heresy. That he was interested in doing so at all seems to indicate a broadness of spirit all too rare in his time. I think that it is further likely that Duran was arguing in an only partially articulate fashion against Maimonides' refusal to allow the category of inadvertent sinning (*shogeg*) to obtain with respect to beliefs. He may not have been clearly aware of the fact that Maimonides' position reflected a new way of defining the meaning of faith in Judaism but he may none the less have been aware of its incongruence with rabbinic perspectives.

Duran's claim that in effect Judaism had only one principle of faith, to believe in all the teachings of the Torah, or that Judaism has as many principles as it has commandments or teachings was adopted by Abravanel in chapter xxiii of his *Rosh Amanah*. Abravanel, of course, derived from this position consequences utterly at variance with those derived by Duran: for Abravanel the denial of any of the beliefs of the Torah, whether purposefully or innocently, constitutes heresy. It is not known if Abravanel was influenced by Duran in this regard. He does not cite Duran in any of his published writings, but that proves very little; he does not cite Abraham Bibago, either, but felt free to incorporate many passages from Bibago's writings into his own without giving any hint as to their source.

Duran's contribution to the medieval discussion of the principles of Judaism, we may say in conclusion, seems to have been sadly misrepresented over the years and seriously undervalued. In terms of the originality of his position he stands with Maimonides and Crescas at the forefront of those who dealt with the issue.

4

Ḥasdai Crescas

1. Introduction

Rabbi Don Ḥasdai Crescas was one of the most prominent religious and communal leaders of Aragonese Jewry in the latter part of the fourteenth century.[1] He died around 1412 in Saragossa. Crescas was a student of Rabbenu Nissim ben Reuben Gerondi (*c*.1310–75)[2] and a highly respected friend of Rabbi Isaac bar Sheshet Perfet (1326–1408).[3] He and Shimon ben Ẓemaḥ Duran were apparently at least acquainted with each other, although there is no evidence that he was aware of Duran's philosophic work.[4] Crescas's many communal activities left him little time for writing, but four works composed by him have come down to us: a chronicle concerning the massacres of 1391,[5] a Passover sermon dealing with the question of free-will,[6] a Hebrew translation or paraphrase of his Catalan *Refutation of the Principles of Christianity*,[7] and his philosophic/dogmatic treatise, *Or Adonai*.[8]

The *Or Adonai* ('Light of the Lord') was intended to be the first part of a comprehensive philosophic and halakhic work, *Ner Elohim*. The second part of this work, *Ner Miẓvah*, was never composed. Crescas, however, did write an introduction to the whole work, in which he describes the proposed project and explains why he came to write it.[9] The *Or Adonai* was completed in 1410 although Crescas was occupied with the writing of it over many years.[10] In planning a work which combined both dogmatic and halakhic elements, Crescas adopted the model of Maimonides, who began his halakhic compendium, the *Mishneh Torah*, with 'Laws of the Foundations of the Torah'.

Crescas's *Or Adonai* is structured according to its author's dogmatic system. The book is divided into four treatises. The first treatise deals with the *shorashim* ('roots') of religious belief — the doctrines of God's existence, unity, and incorporeality — and is divided into three sections (*kelalim*); the first of these presents the positions of Aristotle and Maimonides, the second consists of a critique of those positions, while in the third Crescas presents his own position. The second treatise deals with the *pinnot* ('corner-stones') of the Torah, and is divided into six sections, one part for each belief which Crescas denominates as a 'corner-stone of the Torah'. The third treatise deals with those true beliefs taught by the Torah and is divided into two parts (*halakim*), the first dealing with those beliefs not implied by specific commandments and the second dealing with those beliefs which are implied by specific command-ments. The first part has eight sections (corresponding to eight beliefs) and the second, three. The fourth treatise of the book deals with thirteen questions of a religious nature not conclusively answered by Torah and tradition.

Crescas, then, presents what may be called a multi-tiered, hierarchical system of dogma.[11] The first layer is that belief presupposed by religion: the doctrine of God's existence, unity, and incorporeality. The second level is comprised of those beliefs implied by the concept, 'Torah from heaven'. The third level consists of those beliefs which are in fact taught by the Torah — and as such must be accepted — but which are not such that their denial leads to the collapse of the Torah. In the fourth layer we have beliefs the acceptance or rejection of which is not determined by the Torah and which may, therefore, be determined by reason alone.

Crescas opens his account of the principles of Judaism and the *Or Adonai* by debating Maimonides' claim that belief in God is a commandment of the Torah, indeed the first of all the command-ments. Crescas does not deny, of course, that Jews must believe in God. He holds, rather, that acceptance of God's existence is a presupposition of all religious belief. It follows that if belief in God is a presupposition of the Torah, it cannot be commanded in the Torah; thus, there can be no command to believe in God.

The significance of this may be appreciated if we take note of some points raised by Zev Harvey.[12] In 'Laws of the Foundations of the Torah', i. 1, Maimonides codifies as law the proposition that every Jew must know that God exists. But Maimonides also implies, in the introduction to part ii of the *Guide*, that in order to know that God exists one must fully understand the twenty-six propositions of Aristotelian physics and metaphysics listed there. It follows, therefore, in Harvey's words, that for Maimonides, as he was understood by Crescas, in order 'to be a good Jew, one must be a good Aristotelian'.[13]

This is precisely the point which Crescas rejects; this rejection informs the entire *Or Adonai*. Maimonides claimed that God's existence and unity are rationally demonstrable and that human beings may, in principle, be commanded to accept their truth. Maimonides thus sought to demonstrate the essential unity of halakhah and philosophy (and thus grounded the first commandment and the first foundation of the Torah — belief in God — in philosophy). Crescas, on the other hand, disputed this claim, argued against the demonstrability of God's unity, at least, and sought to divorce religion from philosophy, in an attempt to secure the autonomy of the former from the latter, and to establish it on independent grounds.[14]

We may now turn to Crescas's texts themselves.

II. The Texts

Preface

'O house of Jacob, come ye, and let us walk in the light of the Lord' [Isa. 2: 5]

The foundation of beliefs and the root of first principles which direct one to the knowledge of truth concerning the corner-stones of the divine Torah is belief in the existence of God.[15] In that the intention of this part[16] is the verification of the corner-stones and views of the divine Torah[17] we ought to investigate this root and how we come to understand it.[18] In that the root of the first principles of the divine Torah is belief in the existence of God it is self-evident that the Torah is arranged and commanded by an Arranger and Commander; and its being 'divine' means nothing other than that its Arranger and Commander was God.[19]

Thus, he who counted belief in God's existence as a positive commandment committed a notorious error.[20] This is so because commandments are relational and no commandment can be supposed without a known commander. Thus, if we posit belief in God's existence as a commandment we [must] have already posited belief in the existence of God prior in knowledge to the belief in the existence of God! But if we also posit as a commandment this prior belief then one would have to have still another prior belief in God and so on *ad infinitum*. From this it would follow that belief in the existence of God is an infinite number of commandments; but all of this is absurd. It is thus established that one ought not to count belief in God's existence as a positive commandment.[21]

This may be seen from a number of [other] aspects. It will be seen from the meaning and definition of the word 'commandment' that it may be used only of things subject to will and choice. If [putative] commandments applied to beliefs and teachings — which are not subject to will and choice — the meaning of the term 'commandment' could not apply to them. This is one of the subjects we will investigate in what follows, with God's help.[22]

[Furthermore], how could it be since it is clearly established that this belief is the root and first principle of all the commandments? If we count it as a commandment it will of necessity be a first principle of itself which is absolutely absurd.[23]

They were brought to this — that is, to counting this root as a commandment — by the dictum at the end of Gemara Makkot which says: 'Six hundred and thirteen commandments were communicated to Moses at Sinai . . . What is the text for this? "Moses commanded us a Torah" [Deut. 33: 4].' They asked, 'The numerical value of "Torah" is only six hundred and eleven!' They answered, ' "I am" [Exod. 20: 2] and "Thou shalt have no" [Exod. 20: 3] [are not counted since] we heard them from the mouth of the Almighty.'[24] Because of this they thought that 'I am' and 'Thou shalt have no' were two [distinct] commandments; they therefore counted belief in God's existence as a commandment. It is clearly established that this does not follow since what is meant there is that [the] God who is called thus is the Deity and Leader who brought us out of the land of Egypt.[25]

Maimonides properly followed this approach in his *Book of Commandments*, in which he counted the first commandment as involving belief in the Divinity: 'By this injunction we are commanded to believe in God: to believe that there is a Supreme Cause which is the Creator of everything in existence. It is contained in His words — exalted be He — "I am the Lord thy God".'[26] He thus explained God's divinity in terms of His having created all existent beings. Because of this God said, 'Who brought thee out of the land of Egypt' [Exod. 20: 2], by way of proving this belief: from it we come to understand God's power, and that all existent beings are, when compared to Him, 'as clay in the potters hand' [Jer. 18: 6].[27] On this account the commandment relates to the belief that it was God who brought us out of the land of Egypt.

But this way of understanding the verse is in itself demonstrably false.[28] This is so because the reference[29] to 'I am' and 'Thou shalt have no' may readily be seen to include all of the utterance which continues as far as '. . . of them that love Me and keep My commandments' [Exod. 20: 6]. Since both these utterances are spoken in the first person, as it is said, 'I am the Lord . . . who brought thee out' [Exod. 20: 2], 'before Me' [Exod. 20: 3], 'for I the Lord thy God' [Exod. 20: 5], and 'of them that love Me and keep My commandments' [Exod. 20: 6]; and since the rest of the utterances are spoken in the third person, as it is said, 'for the Lord will not hold him guiltless' [Exod. 20: 7], 'for in six days the Lord made' [Exod. 20: 11] and 'He ceased from work and rested' [Exod. 31: 17],[30] [the Sages therefore] held that 'I am' and 'Thou shalt have no' were heard from the mouth of the Almighty.

Since all the authors who enumerate *Azharot*[31] saw fit to count 'Thou shalt not make unto thee a graven image, nor any manner of likeness' [Exod. 20: 4] and 'Thou shalt not bow down to them' [Exod. 20: 5] as two separate admonitions — and this is the true position — were we to count 'I am' as a commandment, there would then be three commandments which we heard from the mouth of the Almighty[32] and [the total number of commandments] would then rise to six hundred and fourteen.[33] If we consider 'Thou shalt have no other gods' [Exod. 20: 3] as an admonition not 'to believe in, or ascribe deity to, anyone but Him', as Maimonides wrote,[34] [then the number of commandments] would rise to six hundred and fifteen.[35]

We ought to say, therefore, that it was not the intention of those who said, '"I am" and "Thou shalt have no" we heard from the mouth of Almighty,' that each [verse] be considered a commandment. Rather, they explained that we have heard them from the mouth of the Almighty, because both were spoken in the first person, as [said] above. It follows that the two admonitions in the utterance 'Thou shalt have no' — which are 'Thou shalt not make unto thee a graven image, nor any manner of likeness' [Exod. 20: 4] and 'Thou shalt not bow down unto them' [Exod. 20: 5] — are those which we heard from the mouth of the Almighty. These with the six hundred and eleven we heard from the mouth of Moses add up to six hundred and thirteen.

All that remains to be explained is why they[36] did not count 'Thou shalt have no other gods before Me' [Exod. 20: 3] as an admonition which would then make three admonitions in that utterance. This is easily explained. If will and choice did not apply to beliefs, the term 'admonition' could not be applied to them. But if the term 'admonition' is withal applied to them the explanation of 'Thou shalt have no' would be that one should not accept any other thing as God.[37] [Indeed,] it has been established in the tractate Sanhedrin that one who does so is culpable.[38] They did not see fit to consider 'Thou shalt have no' and 'Thou shalt not bow down unto them' as two [separate commandments], for the root of them both is one, viz., the acceptance of the Divinity. But 'Thou shalt not make unto thee a graven image' [Exod. 20: 4] [applies] even if one did not worship [the image] or accept it as a god. They were therefore counted as two separate commandments. But it never occurred to them to consider 'I am the Lord thy God' as a commandment, since it is the root and first principle of all the commandments, as stated above.[39]

Once it is clearly established that this belief is the root and first principle of all the Torah beliefs and commandments we ought to investigate this root and [see] how we come to understand it.

Now then, some Torah beliefs are corner-stones and foundations of all the commandments[40] and some are not corner-stones and foundations but are true views.[41] But they are all alike beliefs which a believer in a divine Torah ought to believe; one who denies them is like one who denies the whole Torah.[42] Some of them are theories which the mind tends to accept but one who does not believe them is not called a heretic.[43] In that the intention of this part is the verification of the corner-stones and teachings of the divine Torah we have seen fit to divide it into four treatises. The first deals with the first root which is the first principle of all the Torah beliefs. The second deals with the beliefs which are corner-stones and foundations of all the commandments. The third deals with the true views which we who believe in the divine Torah [ought to] believe. The fourth deals with those theories which the mind tends to accept.

There are two ways to discuss this subject. The first is an explanation of its meaning as decreed by the Torah. The second is how we come to understand them.[44]

Treatise II. Concerning the corner-stones of the Torah, i.e., the foundations and pillars upon which the house of the Lord rests. With their existence, the existence of the Torah as ordered by God is conceivable; could we conceive the lack of one of them the entire Torah would collapse, heaven forfend.[45]

Upon investigating them we found them to be six: (1) God's knowledge of existents; (2) His providence over them; (3) His power; (4) prophecy; (5) choice;[46] and (6) purpose.[47] This is so since, in so far as the Torah is [the product of] a volitional activity from the Commander, who is the Agent, to the commanded, who is acted upon, it necessarily follows that the Agent knows, wills, and has power and that which is acted upon wills and chooses and is neither determined nor compelled. Furthermore, in so far as there is an activity produced by the Agent upon those acted upon, there must necessarily be some relationship between them. It is necessary that there be some relationship and conjunction between them; this is prophecy. In so far as every natural and artificial activity — and *a fortiori* the volitional activity of an infinitely perfect Agent — has some known purpose there is no escaping the fact that this perfect activity must have some important purpose.

For this reason we have seen fit to divide this treatise into six sections.[48]

Treatise III. Concerning true beliefs which we who believe in the divine Torah believe and which are such that if one denies one of them one is called a sectarian.[49]

Upon investigation we found that these [beliefs] fall into two groups beyond the six corner-stones included in treatise II. The first group is comprised of beliefs independent of specific commandments. The second is comprised of beliefs dependent upon specific commandments. With respect to the first group we found it to contain eight beliefs: (1) creation of the world; (2) immortality of the soul; (3) reward and punishment; (4) resurrection of the dead; (5) eternity of the Torah; (6) the difference between Mosaic prophecy and that of the rest of the prophets; (7) that the High Priest is answered through the *Urim* and *Tummim*; and (8) the coming of the Messiah. We thus divided this part [of treatise III] into eight sections.

We did not see fit to include these beliefs among the corner-stones of the Torah since, even though belief in them is obligatory and denial of them is such great rebelliousness that one who denies them is included among the sectarians, belief in the Torah is conceivable without them. We thus did not consider them to be foundations and roots of the Torah.

One must wonder at Maimonides who, in his commentary to *Perek Ḥelek*, laid down thirteen principles which he counted as foundations of religion. Now, if he called a 'principle' the true beliefs the denial of which constitutes sectarianism they will be found to be more than fifteen[50] and if he called a 'principle' the corner-stones and foundations of the religion which are such that it cannot be conceived without them then they are no more than seven when we count among them God's existence[51] or eight if we also count among the corner-stones that the Torah is a divine Torah from heaven.[52]

It may be objected on the basis of what is generally accepted and what is well known to be the opinion of some of our predecessors,[53] that belief in creation is the axis of the Torah around which it revolves since belief in it necessitates God's power and [the belief] that all existent beings are, from His perspective, 'like clay in the potter's hand' [Jer. 18: 6], for without this [belief] the existence of the Torah in and of itself in general, and of the signs and demonstrations found in it in particular — these being its foundations and pillars — could not be conceived. According to the believers in eternity, who see the world as derived necessarily from God, the existence of the Torah cannot be conceived at all.[54] Were this so it would indeed be appropriate to count this belief as a great pillar and corner-stone among the other corner-stones in the second treatise. But the solution of this objection is not difficult once we establish that God's power can be accepted even according to the believers in eternity. This is what was hidden from the eyes of our predecessors.[55]

How this can be established is what we will discuss in what follows, according to the decree of God. However, since the necessity of believing in creation is established by Torah and tradition, we must investigate, as is our custom, how it ought to be believed, and how we come to know it. We have placed it in the first section of this treatise.[56]

[Treatise III, part i, section 8, chapter 3]

Chapter 3. An explanation that the roots included in this treatise, notwithstanding the fact that they are true and that there is no doubt concerning their truth, are not corner-stones and foundations of the Torah such that it could not be conceived without them.

This may easily be shown by way of induction. With respect to the first root, creation, we have already established that even believers in eternity must necessarily believe in God's omnipotence, in His knowledge, and in His will.[57] With these the divine Torah may be conceived. Similarly, the existence of the Torah can be conceived without [belief in] immortality and retribution since, as has been established, true worship is not performed in order to earn a reward. All this certainly applies to the resurrection of the dead. Similarly with the eternity of the Torah; were it temporal its existence would still be conceivable. Similarly with the difference between the prophecies of Moses and the [other] prophets; for even if there were no difference between them and, even if the possibility of a prophet greater than Moses could be imagined, the existence of an eternal, divine Torah would still be conceivable since it is impossible that a prophet — even were he greater than Moses — would deny [even] one thing said by any [other] prophet, even were the latter greatly inferior to him. Similarly concerning the Messiah; with his absence the existence of the Torah could still be conceived.

There is no doubt concerning the roots dependent upon specific commandments[58] that if the absence of those commandments were conceived, the existence of the divine Torah would still be conceivable.[59]

We thus included the roots contained in this treatise in the number of the true roots which are such that if one denies any of them one is called a sectarian but we did not include them among the corner-stones and foundations which are such that the existence of the Torah cannot be imagined without them.[60]

This is what we wanted to establish. With this the first part of this treatise is concluded.

Praise to the Lord who alone is exalted 'above all blessing and praise' [Neh. 9: 5]. Amen and amen.[61]

[III. ii, introduction]

Part ii. Concerning beliefs dependent upon specific commandments. Upon investigation we discovered these to be three: (1) prayer and the priestly blessing;[62] (2) repentance;[63] and (3) the Day of Atonement and the four divisions of the year established as holidays for the Lord.[64] We have therefore included three sections in this part.

We did not see fit to include the belief dependent upon the act of the Sotah[65] since it is a particular commandment. Similarly with the beliefs dependent upon the pilgrim festivals and joyous occasions since the rewards promised for them refer to physical good — even though it will be balanced with spiritual good — they are to be treated like other commandments and their promised rewards.[66]

Treatise IV. Concerning traditional doctrines and conjectures which the mind tends to accept.[67] There are thirteen issues here: (1) is the world eternal *a parte post*? (2) can another world or worlds exist? (3) are the spheres living and rational? (4) do the movements of the heavenly bodies influence the fates of men? (5) do amulets and charms have effects on the activities of men? (6) concerning demons; (7) can a human soul move? this is what one school of scholars calls transmigration; (8) is the soul of uneducated youth immortal? (9) concerning paradise and hell; (10) does *Ma'aseh Bereshit* refer to physics and does *Ma'aseh ha-Merkavah* refer to metaphysics, as some of the scholars of our people have held? (11) are the intellect (*sekhel*), the intellectually cognizing subject (*maskil*), and intellectually cognized object (*muskal*) identical or not? (12) concerning the Prime Mover; (13) concerning the impossibility of knowing God's essence.

Since the correct position on these issues — whether positive or negative — was not explicitly established by the Torah we shall investigate them by showing the elements of probability on each side of each pair of contradictories so that it will be easy for the reader to distinguish what is correct from what is incorrect.[68]

III. Crescas's System of Principles

The texts presented here constitute, by and large, Crescas's introductions to the various parts of his *Or Adonai*. It is in these introductory passages that Crescas explicitly comments on his system of principles of faith. The book itself is given over to analyses of the various beliefs included in Crescas' dogmatic system, while the structure of the book is determined by that system.

In the preface to the *Or Adonai* Crescas argues against Maimonides' claim that belief in God is both a foundation of the Torah and a commandment. We noted above that Crescas rejects Maimonides' position here because of its implicit attempt at joining Torah and philosophy. Crescas, however, did not phrase his dispute with Maimonides in those terms, arguing on other grounds altogether that it is illegitimate to count belief in God as a commandment.

Crescas's first argument is based on the logic of the situation.[69] We cannot make sense of the idea of a commandment without assuming the antecedent existence of a commander. Thus if God commands that we believe in Him, we end up like dogs chasing our tails, unless we prefer the chicken and egg problem and posit an infinite series of antecedent beliefs.

Crescas's second argument is based upon his analysis of the concept 'belief'. Crescas held that we cannot *choose* to believe things. But the concept 'commandment' only makes sense in the context of will and choice: we cannot be commanded to do things which we cannot choose to do or refrain from doing. So we cannot be commanded to believe anything.[70]

Now, if Crescas is a strict physical determinist,[71] how can he maintain (as we saw him doing above) that commandments make sense only in a context where will and choice obtain? With respect to our actions there are simply no contexts where will and choice obtain! And if that is the case, why can we not be commanded to accept certain beliefs? Objectively speaking, we have no more control over the beliefs we accept than over the things we do.

But that, I think, is precisely the point: what does Crescas mean by saying that commandments make sense in a context where will and choice obtain? He means, I submit, that commandments make sense only where we feel free to do or to desist from doing, i.e., in contexts where we are not aware of being determined. In such a context the term 'commandment' makes some sense; in contexts where we cannot choose to obey or disobey, it makes no sense at all to use the term. Now, we do not feel compelled when we act; the use of the term 'commandment' in such a context, according to Crescas, is not on the face of it ridiculous. But we do feel compelled when we adopt or reject beliefs; if we find the evidence compelling we cannot choose to disbelieve the conclusion it brings us to, at least so far as Crescas is concerned.

We must say that Crescas adopted this analysis of the term 'commandment' for, were he willing to admit that commandments made sense in a context where will and choice do not obtain, he could have allowed for the commanding of beliefs (as did Maimonides).

Returning to the issue at hand, we find that Crescas's third argument is based on the idea that belief in God is the 'root and first principle' of all the commandments and cannot, therefore, itself be one of the commandments. The 'first principle'[72] of a science is not itself part of that science. The 'science of Judaism'[73] cannot include its own first principles in it and therefore the existence of God cannot be counted as either a commandment or, when we understand the concept of a principle of religion as Crescas understands it, as a 'foundation of the Torah' either.

It might be objected that this argument of Crescas is circular, since it assumes as a given exactly what Crescas wants to prove, namely, that belief in God's existence cannot be counted as part of the Torah since it is the 'first principle' of the Torah. This charge, however, ignores the fact that in his first argument Crescas had already established that God's existence had to be accepted antecedent to the Torah. His argument here builds upon the conclusions established by the first argument and is thus not circular.

Crescas then goes on in effect to exculpate those who count God's existence as a commandment on the grounds that they were led to this position by a mistaken exegesis of Scripture and Talmud. In the tractate *Makkot* of the Babylonian Talmud (23b–24a) we read:

R. Simlai when preaching said: 'Six hundred and thirteen precepts were communicated to Moses, three hundred and sixty-five negative, corresponding to the number of solar days (in the year), and two hundred and forty-eight positive, corresponding to the number of members of man's body.' Said R. Hamnuna: 'What is the (authentic) text for this? It is, *Moses commanded us Torah, an inheritance of the congregation of Jacob* (Deuteronomy 33: 4), *Torah* being numerically equal to six hundred and eleven,[74] *I am* (Exodus 20: 2) and *Thou shalt have no* (Exodus 20: 3) (not being reckoned, because) we have heard (them) from the mouth of the Almighty.'

This idea that the Torah contained exactly six hundred and thirteen commandments became widely accepted in the Jewish tradition and gave rise to a whole genre of literature dedicated to identifying and enumerating the six hundred and thirteen commandments. One of the first books actually to contain such a list is the *Halakhot Gedolot* attributed to Simeon Kayyara (ninth century).[75] Scores of liturgical poems, known as *Azharot*, were composed during the Middle Ages, all of them embodying enumerations of the six hundred and thirteen commandments. These poems were meant to be recited on the Festival of Weeks

(*Shavuot*), traditionally regarded as the anniversary of the revelation at Sinai.

One of the most important attempts to enumerate the six hundred and thirteen commandments is that of Maimonides. In his *Book of Commandments* he lists and explains the principles which guided him in his choice of precepts for inclusion in his list.

Maimonides opens the *Book of Commandments* with positive commandment number 1:

BELIEVING IN GOD. By this injunction we are commanded to believe in God, that is to say, to believe that there is a Supreme Cause which is the Creator of everything in existence. It is contained in His words — exalted be He — *I am the Lord thy God, who brought thee out of the land of Egypt,* etc. [Exod. 20: 2].

At the end of Tractate *Makkot* it is said: 'Six hundred and thirteen commandments were declared unto Moses at Sinai, as it is said, *Moses commanded us a Torah* [Deut. 33: 4]', that is to say, He commanded us to observe as many commandments as are signified by the sum of the numerical values of the letters of *Torah*. To this it was objected that the numerical value of the word Torah is only six hundred and eleven; to which the reply was: 'The two commandments, *I am the Lord thy God*, etc., and *Thou shalt have no other gods before Me* we have heard from the Almighty Himself'.

Thus it has been made clear to you that the verse *I am the Lord thy God*, etc., is one of the 613 commandments, and is that whereby we are commanded to believe in God, as we have explained.[76]

Maimonides reiterates this position at the very beginning of his great law code, the *Mishneh Torah*:

The foundation of all foundations and the pillar of all sciences is the realization that there is a First Being who has brought every existing thing into being. All existing things, whether celestial, terrestrial, or belonging to an intermediate class, exist only through His true existence.

To acknowledge the truth of this is an affirmative precept, as it is said, *I am the Lord thy God*. And whosoever permits the thought to enter his mind that there is another deity besides this God, violates a prohibition, as it is said, *Thou shalt have no other god before Me*, and denies the essence of religion, this doctrine being the great principle on which everything depends.[77]

These texts clearly demonstrate that Maimonides understood Exod. 20: 2, 'I am the Lord thy God', to express a commandment.

It is logically the first positive commandment in the Torah and 'the great principle on which everything depends'.

Maimonides' position here can be explained in terms of a statement he makes in the *Guide of the Perplexed* (ii. 33):

> This is their dictum: 'They heard *I am* and *Thou shalt have no* from the mouth of the Almighty.' They mean that these words reached them just as they reached Moses our master, and that it was not Moses our master who communicated them to them. For these two principles, I mean the existence of the Deity and His being one, are knowable by human speculation alone. Now with regard to everything that can be known by demonstration, the status of the prophet and that of everyone who knows it are equal; there is no superiority of one over the other. Thus these two principles are not known through prophecy alone. The text of the Torah says *Unto thee it was shown*, and so on [Deut. 4: 35]. As for the other commandments, they belong to the class of generally accepted opinions and those adopted by virtue of tradition, not to the class of the intellects.[78]

It is Maimonides' claim, therefore, that God's existence and unity are rationally demonstrable and that human beings may, in principle, be commanded to accept their truth.[79]

Crescas brings the preface to a close by summarizing the different types of beliefs included within his system of principles. The system is multi-tiered. On the most fundamental level we have the 'first principle of all the Torah beliefs and commandments', belief in God's existence, unity, and incorporeality. There are then those beliefs taught by the Torah which are 'corner-stones and foundations of all the commandments'. This second tier is distinguished from the third tier of beliefs which 'are not corner-stones and foundations but are true views'. Last, there are those beliefs — many the subject of considerable debate in Crescas's time — which 'the mind tends to accept' and which may or may not be taught by the Torah.

We ought to note the following points. Belief in God is the 'first principle' of all Torah beliefs and commandments; this may be distinguished from beliefs of the second variety which are foundations of the commandments, but are not themselves foundations of other Torah beliefs. That is to say, these beliefs are not logically related to the other teachings of the Torah in any particular way. They are, however, related to the commandments in that the Torah as a system of commandments cannot be accepted if even one of these beliefs be denied. The third tier of beliefs are those which the Torah teaches but are such that if one of them be denied the Torah as a whole would not collapse. The second and third group of beliefs have one important characteristic in common: denial of any one of these beliefs is like denying the whole Torah and constitutes heresy. Although Crescas does not make this explicit, we may assume that he held that heretics lose their share in the world to come. That he fails to make this explicit is significant, as will be seen below.

Table: A summary of Crescas's system

Treatise	Level	Term	Definitions	Beliefs
I	I	*Shoresh* (root) or *Hathalah* (1st Principle)	Presupposition of revelation in general	God's existence, unity, incorporeality
II	II	*Pinnot* (corner-stones)	Beliefs the acceptance of which makes belief in revelation in general possible	1. God's knowledge of particulars 2. Providence 3. God's power 4. Prophecy 5. Choice 6. Purposefulness of the Torah
III part i	III	*De'ot Amitiot* (true doctrines) or *Emunot Amitiot* (true beliefs) (independent of specific commandments)	Beliefs actually taught by the Torah of Moses	1. Creation *ex nihilo* 2. Immortality 3. Reward and punishment 4. Resurrection 5. Eternity of the Torah 6. Mosaic prophecy 7. *Urim ve-Tummim* 8. Messiah
III part ii	III	*Emunot ha-Nitlot ba-Mizvot* (beliefs dependent upon commandments)	same as above	1. God answers prayers and the priestly blessing 2. Efficacy of repentance 3. Day of Atonement and the four divisions of the year arouse us to worship God
IV	IV	*De'ot u-Sevarot* (views and theories)	Beliefs concerning which the teaching of the Torah is not conclusive	See p. 116.

We may summarize Crescas's system, to the extent to which it is outlined in the preface to the *Or Adonai*, as follows: Level I belief (God) makes possible the Torah as a system of teachings and commandments. Level II beliefs answer the analytic question, which of the Torah beliefs must be held if any Torah as a system of divine commandments is to be possible? Level III beliefs answer the empirical question, what other beliefs are in fact taught by the Torah of Moses? We may express it in another way (see Table).

Level I: The presupposition of revelation.
Level II: beliefs the acceptance of which makes belief in Revelation possible.
Level III: beliefs which are in fact taught by the Torah of Moses.
Level IV: beliefs which are not conditions for revelation and which the Torah of Moses neither affirms nor denies explicitly.

In the introduction to treatise II Crescas further defines the 'corner-stones of the Torah' and lists them. Crescas's analysis goes something like the following: assuming the Torah to be '[the product of] a volitional activity from the Commander, who is the Agent, to the commanded, who is acted upon', we may then ask, what beliefs must be accepted in order to make such an entity as the Torah possible? We must assume, Crescas answers, that the Agent has knowledge, will, and power. If the Agent commands, He must have knowledge of those He is commanding, He must have a will expressed in the commands, and He must have power. By 'power', Crescas explains in another context,[80] he means that God, if He commands us, must have power over us and further, since the Torah revolves around the axis of 'signs, demonstrations, and promises', God must have the power to perform the miracles described in the Torah and keep the promises made therein. So much for God. We must further assume, Crescas continues, that there is some 'relationship' between God and those whom he commands, and thus we are forced to assume the existence of prophecy. Every natural and artificial activity, Crescas says, has some end or purpose. This being so, it is evident that the 'volitional activity of an infinitely perfect Agent' must surely have some end or purpose; thus the Torah must have an end or purpose. This purpose, it turns out, is twofold: from the perspective of God the end of the Torah is the granting of goodness to His creatures; from the perspective of the commanded the end of the Torah is the true worship and love of God, in which lies man's ultimate felicity.[81] Furthermore, if man is commanded, he must be able to choose to obey or not to obey; we must therefore assume that man has some power of choice. Crescas does not here say explicitly why we must assume God's providence in order to make possible the existence of the Torah. But since the end of the Torah is the good of mankind, the Torah itself must be seen as an example of God's providential care over man, and thus could not exist without providence. Alternatively, Crescas may see God's providence as an expression of God's will, which he does here explicitly connect to the possibility of Torah from heaven.

Crescas includes among the six beliefs which he construes as 'corner-stones and foundations' of the Torah only those beliefs the denial of any one of which would cause the Torah 'to collapse'. There are other beliefs, however, which are taught by the Torah of Moses, and the denial of which is heresy and rebelliousness, but are not such that if one denied them one would be logically bound to deny the possibility of Torah from heaven. These beliefs are discussed in treatise III of the *Or Adonai*. In his introduction to that treatise Crescas points out that these beliefs fall into two classes: those taught by the Torah and those implied by the commandments of the Torah. Treatise III is thus divided into two parts, the first dealing with the 'true doctrines' not dependent upon specific commandments and the second dealing with those teachings implied by specific commandments.

There are eight beliefs in the first category: creation of the world *ex nihilo*, immortality of the soul, reward and punishment, resurrection of the dead, eternity of the Torah, the difference between Mosaic prophecy and that of the rest of the prophets, that the high priest is answered through the *Urim* and *Tummim*, and Messiah. These Crescas explicitly tells us are not 'corner-stones of the Torah' because 'belief in the Torah is conceivable without them'. Crescas makes the point clear in the last chapter of treatise III, part i,[82] where he shows how each one of these beliefs is such that were it denied the Torah would not collapse.

Crescas makes a special point of discussing belief in creation in this connection. Maimonides and Naḥmanides had both claimed that belief in creation was an absolute prerequisite for belief in the Torah.[83] Crescas dismissed this claim on the grounds that there are other theories concerning the generation of the world which make possible God's volitional and powerful intervention in the world. The doctrine of eternal emanation by will, for example, would make Torah from heaven possible. That being the case, belief in creation *ex nihilo* is not analytic to the concept, 'Torah from heaven' and cannot be counted as a 'corner-stone and foundation of the Torah'.[84]

In his introduction to treatise III Crescas takes Maimonides to task for his account of the principles. Maimonides' list is either too long or too short, Crescas says. If by 'foundation of the Torah' he meant what Crescas means by 'corner-stone of the Torah' then his list is too long since there are only six such beliefs, or seven, if we include among them God's existence, or eight, if we include among them that belief which they make possible, Torah from heaven; but there are certainly not thirteen. On the other hand, if by 'foundation of the Torah' Maimonides meant those beliefs the denial of which constitutes sectarianism, Crescas continues, then there are more than fifteen: six 'corner-stones', eight 'true doctrines' independent of specific commandments, and belief in God. Crescas says 'more than fifteen' because there are also three 'true doctrines' implied by specific commandments which he has not yet introduced.

Crescas does introduce these beliefs in the introduction to part ii of treatise III, where he says that there are three such beliefs: belief in the efficacy of prayer and the priestly blessing, in the efficacy of repentance, and in the efficacy of the Day of Atonement and other seasons set aside for atonement and repentance. It is obvious that these beliefs should not be counted as 'corner-stones of the Torah' since, related as they are to particular commandments, the Torah as a whole would not collapse with their refutation.

Crescas goes on to distinguish these three beliefs from other beliefs, also connected to specific commandments, which we might have thought warranted inclusion in the category of 'true doctrines'. He rejects the beliefs associated with the act of the *Sotah* since 'it is a particular commandment'. I do not understand his purpose here. Clearer is his refusal to count in this category the beliefs dependent upon the festivals and holidays. The belief involved is that we will be rewarded for their observance; but this, Crescas observes, is the case with every commandment and there is no reason for singling these out.

Crescas's final treatise deals with beliefs not determined explicitly by the Torah one way or the other. These are 'traditional doctrines and conjectures which the mind tends to accept'.

IV. Crescas's Use of the Concept 'Principle of Faith'

Analysis of these texts makes it evident that Crescas did not use the term 'corner-stone' in the way Maimonides used the term 'foundation of the Torah'. Maimonides, as we saw above,[85] was interested in dogmatic/religious questions: what must one believe in order to be counted as a Jew and merit a share in the world to come? Like Duran, Crescas is basically uninterested in the question of salvation, and even emphasizes that there is no difference between denying a principle of the Torah and denying any other belief taught by the Torah. May we say then that he understood the principles of Judaism on some sort of axiomatic model?

There are many reasons for saying that we ought indeed so to interpret Crescas. Although arguments from authority prove nothing, it is worth noting that this is the way Abravanel, surely an acute and sophisticated student of the whole question of dogma in Judaism, understood him. Abravanel argued that both Crescas and his student Joseph Albo

were brought to postulate principles in the divine Torah only because they were drawn after the custom of gentile scholars as described in their books. For they saw in every science, whether natural or mathematical, roots and principles which ought not to be denied or argued against.[86] . . . Our scholars, having been dispersed among the nations and having studied their books and sciences, learned from their deeds and copied their ways with respect to the divine Torah. They said, '*How do these Gentiles pursue*[87] their sciences? By positing first principles and roots upon which a science is based. I will do so also and postulate principles and foundations for the divine Torah'.[88]

Abravanel thus understood Crescas and Albo both to be using the concept of a principle of faith in an axiomatic sense.

There are other reasons for assuming that Crescas defined his corner-stones in an axiomatic sense. First, he defines them as 'the foundations and pillars upon which the house of the Lord rests. With their existence, the existence of the Torah as ordered by God is conceivable; could we conceive the lack of one of them the entire

Torah would collapse, heaven forfend.'[89] That definition certainly makes the corner-stones sound like axioms, beliefs upon which the very existence of the Torah rests.

Second, adopting Abravanel's interpretation allows us to see an interesting and suggestive parallelism between the critical and constructive portions of Crescas's *Or Adonai*: in the first treatise he criticizes the axioms of Aristotelianism while in the second he analyses and defends the axioms of Judaism, which he proposes as a replacement for Aristotelianism.

This interpretation of Crescas, then, is certainly cogent, but I do not think that it is entirely satisfactory. Terminologically, we must ask why Crescas, if he meant his principles to be construed as axioms, chose to call them *pinnot* ('corner-stones') rather than *hakdamot*, the accepted term for Euclid's axioms, and the term he himself uses for those axioms of Aristotelianism which he criticizes in the *Or Adonai*.[90]

More important, however, we must note that, for Crescas, acceptance of the Torah precedes acceptance of the corner-stones; it is not deduced from them. In his introduction to treatise II, which deals with the corner-stones of the Torah, Crescas deduces them from the concept, 'Torah from heaven'; he does not base our belief in Torah from heaven on our antecedent acceptance of these beliefs; this would have been the proper approach were he dealing with axioms of the Torah.

Third, if Crescas did understand his 'corner-stones' in an axiomatic sense, then we must ask why he repeatedly refuses to admit that they are any more important than other Torah beliefs with respect to the question of heresy. One would expect him to argue that axioms are more fundamental, more important, more crucial, than derivative beliefs. Yet he does not. This raises another and related point: Crescas — unlike Albo, who did adopt an axiomatic model — does not present his secondary beliefs ('true doctrines') as being derived from his 'corner-stones'. There is no logical relationship between them whatever. Rather, the 'corner-stones' are those beliefs which we must accept if we accept Torah from heaven and wish to be consistent; the 'true doctrines' are those beliefs which the Torah happens to teach.

We may phrase the point in another way. In discussing the 'corner-stones' of the Torah, Crescas analysed the concept of revelation without specific reference to the Torah of Judaism (he even defines it in remarkably neutral terms: 'a volitional activity from the Commander, who is the Actor, to the commanded, who is acted upon . . .'[91]). In discussing the 'true doctrines' he is discussing those beliefs actually taught by the Torah of Moses. Thus, the questions that Crescas is answering in his discussion of the principles of Judaism are not, in the first instance, strictly religious questions. Unlike Maimonides, he is not attempting to determine who is a Jew or who is eligible for a portion in the world to come. The issue of salvation and the world to come does not arise in Crescas's discussions at all.

Crescas's position is perhaps best summarized in Kantian terms: we may say with Zev Harvey[92] that Crescas sought to discover those beliefs which were analytic to the concept 'divinely revealed Torah' or, further in the Kantian vein, we may say with Shalom Rosenberg that Crescas sought to provide a transcendental deduction of the term 'Torah'.[93]

Crescas's understanding of the nature of his principles is reflected clearly in his comments on the place of creation in his scheme. He counts creation *ex nihilo* not as one of the corner-stones of the Torah, without belief in which the Torah cannot be conceived, but among the 'true doctrines', those beliefs which are in fact taught by the Torah. There are those, he says, who might criticize him for this on the ground that without belief in creation belief in the Torah is impossible. But is this really so, Crescas asks, and goes on to prove that we can still believe in a God possessing power and will even if the world exists coeternally with him. This being so, it is evident that belief in creation is not a belief without which the Torah cannot be conceived.

v. Does the Torah Command Belief?

We saw above that Crescas rejected Maimonides' claim that *I am the Lord thy God* [Exod. 20: 2], the first verse of the Decalogue, is the textual source for a commandment to believe in God's existence.[94] Crescas argues against Maimonides' position, in part, on the ground that beliefs cannot be commanded. It makes sense to speak of commands, he says, only where the person commanded feels that he can choose to obey or not obey. For example, it makes no sense to command a person not to digest food already swallowed; the issue is out of the hands of the person being commanded. Our beliefs are not matters over which we have conscious control any more than is our digestion: we do not will or choose to believe or not to believe. It follows therefore, that we cannot be commanded to believe or disbelieve something.

Having made this claim, Crescas turns right round and posits a series of 'roots', 'corner-stones', and 'true doctrines', which every Jew must hold on pain of being convicted of 'sectarianism' and 'rebelliousness'. This smacks of contradiction. If the Torah does not command beliefs, why must a Jew believe in the 'roots', 'corner-stones', and 'true doctrines' of the Torah?[95]

The solution to this conundrum lies, I believe, in the fact that Crescas sincerely believed that the Torah did not command beliefs; it commands actions. Nowhere does the Torah say, 'You must believe in God!' or 'Thou shalt believe in creation *ex nihilo*!' or even 'Cursed be he that doth not believe in the resurrection of the dead!'[96] Rather, there are certain beliefs which we must logically accept if we accept the Torah (the 'corner-stones') and certain beliefs which we must logically accept if we do not wish to say that the Torah preaches falsehood (the 'true doctrines'), for, although the Torah nowhere explicitly commands belief in the Messiah, for example, one cannot reject belief in the Messiah without giving the lie to many passages in the Torah.

Thus, the Torah does not command beliefs; but there are beliefs which cannot be rejected without rejecting the Torah, either because the concept of the Torah is logically incoherent if we reject these beliefs ('corner-stones') or because the Torah itself implicitly or explicitly teaches these beliefs. Once the Torah is accepted, these beliefs must logically be accepted. Thus, all Crescas's principles relate, in the final analysis, to the acceptance of the Torah of Moses from heaven.[97] I say 'Torah *of Moses* from heaven' because, while the 'corner-stones' relate only to the possibility of divine revelation generally, the 'true doctrines' relate specifically to the divine revelation to Moses.

Now then, the Torah does not command belief in itself, any more than God commands belief in Himself. But once we do accept the Torah, we accept the 'corner-stones' and 'true doctrines' not because we are commanded to do so, but because not to accept them would involve self-contradiction. Crescas nowhere tells us why we ought to accept the Torah; that is a question of apologetics, not of systematic dogmatic analysis, and it is the latter which occupies Crescas in the *Or Adonai*, not the former.[98]

I do not think that this is a matter of playing with words, as it might, at first blush, appear to be. There is nothing inconsistent or even surprising in the idea that one might accept a given belief as true simply because not to accept it would willy-nilly involve the rejection of other beliefs, already firmly held. One can believe in the Torah without being fully aware of everything that belief entails and with the expectation that one will accept entailments of that belief as one discovers them. This, I think, is the typical attitude of most believers.

In brief, once the Torah is accepted, the 'corner-stones' and 'true doctrines' do not have to be commanded, since one cannot reject them without rejecting the Torah. Thus, it appears, Crescas does not contradict himself by rejecting the possibility of a command-ment to believe in God on the one hand and positing a system of the principles of Judaism (including belief in God) on the other hand.

vi. Crescas on Inadvertent Heresy

As established in the previous chapter, Duran allowed for the possibility of inadvertence (*shegagah*) with respect to beliefs, maintaining that there is no teaching so basic that if one makes an honest mistake about it one is thereby condemned as a heretic.[99] As noted, Bibago and Abravanel explicitly reject this position; in the next chapter it will be shown that Joseph Albo was ambivalent on the issue. One could easily get the impression that Duran and possibly Rabad were alone in resisting this hard line on heresy in the Jewish Middle Ages. I think that this impression may be mistaken; a careful reading of Ḥasdai Crescas's comments on the matter of belief suggests that he may have held a position similar in important respects to that Duran.

My proposal concerning Crescas may appear surprising in light of Crescas's explicit statement that if a person denies even one of the beliefs which he lists as principles then that person is a sectarian.[100] Crescas does not state that such disbelief must be intended as heresy in order to count as heresy. Despite all this, a close examination of Crescas's analysis of the possibility of commanding belief in God opens up the possibility that he may have allowed for non-heretical disbelief, even concerning the principles of the Torah.

Maimonides had asserted that belief in God was not only a 'foundation of the Torah'[101] but that it was also the first and most fundamental of the commandments.[102] But 'he who counted belief in God's existence as a positive commandment', Crescas insisted, 'committed a notorious error.'[103] Crescas, as we have seen, presents a number of arguments against Maimonides' claim that belief in God could be counted as a commandment. He phrases the second of these arguments as follows:

> It will be seen from the meaning and definition of the term 'commandment' that it may be used only of things subject to will and choice. If [putative] commandments applied to beliefs and teachings — which are not subject to will and choice — the meaning of the term 'commandment' could not apply to them. This is one of the subjects we will investigate in what follows, with God's help.[104]

Crescas's argument may be rephrased as follows: we cannot will to believe things. But the very concept of a commandment makes sense only in the context of will and choice: we cannot fairly be commanded to do things which we cannot choose to do or refrain from doing. So we cannot fairly be commanded to believe anything.

Crescas promises, we have just seen, to investigate further the issue of will and choice with respect to commandments. This he does in *Or Adonai*, II. v. 5. Crescas, it is well known, maintained a doctrine of strict physical determinism. In the chapter under discussion he raises the question, how is it possible to reconcile God's justice in reward and punishment with a position that holds that all of our acts are determined in accord with the laws of causality before they are done?

Crescas introduces the distinction between 'determinism accompanied by a feeling of compulsion and necessity' and 'Determinism unaccompanied by a feeling of compulsion and necessity'.[105] We are subject to 'determinism accompanied by a feeling of compulsion and necessity' when we are aware of the fact that we act, not freely, but in accordance with or as a result of causes over which we have no control; that is to say, we *feel* compelled, not free. It might be urged on this basis that reward and punishment justly apply in cases where we are not aware of the fact that our actions are determined. Crescas rejects this approach on the grounds that reward and punishment cannot depend upon whether or not we *feel* determined, because, in fact, we *are* determined.[106]

Crescas rejects this approach on the further grounds that it makes it impossible to account for the fact that we are rewarded and punished for our beliefs. How so? Well, for one thing, will and choice play no role in beliefs (i.e., we cannot choose to believe or disbelieve), and we are aware of the fact that our beliefs are determined. That is to say, we all realize full well, Crescas maintains, that we cannot choose to believe or disbelieve. Therefore, if the feeling of being free played some role in making possible just reward and punishment, we could not be rewarded for our beliefs since we do not even feel that we are free to accept them or reject them.

Well, then, if our actions are determined, and if our awareness or lack of awareness of that determination plays no role in the justice of rewarding and punishing us for actions over which we have no control, how can we then be rewarded for observing the commandments and punished for violating them? Crescas's answer is simple. Actions are subject to choice and will and that — as opposed to the physical/causal freedom of our choice and will — is the criterion that makes them fit objects of reward and punishment.

Fine and good: but what about beliefs? They are not subject to choice and will.[107] Here the main issue in Crescas's discussion comes into play: we are not rewarded for holding certain beliefs, but for the pleasure and joy we feel in holding them. This joy, Crescas holds, is the result of choice and will. There is also a further point to be noted: we can choose to hasten the process of adopting a belief (through study and reflection, it seems[108]) and for this we can also be rewarded.

We may now revert to the question of inadvertent heresy. In order to understand what might be Crescas's position here it will be helpful to distinguish among the following cases:

(*a*) a person commits a crime — let us say murder — in the mistaken belief that he is commanded by the Torah so to act.

(*b*) a person knows that the Torah teaches a certain belief, strives to adopt that belief, does not succeed in adopting it, and feels anguish over the fact.

(*c*) a person mistakenly thinks that the Torah teaches a certain belief (e.g., God's corporeality), holds that belief, and feels joy over the fact that he holds a Torah belief.

In each of these cases the Torah is being violated unintentionally. What can Crescas say about them? These are not cases with which he explicitly deals, but perhaps we can extrapolate from what he does say to what he might or ought to say. With respect to the first case we may make the following comments. According to Crescas we are rewarded and punished for our actions.[109] Murder is an action and it is reasonable to assume that Crescas would hold in this case that the murderer would be punished. But, according to Crescas, we are also rewarded for our intentions.[110] Thus, one might expect him to say that the proper intention with which the murder was done, while not a cause for reward, perhaps, should at least mitigate the severity of the punishment. But, on the other hand, Torah and tradition are quite clear on what ought and ought not to be done. There seems to be little room for mitigation here, therefore.

With respect to the second case, that of the anguished non-believer, it would seem that consistency would demand that if we are rewarded for the joy we feel in holding correct beliefs, perhaps we ought also to be rewarded for the anguish we feel when we are unable to hold those correct beliefs. This may be going a bit far but it is certainly reasonable to suggest that Crescas would see the anguish as exculpating the sin of the person in question at least to some degree and quite properly mitigating the severity of his punishment.

The third case is that of the inadvertent or well-intentioned misbeliever. This is the misbeliever condemned by Maimonides and Abravanel and exonerated by Duran (and, at least in the case of corporeality, by Rabad). Crescas says nothing about such a case. We can, however, attempt to construct a position which is consistent with and perhaps derived from other statements of Crescas.

We ought to take note of the following facts. Crescas himself admits that the basic teachings of the Torah are not as well known as they should be. In the introduction to the *Or Adonai* he writes:

And yet one more, for it is great: concerning the fundaments of belief and the foundations of the Law and the principles of its roots. Until the completion of the Talmud, there never occurred any division of opinion with regard to them but they were well-known and agreed upon among the sages of our nation — with the exception of the secrets of the Law, including the Account of Creation and the Account of the Chariot, which were in the hands of the exceptional individuals, the modest ones, and the modest ones transmitted them to their disciples at certain times and under certain conditions. However, when the generations became weak, and the hands of those who held the received Oral Law and the concealed things of its mysteries and secrets became feeble, the wisdom of our wise men perished and the understanding of our prudent men became hidden.[111]

Confusion and ignorance surround the principles of the Torah so much that, according to Crescas, even Maimonides strayed from the truth:

And many among the sons of our people exalted themselves to interpret [true prophetic] visions and shut up the sealed words of prophecy by means of dreams and vanities and by means of the children of strangers. It came to the extent that some of the greatest of our sages were drawn after their words, and they prettified themselves with their discourses and adorned themselves with their proofs. And among them at their head was the great master, our Rabbi Moses ben Maimon of blessed memory, who, even with the greatness of his intellect, the extraordinarily encompassing scope of his Talmudic knowledge, and the breadth of his mind, when he meditated upon the books and discourses of the philosophers, they seduced him and he was seduced! From their weak premises, he made columns and foundations to the mysteries of the Law, in his book which he called *Guide of the Perplexed*.[112]

Maimonides may have been mistaken, but at least his mistakes were prompted by the best intentions. Such was not the case with those who arose after him, claiming to be his students:

Now, whereas the intent of the Master in this was desirable, there have arisen today rebellious servants, and they have turned into heresy the words of the living God. They mutilated holy sacrifices. They inflicted upon the words of the Master blemish in the place of beauty.[113]

From these passages we learn a number of suggestive facts. First, confusion and ignorance dominate discussions of the principles of Judaism. From this we might expect that Crescas would exonerate a person whose misbelief was not occasioned by rebelliousness. This leads to our second point: Crescas does exactly that. He exonerates Maimonides for his mistaken approach to the basic teachings of the Torah, since his intentions were pure. Those who claim to follow Maimonides, and this is our third point, Crescas condemns on the grounds that their deviations from Torah teachings were not well intentioned. In other words, Maimonides may actually have been guilty of misbelief but since (*a*) his misbelief was well intentioned and (*b*) he had reason to be confused about the basic teachings of Judaism, his misbelief can be excused.

This is fine and good with respect to Maimonides. Can we assume that unintentional misbelief on the part of all Jews would also be excusable? I think that the probable answer to that question is yes. As noted above, Crescas maintains that one is rewarded for the joy one feels at holding Torah teachings. In particular, he says:

Chapter 6: an explanation that what has been established here speculatively accords with the doctrine of the sages. This is so, for two matters have been established here. The first is that the belief concerning doctrines is acquired without will and the second is that reward and punishment are connected to the will, whether we have reference to the reward for the desire, for labour invested in, and happiness at being of this religious sect, or if we have reference to the punishment for the opposite.[114]

What particular joy is it, then, which merits reward? The joy of holding a Torah teaching which makes one 'of this religious sect'. This joy is contrasted with the cause of punishment which is the opposite of the feeling of joy at membership in 'this religious sect'. From this it seems we are punished for our conscious rejection of 'this religious sect'. What then can we say of a person who holds a certain belief because he thinks it is taught by the Torah (when in fact it is not), thereby identifying himself with the Jewish 'religious sect', and feeling great joy at the holding of that belief and that identification with Judaism? The very strictest consistency would seem to demand that such a person actually be rewarded. Demanding such consistency of Crescas may be asking too much of him. But, given his comments quoted above from the introduction to the *Or Adonai* and his emphatic assertion that the reward for beliefs depends upon the joy with which they are held, it seems not altogether unlikely that were Crescas confronted with a Jew who held mistaken beliefs concerning the principles of Judaism but held these beliefs because he thought that they were Torah teachings, and felt joy at thus fulfilling his obligations as a Jew, that he (Crescas) might very well admit that, at the very least, this mistaken but well intentioned Jew would not be punished for what, objectively speaking, is heresy. In other words, it seems that on the issue of unintentional sinning with respect to heresy, Crescas might side with Duran and not with Maimonides and Abravanel.

There are a number of reasons for suspecting that Crescas might not find this consequence of his position at all upsetting. We noted above that Maimonides presented his principles as 'foundations of the Torah', supporting them with verses drawn from Scripture. He furthermore makes attaining a portion in the world to come dependent upon acceptance of his principles and defines a Jew by that acceptance. In his discussion, we may thus say, Maimonides was asking a religious or theological question: what beliefs does the Torah demand that Jews accept as fundamental? Rejecting the principles involves the violation of Torah commands. Thus it is not surprising that Maimonides repeatedly decries as heretics those who question or reject his principles and condemns them to exclusion from the world to come.

Crescas, on the other hand, was not asking a religious question so much as a logical or structural one: what beliefs must a Jew accept as fundamental in order to be consistent? And, where Maimonides emphasizes the centrality of the question of salvation (asking, what principles must one accept in order to merit a share in the world to come), the question barely comes up in Crescas at all.[115] This may be some indication that Crescas had no compelling interest in excluding from the fold (and from the world to come) Jews who did not accept the principles as he promulgated them, especially if they did not mean thereby to rebel against the Torah.

We ought to note further that the Maimonides–Abravanel 'hard-line' position ignores the category of unintentional transgression altogether. It seems odd that halakhah should allow that category to obtain with respect to actions but not with respect to belief.[116] This point brings us to another reason why Crescas might have been happy with the position I have imputed to him in this chapter.

Speaking in the very broadest terms and recapitulating the points made above in the introduction[117] we may say that when Maimonides posited his principles of faith (an act for which he had no clear-cut precedent within the Jewish tradition) he gave expression to a conception of faith radically at variance with biblical–talmudic usage. For the Bible and Talmud Judaism was not a series of propositions which could be either affirmed or denied. The Torah and Sages do not demand belief *that* certain propositions are true or false; they do demand belief *in* God. The Bible and Talmud do not conceive of Judaism as a science affirming propositions which could be true or false.

Where does Crescas fit into this picture? There is no doubt that many of the same forces which brought other Jewish thinkers to adopt basically alien categories of thought in their own understanding of Judaism were operative in Crescas's case. It is unlikely that any medieval Jew was aware of the ways in which his conception of Judaism differed from that of the Bible and Talmud. It is only our hindsight which makes that possible. But there are indications that Crescas, more self-consciously than any other medieval Jewish thinker, resisted the Hellenization of Jewish thought, one of the clearest expressions of which was Maimonides' creed.

Among these we may note, in addition to Crescas's explicit comments in the introduction to the *Or Adonai*, the fact that for Maimonides human perfection, human felicity in the greatest measure possible, and the purpose of the Torah were all one and the same: intellectual perfection. This is as it should be: if Torah faith is defined as a series of propositions then the more perfectly one adheres to the Torah the more perfect is one's acquisition of the truths contained in those propositions.

Crescas subjects this conception of human perfection and the purpose of the Torah to devastating criticism.[118] To the Maimonidean ideal Crescas opposes another, one far removed from a conception of faith understood in propositional terms and much closer to classic rabbinic conceptions of man's proper relationship to God: love. The end of human existence, the purpose of the Torah (and of creation), and the greatest felicity to which a human being can aspire is the love of God — not the cold, intellectual love of Maimonides, attainable only by the philosopher, but warm, passionate love, the route to which was the observance of the commandments; love not of the intellect but of the emotions.

If I am correct in seeing Crescas's analysis of the end of man and the Torah as an attempt to resist Greek categories of thought and revert to a more pristinely Jewish approach, and if I am further correct in suggesting that this second approach was by its very nature open to the concept of unintentional sinning with respect to misbelief, then we have further grounds for accepting the interpretation of Crescas offered above and may more safely assert that in the question of what we may call inadvertent heresy the logic of his position forces him to stand with Duran in opposition to Maimonides and Abravanel.

VII. Crescas, Rabbenu Nissim, and Duran

In the course of the preceding discussion we have taken note of a number of places in which Crescas's thought bears the apparent impress of that of his teacher, Rabbenu Nissim.[119] Attention has been drawn to this issue through the writings of Sara Klein-Braslavy.[120] Rabbenu Nissim had no system of principles of faith of his own;[121] Crescas, however, apparently adopted some of Rabbenu Nissim's scattered ideas in working out his own system. Among the ideas which the two thinkers share in common, and which it is safe to assume Crescas adopted from his master, we find the following. First, the anti-Maimonidean claim that halakhah and philosophy are autonomous, the former in no way dependent upon or derivable from the latter, is a central idea shared by both thinkers.[122] Second, Klein-Braslavy demonstrates that Crescas's hierarchical system of principles of faith was suggested to him by Rabbenu Nissim's analysis of belief in creation.[123] Rabbenu Nissim, followed by Crescas, argued that creation *ex nihilo* was not the only theory concerning the coming to be of the world consistent with belief in God's power to work the wonders described in the Bible. Therefore, although belief in creation *ex nihilo* is certainly correct (because the Torah affirms it), it is not so centrally important dogmatically as Maimonides and Naḥmanides had insisted.[124] Klein-Braslavy maintains that Crescas derived the idea for a hierarchical system of dogmas from this analysis of creation, suggesting as it does a difference between beliefs affirmed by the Torah and beliefs without which the Torah cannot be accepted. Third, both Rabbenu Nissim and Crescas affirm the dogmatic centrality of belief in Torah from heaven; indeed, Crescas's whole system 'revolves around the axis of belief in Torah from heaven'.[125] Lest it be objected that it is hardly surprising that a Jewish theologian should emphasize the dogmatic centrality of belief in Torah from heaven, let it be recalled that for Maimonides the most important principle of faith, it would seem, was belief in God's existence. This emphasis on the dogmatic centrality of belief in Torah from heaven that we find in Rabbenu Nissim, Duran, and Crescas marks a distinct turning-point in the discussion of the principles of faith in medieval Judiasm. Fourth and finally, Crescas's claim that belief in God cannot be a commandment of the

Torah, since it is presupposed by the Torah, mirrors a position maintained by Rabbenu Nissim.[126]

While there is every reason to believe that the similarities found by Klein-Braslavy between the ideas of Rabbenu Nissim and Crescas are the result of the former's influence upon the latter, there is no reason to believe that the similarities we find between some of the ideas of Duran and some of the ideas of Crescas are the result of anything more than the influence of their common cultural milieu. Duran was a disciple of a disciple of Rabbenu Nissim and knew of Crescas, at least by reputation. We have no evidence, however, that Duran knew of Crescas's theological work when he composed his own account of the principles or that he had read Rabbenu Nissim's *Derashot* and Bible commentary.

We have noted various similarities between Crescas and Duran. Both emphasize the dogmatic centrality of Torah from heaven as opposed to emphasizing the dogmatic centrality of God's existence.[127] They both use the same neutral term *po'al* to describe the Torah, implying, more clearly in Crescas than in Duran, that in those contexts they are dealing with revelation in general, not the Torah of Moses.[128] Both Crescas and Duran frame at least parts of their discussions in terms of beliefs which must be held in order to avert the 'collapse' of the Torah.[129] Both deny that the Torah commands beliefs, and both insist that the principles of the Torah are not to be numbered among its commandments.[130]

Yet these similarities are ultimately less important than the differences between their respective dogmatic systems. There are, I think, three substantial differences between Duran and Crescas. In the first place, Duran's main interest in positing the principles of Judaism is religious or theological: he is primarily interested in defining what makes a good Jew. Crescas's main interest, on the other hand, is more logical or analytic: he is interested in discovering what beliefs a Jew must hold in order to be consistent.

Second, where Duran does betray a logical or analytical interest, he frames his discussion in axiomatic terms: from what beliefs may the Torah be derived, and which beliefs may be derived from other beliefs? Crescas eschews the axiomatic model, denying that Torah from heaven or the 'true doctrines' of treatise III can be derived from the 'cornerstones' of treatise II.

Third, Duran's own final position is that Judaism has no principles of faith beyond the acceptance of the Torah and all that it teaches. This is a position with which Crescas cannot possibly agree.

As we will see in the coming Chapter, Albo, although he was Crescas's student, was decisively influenced by Duran and followed him both in framing his discussion, at least partially, in terms of defining who a good Jew is and in adopting the axiomatic, not analytic model of principles of faith.

5

Joseph Albo

1. Albo's System of Principles

Although Joseph Albo wrote one of the most enduringly popular works of medieval Jewish philosophical theology, the *Sefer ha-Ikkarim*,[1] very little is actually known about his life. He himself informs us that he was a student of Ḥasdai Crescas[2] and Abravanel mentions that Albo studied under Rabbenu Nissim.[3] It is reported that he was alive in 1435.[4] He represented the Jewish community of Daroca (southwest of Saragossa in Aragon) at the disputation of Tortosa (1413–14)[5] and himself records that he wrote at least the first treatise of the *Sefer ha-Ikkarim* while residing in Soria (west of Saragossa in Castile).[6]

The *Sefer ha-Ikkarim*, like Crescas's *Or Adonai*, is a broad-ranging conspectus of theological and philosophical discussions organized according to the author's dogmatic system. But, while only the framework of Crescas's work is determined by his system of principles, much of the content of Albo's work, at least in the first treatise, is given over to substantive discussions of principles of faith.

Albo opens his discussion by citing Aristotle to the effect that human felicity (*haẓlaḥah*) depends upon philosophical knowledge and proper conduct.[7] But the unaided human intellect cannot fully determine which views are true and which actions are praiseworthy.[8] It follows, therefore, that human beings cannot achieve felicity on their own. Albo apparently takes it as a given that the achievement of felicity is possible because he goes on to assert that there must, therefore, exist something higher than the human intellect which defines praiseworthy acts and true views in a manner which leaves no room for doubt. This, he says, is divine guidance. As a matter of historical fact, however, it turns out that there are a number of competing systems of law (*dat*),[9] each of which claims uniquely to embody the divine guidance upon which the attainment of human felicity depends. In order to achieve such felicity, then, one must know which of all the putatively divine laws is in truth divine. At this juncture Albo posits the point which forms the basis for his entire work: in order to determine which law is truly divine one must determine those principles (*ikkarim*) without which a divine law cannot exist.

The apologetic intent of the work is evident from the outset. Although masquerading as a disinterested study of the principles of divine law in general, the *Sefer ha-Ikkarim* is a thinly disguised apology for Judaism: no reader can be surprised at Albo's conclusion (at I. 20, p. 173) that of all contemporary candidates for the status of divine law, only the Torah of Moses actually conforms perfectly to all the criteria of a divine law.

The *Sefer ha-Ikkarim*, therefore, seeks to explain 'those principles which pertain to a divine law generally, principles without which a divine law cannot be conceived'.[10] Every divine law must have general principles without which it would not be divine law and particular principles, special to it, the denial of which would lead to the collapse of that specific law, but not of divine law in general. In order to determine the general principles of any divine law, Albo proposes to study that single divine law which all agree is divine: the Torah of Moses.[11] Upon investigation Albo discovers that the Torah of Moses has certain characteristics which he takes as paradigmatic for all divine laws. It has general principles in so far as it is divine and special principles in which its distinctiveness lies. The general principles are called *ikkarim* (literally: 'roots', but better understood as 'dogmas') and the special principles are called *anafim* ('branches'). It also turns out that the general principles have certain derivative principles, *shorashim* ('roots'), which branch out from them and which are dependent upon them.[12]

All truly divine laws, Albo asserts, affirm three fundamental or general principles: the existence of God, Torah from heaven, and reward and punishment.[13] Albo, beyond providing scriptural, liturgical,[14] and talmudic[15] grounding for these three beliefs, does not in the first instance really essay a proof that they are indeed the fundamental and general principles of all truly divine religions. Indeed, he even introduces the three principles with the following words: '*It seems to me* that the correct way of counting the principles which are roots and foundations of the divine Torah [is to assert] that the general and necessary principles of the divine Torah are three . . .'[16] After distinguishing among different sorts of law, however, Albo offers the following argument for his basic principles:

There is no doubt that these three are necessary presuppositions [*hathalot*] of divine law *qua* divine. For if we assume the removal of one of them the law will collapse entirely.[17] This is obvious from the nature of the principles. Thus if we do not believe in the existence of God Who commands the law, there is no divine law. And if we do not believe in the existence of God, and do not believe in Torah from heaven, there is no divine law. And if there is no corporeal reward and punishment in this world and spiritual in the next, what need is there of divine law?[18]

It is interesting that Albo here follows Duran and Crescas in emphasizing the dogmatic centrality of belief in Torah from heaven,[19] for as it turns out, of course, the only truly divine law among all those which compete for the title in the contemporary world[20] is the Torah of Moses. Albo's argument, therefore, runs essentially as follows: without belief in God we cannot believe in the revelation of the Torah; and without belief in reward and punishment we cannot believe in the Torah since otherwise it would serve no purpose.

In continuing his analysis of divine law and its principles, Albo argues in i. 13 that the three general principles — God, Torah from heaven, and retribution — do not themselves exhaust all the beliefs which one must hold if one is to be considered a believer in divine law in the fullest sense of the term and if one wishes to earn a share in the world to come. 'But one may acknowledge these principles', he says, 'and yet have no share in the world to come. He must in addition believe in the derivative principles [*shorashim ha-nitlim*] which branch out of them. If he denies any of the derivative principles, it is tantamount to a denial of the fundamental principle from which the former is derived.'[21]

Before proceeding to give a complete account of the derivative or subordinate principles, Albo explains by which criteria we ought to be guided in selecting them. This forms the substance of chapter 14. First, following Duran,[22] he asserts that 'none of the commandments of the Torah should be counted as principles, whether fundamental or derivative'.[23] Simple disobedience (as opposed to that of one who denies that a commandment is truly God-given) is punishable but does not constitute heresy and does not cost one his share in the world to come.[24] Albo continues the chapter with an analysis of various possible counter-instances to his claim,[25] with a critique of some of Maimonides' principles,[26] and concludes the chapter having told us what not to count as a principle, fundamental or derivative, but without having told us what beliefs ought to count as derivative principles.

Albo opens his next chapter (i. 15) by launching directly into an account of the secondary or derivative principles. 'The derivative principles [*shorashim*]', he announces,

> which are dependent upon the three fundamental principles [*ikkarim*] which we have mentioned are eight. From the first principle, existence of God, are derived four secondary principles, including all of those things implied in the existence of God, Who is a necessary existent. They are as follows: (1) unity, as we explained it above;[27] (2) that He is neither a body nor a corporeal force; (3) that He is independent of time; and (4) that He is free of defects. . . .
>
> The derivative principles which are dependent upon and branch out of the second fundamental principle, Torah from heaven, are three: (1) God's knowledge; (2) prophecy; and (3) the genuineness of the divine messenger. . . .[28]
>
> As to the third fundamental principle, reward and punishment, the secondary principle which is prior to it and related to it necessarily is providence.[29]

Albo spends much of chapter 15 showing how these eight derivative, secondary, or subordinate principles relate to the three fundamental principles. We will take up this question in some detail below.

It is worthy of note that, while Albo's division of the principles of the Torah into three, his argument that each of the three corresponds to a term in Mishnah Sanhedrin x. 1, and his attachment of subordinate principles to the fundamental principles all seem to have been taken over from Duran, his naming and division of the subordinate principles seems to be his own. Where Duran had actually done no more than divide Maimonides' principles into three classes, Albo reworked the Maimonidean list in a new way.

The first five of Maimonides' principles (God's existence, unity, incorporeality, ontic priority, and that He alone may be worshipped) are taken over with only modest changes by Albo: in place of God's ontic priority Albo's fourth principle has God's independence from time (in order to include God's existence *a parte post* as well as *a parte ante*, Albo informs us[30]), and in place of the principle dealing with God's worship Albo's fifth principle deals with God's perfection, a point emphasized by Maimonides in his statement of his fifth principle.[31]

Where Duran's second group of principles simply restates principles 6, 7, and 9 from Maimonides' list (prophecy, Mosaic prophecy, and immutability of the Torah, the eighth principle being Torah from heaven), Albo subordinates to Torah from heaven the following: God's knowledge, prophecy, and the authenticity of the prophet's mission. Albo argues that the special nature of Mosaic prophecy and the immutability of the Torah are 'neither fundamental nor derivative principles, because they are not essential to divine law. They are merely like branches issuing from the belief in the autheniticity of the prophet's mission. If they are principles at all, primary or secondary, they are peculiar to the Torah of Moses, and not common to all divine law.'[32] Albo includes God's knowledge in this category 'for if God does not know terrestrial existence, prophecy cannot come from Him, nor a revealed Torah'.[33] He goes on to include the genuineness of the messenger as a principle since even with prophecy acknowledged, 'men would not have to obey the alleged prophet unless it is proven that he is a divine messenger sent to communicate to the people the commands of God'.

Duran's third group consists of beliefs dependent upon the principle of reward and punishment (number 11 in Maimonides' list); God's knowledge, Messiah, and resurrection. Albo lists God's knowledge under the heading of Torah from heaven, and denies that Messiah and resurrection are principles common to divine law as such. As a prerequisite of reward and punishment he lists God's providence which, unlike Maimonides, he counts as distinct from God's knowledge.[34]

Albo's insistence, then, on counting as principles of faith only those beliefs which he took to be common to divine laws as such led him to posit a list of principles which differed in various ways from that of Maimonides and Duran, while remaining fundamentally loyal to its overall structure. This is, perhaps, an expression of Albo's basically ambivalent attitude towards Maimonides' system of principles, as will be noted below.

In addition to his three fundamental principles and eight

derivative principles, Albo also includes in his list six 'beliefs which everyone professing the Torah of Moses is obliged to believe, which are connected with the three fundamental principles that we laid down, even though they are not derivative principles of them'.[35] These beliefs are not beliefs common to divine law as such but, rather, are beliefs which are as a matter of historical fact taught by the Torah of Moses. They are not, then, properly, principles of divine law.

The six beliefs are: (1) creation *ex nihilo*; (2) that the prophecy of Moses is superior to that of all other prophets; (3) that the Torah of Moses will neither be repealed, nor changed, nor exchanged; (4) that (a measure of) human perfection can be attained by fulfilling even a single one of the commandments of the Torah of Moses; (5) resurrection; (6) Messiah.

With respect to each of these beliefs Albo argues that while they are indeed taught by the Torah, and while they may be seen to be connected in some sense to the three fundamental principles, they are not beliefs such that we could not conceive of divine law in general or the Torah of Moses in particular without them.

Among the various beliefs taught by the Torah, why does Albo specify these six as having special significance? He answers the question in the following way:

We did enumerate specially the six beliefs above mentioned, because they are accepted beliefs among our people[36] necessary for the maintenance of the fundamental and derivative principles of the Torah. The fulfilment of the Torah is dependent upon them even though they are not principles [*shorashim*], since the Torah can exist without them, as we explained above. He who denies them is called a sectarian, even though he does not deny the Torah, and has no share in the world to come.[37]

These then are beliefs connected in one way or another with the fundamental and derivative principles and 'necessary for their maintenance'. This 'necessity' seems to spring from the fact of their wide acceptance among the Jewish people and the way in which they substantiate or exemplify the fundamental and derivative principles.

There is another distinguishing feature of these six special beliefs: they are neither dependent upon specific commandments[38] nor 'included in the belief in the biblical miracles generally'.[39]

Albo then, like his teacher Crescas, proposes a tripartite scheme of dogma: fundamental principles, derivative principles, obligatory beliefs. But beyond their both dividing their principles into three tiers there are very few similarities between the two systems. Crescas's first level consists not so much of principles of the Torah as of the presupposition upon which belief in any Torah must be based: belief in God's existence. Albo's first level, on the other hand, consists of those general beliefs common to any divine law. Crescas's second level consists of those beliefs which we must hold if we are to hold belief in Torah from heaven without self-contradiction. There is no specific logical relationship between Crescas's first and second strata. This is opposed by Albo who derives his second group of principles from the first. Crescas and Albo are closest in their definitions of their third group of principles, although here they differ radically on what beliefs they count in that group. This last is a reflection of the more polemical nature of Albo's book.

II. *Ikkarim, Shorashim*, and *Anafim*

Having enumerated which beliefs Albo counts under his various headings it is worthwhile trying to clarify a number of questions. First, what is the exact relationship which obtains among the general principles (*ikkarim*), derivative principles (*shorashim*), and particular principles (*anafim*)? Second, what is the exact relationship between the general principles and the rest of the Torah of Moses?

With respect to the first question, we find that Albo himself provides a number of different accounts of the relationship which holds between the general and derivative principles. When first introducing the subject he writes:

Not every law which maintains the three principles mentioned, viz., existence of God, reward and punishment, and Torah from heaven, which are the general principles [*ikkarim kolelim*] of divine law, as we have seen, is divine in the full sense of the word, so that a believer in it can be called a believer in divine law without qualification and has a share in the world to come. The truth of the matter is that these three are general principles of all divine law in the sense that one who denies any one of them is excluded from the class of those who profess divine law, and has no share in the world to come, because he does not believe properly in divine law. But one may acknowledge these principles and yet have no share in the world to come. He must in addition believe in the derivative principles [*shorashim*] which branch out of them. If he denies any of the subordinate principles, it is tantamount to a denial of the fundamental principle from which the former is derived.[40]

We are told here, then, that in addition to the three general or basic principles (*ikkarim*) of divine law, one must also accept those derivative (literally: 'dependent') principles which 'branch out' from the basic principles.

In what sense do the derivative principles depend upon and branch out from the basic principles? Albo hastens to answer, without, however, really throwing a great deal of light upon the subject. The derivative principles, we are told, 'follow from' (*yoz'im min*) or are 'dependent upon' (*nitlim*) the basic principles such that if one accepts the basic principle one 'must' (*zarikh*) accept the derivative principle and such that if one denies the derivative principle it is 'as if' (*ke-ilu*) one denies the basic principle.

This is not terribly clear because, even after this clarification, a number of possibilities remain concerning the exact nature of the relationship between the fundamental and derivative principles. The derivative principles may be logical consequences of the fundamental principles or they may be the presuppositions of the fundamental principles. Albo, it seems, was not particular about this issue. He counts as derivative principles of the first principle, belief in God, the belief in God's incorporeality, for example, a belief which follows from belief in the necessary existence of God. With respect to the second principle, Torah from heaven, we find that prophecy (i.e. the possibility of communication between God and man), clearly a presupposition of revelation, is counted as one of his derivatives. Similarly, God's knowledge of particulars is counted as a derivative principle of the principle of reward and punishment, even though divine reward and punishment are impossible without divine knowledge of particulars[41] while divine knowledge of particulars is possible even if God does not reward or punish those over whom His knowledge extends.[42]

In I. 15 Albo explicitly states that the derivative principles of the first two fundamental principles 'follow necessarily from' (*mithay-vim*) the fundamental principles.[43] In the same context he explicitly states that 'nothing should be regarded as a fundamental principle unless a divine law cannot be conceived without it,[44] nor as a secondary principle, unless it follows necessarily from a fundamental principle'.[45] Here he makes himself perfectly clear that the derivative principles are logically dependent upon the fundamental principles. In the same chapter, however, he tells us that providence, even though it is a derivative principle of the third fundamental principle, reward and punishment, is 'prior and essential to' (*ha-kodem lo ve-ha-mithayev elav*) it. This inconsistency did not seem to trouble Albo in the least.

At the end of treatise i Albo reiterates the claim that the derivative principles are logically dependent upon the fundamental principles, although he uses a different vocabulary there:

The result of our discussion in this Treatise is that the number of fundamental principles of a divine law is three, existence of God, Torah from heaven, and reward and punishment. Without these we cannot conceive of a divine law. Subordinate to these three are other secondary principles derived from them and related to them as species are to their genera, namely, that if you remove one of the derivative principles you do not remove thereby the fundamental principle, but if you remove the fundamental principle, the derivative principles disappear also, as we have explained.[46]

Once again we see Albo asserting that the derivative principles are in some way dependent upon the fundamental principles; only here the dependence is not expressed in logical terms of consequent to antecedent but in terms of prerequisites for existence: if some species of a particular genus were destroyed, the genus would not be destroyed thereby; but if the genus were to disappear, its species would also disappear.

When speaking in general terms, therefore, Albo insists that the derivative principles (*shorashim*) are derived from or at least dependent upon the fundamental principles (*ikkarim*). But, as we have noted, he is not consistent in applying this conception when it comes to the actual enumeration of his fundamental and derivative principles.

Albo himself takes note of this problem in the third treatise of the *Sefer ha-Ikkarim*. It might be supposed, he says that prophecy ought to be considered fundamental and Torah from heaven derivative;[47] similarly, 'one might say that since providence precedes reward and punishment, the latter is derived from it'.[48]

Albo answers these objections in the following way. The purpose of prophecy, he says, is to guide human beings to their ultimate and eternal felicity through the revelation of the Torah. Thus revelation of the Torah 'must be a fundamental principle, because it is that which makes prophecy necessary'.[49] The purpose of providence over human beings, Albo asserts, is reward and punishment. 'Hence we considered reward and punishment a fundamental principle and providence a subordinate principle derived from the former . . .'[50]

On this analysis, the fundamental principles are not those which are in some logical or definitional sense antecedent to the derivative principles, but are, rather, those principles through the existence of which the derivative principles gain their importance and value. Whether or not one finds Albo's answers here convincing,[51] there is no doubt that they are inconsistent with the general position adumbrated in treatise i.[52]

III. Judaism as a Science

We may now take up the question raised above, what is the relationship between the general principles and the rest of the Torah of Moses?

Albo's account of the relationship between the fundamental and derived principles as it is presented in treatise i is part of his understanding of what we would call theology. Albo opens the *Sefer ha-Ikkarim* with the following statement:

To know the fundamental principles upon which laws in general are based is both easy and difficult. It is easy, because all the people that we know of in the world today possess a law, and it is inconceivable that a person should be subject to or identified with a law without knowing its principles or having some notion of them sufficient to induce belief in them, as we do not call a person a physician who does not know the principles of medicine, nor do we call one a geometrician who does not know the principles of geometry or who does not at least have some notion of them.[53]

The *Sefer ha-Ikkarim* deals with divine law. At the very beginning of the book we find that Albo understands divine law to be similar, in at least one very important respect, to sciences such as medicine and geometry. The similarity rests in this: divine law, like the sciences, has principles upon which it is based. The Torah, in other words, is likened to the sciences, at least with respect to its logical structure. Albo makes this point clearer in i. 11:

Just as in every science the principles are first laid down upon which the science turns and by which are proved all the other propositions that come in that science, so in the weekly reading *Bereshit*[54] are recounted three matters,[55] different from each other, every one explaining one of the principles to indicate that they are the principles and foundations of divine law upon which it and all its contents turn.[56]

In this brief passage we learn, first, that Albo considers divine law to be structurally analogous to the sciences; second, that the principles of a science ought to be enunciated at the beginning of any exposition of that science and that the Torah does indeed do that; third, that the principles of a science are those propositions by which are proved all the other propositions of a science; and fourth, that the Torah has principles in exactly that sense — i.e., the Torah has axioms which are necessary for the derivation of all the other propositions (beliefs and commandments) of the 'science of the Torah'.

The point is reiterated again in i. 17:

Every science makes use of principles [*hathalot*] and postulates [*hanahot*] which are not self evident, but are assumed as true and borrowed from another science in which they are proved. Upon these principles are built all the proofs of the science in question . . . So every theoretical science necessarily assumes at the beginning certain principles and postulates which are proved in another science, as is explained in the *Posterior Analytics*.[57] Upon these principles or upon the first principles [*ha-muskalot ha-rishonot*] are built all the proofs of that science. This being so, it is proper to inquire where divine law takes its principles.[58]

Here again we see that for Albo divine law is a science like every other science, having principles of its own upon which is based the rest of the science. The principles or foundations of the Torah, therefore, may be likened to the axioms of geometry: propositions accepted within the science and from which are derived the rest of the propositions of the science. This understanding of the principles of the Torah was introduced into Jewish discussions of dogma, as we noted above, by Duran.[59]

Albo's use of this account, however, presents some problems. Which beliefs are the axioms of Judaism: the three fundamental principles (*ikkarim*) alone, or the fundamental and derivative principles together? If the three fundamental principles alone are the axioms of Judaism, how do the derivative principles differ from the rest of the beliefs of Judaism? But if all the principles of the Torah — fundamental and derived — are the axioms of Judaism, how then do they differ from one another?

Albo does not provide clear-cut answers to these questions and seems, in fact, to have been unaware of them. The basic difficulty seems to stem from his ambivalent attitude towards Maimonides' account of the principles of Judaism. On the one hand, he rejects it, and indeed, subjects it to repeated criticism.[60] On the other hand, he also tries to show how close to Maimonides' system his own really is, and in so doing blurs the distinction between the fundamental and derivative principles.[61] In those passages where Albo is concerned to emphasize his originality and his independence of Maimonides, he emphasizes the important differences between fundamental and derivative principles.[62] In others where Albo emphasizes the similarity between his system and that of Maimonides, he lumps the two kinds of principles together, coming up with a list very little different from that of Maimonides.[63]

IV. Heresy

One way of approaching the question of the relative status and importance of the fundamental and derivative principles in Albo's system is by examining his comments concerning their importance with respect to the question of salvation, and with respect to the consequences of what we may call 'accidental heresy'.

In the first chapter of the first treatise of the *Sefer ha-Ikkarim* Albo asserts that 'the investigation of fundamental principles is very dangerous'.[64] He explains the danger in the following way: religions more or less agree on the general, fundamental principles of divine law; they disagree, however, with respect to particular principles, and one who denies the particular principles held by a certain religion excludes himself from that religion. The danger involved in being excluded from a religion is that if that is the true religion, then one is thereby excluded from the world to come. This becomes clear from Albo's analysis of the notorious statement attributed to R. Hillel: 'the Jews will have no Messiah, since they have already enjoyed the benefits of the Messiah in the days of Hezekiah, King of Judah.'[65] After analysing a number of explanations for the startling pronouncement, Albo concludes that R. Hillel 'did not believe in the coming of the Messiah at all, and if despite this he was not classed as an unbeliever, it is because the coming of the Messiah is not a fundamental principle of the Torah of Moses'.[66] It is safe to assume from this that were belief in the Messiah a fundamental principle of the Torah then R. Hillel would indeed have been considered to be an unbeliever (*kofer be-ikkar*) and as such no longer a member of the community of Israel, in this world and in the next. Albo makes the point at the end of the chapter: 'For this reason we said that there is grave danger in the investigation of principles. For how can one tell what those things are, the denial of which, and of their fundamental character, constitutes one an unbeliever?'[67]

It would seem to follow from all this that Albo's position is simple and straightforward: denial of any of the fundamental or derivative principles of the Torah constitutes heresy. There is no such thing as accidental heresy: even if a person were convinced that he was denying beliefs denied by the Torah, so long as he is in fact wrong he is a heretic and, it seems, will have no share in the world to come.[68]

But now we find something truly strange. In the very next chapter of his book Albo seems to allow for the possibility of unintentional disbelief not counting as heresy! He seems in this chapter to have taken over whole Duran's position concerning unintentional heresy. He opens the chapter with the following statement:

It is proper to say this in justification of those Jewish scholars who deal with this subject.[69] Every Israelite is obliged to believe that everything that is found in the Torah is absolutely true, and anyone who denies anything that is found in the Torah, knowing that it is the opinion of the Torah, is a heretic . . . But a person who upholds the Torah of Moses and believes in its principles, but when he undertakes to investigate these matters with his reason and scrutinizes the texts, is misled by his speculation and interprets a given principle otherwise than it is taken to mean at first sight;[70] or denies the principle because he thinks that it does not represent a sound theory which the Torah obliges us to believe; or erroneously denies that a given belief is a fundamental principle, which however he believes as he believes the other dogmas of the Torah which are not fundamental principles;[71] or entertains a certain notion in relation to one of the miracles of the Torah because he thinks that he is not thereby denying any of the doctrines which it is obligatory upon us to believe by the authority of the Torah,[72] — a person of this sort is not a heretic. He is, rather, classed with the sages and pious men of Israel, though he holds erroneous theories. His sin is due to error and requires atonement.[73]

In this passage Albo adopts Duran's principle that at basis one is obliged to accept that all that the Torah teaches is true. But, once one does accept that, if one is led — either by philosophical speculation or honest exegesis of Scripture — to adopt certain types of heterodox positions one does not thereby become a heretic, forfeiting one's share in the world to come. Albo discusses four types of heterodox position to which one might be led by faulty speculation or faulty exegesis and which do not remove one from the community of Israel: (1) misinterpretation of a principle; (2) denying the truth of a principle; (3) denying that a particular belief is a principle, while not denying that the belief is true and truly taught by the Torah; and (4) misinterpreting a miracle. Persons who err in any of these ways are not heretics, are not excluded from the community of Israel (indeed, they may be classed among 'the sages and pious men of Israel') and, although they have sinned and must expiate their sin, are not denied a share in the world to come.

Albo goes on to give various examples of 'sages and pious men of Israel' who, misled either by philosophy or their failure properly to understand Scripture, adopted one or more of the heterodox positions listed above. 'We say, therefore,' he concludes,

that a person whose speculative ability is not sufficient to enable him to reach the true meaning of scriptural texts, with the result that he believes in the literal meaning and entertains absurd ideas because he thinks they represent the view of the Torah, is not thereby excluded from the community of those who believe in the Torah, heaven forfend! Nor is it permitted to speak disrespectfully of him and accuse him of 'perverting the teaching of the Torah'[74] and class him among the heretics and sectarians.[75]

Thus we find Albo staunchly defending those Jews who are led to mistaken beliefs by honest mistakes in their understanding of Scripture. 'That man alone', Albo tells us after citing the case of Elisha Aḥer,

who knows the truth and deliberately denies it, belongs to the class of the wicked whose repentance is rejected. But the man whose intention is not to rebel, nor to depart from the truth, nor to deny what is in the Torah, nor reject tradition, but whose sole intention is to interpret the verses according to his opinion, though he interprets them erroneously, is neither a sectarian nor a heretic.[76]

Albo concludes this chapter with the following declaration:

It is clear now that every intelligent person is permitted to investigate the fundamental principles of religion and to interpret the verses [of the Torah] in accordance with the truth as it seems to him. And though he believe concerning certain things which earlier authorities regarded as principles, like the coming of the Messiah and creation, that they are not fundamental principles, but merely true doctrines, which the believer in the Torah is obliged to believe, . . . he is not a denier of the Torah or its principles . . .[77]

It does indeed seem, therefore, that chapter 2 of treatise i of the *Sefer ha-Ikkarim* stands in blatant contradiction to chapter 1 of that treatise. The implication of chapter 1 is that denial of one of the principles of the Torah, or even the affirmation of a belief constituting a principle coupled with the denial that that belief is actually a principle (as opposed to simply being a true belief taught by the Torah) constitutes heresy. The upshot of chapter 2, however, is that if one denies a belief which constitutes a principle, or denies that a certain true belief is a principle, when in fact it is, but does so because of an honest mistake and not out of any intention to rebel, then one may still be classed among 'the sages and pious men of Israel'.[78]

It may be argued, however, that chapter 2 does not contradict chapter 1, but explains it: in chapter 1 Albo asserts that denial of the principles constitutes heresy, while in chapter 2 he explains what *sort* of denial of the principles constitutes heresy. But Albo opens chapter 1 by warning that 'the investigation of fundamental principles is *extremely dangerous*'.[79] If honest mistakes concerning the principles did not constitute heresy and cost one one's share in the world to come, wherein lies the extreme danger in investigating the principles? It does not seem possible, therefore, to reconcile the two approaches outlined in chapters 1 and 2 of treatise i. It seems to me that chapter 1 is more consistent with Albo's overall approach than is chapter 2: throughout the book Albo speaks of denial of any of the principles of Judaism as heresy, without qualifying it with respect to intention.[80] Chapter 2 is more or less taken over whole from Duran. I suggest that Albo included it in his book so that his analysis would not be taken to imply that he held that any of his predecessors among the Jewish scholars who dealt with the principles of Judaism were heretics, even though they differed from him in their account of the principles. It might be further suggested that Albo's comments in chapter 2 show how fundamentally uncomfortable he was with the new propositional definition of 'belief' and its corollary rejection of the possibility of inadvertence (*shegagah*) with respect to heresy.[81] It may very well be that chapter 1 reflects a Maimonidean (and, as we shall see, an Abravanelian) position on the question while chapter 2 reflects Albo's reservations concerning a position which he may have not quite clearly recognized as radical and unconventional in the context of traditional rabbinic Judaism.

v. Duran, Crescas, and Albo

This discussion of Albo's sometimes conflicting statements on the dogmas of Judaism can be conveniently summarized by pointing out those elements of Albo's position which were borrowed from other authors and those elements which represent his own original contribution. From Duran Albo borrowed the conception that the basic principles of Judaism could be reduced to three: God, Torah, retribution. From Duran as well he borrowed the ideas that Maimonides' thirteen principles could be reduced to these three, that each could be attached to a term in Mishnah Sanhedrin x. 1, that the principles can be divided into fundamental and subordinate classes, and that the principles may not be taken from the commandments in the Torah. Albo also followed Duran (and Crescas) in emphasizing the dogmatic centrality of belief in Torah from heaven as opposed to belief in the existence of God.

From Crescas Albo borrowed at least two ideas: the tripartite structure of the principles, and the definition of a principle as a belief without the acceptance of which belief in Torah from heaven (for Crescas) or divine law in general (for Albo) cannot be maintained. Of course, Crescas pictured the relationship in basically horizontal or analytic terms while Albo pictured the relationship in basically vertical or geometrical terms.

Albo's own contribution seems to have been in the emphasis he placed on picturing the Torah as a science (an idea the germ of which we find in Duran), in his definition of principles in terms of divine law in general, and in the logical relationship he posited between the fundamental and subordinate principles. These ideas were not, however, formulated rigorously, and confusion remains concerning the exact nature of the relationship between fundamental and subordinate principles, concerning the issue of unintentional heresy, and concerning Albo's attitude towards Maimonides' statement of the principles.

6

Shalom, Arama, and Yavez̧

The three figures whose writings on the principles of Judaism will be surveyed briefly in this chapter have a number of things in common. All late fifteenth-century Spanish Jews, they each composed theological works in which dogmatic questions are given fairly brief and unsystematic attention. In this they differ markedly from their contemporary countrymen, Bibago and Abravanel, each of whom devoted extensive attention to the principles of Judaism.

1. Abraham Shalom

Abraham Shalom (d. 1492) apparently lived in Catalonia. He is the author of *Neveh Shalom*, a work ostensibly devoted to justifying the Aggadic portions of the Talmud but which also includes a series of philosophic discussions devoted to discovering which teachings of philosophy accord with the Torah.[1] These discussions reflect Shalom's desire to defend Maimonides from Crescas's critique that he was too radical and from Gersonides' critique that he was too conservative.

Shalom makes a number of passing references to beliefs which he calls variously *ikkarim* and *yesodot*. All told, the different beliefs which he mentions in this fashion are the following:

(1) the necessary existence of God
(2) reward and punishment
(3) divine providence
(4) creation of the world
(5) divine omnipotence
(6) revelation
(7) prophecy
(8) Messiah
(9) that God is omniscient and man has freedom
(10) resurrection.

Shalom also mentions the immutability of God and eternity of the Torah as beliefs which may be considered as principles even though he does not explicitly call them *ikkarim* or *yesodot*.[2]

The first four beliefs appear to be Shalom's basic list of principles. The list appears three times in the *Neveh Shalom* (although in the first occurrence, divine omnipotence is listed in place of providence).[3] The other beliefs are listed in various contexts, almost haphazardly. A distinguishing feature of Shalom's account of the principles of Judaism is the heavy emphasis he places on the centrality of belief in creation. It is, he says, 'the foundation which precedes all of the Torah, upon which the latter built its house, and upon which all its foundations stand'.[4] This opinion concerning the importance of creation, we shall see, was shared by all of Shalom's contemporaries who dealt with the principles of Judaism.

Claiming that creation is so important, Shalom must answer why Maimonides failed to include it in his account of the principles of the Torah. He argues that Maimonides did not count creation among the principles 'because it is their foundation. There is a great difference between a foundation [*yesod*] and a principle [*ikkar*]: every foundation is a principle but not every principle is a foundation . . .'[5] Shalom's ingenious argument claims that belief in creation is a foundation of faith while the beliefs listed by Maimonides are merely principles of faith, all logically posterior to belief in creation. This argument founders on the fact that Maimonides himself uses the same term, *qa'ida* (foundation) to refer both to creation and to his thirteen principles.[6] Furthermore, Maimonides added creation to his thirteen principles towards the end of his life.[7] Be that as it may, the relevant point here is that Shalom emphasized the centrality of belief in creation and at the same time felt called upon to defend Maimonides' formulation of the principles of Judaism.

Shalom felt constrained to do this because he apparently accepted Maimonides' thirteen principles as the standard account of Jewish dogmatics. He refers to them as '*the* thirteen principles of religion'[8] and seems to accept it as obvious that they are the principles of Judaism. This fact, coupled with the seeming informal way in which various beliefs are listed as principles of faith shows that Shalom's account was in no way intended to replace that of Maimonides.

In sum we may say that Shalom's account adds little to the discussion of the principles of Judaism in late medieval Judaism. It also seems not to have influenced any other writer.

11. Isaac Arama

Isaac Arama (1420–94) wrote a popular homiletical commentary on the Pentateuch, *Akedat Yizhak*.[9] Arama, an older friend and colleague of Abravanel's, shared the latter's fate and went into Italian exile after the Expulsion.

The one hundred and five sermons into which the *Akedat Yizhak* is divided contain extended discussions of most of the important philosophical and theological issues which exercised the Jewish community in Arama's day.[10] It is no surprise, therefore, to discover that Arama takes up the question of principles of Judaism. He raises this issue most systematically, albeit briefly, in the sixty-seventh sermon.[11]

This sermon discusses the order of the festivals laid down in Leviticus 23. Arama claims that the festivals are listed here, and their major ceremonials summarized, so that even the simplest Jew will know something concerning the 'root corner-stones' of the Torah.[12] The festivals, then, unique as they are to Judaism, summarize or hint at the basic beliefs of the Jewish faith. This is so, Arama urges, because

not every belief which is necessary so that one can conceive the existence of the Torah is a principle specific to it.[13] For, were this so, the existence of nature, that man is rational, or that man has choice would be principles of it, for no Torah is possible without them.[14] However, since these things are shared by adherents of the Torah, and by others, among the philosophers and among adherents of other faiths, they ought not to be considered as principles specific to it.[15]

For this same reason it is also clear that God's existence, unity, and incorporeality, — even though the Torah lays them down and emphatically admonishes [us] concerning them, just as it admonished [us] concerning murder, adultery, etc. — are not principles specific to it for all of the philosophers proved the necessity of their truth with absolute demonstrations[16] even though they did not admit the truth of the divine Torah.

It is appropriate that this divine Torah and the principles specific to it be related in the way in which a term defined is related to its definition so that we may say that every adherent of the divine Torah will believe them and all who believe them will be adherents of the divine Torah.[17]

In this passage Arama introduces an entirely new conception of what a principle of Judaism is. Principles of Judaism are not dogmas, as they were for Maimonides, they are not propositions analytic to the concept 'Torah from heaven' as they were for Crescas, and they are not the axioms of divine science as they were for Albo; rather, the principles of Judaism are those beliefs which distinguish Judaism from philosophy on the one hand and from other religions on the other. They are, it might be said, the defining characteristics of Judaism: a Jew is a person who accepts the principles and acceptance of the principles makes one a Jew.[18] This being so, it makes excellent sense to claim that the principles of Judaism, specific as they are to Judaism, are embodied in the practices specific to Judaism, its ceremonials. This is exactly the tack taken by Arama, who argues that each one of the festivals described in Leviticus 23 hints at one of the principles of the Torah. This approach fits well into Arama's claim that it is actions (the fulfilment of the commandments) and not intellectual perfection which bring a person to felicity.[19]

Arama relates six beliefs to the festivals listed in Leviticus 23 in the following way:[20]

Sabbath: creation
Passover: God's power
Shavuoth: prophecy and Torah from heaven
Rosh ha-Shanah: providence
Yom Kippur: repentance
Sukkot: world to come (i.e., human immortality)

Of these six beliefs, Arama repeatedly emphasizes the special importance and centrality of the first, belief in creation of the world. He writes:

The greatest of them and the first of them all is belief in the creation of the world; it says, 'Six days shall work be done; [but on the seventh day is a sabbath of solemn rest, a holy convocation; ye shall do no manner of work; it is a sabbath unto the Lord in all your dwellings]' [Leviticus 23: 3]. For the most important thing the truth of which every adherent of the divine religion must affirm is that God brought the world into existence and created it after it did not exist by His absolute will at the very moment He desired to do it and in the way in which the Creator saw as appropriate in which to do it. For, with this belief one can accept and establish all the other principles which it[21] posits afterwards; this is doubtless the reason the Torah began with it . . .[22]

In emphasizing the importance of belief in creation, Arama, we shall see, is at one with all the other late fifteenth-century Jewish thinkers who dealt with the subject of the principles of Judaism. Belief in creation, however, is not more distinctive to Judaism than are the other beliefs which Arama lists. On his own definition, therefore, it cannot be more important as a principle than the other beliefs. In that it precedes the others logically, however, since they are only possible if the world is created, we may say that it is 'first among equals'. Arama emphasizes the prime importance of creation in sermon 55 where he deals with the Sabbath. There he derives not only creation from the Sabbath, but God's power as well. Indirectly, he also derives the other four principles from the Sabbath, emphasizing in this fashion the fundamental role of the Sabbath *vis-à-vis* the other principles of faith.[23]

It may be objected to Arama's account of the principles that while his six dogmas do indeed distinguish Judaism from orthodox Aristotelianism, they do not distinguish Judaism emphatically from Islam and Christianity, faiths which accept belief in creation, God's power, prophecy and revelation, providence, repentance, and the world to come. The answer to this objection, it seems to me, lies in Arama's emphasis upon the connection between the principles and the festivals which embody them. The principles of Judaism find their expression in the commandments of Judaism. Christianity and Islam on the one hand, and philosophy on the other hand, reject these commandments. It is in this fashion that the principles of Judaism distinguish it from other faiths and from philosophy.

This emphasis on the connection between the principles and ceremonials and the understanding of a principle as a defining characteristic of Judaism constitutes Arama's most interesting contribution to the late medieval debate on the principles of Judaism.

III. Joseph Yavez

R. Joseph ben Ḥayyim Yavez (1438–1507), like his brother-in-law Isaac Arama and his sometime teacher Isaac Abravanel, was a victim of the Expulsion from Spain and, along with these two more famous contemporaries, he settled in Italy after being forced to abandon his homeland. In Italy he became an itinerant preacher, polemicizing against philosophy and seeking to strengthen the faith of the Jewish people in the aftermath of the catastrophe of 1492. As with Abravanel, the bulk of Yaveẓ's activity dates from the period of his sojourn in Italy.[24]

Yaveẓ devoted two short works to the principles of Judaism. It is perhaps more correct to say that he composed two treatises in which his account of the principles of Judaism provides a structural framework and springboard for his anti-philosophic homilies. These two works are *Ma'amar ha-Aḥdut* and *Yesod ha-Emunah*. Yaveẓ also makes reference to his principles in *Or ha-Ḥayyim* and in his *Commentary on Psalms*.[25]

'The principles of faith', Yaveẓ asserts categorically at the beginning of his *Ma'amar ha-Aḥdut*,

are not thirteen as Maimonides posited, nor are they seven as R. Ḥasdai posited, nor are they the three which Rabbi J. Albo, author of the *Ikkarim*, posited. Rather they are three which comprise an explanation of the great and glorious 'name of being'[26] and they are themselves an explanation of the term 'one' . . . One-ness is divided into three parts. The first is absolute one-ness, expressed in the idea that God alone is Creator, for there is none other with Him . . . The second part of God's one-ness is that he alone is the true Provider;[27] there is none beside Him . . . The third part [of God's one-ness] is not in this time but in that future to which we look forward when He alone will be worshipped . . .[28]

Here Yaveẓ explicitly rejects the dogmatic schemes of Maimonides, Crescas, and Albo, and insists that Judaism has only three principles: creation, providence, and that in the end of days God will be universally acknowledged.[29] This last principle Yaveẓ refers to also as the principle of unity[30] and as belief in reward at the end of days.[31]

Yaveẓ presents the three principles as contributing to an elucidation of God's unity as expressed in the Tetragrammaton ('name of being'). The first principle refers to the past tense of the verb 'to be' since before creation God *was* alone. The second principle refers to the present tense of the verb 'to be' since God *is*, and is the only true source of providence. The third principle refers to the future tense of the verb 'to be' since ultimately God will be the only deity worshipped in consequence of the fact that His unity will be universally acknowledged.[32]

Even though in *Ma'amar ha-Aḥdut* Yaveẓ introduces his principles by way of supplanting those of Maimonides, in *Yesod ha-Emunah* he attempts to show how his three principles actually do include all of Maimonides' thirteen.[33] In order to do so he groups Maimonides' principles in the following fashion:

Creation	God's existence (principle 1) God's eternity (principle 4)
Providence	reward and punishment (principle 11) prophecy (principle 8) Mosaic prophecy (principle 7) Torah from heaven (principle 8) God's knowledge (principle 10)
Unity	reward for souls (principle 11) that God alone may be worshipped (principle 5) eternity of the Torah (principle 9) Messiah (principle 12) resurrection (principle 13).

In this categorization Yaveẓ leaves out Maimonides' second and third principles (God's unity and incorporeality) and divides his eleventh principle into two. These matters are of little importance, I think. Yaveẓ presents this division in a thoroughly informal way and, I am sure, did not mean it to be examined too closely. It is significant, however, that while he felt the need to show how his system could be harmonized with that of Maimonides, he rejected the systems of Crescas and Albo out of hand. Along with his contemporaries Bibago and Abravanel, Yaveẓ apparently felt that he could not simply reject Maimonides' formulation of the principles of Judaism.

Although Yaveẓ seems to find his second principle, that of providence, to be the most important of the three,[34] he follows Duran, Shalom, Arama, Bibago, and Abravanel[35] in emphasizing at least the logical priority of belief in creation as the 'principle of principles'.[36] Belief in creation necessitates belief in providence, while the two together necessitate belief that God's unity will ultimately be acknowledged by all men.[37] The three principles are interrelated in another way: they are progressively harder to believe.[38] Yaveẓ emphasizes that they are matters of belief, as befits principles one of whose aims is to distinguish Judaism clearly from philosophy.[39]

This emphasis on the distinguishing character of the principles is one of several ways in which Yaveẓ's discussion is similar to

Arama's. Not only does Yaveẓ see his principles as distinguishing Judaism from philosophy and other faiths, but he also insists that they be implemented in Jewish ceremonials. Yaveẓ, for example, sees the three Sabbath meals as symbols for his three principles.[40]

We have before us, then, three thinkers who developed in the same milieu, who were almost precise contemporaries, who composed works of Jewish theology, and who touched, however briefly, on the question of the dogmas of Judaism. They are similar in all these respects but one to Bibago and Abravanel. These latter authors also grew to maturity in late fifteenth-century Christian Spain and composed works on Jewish theology. They both, however, dealt with the principles of Judaism systematically and at length and will, therefore, be treated separately.

With respect to the content of their teachings on the principles of Judaism, our three writers have at least two points in common. They all agree, indeed, they take it as given, that Judaism has principles of faith, and all agree that creation is the most important of Judaism's dogmas. Shalom and Yaveẓ, furthermore, agree in their more or less informal acceptance of Maimonides' thirteen principles as *the* standard account of the principles of Judaism while Arama and Yaveẓ agree in their claim that for Judaism, actions take precedence over beliefs.

7

Abraham Bibago

I. Bibago's System of Principles

Abraham Bibago[1] (d. *c*.1489) served as a rabbi, seminary head, and communal leader in Huesca and Saragossa.[2] Although he was a prolific writer, only two of his works were ever published.[3] Bibago was highly regarded by many of his contemporaries and successors, some of whom used extensive portions of his work without attribution.[4]

Bibago completed his most important work, *Derekh Emunah* (*Path of Faith*), about 1480.[5] This work is based upon Bibago's contention that human felicity (*haẓlaḥah*) depends upon intellectual perfection and that there are two separate routes to that goal: the path of philosophic investigation and the path of faith. The path of faith, when coupled with the path of investigation, is superior to the path of investigation alone. On its own, the path of faith is not inferior to the path of investigation.[6] We see here a position which, while resembling that of Maimonides on the surface, is actually far removed from it. Bibago agrees with Maimonides' contention that human felicity depends upon cognition of the intelligibilia but goes on to add that such felicity may also be achieved through faith alone. This analysis leads Bibago to examine the concept 'faith' (*emumah*). This examination constitutes the subject matter of part of the second and all of the third and final treatise (*ma'amar*) in the *Derekh Emunah*. In clarifying the concept 'faith' Bibago is led to take up the question of the content of faith; after all, how can one properly call oneself a 'believer' if one cannot specify one's beliefs?[7] It is by way of specifying the content of Jewish faith that Bibago discusses the dogmas of Judaism.

A number of noteworthy motifs emerge in Bibago's analysis of the principles of the Torah. First, he — more explicitly than any of his predecessors — adopts a scientific model of Judaism.[8] Second, like Albo, he is concerned in the first instance not to define Judaism so much as to define 'faith' in general; unlike Albo, however, whose work is clearly motivated by apologetic and polemical concerns,

Bibago's discussion of faith and its presuppositions is largely disinterested and academic.[9] Third, like Crescas and Albo, Bibago discusses different 'levels' of principles. Finally, like almost every one of his fifteenth-century predecessors, contemporaries, and successors, Bibago emphasizes the dogmatic centrality of belief in creation.

The third treatise of the *Derekh Emunah* is divided into five chapters. In the first Bibago discusses the axioms (*hathalot*)[10] of faith and discovers that they are of two kinds: they may be called epistemological (bringing us to accept religion) and logical. The first he determines to be miracles and the second creation. Chapters 2 and 3, therefore, are devoted to discussions of these subjects. In chapter 4 Bibago defines the term 'principle' (*ikkar*) while in the fifth and final chapter he discusses the specific principles of Judaism.

Bibago opens *Derekh Emunah*, iii. 1 by affirming that the speculative sciences, for all their differences, share four characteristics in common. First, each has its own particular subject matter (e.g., being *qua* being in the case of metaphysics); second, each science deals with the accidents specific to its subject (e.g., unity, multiplicity, potentiality, and actuality in the case of metaphysics); third, each science has questions unique to it (e.g., in the case of metaphysics can being *qua* being be divided into unity and multiplicity?); fourth, each science has axioms and theorems (*hakdamot*) which are either self-evident or derived from another science.[11]

Having established this, Bibago goes on to take up the question of how these four characteristics of science are found in religion (*emunah*).[12] But first, religion itself must be defined. 'It is known and established', Bibago writes,

that religion teaches views concerning divinity, for this is its purpose and upon this it labours. This is something common to all religions *qua* religions: they seek to bring a person to felicity. Religion being so, its roots and pillars all seek to direct adherents [*ma'aminim*] to believe true opinions concerning Prime Being. This is something common to all religions without exception, irrespective of their being true or false.[13]

Religion is a science, therefore, which takes as its subject-matter Divinity or Prime Being and which aims at directing individuals to their felicity. It may be compared to the science of medicine — the

subject-matter of which is the functioning of the human body and
the aim of which is the attainment and preservation of health.

Since religion in general seeks to inculcate in us true views, it is
not surprising that Bibago insists that the Torah (being the teaching
of the one truly divine religion) teaches true beliefs through its
commandments and narratives.[14]

The axioms of religion can be of four kinds: sensible (e.g., the sun
rises and sets), experiential (e.g., opium sedates), rational (e.g., the
whole is greater than its parts), and traditional (e.g., creation).[15] An
analysis of these four kinds of axiom brings Bibago to argue:

. . . that the axiom of the creation of the world is an axiom upon which the
Torah is built. It is a general theorem [*hakdamah*] of all the specific beliefs
found in the Torah since upon its basis we accept the existence of a
powerful Creator who commands us to believe. . . . It is an axiom upon
which are built the Torah, its principles, and its [other] beliefs. This is the
reason why the divine Torah began with it, in the manner of all sciences
which put their axioms 'in the beginning' [Gen. 1: 1].[16]

Bibago goes on to distinguish

two types of axiom of religion: the first [type] brings one to accept the
religion — these are the miracles; the second is the axiom upon which it is
based — this is creation of the world. This is the reason that the Torah
opened with the first and closed with the second. It opened with the
first — 'In the beginning God created the heaven and the earth' [Gen. 1:
1] — and closed with the second — 'In all the signs and wonders [which
the Lord sent him to do in the land of Egypt . . .]' [Deut. 34: 11].

It is therefore necessary that I speak about these two before I speak
about the principles of faith, how many they are, and what they are. For
axioms ought to take precedence over what comes after axioms.[17]

There are, then, two axioms of religion: miracles and creation. The
first we may denominate an epistemological axiom: miracles are not
logically prior to other beliefs of religion, but they are epistemologi-
cally prior in that they bring us to accept religion. It is that sense in
which they are axiomatic. The second axiom, creation, is indeed
logically prior to the other beliefs of religion and it is in that sense
that creation is an axiom of religion.

Derekh Emunah, iii. 2 is given over to a discussion of miracles.
Bibago opens the following chapter (iii. 3) with this statement:

In that I have discussed in the previous chapter the axiom of religion, the
one which brings one to the Path of Faith [*Derekh Emunah*], it being the

demonstrations and wonders . . . it is appropriate to discuss another axiom, the creation of the world. It was established above that this is an axiom of religion and its first foundation since through it is established the existence of the First Creator. . . . and it makes possible wonders, that God acts volitionally, that God extends providence, and all the other specific principles of divine religion.[18]

In this passage Bibago makes clear his reasons for positing creation as an axiom of religion. Following his understanding of Maimonides' position in *Guide*, ii. 25, Bibago asserts that only by accepting belief in creation of the world is it possible to accept belief in miracles, God's volitional actions, providence, etc.[19] We see here that at least in logical terms Bibago's second axiom, creation, precedes his first axiom, miracles. He reiterates the importance of belief in creation a few pages further on:

Behold, therefore the root of creation 'is the joy of our way' [Job 8: 19] and the axiom of our Torah upon which is built our religion and by virtue of which 'we are called by the name Israel' [after Isa. 44: 5].[20]

Having discussed the axioms of religion in chapters 2 and 3, Bibago turns in chapter 4 to the principles of religion. 'It is proper that we establish the number of principles and roots upon which the divine Torah is built', he says. 'But this can only be done if we first make known what the word "principle" signifies.'[21] In order to determine what things are properly called principles, Bibago distinguished among (*a*) those characteristics of an entity 'which are of its essence and without which its existence cannot be conceived', (*b*) characteristics which aid the entity to maintain its existence without being absolutely necessary for its survival, and (*c*) characteristics which are conducive to the 'perfection, praiseworthiness, and beauty' of the entity.[22] Bibago cites as examples (*a*) the heart, liver, and brain, without which a man's existence is inconceivable, as opposed to (*b*) the stomach and lungs, which help maintain one's existence without being absolutely necessary to it, and (*c*) one's eyes, hands, feet, and ears, which only serve the end of furthering man's perfection, praiseworthiness, and beauty.

'Thus', he says,

it is proper that there be found in the divine Torah elements which are primary and are such that without them the Torah would not be a divine Torah, and elements which are secondary and are such that they help bring the adherent to belief in the primary elements, and tertiary elements which are certainly found there [only] for perfection, praiseworthiness, and beauty and are such that when their beauty is apprehended they will certainly arouse those who slumber to believe in the true beliefs.[23]

Examples of the primary elements are beliefs such as God's existence and unity. The commandments, whose purpose is to bring adherents of the Torah to correct belief, represent the secondary element, while the narrative portions of the Torah — which arouse the reader to accept the teachings promulgated by the Torah and expressed in the miẓvot — are the tertiary element.[24] The principles of the Torah constitute the primary element.[25]

At this point Bibago allows himself to get side-tracked into one of the many long digressions which make the *Derekh Emunah* so difficult to follow and only several pages later does he return to his subject, there writing:

It is established by all this that the foundations of the Torah are those specific beliefs [*ḥelkei ha-emunah*] by virtue of [the acceptance of] which an adherent is an adherent. Generalizing, I assert that what will be called principles of Torah are those foundations relating to belief without which the religion would not be a religion. They are those [beliefs] by virtue of which he who believes them is called an adherent, and he who denies them will be called a heretic and will be denied a share in the world to come.[26]

Bibago tells us here that a principle of the Torah is a specific belief (lit. 'part of faith') the acceptance of which is absolutely necessary for anyone who would be called a Jew. We learn here, then, that there are certain beli s the rejection of which is tantamount to the rejection of the Torah as a whole. From this it would seem to follow (and this is a conclusion explicitly rejected by Abravanel, as we shall see in the following chapter[27]) that there are teachings of the Torah the rejection of which is not tantamount to the rejection of the Torah as a whole.

But what sorts of belief are those the rejection of which is tantamount to the rejection of the Torah as a whole? To this question Bibago gives an answer which reflects the scientific model by which he described religion. Principles are those foundations, Bibago informs us, 'upon which the religion rests, they being roots such that if they fall the whole religion will fall, it being impossible for it not to. An example of this is the existence of God . . .'[28]

In the context of the description of religion given at the beginning of *Derekh Emunah*, iii there can be no doubt that Bibago is offering here a deductive/geometric account of the principles similar to that of Albo.[29]

II. Bibago's Analysis of Maimonides' Principles

Having defined the term 'principle' in chapter 4, Bibago goes on in the next and closing chapter to discuss which beliefs are principles of the Torah. He starts, reasonably enough, by examining the positions adopted by earlier scholars. He presents a long and detailed exposition of Maimonides' thirteen principles, concluding with this impassioned statement: 'Since I love my Master Maimonides, repeat his teaching,[30] follow in his footsteps, and lie at his feet, I come to urge his case and to show [the correctness of] his views so far as it is possible for me to do.'[31] Bibago goes about urging Maimonides' case by showing in a variety of ways how Maimonides' thirteen principles actually do constitute all the beliefs which ought to be counted as principles and by showing in a number of ingenious if sometimes far-fetched ways how Maimonides' enumeration of the principles reflects normative texts and traditions.

Bibago observes that

an adherent's faith in the divine Torah cannot but involve belief in God or in His works for nothing exists but God and His works, as Maimonides established. Now that which we ought to believe about God is negative belief and not positive belief for no attribute may be predicated of God as Maimonides expounded at length[32] and as Solomon described when he said, 'be not rash with thy mouth, and let not thy heart be hasty to utter a word before God; for God is [in heaven, and thou upon the earth; therefore let thy words be few]' [Eccles. 5: 1]. By this he means to say that one should not be hasty, whether in speech or thought, to predicate positive attributes of God, 'for God is in Heaven', absolutely beyond our ken[33] and we are material. Therefore His attributes are not like ours; they are absolutely different. It is therefore fitting that 'thy words be few', that is, exclusionary and negative . . .[34]

Bibago indicates here that Maimonides' principles fall into two categories, indeed that they fall into the only two categories possible. They all deal either with God or with His actions. Furthermore, the principles are seen to accord with Maimonides' account of God's attributes, since they deal either with negations or with actions.

Bibago divides Maimonides' principles according to the following schema:

(*I*) negations

> (*A*) negation of non-existence (principle 1)
> (*B*) negation of multiplicity (principle 2)
> (*C*) negation of composition (principle 3)
> (*D*) negation of coming to be (principle 4)

(*II*) Fit actions of God's creatures (principle 5)

(*III*) God's actions

> (*A*) continuing actions
> > (*1*) on the living (providence: principle 10)
> > (*2*) on the dead (retribution: principle 11)
>
> (*B*) completed actions
> > (*1*) affecting part of the world
> > > (*a*) affecting part of all the world (prophecy: principle 6)[35]
> > > (*b*) affecting part of part of the world (Mosaic prophecy: principle 7)[36]
> >
> > (*2*) affecting all the world
> > > (*a*) single, specific actions (revelation: principle 8)
> > > (*b*) preserving an action (eternity of the Torah: principle 9)
>
> (*C*) future actions
> > (*1*) upon the living (Messiah: principle 12)
> > (*2*) upon the dead (resurrection: principle 13).[37]

However convincing we find this analysis it is clear that Bibago proposed it in order to demonstrate to the reader that Maimonides' account of the principles of the Torah is exhaustive and indeed summarizes the basic elements of Torah teaching. The Torah teaches nothing other than truths concerning God and His actions; there is nothing else in the world for it to teach about. Its teachings concerning God are all negations, as they would be understood by any good Maimonidean. The teachings concerning God's actions are themselves divided into two parts. The first deals with the appropriate actions of God's creatures ((*II*) above) who are, themselves, after all, nothing other than God's actions, while the second deals with God's actions upon His creatures ((*III*) above). God's actions upon His creatures are themselves divided into continuing, completed, and future actions. This division is as exhaustive as the previous ones. Finally Bibago divides each of these categories further, in ways which he clearly expects us to take as exhaustive. The intent of Bibago's exercise here is to demonstrate that Maimonides' principles cover all bases. That being the case, one can neither add to nor subtract from Maimonides' principles. They are thus proven to be *the* principles of the Torah.

Having shown the adequacy of Maimonides' account on these grounds Bibago next adduces traditional support for them. He shows how the principles are found in the prayers,[38] and in the Scroll of Esther.[39] He further shows how they are indicated by the rite of circumcision,[40] and mentions that some other, unnamed scholar, connected them to God's thirteen attributes.[41] He closes this list of traditional supports for Maimonides' principles by finding them hinted at by two talmudic texts.[42]

Bibago's intention to this point has been to argue for the adequacy of Maimonides' account of the principles of Judaism. Further to that end he next proceeds to raise a series of problems with Maimonides' account. By refuting these objections he hopes further to strengthen Maimonides' case. Bibago raises the following objections:

(*1*) How can Maimonides count the coming of the Messiah as a principle when R. Hillel (Sanhedrin 99a) denied the coming of the Messiah?[43]

(*2*) Why should one be considered a heretic for denying a principle if one's denial is not motivated by rebelliousness?[44]

(*3*) Why did Maimonides fail to count as a principle (*a*) that God is not complex; (*b*) that God is neither generated nor corrupted; (*c*) that God is not multiple; (*d*) Israel's chosen-ness;[45] (*e*) the obligation to follow ancestral tradition;[46] (*f*) the obligation to accept the oral Torah; (*g*) the obligation to believe in the 'assembly at Sinai';[47] (*h*) that human beings have choice?[48]

(*4*) Why did Maimonides count as a principle the obligation to worship God, seeing that (*a*) it is a specific commandment[49] and (*b*) that the Torah would not fall if man prayed to God through intermediaries?[50]

Bibago prefaces his responses to the objections with the following observation: there are four signs of the divinity of a system of laws or *nomos* (*hanhagah*). The first is the perfection of the promulgator; the second is the perfection of the *nomos* itself; the third is that it makes provisions for those being led by it to recognize its perfection so they will indeed follow it; the fourth is that the *nomos* actually does lead those who follow it to their personal perfection and felicity. Maimonides' thirteen principles embody these four signs of the divinity of a *nomos* and thus are truly necessary to it since if any of them was dropped the Torah would lose part of its claim to divinity.

The first four principles, Bibago says, demonstrate the perfection of God, the promulgator of the Torah. The obligation to worship God brings the followers of the Torah to accept its perfection and divinity and thus accustoms them to being led by it (Bibago's third sign above). Similarly with principles 6 to 9, all of which deal with perfection of the Torah itself, Bibago's second sign. The principles concerning God's providence and the Messiah (numbers 10 and 12) and the principles concerning retribution and resurrection (numbers 11 and 13) deal, respectively, with human perfection and felicity in this life and human perfection and felicity after this life. Each of Maimonides' principles is thus shown to contribute to the recognition of the divinity of the Torah.

'From this we see', Bibago concludes, 'that none of the thirteen principles of the Torah ought to be called a specific belief[51] for every one of them is general with respect to the Torah or its perfection.'[52] That is to say, each and every one of the principles is a principle of the whole Torah, upon which the Torah depends for its divinity; they are thus more than just specific teachings which the Torah, as it were, happens to teach. Here we find that the principles of the Torah, rather than being depicted as axioms in a geometric system, as they were above,[53] are depicted as signs of its divinity and in that sense more general and fundamental than the other teachings of the Torah. This understanding of the principles is found in no other writer on the subject.

On this basis, along with positions already taken, Bibago is able to answer the objections he had raised above. Miracles are not principles of the Torah, but its axioms; therefore the assembly at Sinai, miraculous to be sure, ought not to be counted as a principle.[54] Choice ought not to be counted as a principle since it precedes all human activities and it is thus not specific to the Torah.[55] R. Hillel's rejection of belief in the Messiah is no problem because it is not the normative position of the Talmud. Indeed, R. Hillel was not a great scholar but among the last of the Amoraim and was castigated by his colleagues for this belief. They even prayed that God might forgive him for his sinful lack of belief in the Messiah.[56]

With respect to the objection raised by Rabad — why should incorrect belief cost one his position in the world to come — Bibago argues as follows:

Rabad's statement is really amazing to me since if it were correct everyone who denied a principle without meaning to would have an excuse and a portion in the world to come. [Even] the belief of the Christians would not be inconsistent with true felicity since they understand Scripture literally and they think that the intention of the verses is as they believe it. [On this basis] they would not thereby be called heretics and sectarians. It would be possible to find a man who does not believe in any one of the principles or beliefs of the Torah because of his failure to understand the meaning of the Torah. [On this position] such a one would be called neither a sectarian nor a heretic. All this opposes reason and faith.[57]

Bibago's position here would have led him to reject not just the opinion of Rabad concerning inadvertent heresy, but also the opinion of Duran.[58] In this Bibago was followed by Abravanel who, here too, borrowed from him word for word without acknowledging his source.[59] Bibago follows Maimonides here in explicitly making acceptance of the principles as correctly promulgated a necessary condition for enjoying a portion in the world to come. Maimonides, as we saw above,[60] also made it a sufficient condition; Bibago is silent on that issue. But there can be little doubt that he rejects the position of Duran (and probably Crescas) on inadvertent heresy. In this regard, at least, he is a true disciple of Maimonides.

Having solved the objections raised by other thinkers against Maimonides' principles, Bibago raises an objection of his own. If the Torah does not change (principle 9), how can Messiah and resurrection be posited as principles, since with the coming of the Messiah and the occurrence of resurrection we will no longer be obligated to believe in the future coming of the Messiah and the future resurrection of the dead, as we are today? But if that is true the Torah will have changed![61] Bibago resolves this objection by asserting that the principles of Messiah and resurrection are independent of time: we are obliged to believe in the coming of the

Messiah and in the resurrection but we are not obliged to believe in the future coming of the Messiah or the future resurrection of the dead.[62]

That being so, Bibago asks, why did Maimonides phrase the principle of the coming of the Messiah in the future tense?[63] This, Bibago answers, was to refute the beliefs of the Christians, who maintain that the Messiah has already come.

Bibago raises one final objection: why did Maimonides not count as a principle that God acts by will, not by necessity?[64] This is not a principle, Bibago replies, because it is presupposed by miracles, which are themselves the axioms of religion, not its principles.

Bibago closes the third treatise, and the *Derekh Emunah* as a whole, with a few comments concerning the dogmatic systems of Crescas and Albo. The first he rejects and the second he accepts as an attempt to compress Maimonides' thirteen principles into three.

III. Bibago, Maimonides, and Abravanel

Bibago's discussion of the principles of Judaism does not represent a truly independent analysis of the question of dogma in Judaism. Rather, it is a defence of Maimonides' principles. This is clear even where Bibago seems to diverge from the teachings of his master, as in his claim that underlying the thirteen principles of Maimonides there are the axioms of miracles and creation. By positing these two beliefs as more fundamental than the thirteen principles themselves Bibago is able to account for the fact that Maimonides did not include them in the principles, and is thus able to further his defence of Maimonides.[65]

That Bibago was not laying down an independent system of dogmas for Judaism is also clear from the rather casual, almost haphazard manner in which he defines the term 'principle' in different ways. First, principles are defined as those characteristics of an entity 'which are of its essence and without which its existence cannot be conceived'.[66] This definition sounds very similar to that offered by Crescas for his *pinnot* (corner-stones) of the Torah.[67] In line with this definition Bibago analyses the thirteen principles of Maimonides showing how they are all necessary for the Torah to be understood as a divine *nomos*.[68]

Second, principles are characterized as those beliefs the holding of which define their holders as Jews.[69] We may say that this is not a new definition of the term 'principle' so much as an explication of the first definition. If this is the case, then we may see that Bibago is here following Maimonides, who made the holding of his principles a necessary (and sufficient) criterion for one's being considered a Jew and for thus meriting a share in the world to come.[70] A consequence of this definition is the position that the rejection of certain beliefs is heresy. Bibago accepts this consequence and rejects, therefore, the position of Duran and Crescas which saw the criterion of heresy not as which beliefs were rejected, but the reasons for which a belief was rejected.[71]

Third, principles are defined as those beliefs 'upon which the religion rests, they being the roots such that if they fall the whole religion will fall, it being impossible for it not to'.[72] This definition, clearly influenced by Albo, posits a deductive relationship between the principles on the one hand and the body of Torah beliefs on the other hand. It may be urged, however, that Bibago thought of this definition as merely developing, rather than supplanting, the first definition. If this is indeed the case it is easier to understand why Bibago does not attempt to demonstrate that the other beliefs of Judaism may truly be derived *more geometrico* from the thirteen principles. He may simply have seen his third definition as being an alternative way of saying that without accepting the principles of Maimonides one could not conceive of the Torah as a divine *nomos*.

This may be the case; if it is it does not demonstrate that Bibago was consistent despite his use of different definitions of the term 'principle'. Rather, it suggests that he was using different definitions of the term 'principle' without being aware of the differences.

Bibago's most interesting contributions to the discussion of the principles of Judaism is his analysis of the structure of Maimonides' principles. His claim that they all relate to God as either negations or as attributes of action is ingenious if not, as suggested above, ultimately convincing.[73]

Bibago's indebtedness to Albo for the geometric model of the principles and to both Crescas and Albo for the idea of a multi-tiered system of dogma is obvious. More important than his indebtedness to earlier writers, however, is Bibago's influence on those who came after him. Abravanel's use of unattributed passages from the *Derekh Emunah* in his own discussion of dogma, *Rosh Amanah*, was discovered in the last century.[74] What has not been noted, however, is the more general way in which Bibago may have influenced Abravanel.

Bibago structures his discussion of the principles of the Torah in *Derekh Emunah*, iii. 5 in the following way:

(*a*) statement of Maimonides' thirteen principles with extensive explanations
(*b*) defence of Maimonides' principles
(*c*) objections to them raised by other scholars
(*d*) observation (*haza'ah*) concerning the principles necessary for the refutation of the objections
(*e*) solutions to the objections
(*f*) Bibago's own objections and their solutions
(*g*) critique of Crescas and Albo.

The overall structure of the *Rosh Amanah* bears a striking resemblance to this approach. It may be outlined as follows:

(*a*) statement of Maimonides' thirteen principles (chapter 1)
(*b*) positions of Crescas and Albo (chapter 2)
(*c*) objections to Maimonides' principles raised by Crescas, Albo, and other scholars (chapters 3, 4)
(*d*) Abravanel's own objections (chapter 5)
(*e*) propositions (*hakdamot*) concerning the principles necessary for the refutation of the objections (chapters 6–11)
(*f*) solutions to the objections (chapters 12–21)
(*g*) critique of Crescas and Albo (chapter 22)
(*h*) Abravanel's own positions (chapters 23, 24).

The similarities are too striking to be coincidental, especially in light of the textual evidence that Abravanel had carefully read the *Derekh Emunah* before writing the *Rosh Amanah*.

Abravanel, it seems, wrote the *Rosh Amanah* at least in part in order to do better the job attempted by Bibago in the *Derekh Emunah*. Improving upon Bibago, however, did not mean that Abravanel could not make use of the overall way in which Bibago structured his discussion[75] nor adopt a number of his specific ideas. Abravanel's outright refusal to cite Bibago's name[76] appears to reflect a certain measure of disdain which he apparently felt for the author of the *Derekh Emunah*. This disdain may be rooted in the poor job which Abravanel thought Bibago had made of defending Maimonides' principles.

From what Abravanel included and failed to include in the *Rosh Amanah* we may glean some idea of what he disliked about the

Derekh Emunah. Abravanel eschews the long discussion of each principle in which Bibago indulged (if Abravanel felt that Bibago's discussions did not significantly enhance our understanding of Maimonides' intentions, he was correct). Abravanel is much more exhaustive in listing objections to the thirteen principles than was Bibago and more careful in his laying of the groundwork for his solutions to the objections. Moreover, Abravanel passes over without mention the many imaginative, one is tempted to say fanciful, ways in which Bibago connects Maimonides' thirteen principles to normative Jewish texts and ceremonies.

In sum, Bibago demonstrates once again how profoundly Maimonides dominated discussions of Jewish dogma, especially in the fifteenth century. His own analyses may not have advanced the discussion significantly but, by providing a catalyst for Abravanel's more sophisticated analysis, they have enduring importance. It is to Abravanel's account of the principles of Judaism that we now turn.

8

Isaac Abravanel

1. Abravanel's Analysis of Maimonides

Rabbi Isaac Abravanel (1437–1508) was the last medieval Jewish thinker systematically and extensively to deal with the question of the principles of Judaism.[1] Indeed, he devoted an entire book to the subject, the *Rosh Amanah*.[2] This book is ostensibly devoted to defending Maimonides' thirteen principles in the face of the criticisms levelled against them by Crescas and Albo. But, paradoxically, and despite its avowed aim, the *Rosh Amanah* is best known for Abravanel's claim that Judaism has no principles of faith at all.

This was the situation which confronted Isaac Abravanel when he sat down to write his *Rosh Amanah* in 1494: the Jewish people had just suffered its greatest calamity since the destruction of the Second Temple and, in turning to their religious leaders in search of a clearly enunciated statement of what Judaism demanded of them, met with chaos. All of Abravanel's post-Expulsion literary activity was connected in one way or another with his attempt to encourage and console the shattered people. The *Rosh Amanah* fits into that pattern: in the place of conflicting and confusing opinions concerning the principles of Judaism, Abravanel sought to establish one system, that of Maimonides, as normative. In doing so he provided the most thorough analysis of Maimonides' principles yet written.

Abravanel opens the book by quoting Maimonides' statement of the principles in an otherwise unknown Hebrew translation.[3] In the second chapter Abravanel briefly summarizes the dogmatic systems of Crescas and Albo. He claims that these scholars diverged from Maimonides' account of the principles because of certain problems they found in his account. Abravanel saw fit, therefore, in chapters iii and iv to list these objections. We ought to note two points here. First, there is little doubt that Abravanel was wrong: Crescas and Albo did not reject Maimonides' system because of specific problems they found with it, but because they defined the term 'principle' differently from Maimonides. Maimonides, as we have seen, used the term in a dogmatic sense, Crescas in an analytic sense, and Albo in a geometric sense. It is remarkable that Crescas and Albo were unaware of the way in which their usage of the term 'principle' differed from that of Maimonides and from each other.

Second, we must ask why Abravanel took account only of the works of Crescas and Albo. He was certainly aware of Bibago's writings on the subject[4] and it is likely indeed that he was familiar with what his friend Isaac Arama had written about it.[5] It is reasonable to assume that he was also familiar with R. Shimon ben Zemaḥ Duran's account of the principles.[6] The simplest answer to this question seems to me to be twofold: both Crescas and Albo, unlike the other authors mentioned, had explicitly criticized Maimonides; in addition, both had devoted entire books to the exposition of their dogmatic systems and were relatively well known. The fact that Crescas and Albo are the only two critics of Maimonides' principles mentioned by Bibago lends further support to my suppositions about Bibago's influence on Abravanel, raised at the end of the last chapter.

Abravanel lists seventeen objections to Maimonides' statement of the principles of the Torah in chapter iii of the *Rosh Amanah*. Many of these objections are based upon the fact that Maimonides had no clearly enunciated criterion by which he chose which beliefs to include among his principles. Other objections are based upon the claim, which Albo had borrowed from Duran,[7] that specific commandments ought not to be counted as principles of the Torah. With two exceptions, the first fourteen of these objections are drawn from Albo's *Sefer ha-Ikkarim*; objections 7 and 13 are drawn from Bibago, although Abravanel does not cite his source. The last three objections ask why Maimonides did not count as principles various of the beliefs so counted by Crescas.[8]

In chapter iv Abravanel lists three objections first raised by Crescas, all three of which relate to the fact that Maimonides had counted his first two principles (God's existence and unity) as commandments. The issue relates to the well-known debate between Maimonides and Crescas on whether or not beliefs can be commanded.[9]

In raising these twenty objections Abravanel was following his favourite approach to writing commentaries: first one marshals every possible objection and question that can be raised in connection with the text to be explained and then one explains the text by answering the questions. He was also following the pattern established by Bibago. Following that methodology here, then, Abravanel adds, in chapter v, eight objections of his own to Maimonides' system of the principles of Judaism. Several of these objections relate to questions concerning the relationship between Maimonides' account of the principles in his commentary on *Ḥelek* and in his account of them in the *Book of Knowledge*, both in 'Laws of the Foundations of the Torah' and in 'Laws of Repentance'.[10]

After raising these objections Abravanel lists and explains nine propositions (*hakdamot*); these are all points upon which he will draw in his defence of Maimonides. The first proposition, the subject of chapter vi, distinguishes among the meanings of terms *ikkar* ('principle', lit. 'root'), *shoresh* ('root'), and *yesod* ('foundation'). Whereas the latter two terms always signify something which serves as a basis or foundation for something else, Abravanel says, the term *ikkar* can also be used to signify a praiseworthy thing, even if it is not a basis or foundation for anything else. The beliefs listed by Maimonides in his thirteen principles were not all of them meant to be understood as *yesodot* in the strict sense (as Albo understood them); rather, Maimonides listed thirteen beliefs which he considered to be particularly important to Judaism. In this proposition, then Abravanel notes something missed entirely by Crescas and Albo: that Maimonides and his critics were using the same term (*ikkar*) to mean different things.

The second of Abravanel's propositions (chapter vi) is that Maimonides' first principle teaches, not that God exists, but that God exists necessarily. In positing this principle Abravanel was seeking to solve the problem raised by Crescas (and cited by Abravanel in chapter iv): if we construe Exodus 20: 2 ('I am the Lord thy God') as a commandment, we are forced to assume that God commanded belief in Himself, an idea which Crescas rejects as paradoxical. Maimonides' position as expounded by Abravanel here, however, is not that God in one breath, as it were, is both introducing Himself to the Israelites and demanding that they believe in Him; rather, God, whose existence the Israelites already acknowledged, commanded them to believe that He exists, not contingently, but necessarily. In explaining this proposition Abravanel provides a brief summary of the various ways in which Exodus 20: 2 had been understood by other scholars.

Rosh Amanah, chapter viii, expounds the third proposition. In this proposition Abravanel argues that each of Maimonides' principles contains at least two distinct teachings. In this way Abravanel manages to inject into Maimonides' listing many beliefs which did not appear in the list as first understood.[11]

The fourth proposition is found in the following chapter. Here Abravanel argues that some of Maimonides' principles are included in others of them. Maimonides listed them separately, however, because they were praiseworthy beliefs, important for the perfection of the common people. In this way Abravanel meets Albo's objection that some of the principles are redundant.

In the fifth proposition (chapter x) Abravanel takes up the question of the order and internal relationship of the principles. In this discussion he demonstrates two sides of his character which would seem to be somewhat inconsistent. On the one hand he shows insight and sophistication; on the other hand, he copies shamelessly from the writings of other thinkers.

The questions which occupy Abravanel in this chapter are, why did Maimonides choose thirteen principles (as opposed to some other number) and what can we learn from their ordering and interrelationship? As Abravanel states it, he is concerned in this chapter to prove

that the number of foundations and principles of faith as stated by Maimonides was neither accidental nor inadvertent; nor [did Maimonides choose the number thirteen] in order to match the thirteen attributes of God's mercy or the thirteen hermeneutical principles of Torah exegesis. Rather, with this number Maimonides intended to teach one or all of three lessons and great speculative teachings.[12]

The chapter itself is given over to a discussion of the three 'lessons' taught by the order and interrelationship of the thirteen principles.[13]

The last four propositions presented by Abravanel are grouped together in chapter xi. The sixth proposition states that the principles of faith ought not to be taken from the practical commandments of the Torah. Only beliefs ought to be counted as principles. In positing this proposition, Abravanel followed Duran and Albo.

The seventh proposition maintains that the principles of the Torah ought to be unique to it.[14] The eighth proposition teaches that the principles relate only to God and His actions, not to beliefs concerning the nature of man and the world, true though they may be. With these two propositions, Abravanel is able to respond to some of those objections which ask why Maimonides excluded certain beliefs from his list of principles.

The ninth and last proposition states that while individuals cannot be commanded to believe things, they can be commanded to make those preparations (i.e., learn the relevant facts) which make the acceptance of certain beliefs possible and likely. Abravanel uses this proposition in order to answer Crescas's objection concerning the impossibility of commanding belief.

In chapters xii to xxi Abravanel takes up the twenty-eight objections he had raised and, using his propositions, answers them one after the other. The answers by themselves contain few surprises: they are mostly a matter of applying the relevant propositions. But in answering the objections Abravanel does raise some interesting points which ought to be noted in the present context.

One of these points concerns Abravanel's uncompromising stand concerning heresy. Rejecting the view of Rabad, who had maintained that one who held mistaken beliefs — even on the issue of God's corporeality — without intention to rebel ought not to be considered a heretic,[15] Abravanel follows Maimonides[16] in insisting upon absolute doctrinal orthodoxy. In this he once again borrows from Bibago, quoting extensively, and without attribution, from the *Derekh Emunah*.[17] Bibago and Abravanel were rejecting a position which found its most clear-cut expression in the writings of Shimon ben Ẓemah Duran,[18] which may have been held by Crescas and on which Albo was ambivalent.[19] According to Abravanel, if one rejects a belief of the Torah or adopts a belief rejected by the Torah, one is a heretic and loses one's share in the world to come. Given this position it is easy to understand why Abravanel was so concerned about the correct enunciation and formulation of the principles of the Torah.

Abravanel rejects Rabad's position in the following words (most of which are Bibago's):

But upon examination this position may be seen to be clearly false, for according to it, [even] one who unintentionally denies every principle will acquire [a portion in] the world to come. Thus, the belief of the Christians — who took the words of Torah and prophecy literally, and believed their meaning to be as they understood it — would not deprive them of the true felicity and we may not say that they are heretics and sectarians. It would be possible, according to this, to find a man who does not believe in any one of the principles or beliefs of Torah and yet who should not be called a sectarian or heretic if he were brought to this blind foolishness by his failure to understand the meaning of the Torah. These things are intolerable, according to both the faith of Torah and correct reason. For a false doctrine about any one of the principles of faith turns the soul from its true felicity and will not bring [one] to life in the world to come, even if the opinion is held without intention to rebel. It is like poison which consumes the spirit of him who eats it, *and his spirit will be gathered to God* (Job 34: 14), even if he ate it thinking that it was good and healthy food. Similarly, heresy and false beliefs in the matter of principles of religion will expel the soul of man and without a doubt make it impossible for him to inherit the world to come.[20]

It is thus clear that Abravanel, along with Maimonides and Bibago, does not allow for inadvertent heresy. In this he is opposed by Duran and probably Crescas; Albo adopted both sides of the issue.

II. Does Abravanel Truly Reject the Claim that Judaism has Principles of Faith?

Having concluded his defence of Maimonides' principles by refuting the twenty-eight objections, Abravanel takes the offensive and, in chapter xxii, attacks the creedal formulations of Crescas and Albo, raising a variety of problems found in them. He then goes on to argue,

Were I to choose principles to posit for the divine Torah I would only lay down one, the creation of the world. It is the root [*shoresh*] and foundation [*yesod*] around which the divine Torah, its cornerstones, and its beliefs revolve and includes the creation at the beginning, the narratives about the Patriarchs, and the miracles and wonders which cannot be believed without belief in creation. So, too, with belief in God's knowledge and providence, and reward and punishment according to [one's observance of] the commandments, none of which can one perfectly believe without believing in the volitional creation of the whole world.[21]

In emphasizing the dogmatic importance of belief in creation Abravanel was following in the footsteps of almost all the previous and contemporary writers on the subject of the principles of Judaism.[22] He was also being consistent with a position he adopted in two of his other works, *Shamayim Ḥadashim* and *Mifalot Elohim*. In the first he wrote that 'belief in the creation of the world is the corner-stone [*pinnah*] and foundation [*yesod*] upon which the whole Torah depends'.[23] Abravanel devotes all of *Mifalot*, i. 3 to arguing that belief in creation is a fundamental principle. Thus, for example, he writes:

We ought to know the relative importance of belief in the creation of the world as recounted by the Torah relative to the other narratives of the Torah. I say that the importance of belief in this divine narrative relative to the other narratives of the Torah and its commandments is like the importance of a foundation [*yesod*] and root [*shoresh*] relative to what is founded and built upon it.[24]

While Abravanel's claim that belief in creation is a *yesod* of Judaism may be consistent with generally accepted attitudes, and consistent with his other writings, it blatantly contradicts the position he adopts in the very next chapter of the *Rosh Amanah*! It is in that chapter that Abravanel makes his notorious — and, in the context of a defence of Maimonides' principles very surprising — claim that Judaism has no principles of faith at all. He writes:

Our scholars, having been dispersed among the nations and having studied their books and sciences, learned from their deeds and copied their ways and customs with respect to the divine Torah. They said: '*How do these gentiles pursue*[25] their sciences? By positing first principles and roots upon which a science is based. I will do so also and postulate principles and foundations for the divine Torah.'

But to my eyes the 'conclusion is not similar to the premise'[26] for the sciences of the gentiles and their books are pursued by way of investigation and speculation. In order that their speculations would not become confused with the explanation of their premises they were forced to postulate accepted first principles which would be accepted by the student of science without the demand for demonstration and evidence. Those first principles in turn would be explained by a different, more general, science, or they would be self-evident, like the primary intelligibles. God, however, understands the way of the divine Torah; He gave it to His people to be accepted in faith, according to what he saw as necessary for their perfection. For this reason He did not have to set down in it some beliefs as more fundamental than others, or some as more acceptable than others: nor did He establish the relative importance of the commandments, since they were all *given by one Shepherd* [Eccles. 12: 11]. Nor is there any other Torah, or any science or divine understanding more general than or prior to our Torah, such that we would derive first principles for the Torah from it, or explain or validate them through it.

Therefore, I said, *this I recall to my mind* [Lam. 3: 21] that the divine Torah, with all its beliefs, is completely true. All of its commandments were divinely revealed. The validation and substantiation of all the beliefs and commandments, minor as well as major, is the same. The validation of one is like the validation of another. I, therefore, believe that it is not proper to postulate principles for the divine Torah, nor foundations in the matter of beliefs, for we are obliged to believe everything that is written in the Torah. We are not permitted to doubt even the smallest thing in it that it should be necessary to establish its truth with those principles and roots. For he who denies or doubts a belief or narrative of the Torah, be it small or great, is a sectarian and *epikoros*. For, since the Torah is true, no belief or narrative in it has any advantage over any other.[27]

In this passage Abravanel argues on two levels — the dogmatic and the axiomatic — against the thesis that Judaism has principles of faith. The Torah does not specify any beliefs as being salvifically superior to any others; which is to say that it does not list any dogmas. Nor, Abravanel further argues, is Judaism a science which would collapse with the refutation of its first principles. That is to say that none of the beliefs or teachings of Judaism may be considered to be axioms of the faith.

Abravanel's position here not only contradicts the claim he advanced in chapter xxii concerning the status of belief in creation, but, more importantly, it seems to stand in out and out contradiction to the rest of the *Rosh Amanah*, which was, after all, written to *defend* Maimonides' formulation of the principles of the Torah. This apparent contradiction is one of the best-known facts concerning the *Rosh Amanah* and many scholars have attempted to explain it.[28] I believe, however, that the contradiction is apparent rather than real.

We have seen how Maimonides and Duran present what I have called a doctrinal or dogmatic interpretation of the principles of Judaism, how Crescas takes them in an analytic sense and how Albo understands them in what may be called a logical or axiomatic sense. There is, however, another understanding of the principles, one which sees them not as doctrines which must be held in order to merit salvation, nor as beliefs which must be held to avoid self-contradiction, nor as axioms from which the other beliefs of the religion follow. This interpretation of the principles sees them as nothing more than pedagogical devices, designed to help the ignorant learn some important truths about their faith. This may be called the heuristic interpretation of the principles. It is on this basis that Abravanel approves of Maimonides' principles and defends them from the attacks of Crescas and Albo.

Abravanel rejects the doctrinal or dogmatic interpretation of the principles, at least as it is held by Maimonides and Duran, on the grounds that all of the beliefs of Judaism are doctrinally essential. Actually, Abravanel does not deny the claim that certain beliefs must be held in order to merit salvation. He simply elevates every belief of Judaism to the status of necessary dogma. He says:

... there is no need to lay down principles for the Torah of God which ought to be believed by every Israelite in order to merit life in the world to come as Maimonides and those who follow after him wrote, for the entire Torah, and every single verse, word, and letter in it is a principle and root which ought to be believed.[29]

Abravanel rejects the axiomatic or logical interpretation of the principles which he thought was held by both Crescas and Albo, and not by Albo alone, on the grounds that, with one possible exception, Judaism has no axioms such that the religion would collapse with their refutation. He further argues that the thinkers who adopted this understanding of the principles of Judaism did so because they were unduly influenced by the example of secular science.

Judaism, according to Abravanel, thus has no principles in the sense of dogmas (as Maimonides and Duran had thought) and it has no principles in any logical sense (as he maintained Crescas and Albo has both thought). It does, however, have great, praiseworthy, and important beliefs which may be singled out for the edification and improvement of the masses. These beliefs may be called principles, but only in a heuristic sense. It is Abravanel's contention that Maimonides presented his principles certainly as dogmas, but also as pedagogical guides for the unlearned. It is in this latter sense, and in this sense only, that he defends Maimonides' principles.

This point may be clarified by summarizing the ways in which Maimonides and Abravanel agree and disagree. They agree in rejecting the axiomatic or logical interpretation of the principles; they agree that correct adherence to dogma is a prerequisite for salvation; they agree that Maimonides' thirteen principles are great, praiseworthy, and important beliefs. They disagree, however, on one important point: Maimonides maintains that belief in the thirteen principles is sufficient for attaining salvation while Abravanel holds that belief in all of the teachings of Judaism is necessary for salvation.

Abravanel emphasizes this latter point in a number of places in the *Rosh Amanah*. In chapter xii he rejects Rabad's position on the grounds that,

> according to it (even) one who unintentionally denies every principle will acquire a portion in the world to come . . . It would be possible, according to this, to find a man who does not believe in any one of the principles or beliefs of the Torah and yet who should not be called a sectarian or heretic if he were brought to this blind foolishness by his failure to understand the meaning of the Torah. These things are intolerable . . . for a false doctrine about any one of the principles of faith turns the soul from its true felicity and will not bring [one] to life in the world to come, even if the opinion is held without intention to rebel.[30]

If there were as many fundamental principles as there are miracles and promises in the Torah, then intelligent people would not be permitted, in Albo's words, to 'investigate the fundamental principles of religion and to interpret the biblical texts in accordance with the truth as it seems to [them]'.[31]

But this is exactly what Abravanel wants. The idea which Albo rejects appealed to him and he held it tenaciously. His is indeed an orthodox position in the strictest sense of the word. He simply rejects the possibility of any enquiry into any of the teachings of Judaism. Thus, in chapter xxiii of the *Rosh Amanah* he writes,

> Therefore, I said, *this I recall to my mind* [Lam. 3: 21] that the divine Torah, with all its beliefs, is completely true . . . We are not permitted to doubt even the smallest thing in it that it should be necessary to establish its truth with those principles and roots. For he who denies or doubts a belief or narrative of the Torah, be it small or great, is a sectarian and *epikoros*.[32]

Further on in the same chapter he says, 'All of the commandments of the Torah, as well as the attributes and opinions taught therein, are divine. He who denies the smallest of them all, in that he uproots something from the Torah and denies it, is not worthy to be of the world to come.'[33]

It may be that Abravanel rejected the legitimacy of philosophical discussion of religious beliefs because he saw in such discussions a source for the spiritual weakness which he attributed to fifteenth-century Iberian Jewry. It was to combat this weakness and confusion that he wrote the *Rosh Amanah*.[34]

With this in mind we may now see that contrary to what is ordinarily believed, there is no 'about-face' in the *Rosh Amanah* on the issue of creed formulation. Abravanel does not defend Maimonides in twenty-two chapters only to attack him in the twenty-third. Throughout the book he defends Maimonides only to the extent that the latter could be interpreted to have adopted the heuristic interpretation of the principles.

He opens his defence of Maimonides in the first of his nine propositions (chapter vii) by pointing out that the term *ikkar* is not completely synonymous with the terms *shoresh* and *yesod*. All three are terms used to denote principles of faith in discussions of Jewish creedalism. While they can all signify 'a thing upon which the existence and duration of another thing depends and without which it cannot endure'[35] (i.e., principles in the axiomatic sense), the term *ikkar* often means only the most important thing in its class, even if nothing else depends upon it for its existence. Thus, according to Abravanel, Maimonides' thirteen principles ought not to be considered as the axioms of Judaism, but as 'praiseworthy, essential, and fundamental beliefs of exalted degree'.[36]

In chapter ix Abravanel argues that Maimonides put forward his principles for the masses in order 'to perfect men and women who were not perfected by speculative investigation',[37] that is to say, for heuristic purposes. In chapter xxi Abravanel points out that Maimonides did not lay down 'these principles of his for *the wise men who know the times* [Esther 1: 3] but *for all of the people from every quarter, both young and old* [after Gen. 19: 4]'.[38] Abravanel makes the argument at length in chapter xxiii:

We may say in defence of Maimonides that he . . . did not choose principles among them [i.e., the beliefs of the Torah] in order to say that we are obliged to believe these principles but no others. His intention was, rather, correctly to guide those men who neither studied nor served their teachers enough. Since they could not comprehend or conceive of all the beliefs and opinions which are included in the divine Torah, Maimonides chose the thirteen most general beliefs to teach them briefly those matters which I discussed in the fifth proposition in such a way that all men, even the ignorant, could become perfected through their acceptance. From this point of view he called them principles and foundations, adapting [his language] to the thinking of the student, though it is not so according to the truth itself . . . He postulated the principles for the masses, and for beginners in the study of Mishnah, but not for those individuals who plumbed the knowledge of truth for whom he wrote the *Guide*. If this was his opinion, then his intentions were acceptable and his actions were for the sake of heaven.[39]

According to the standard interpretation of the *Rosh Amanah*, Abravanel defends Maimonides' formulation of the principles of Judaism in chapters i to xxii only to turn around in chapter xxiii and attack the entire project of creed formulation (including Maimonides' attempt) altogether. I suggest that this is not Abravanel's intention at all. He is consistent throughout the book.

In chapters i to xxii Abravanel defends Maimonides' heuristic interpretation of the principles in the face of the attacks of Crescas and Albo. In chapter xxiii Abravanel takes the offensive and attacks the axiomatic and doctrinal interpretations of the principles of Judaism. This simply furthers his defence of Maimonides. His attack on creed formulation is a continuation of his defence of Maimonides.

The interpretation of the *Rosh Amanah* offered here is supported by an analysis of chapter xxiii of the book. It is in this chapter that Abravanel is supposed to reverse himself and attack Maimonides after having defended him in the rest of the book. Abravanel opens the chapter by saying that Maimonides, Crescas, and Albo were led to posit principles in the Torah by the example of secular science. He then states and defends his own view that there are no principles of Judaism since its beliefs, narratives, and commandments are all equally true and precious. He then goes on to distinguish Maimonides from Crescas and Albo and thus to exculpate him. This is the passage quoted just above.

Maimonides, Abravanel informs us, had adapted his language to the needs of the uninformed masses. Abravanel faults Crescas and Albo for having taken Maimonides' words at face value. Maimonides had posited the principles for the uninitiated; Crescas and Albo, however, 'took these things literally and put those beliefs at the level of roots and principles, like the first principles of the sciences, as I have discussed.'[40] We see here that it is Crescas and Albo who are faulted for holding the axiomatic view of the principles, not Maimonides. Abravanel follows this with a critique of the axiomatic or logical view, insisting that Judaism is a seamless, entirely interdependent whole: 'the divine Torah would collapse with the denial of any narrative, opinion, or belief in it.'[41] All the beliefs of Judaism are its principles; there are no axioms which underlie the other beliefs, from which the latter may be derived and without which they could not endure. This is the attitude which Albo excoriated as making all philosophical investigation on religious questions impossible.

We see, therefore, that, far from turning around to attack Maimonides here in chapter xxiii, Abravanel continues to defend him. He distinguishes Maimonides' position from that of Crescas and Albo. He rejects the latter, imputes the heuristic view of the principles to Maimonides, and on those grounds he defends him: 'If this was his opinion then his intentions were acceptable and his actions were for the sake of heaven.'[42]

It is now clear that Abravanel is consistent throughout the *Rosh Amanah*. He did not defend Maimonides and the project of creed formulation only to turn around and attack them. He defends Maimonides' principles (as heuristic devices) throughout the book. He sets up his nine propositions so as to make this defence possible and constantly repeats that he is defending Maimonides' principles as praiseworthy beliefs, not as dogmas or axioms of Judaism. In chapter xxiii his attack is directed at the principles not as heuristic devices, but as axioms or dogmas the holding of which is necessary in order to merit life in the world to come.

Having explained Abravanel's position in chapter xxiii we are now able to turn to the problem raised above and explain the apparent contradiction between chapter xxii (where Abravanel cites belief in creation as a *yesod* of Judaism) and chapter xxiii (where Abravanel denies that Judaism has any principles).

It might be thought that Abravanel was being imprecise in his use of language and that he meant to assert merely that creation was an important belief of Judaism, as, for example, Maimonides did in *Guide*, ii. 25, and not that it was an axiom of the faith. This suggestion, however, founders on the fact that Abravanel carefully defines the Hebrew term *yesod*. He distinguishes *yesod* from *ikkar* and defines the former as 'A thing upon which the existence and duration of another thing depends and without which it cannot endure.'[43] Creation is consistently presented as a *yesod*. In *Rosh Amanah*, chapter xxiii Abravanel explicitly denies that Judaism has any *yesodot*.

Another suggestion may be considered which seems to provide a solution for the internal contradiction in the *Rosh Amanah* if not the contradictions between *Rosh Amanah*, chapter xxiii on the one hand and *Shamayim Ḥadashim* and *Mifalot Elohim* on the other. In the bulk of the *Rosh Amanah* Abravanel responds to the criticisms of Crescas and Albo on Maimonides. In chapter xxii, however, he criticizes the positions of his two antagonists. His argument in that chapter may be read as an instance of the talmudic *leda'ateykh* argument:

You, Crescas and Albo, claim that Judaism may be likened to a science with axioms and derivative principles. On that basis you criticize Maimonides, faulting him for having chosen the wrong axioms. But even if you are correct — and you are not — you have yourselves chosen the wrong beliefs to posit as axioms. The only belief truly axiomatic to Judaism when it is — incorrectly — pictured as a science, is creation.

If I am correct in my understanding of his position here, Abravanel did not really put forward belief in creation as an axiom of Judaism in *Rosh Amanah*, chapter xxii. He merely extended his argument against Crescas and Albo.

This suggestion may resolve the internal contradiction within the *Rosh Amanah* itself but it still leaves unresolved the contradiction between Abravanel in *Rosh Amanah*, chapter xxiii and Abravanel in *Shamayim Ḥadashim* and *Mifalot Elohim*. He flatly states in the latter two texts that belief in creation is a foundation (*yesod*) and corner-stone (i.e., axiom) of Judaism while denying that Judaism has any such things in *Rosh Amanah*, chapter xxiii.

If we look at *Shamayim Ḥadashim* and *Mifalot Elohim* in the context of Abravanel's post-Expulsion literary activity as a whole, however, then a possible explanation for Abravanel's strange inconsistency begins to emerge. In literary terms, the sixteen years between the Expulsion from Spain and Abravanel's death were the most productive of his life. Despite the varied types of book which he wrote during this period one theme dominates his non-exegetical and even much of his exegetical writings: consolation and encouragement for the Jewish people in the aftermath of the catastrophe of 1492. Abravanel sought to console and encourage his fellow Jews primarily by instilling in them the fervent belief in the imminent coming of the Messiah. Aside from his three explicitly messianic works, *Ma'ayanei Yeshuah*, *Yeshuot Meshiho*, and *Mashmia Yes-huah*, we find the theme of redemption dominating his commentary on the Passover Haggadah (*Zevah Pesah*) and many of his biblical commentaries (e.g., the commentary on Isaiah). His theodicy, *Zedek Olamim*, sought to justify the ways of God in the light of catastrophes like the Expulsion. *Nahlat Avot*, his commentary on *Avot*, encouraged Jews to remain faithful to the 'inheritance of their fathers'. The *Rosh Amanah* was written to allay the doubts of Jews confused by competing systems of dogmas and also, I might add, to undermine the possibility of Jewish philosophy by elevating every belief of Judaism to the status of an unquestionable dogma.

How do *Mifalot Elohim* and *Shamayim Hadashim* fit into this context? Both works subserve a messianic end. Following his interpretation of Maimonides in *Guide*, ii. 25, Abravanel had to establish the createdness of the world in order to make possible miracles in general and the miracle of redemption in particular. Abravanel's emphasis on the fundamental character of creation, therefore, is part and parcel of his entire messianic project, the dominant theme of his post-Expulsion writing.

It is even possible that Abravanel felt that in the context in which he was writing, creation really did serve as an axiom of Judaism, at least in a psychological way. Without belief in the coming of the Messiah, Abravanel seems to have felt, there is little hope for the continued existence of Judaism. Belief in the Messiah, however, presupposes belief in God's volitional creation of the world. Belief in creation is thus absolutely necessary for the 'existence and duration' of Judaism and is a belief without which Judaism in the post-Expulsion world 'could not endure'.

The Jewish world had undergone its greatest catastrophe since the destruction of the Second Temple. Abravanel was doing everything in his power to minimize the effects of the blow, to console the Jewish people, to keep them faithful to their heritage, and, above all, to give them strength and courage with which to face the future. In asserting the axiomatic character of belief in creation in *Shamayim Hadashim* and in *Mifalot Elohim* Abravanel was indeed contradicting the position he enunciated in *Rosh Amanah*, xxiii. But the times demanded radical action. The *Rosh Amanah* was written for one purpose, *Shamayim Hadashim* and *Mifalot*

Elohim for another. If strict consistency between them was impossible so much the worse, Abravanel must have felt, for strict consistency.

Abravanel brings the *Rosh Amanah* to a close in chapter xxiv by raising and answering an objection to his thesis that Judaism has no principles of faith. 'Someone might object to this contention', he admits, 'and say that the Sages (themselves) laid down principles for the divine Torah in that first mishnah in *Perek Ḥelek*.'[44]

Abravanel's response to this objection was to argue that the point of the mishnah is not to lay down principles for the Torah, but to emphasize that all Jews have a share in the world to come which they can earn through the fulfilment of even one commandment.[45] There are no specific principles, beyond the general acceptance of the Torah, which must be believed in order to merit a portion in the world to come.

It is possible, however, to lose one's share in the world to come. This is the mishnah's second point according to Abravanel. The mishnah cites three beliefs and three actions as examples of ways in which one can indeed lose one's share in the world to come. These all relate to denial of the Torah. One may deny the Torah, Abravanel says, for one of three reasons: because of its Giver (such a person is the *epikoros*); because of the Torah itself (such a person denies Torah from heaven); or because of the nature of the recipient (such a person denies resurrection).

The three forbidden actions mentioned in the mishnah also relate to the three possible ways of denying the Torah. He who reads books of the sectarians is an *epikoros*, denying God. He who pronounces the divine name according to its letters obviously denies the divinity of the Torah, otherwise he would not make light of the honour due the divine name. He who whispers a charm over a wound thinks that he himself can resurrect the dead.

'What follows from all this', Abravanel concludes, 'is that our Sages did not posit roots for the Torah in this mishnah nor did they intend to do so. But by way of admonition they specified those heresies which will restrain a person from life in the world to come.'[46]

Abravanel's position in the *Rosh Amanah*, summarized so succinctly in the sentences just quoted seems to have been motivated by a number of considerations. His fundamentally critical stance toward philosophy led him to elevate every teaching of the Torah to the status of dogma, making philosophical speculation dangerous since mistakes in such speculation might very well cost one his share in the world to come. His desire to assist the Jewish masses in their attempt at coping with the profound uncertainties raised by the catastrophe of 1492 led him both to reject the need for complicated formulations of Jewish beliefs and, since such formulations had already been made, to emphasize the importance and value of that of Maimonides: if there must be articles of creed, he seemed to have thought, let there be only one authoritative list. Abravanel's strict ideas concerning doctrinal orthodoxy, furthermore, led him to a position which condemned as heresy any deviation, no matter how innocently motivated, from the dogmas of Judaism (which were all of the beliefs taught by the Torah).

It is useful to compare Abravanel with Duran on this last point. Both seem to understand the term 'principle of faith' in dogmatic terms. Both agree that in the final analysis there is only one principle of faith: to accept the teachings of the Torah. But they differ radically with respect to the conclusions they draw from these premises. Duran concludes that for a deviation from the teachings of the Torah to be considered heresy it must be intended as such; Abravanel concludes that any deviation from the teachings of the Torah is heresy and costs one his share in the world to come.

It seems likely that Abravanel adopted this uncompromising position at least in part because of his analysis of the nature of the times in which he lived.[47] Jews and Judaism, buffeted as they were, could not afford the luxury of internal divisions: no deviations could be permitted.[48] But beyond that, his position is also a consequence of his adoption of the 'propositional' understanding of 'faith' introduced by Maimonides and used by Bibago. If 'faith' is defined in terms of the acceptance of specific beliefs, and if differentiating in any significant way among the beliefs of the Torah is considered illegitimate, then rejecting any Torah belief — no matter what the reason — makes one's faith defective.

9

Four Minor Figures

Isaac Abravanel was the last Jewish thinker systematically to explore the question of dogma in Judaism. The issue was, however, briefly taken up by four other thinkers, all of whom were roughly contemporaries of Abravanel. For the sake of completeness we will briefly consider their contributions to the debate.

1. Muehlhausen

Yom Tov Lippmann Muehlhausen (d. after 1450) is the only medieval Ashkenazi Jew known to have commented on the principles of Judaism. Muehlhausen included two lists of principles in his well-known anti-Christian polemic, *Sefer Ha-Nizzahon.*[1] Although the printed edition of the work contains sixteen principles in the first list, manuscript evidence shows that Muehlhausen's intention was simply to reproduce Maimonides' thirteen principles.[2] Muehlhausen's second list appears in section 127 of his book (p. 82), in the context of a commentary on Deuteronomy 6: 4. Correcting the printed text in light of the manuscript we find that Muehlhausen's seven 'foundations of our faith concerning God' are:

(1) that God exists
(2) that God is first and last
(3) that He created the world and that the existence of all things derives from Him
(4) that we accept Him as our God
(5) that we worship Him alone, that we should not join any other (deity) to Him, and that we refrain from dualism and the positing of intermediaries between man and God
(6) that we should not ascribe to Him body, corporeality, or limit
(7) that we should not ascribe to Him change of will, anger, laughter, happiness, or sadness.

Muehlhausen was slightly older than Abravanel. Two of his younger contemporaries also dealt with the principles of Judaism.

II. Delmedigo

Elijah ben Moses Delmedigo (*c*.1460–97) was a philosopher and rabbinic scholar active in Italian renaissance circles.[3] In 1496 he composed his *Beḥinat ha-Dat*, a work with strongly Averroist overtones dealing with the relationship between religion and philosophy.[4] Near the beginning of the work Delmedigo laid down principles for the Jewish faith, both because this had become standard practice in Jewish theological treatises and in order to establish which beliefs must be held both by the religious élite and by the masses.[5] Delmedigo's list of 'roots' or 'principles of religion' as he calls it turns out to be nothing other than a reordered version of Maimonides' thirteen principles. The only real difference is that Delmedigo makes no explicit reference to Maimonides' eighth principle, Torah from heaven.

III. David ben Judah Messer Leon

Delmedigo's countryman, Rabbi David ben Judah Messer Leon (*c*.1470–1526),[6] is best known as the author of a responsum, *Kevod Ḥakhamim*, which grew out of a dispute to which he was party in Valonia, Albania. This responsum is an important source of information concerning the contemporary Italian rabbinate.[7]

David ben Judah composed two books in which he paid some attention to the principles of Judaism. The first of these, *Magen David*, was never printed and survives today in only one manuscript.[8] The second, *Tehillah le-David* was published in 1576 in Constantinople. The accounts of the principles found in these two works are different and unrelated.

David ben Judah devotes a substantial portion of *Magen David* to a discussion of the nature of faith. He borrowed much of this discussion directly from Bibago's *Derekh Emunah*, without, however, explicitly naming his source.[9] Related to this discussion is an analysis of Judah Halevi's philosophy at the conclusion of which David ben Judah lists three principles which clearly show the impress of Halevi's thought:[10]

(1) 'That God separated, sanctified, and distinguished the Jewish nation from all nations to guide it'

(2) 'That the Jewish people are distinguished and separated from other nations in that they are guided by God through no intermediary or angel'

(3) '. . . it is proper to love God as He loves us, this love being shared between the two'.[11]

David ben Judah devotes considerable attention to Maimonides' principles in the first part of his *Tehillah le-David*. He analyses and defends them in the same way in which Bibago and Abravanel analysed and defended the principles of Maimonides: he raises and then answers a series of objections to Maimonides' principles.[12] This procedure takes up all of chapters 13–20 (pp. 8b–11b) of *Tehillah le-David*, part i.

In chapter 21 (p. 12a) David ben Judah explains the structure of Maimonides' principles in a way reminiscent of Bibago: the first five principles are said to deal with belief in God while the last eight are said to deal with beliefs concerning His actions.[13] These are in turn divided into beliefs concerning past actions (principles 6, 7, 8, and 9), present or continuing actions (principles 10 and 11), and future actions (principles 12 and 13). David ben Judah goes on to claim that the first part of the *Guide of the Perplexed* deals with the first five principles, that *Guide*, ii deals with principles concerning God's past actions, and that *Guide*, iii deals with principles concerning God's present actions. Since no demonstrative proofs can be given concerning the principles dealing with God's future actions they are not dealt with in the *Guide*.

David ben Judah devotes the greater part of *Tehillah le-David*, ii to a discussion of three beliefs which he considers to be central to Judaism and the acceptance of which defines one as a believer in the Torah. These three beliefs are not susceptible of rational proof and are taught by the oral tradition of Judaism. The three beliefs are creation, prophecy, and miracles.[14] David ben Judah, along with almost all his contemporaries who dealt with the principles of Judaism, emphasizes the centrality and importance of belief in creation. At p. 50b he calls it 'the most essential root'. It enjoys this status because 'it is the root of the Torah in its generality; destroying this belief is like destroying the entire Torah'.

iv. Mabit

The last figure to deal with the principles of Judaism before the Haskalah was Rabbi Moses ben Joseph Trani (1500–80; known as the 'Mabit'), the Safed halakhist. Trani devoted the lion's share of his *Bet Elohim* to an ethical, homiletical, and philosophical commentary on Maimonides' thirteen principles.[15] This discussion takes up the sixty-four chapters of the *Sha'ar ha-Yesodot* of Trani's work. Trani takes it as a given that Maimonides' thirteen principles are *the* principles of Judaism and that their acceptance, coupled with repentance and prayer, define a Jew. Like Duran and Albo the Mabit notes that Maimonides' thirteen principles can be reduced to three; God, Torah, and providence in reward and punishment. After arguing that Maimonides' principles can be established rationally as well as traditionally, Trani examines each one of them from the perspective of reason (*sevara*), experience, and tradition.

10

Summary and Conclusions

1. Statements of the Creed

Before attempting to draw conclusions from the information presented and analysed here it will be useful to summarize some of the main points already discussed.

Moses Maimonides (1135–1204) was the first Jewish thinker systematically and self-consciously to designate certain beliefs of the Torah as qualitatively distinct from other beliefs and to designate them as a special class, the class of principles. He listed and commented on thirteen 'foundations of the Torah' which he declared were those beliefs which every Jew had to hold in order to be counted as a Jew and in order to merit a portion of the world to come. His thirteen beliefs may be summarized as follows:

(1) God's existence
(2) God's unity
(3) God's incorporeality
(4) God's ontic priority
(5) that God alone may be worshipped
(6) prophecy
(7) the special nature of Mosaic prophecy
(8) Torah from heaven
(9) eternity of the Torah
(10) God's knowledge
(11) reward and punishment
(12) Messiah
(13) resurrection.

In the two hundred and fifty years following the death of Maimonides the question of principles of Judaism in general and of Maimonides' principles in particular received almost no serious or sustained attention. Abba Mari Astruc of Lunel (thirteenth century) mentions three principles of the Torah in the introduction to his *Minḥat Kena'ot*:

(1) God's existence
(2) creation

(3) providence.

Abba Mari takes it as given that the Torah has principles of faith; Maimonides' innovation had taken root. Abba Mari posits his principles as those beliefs which must be held if a person is going to maintain unswerving obedience to the Torah. He introduces them as *avot* ('fathers') and derives what may be called subsidiary principles from them: God's eternity, God's incorporeality, God's absolute simplicity, God's unity, revelation of the Torah through Moses, God's knowledge, and human choice.

Shem Tov ben Joseph Falaquera (*c.*1220–90) counted as principles

(1) God's existence
(2) His unity
(3) creation *ex nihilo*
(4) prophecy
(5) miracles
(6) immortality of the soul
(7) reward and punishment.

In another context he listed as examples of true Torah doctrines the following:

(1) God's existence
(2) His unity
(3) creation *ex nihilo*
(4) providence
(5) reward and punishment
(6) miracles.

David ben Samuel Kokhavi d'Estella (thirteenth–fourteenth centuries) posits three 'foundations of the Torah' in his *Migdal David*:

(1) that one must observe the commandments of the Torah
(2) that one must accept the beliefs of the Torah
(3) that one must use philosophy so as better to understand the Torah.

Kokhavi raises seven 'pillars' (*ammudim*) on these foundations:

(1) creation
(2) choice and human will
(3) providence
(4) Torah from heaven
(5) reward and punishment
(6) acceptance of true prophecies concerning the end of days

(7) resurrection of the dead.
Kokhavi, like Abba Mari before him, does not present any clear-cut definition of the concept 'principle of faith'.

David ben Yom Tov ibn Bilia (fourteenth century) adds thirteen principles to Maimonides' original list in his *Yesodot ha-Maskil*:
  (1) Separate Intellects
  (2) creation
  (3) world to come
  (4) God emanates soul
  (5) souls are distinct substances
  (6) the soul undergoes change and development during the course of human life
  (7) perfect reward appertains only to the soul
  (8) the wise man sins from desire, not from his wisdom
  (9) Torah is superior to philosophy
  (10) the Torah contains both exoteric and esoteric levels
  (11) the Torah needs no correction
  (12) the reward for fulfilling a commandment is the opportunity to fulfil another commandment
  (13) the fulfilment of the actional commandments is not the aim of human perfection.

Shemariah ben Elijah ha-Ikriti (1275–1355) mentions five 'foundations of the Torah' towards the end of his *Sefer Amaziah*:
  (1) God's existence
  (2) God's incorporeality
  (3) God's unity
  (4) that God created the heaven and the earth
  (5) that God created the world by His will 5106 years before the date on which Shemariah wrote his book.

The five post-Maimonideans listed here contributed very little to the discussion of principles of faith in Judaism. They do, however, demonstrate that after Maimonides Jewish writers did not feel the need to justify attempts to list the principles of Judaism. These authors are all thinkers of the second rank. None of their more illustrious contemporaries raised the issue of the principles of Judaism at all. The situation changed dramatically in the fifteenth century, a period during which almost every prominent Jewish thinker contributed something to the discussion of the principles of Judaism.

The first of these was R. Shimon ben Zemah Duran (1361–

1444). In the introduction to his *Ohev Mishpat* Duran posits two 'foundations' of the Torah: creation and providence. He thereupon derives providence from creation, in effect reducing the number of 'foundations' to one. Within the context of a discussion of Maimonides' principles (in chapter 8 of the *Ohev Mishpat*) Duran notes that Maimonides' principles can actually be reduced to three fundamental principles:

(1) God's existence
(2) Torah from heaven
(3) providence.

In chapter 9 of the same work Duran remarks that Judaism only demands the acceptance of one fundamental principle: the acceptance of the Torah and its teachings as true.

Duran's older contemporary, R. Ḥasdai Crescas (d. *c.*1412), compiled his dogmatic treatise, *Or Adonai*, after Duran had written his work on the subject. Crescas distinguishes among the *shorashim* ('roots'), *pinnot* ('corner-stones'), and *de'ot amiti'ot* ('true doctrines') of religious belief. The first group are beliefs presupposed by religion: God's existence, unity, and incorporeality. The second group comprise those beliefs which we may call analytic to the concept 'Torah from heaven'; they are those beliefs which must be accepted if one wishes both to accept belief in revelation ('Torah from heaven') and remain consistent. These beliefs are Crescas's principles of the Torah as such and are six in number:

(1) God's knowledge
(2) God's providence
(3) God's power
(4) prophecy
(5) human choice
(6) that the Torah has an end or purpose.

Crescas adds to these roots and corner-stones eleven beliefs which, as a matter of historical fact, are taught by the Torah of Moses. These beliefs are religiously no less significant than the six corner-stones (since they are in fact taught by the Torah), but they are logically less significant since it is possible to reject one or all of these beliefs without being forced to reject belief in revelation. They are:

(1) creation
(2) immortality of the soul
(3) retribution

(4) eternity of the Torah
(5) Mosaic prophecy
(6) *Urim* and *Tummim*
(7) resurrection
(8) Messiah
(9) prayer and the priestly blessing
(10) repentance
(11) Day of Atonement and the four divisions of the year.

Crescas's student, Joseph Albo (fifteenth century), followed his master in dividing the principles of Judaism into a hierarchy of classes. Drawing upon the work of Duran, Albo posits three *ikkarim* ('principles' — literally, 'roots') for the Torah:
(1) God's existence
(2) Torah from heaven
(3) retribution.

From these three beliefs he derives eight *shorashim* ('roots') or secondary principles:
(4) God's unity
(5) God's incorporeality
(6) God's atemporality
(7) God's perfection
(8) God's knowledge
(9) prophecy
(10) verification of God's messengers
(11) particular providence.

The eight beliefs in the second class all follow from or are derived from the three beliefs in the first class. This points up an important feature of Albo's system. Again building upon comments made by Duran, Albo presents Judaism as a geometric science and presents his principles as the axioms and theorems of that science.

Like Crescas, Albo also lists beliefs which happen to be taught by the Torah of Moses. Here Albo follows Crescas in making these beliefs logically and structurally independent of the preceding principles. Albo's six *anafim* ('branches') are:
(1) creation
(2) Mosaic prophecy
(3) eternity of the Torah
(4) that human perfection can be attained through the fulfilment of even one commandment
(5) resurrection

(6) Messiah.

Albo followed Crescas in not emphasizing the central importance of belief in creation in Jewish dogmatics. In this the two were unique in the fifteenth century. Abraham Shalom (d. 1492) asserts that creation is the central 'foundation' of the Torah in a number of places in his *Neveh Shalom*. Additionally, he also lists the following beliefs in various places as 'foundations' (*yesodot*) or 'principles' (*ikkarim*) of the Torah:

(2) God's necessary existence
(3) retribution
(4) providence
(5) God's omnipotence
(6) revelation
(7) prophecy
(8) Messiah
(9) God's omniscience and man's freedom
(10) resurrection.

Albo had criticized Crescas — and in this too he was following Duran — for making specific commandments principles of faith. Isaac Arama (1420–92) derived all of his principles of faith from specific commandments. This was consistent with his avowed aim of denominating as principles only those beliefs which distinguish Judaism from philosophy on the one hand and other religions on the other hand. His six principles are:

(1) creation
(2) God's power
(3) prophecy and revelation
(4) providence
(5) repentance
(6) world to come.

Arama agrees with all his contemporaries in singling out creation as the most important of the principles.

Joseph Yavez (1438–1507) also singles out creation as the central dogma of Judaism. He lists two others: providence and that in the end of days all men will acknowledge God.

Abraham Bibago (d. 1489) accepted Maimonides' thirteen principles as definitive, arguing, however, that they were based upon two 'axioms' (*hathalot*), creation and miracles, and that the second presupposed the first. Bibago, even more explicitly than Albo and Duran, adopted a scientific, geometric model of Judaism.

Bibago's *Derekh Emunah* was quoted without attribution by a number of Jewish scholars among whom was Isaac Abravanel (1437–1508). Abravanel, echoing an idea we found first in Duran, denied that Judaism had any principles of faith. These two scholars arrived at this position from diametrically opposed bases. Abravanel does assert, however, that if he were to posit 'foundations' for the Torah he would posit just one, creation. In this he is consistent with all his contemporaries in also emphasizing the importance of belief in creation.

Ignoring Moses Trani and Elijah Delmedigo, both of whom adopted Maimonides' thirteen principles, we may conclude this survey with Yom Tov Muehlhausen (d. after 1450), the only Ashkenazi to fall under our purview here, and David ben Judah Messer Leon (*c*.1470–*c*.1526).

Muehlhausen lists seven principles:
(1) God's existence
(2) God is first and last
(3) creation
(4) acceptance of God
(5) God is the only fit object of worship
(6) God's incorporeality
(7) God's immutability.

David ben Judah lists three principles in his still unpublished *Magen David*:
(1) Israel is God's chosen people
(2) Israel receives special providence
(3) Israel must love God by way of imitating God's love for her.
He posits three other beliefs as principles in his *Tehillah le-David*:
(1) creation
(2) prophecy
(3) miracles.
David ben Judah is not an Iberian, but, like the entire Iberian school of the fifteenth century (Crescas and Albo excluded), he emphasizes the special importance of belief in creation.

This constant emphasis on the centrality of belief in creation appears as a refrain in the work of Duran, Shalom, Arama, Yavez, Bibago, Abravanel, and David ben Judah. This is an issue which demands our attention. But it is not the only one. Other interesting questions which arise out of this survey include the question of why the multiplicity of dogmatic systems within late medieval Judaism did not give rise to schisms and sects; the curious de-emphasis on belief in Messiah as a principle of faith that we find among almost all of the writers surveyed; and, in general, the question of why we find such an efflorescence of dogmatic systems in the fifteenth century and not before it or after it. It is to these questions that we now turn.

ii. Dogma, Heresy, and Schisms

When we consider theological debate within medieval Judaism against the canvas of medieval theological debate generally we cannot help but be struck by the absence of schisms and sects and by the absence of charges of heresy.[1] This apparent theological unanimity is all the more surprising in the context of the debate concerning the principles of Judaism which we have outlined in the preceding pages. Maimonides, Abba Mari, Falaquera, Kokhavi, ibn Bilia, Shemariah, Duran, Crescas, Albo, Shalom, Arama, Yavez, Bibago, Abravanel, Muehlhausen, and David ben Judah Messer Leon each presents a different account of what, theologically speaking, Judaism demands of its adherents. Yet not one of these sixteen thinkers is the founder of a distinct theological school, let alone sect or other schismatic movement. Not only that, none of these thinkers condemns any of the others as a heretic, sectarian, or schismatic.

In the studies of these individual thinkers which make up the bulk of this volume I have tried to emphasize the different definitions which they adopted for the term 'principle of religion'. Now it is true that these different definitions account in part for the different systems of principles put forward, but this in no way explains the lack of what might be called theological animus in the disputes between the various systems. For that I think we have to look elsewhere.

In the introduction to this study I suggested that we might better understand the reason for the total absence of systems of dogma before Maimonides if we took note of the nature of biblical and talmudic faith. I argued that such faith is best understood in terms of trust in God, as opposed to being expressed in terms of the affirmation or denial of propositions concerning God. Maimonides' enunciation of the principles of Judaism marks a turning point in the history of Jewish thought, emphasizing as it does the adoption of a mode of thought which understands faith primarily in propositional as opposed to attitudinal terms. When faith is conceived in terms of a series of propositions it makes excellent sense to summarize those propositions in the form of principles of faith.

Old ways of thinking, however, die hard. The traditional Jewish approach to faith, which saw faith expressed in terms of acceptance of the Torah generally, trust in God, and observance of the commandments, was not superseded by the new approach, which saw faith expressed best in terms of certain propositions *about* God. Rather, the two approaches continued to coexist side by side. So long as a philosophical orientation was maintained, Jewish thinkers found it congenial to express the basic teachings of Judaism in terms of principles of faith. With the passing of Jewish philosophy in the sixteenth century the older ways of thought reasserted themselves and discussions of principles of faith quite literally disappeared from the Jewish intellectual agenda.

These fairly general considerations can be given flesh if we examine the question of heresy in the context of dogma. In doing this, we will be going over some of the ground already covered in this study, but from a fresh perspective.

We noted above in the first chapter that Maimonides' principles are quite clearly (*a*) beliefs laid down by supreme religious authority (the Torah); (*b*) necessary conditions for membership in the community of Israel; and (*c*) necessary (and sufficient!) conditions for enjoying a share in the world to come.

It should not surprise us to discover that if Maimonides had a strict understanding of what a 'foundation of the Torah' is, he also had a strict understanding of what heresy is. Put simply, heresy consists of questioning (not even denying!) any one of the principles as they were formulated by Maimonides. A person who questions any one of the principles excludes himself from the community of Israel and thus forfeits his share in the world to come.

On Maimonides' account, then, it is easy to determine who a heretic is: it is any person who questions one of the principles of the Torah. Maimonides makes identifying heretics even easier by conveniently and succinctly summarizing those principles which a Jew must accept, on pain of being condemned for heresy.[2]

It should be emphasized that Maimonides' statements here in his Mishnah commentary, and in the parallel text in the *Mishneh Torah*,[3] do not interest themselves at all in the question of why a person questions the principles of faith. In order to be considered a heretic it is sufficient to question the principles for any reason. Maimonides makes no distinction between the adoption of incorrect beliefs intentionally (i.e., rejecting beliefs one knows are taught by the Torah or adopting beliefs one knows are denied by the Torah) and the adoption of incorrect beliefs unintentionally (i.e., rejecting beliefs one incorrectly thinks are rejected by the Torah or adopting beliefs one incorrectly thinks are taught by the Torah).[4]

This interpretation of Maimonides is supported by Rabad of Posquières (*c.*1125–98). In 'Laws of Repentance', iii. 7 Maimonides' codifies as halakhah the assertion that one who believes God has a body is a sectarian and has no share in the world to come. In his gloss to the halakhah Rabad comments:

Why has he called such a person a sectarian? There are many people greater than and superior to him who adhere to such a belief on the basis of what they have seen in verses of Scripture and even more in the words of those *aggadot* which corrupt right opinion about religious matters.[5]

Rabad was not, of course, seeking to validate belief in the corporeality of God.[6] It was his point, rather, that even though God was incorporeal, a simple soul might be led by the highly anthropomorphic accounts of God in the Bible and in the midrashim to believe that God had a body. Such a person whose misbelief, as we might call it, was occasioned by an honest mistake, and who thought that he was believing what the Torah taught, ought not to be considered a heretic. It does not follow from this that Rabad thought that misbelief about principles of faith was excusable — after all, he may not even have held that belief in God's incorporeality was a principle (if he indeed held that the Torah had principles) — but it does follow from this that according to Rabad Maimonides did not allow for the possibility of innocent mistakes with respect to his principles.

Maimonides' position on heresy did not go unchallenged in the Middle Ages. He was criticized from two perspectives: some scholars faulted him for being too liberal while others sought to restrict the concept of heresy in ways in which Maimonides would surely have condemned as being too liberal.

Isaac Abravanel is an example of the first tendency. He agreed with Maimonides that the Torah had principles of faith. He was unwilling, however, to admit that these principles could be reduced to the number thirteen, and insisted that every teaching of the Torah was a principle, the questioning of which constituted heresy:

There is no need to lay down principles for the Torah of God which ought to be believed by every Israelite in order to merit life in the world to come as Maimonides and those who follow after him wrote, for the entire Torah, and every single verse, word, and letter in it is a principle and root which ought to be believed.[7]

Not only is every teaching of the Torah a principle which must be accepted in order to merit life in the world to come, according to Abravanel, but the proper interpretation of the principles must be accepted. He writes, '. . . for a false opinion about any one of the principles of faith turns the soul from its true felicity and will not bring one to life in the world to come, even if the opinion is held without intention to rebel.'[8] This must be so, for were it otherwise,

even one who unintentionally denies every principle will acquire a portion in the world to come . . . It would be possible, according to this, to find a man who does not believe in any of the principles or beliefs of the Torah and yet who should not be called a sectarian or heretic if he were brought to this blind foolishness by his failure to understand the meaning of the Torah.[9]

It is hard to find fault with the logic of Abravanel's argument. Once we accept the claim that all of the teachings of the Torah are not only true, but that each of them is a principle of faith, we cannot allow for mistakes with respect to any Torah beliefs. This is so even if the questioning is not intended as heresy: if a person could mistakenly reject a Torah belief on the grounds that he thought the Torah required it of him and not thereby be called a heretic, and since all the Torah beliefs are equivalent in the sense that they have the same dogmatic status, it would follow that a person who in good faith rejected all of the teachings of the Torah thinking that the Torah required this of him would have to be considered a good and pious Jew!

For the sake of convenience we may characterize the Maimonides/Abravanel position (despite some differences between them) as 'hard line'. This position, with its demand for absolute, uncompromising orthodoxy, dominated discussions of heresy in medieval Judaism. But it was not the only position adopted.

Rabbi Shimon ben Zemah Duran, as noted above,[10] rejected Maimonides' position. He quoted Rabad's gloss with approval, citing him as an authority for his own rejection of the hard-line position.[11] Duran analysed Maimonides' thirteen principles in his *Ohev Mishpat*, proposing that they could be reduced to three. In the final analysis, however, he maintained that formulating specific principles of faith was not fundamentally important:

Know, O ye Reader, that the great principle in all this is to believe what is included in the Torah concerning these matters. He who denies something included in the Torah, knowing that it was the opinion of the Torah, is a denier and is not included in the community of Israel.[12]

Duran here modifies Maimonides' strict position with respect to heresy. One is not considered to be a heretic simply for holding false beliefs. In order to be a heretic one must adopt beliefs which one knows to be rejected by the Torah or reject beliefs which one knows to be taught by the Torah. Duran makes this clear a little further on:

You also ought to know that one who has properly accepted the roots of the Torah but who was moved to deviate from them by the depth of his speculation and who thereby believed concerning one of the branches of the faith the opposite of what has been accepted as what one ought to believe and tries to explain the verses of Scripture according to his belief, even though he errs he is no denier. For he was not brought to this deviation by heresy at all and if he found a tradition from the Sages to the effect that he ought to turn from the position he adopted, he would do so. He only holds that belief because he thinks that it is the intention of the Torah. Therefore, even though he errs he is not a denier and sectarian according to what is agreed upon by our people since he accepted the roots of our Torah as he should.[13]

Duran's position is precisely the opposite of Abravanel's. For Abravanel, deviation from any Torah teaching, whether intentional or not, constitutes heresy. For Duran, there is no teaching so basic that if one makes any honest mistake about it, one is thereby condemned as a heretic.[14]

Duran's teaching in this regard did not find many sympathetic listeners in the late Middle Ages. It was explicitly criticized by Abraham Bibago[15] and Isaac Abravanel[16] (although they both attributed the position to Rabad, ignoring Duran altogether), and Joseph Albo could not make up his mind about it.[17] One could easily get the impression that Duran and possibly Rabad were alone in resisting the hard line on heresy in the Jewish Middle Ages. But, as we argued above in chapter 4, a good case may be urged for maintaining that Crescas sided with Duran against Maimonides and Abravanel.

All this said, it ought to be emphasized, to avoid misunderstanding, that the position attributed here to Duran and probably to Crescas — that one who rejects a Torah belief by mistake and with no intention to rebel against God is neither cut off from the community of Israel nor excluded from the world to come — is not a position of theological anarchy. This position does not maintain that there are no correct beliefs (i.e., it does not deny the concept of orthodoxy); rather, it maintains that the criterion of true orthodoxy is not the rigid acceptance of certain carefully formulated, catechismal beliefs so much as the general acceptance of the Torah and trust in God.

It ought to be further noted that the position attributed here to Duran and probably to Crescas does not maintain that a person who mistakenly rejects a belief taught by the Torah, or a person who mistakenly accepts a belief rejected by the Torah, ought to be allowed to persist in his mistake. Such a person must be corrected, but ought not to be castigated as an unbeliever and condemned to perdition.

If the analysis presented here is correct, then while Maimonides and Abravanel would reject as heretics persons who even mistakenly adopted incorrect beliefs, Duran and possibly Rabad, Crescas, and Albo would condemn as heretics only those Jews who consciously rejected Torah teachings as an act of rebellion against God. This second approach is more consistent with biblical-talmudic ways of thought than is the Maimonides–Abravanel approach and, I submit, underlies the fact that despite the disparity of approaches to the question, 'what is a principle of Judaism?' schisms and sectarian movements did not arise in medieval Judaism. After all, if the acceptance or rejection of a particular belief does not make one a heretic — as opposed to the reasons for which one accepts or rejects those beliefs — then there is little reason for denouncing as sectarians those who do not accept the beliefs. There is no way of determining how Abba Mari, Kokhavi, ibn Bilia, Shemariah, Shalom, Arama, Yavez, David ben Judah, Messer Leon, and Muehlhausen would stand on this issue but it is not unreasonable to suggest that they, like Duran and possibly Rabad, Crescas, and Albo, would excuse inadvertent heresy, despite the fact that each of them propounded his own system of principles of faith.[18] In sum, Maimonides' attention to the principles of Judaism reflects a new concept of 'faith'. He succeeded — if only temporarily — in inserting the issue of creed formulation into the agenda of medieval Jewish intellectuals. He had much less success in implanting the new conception of the content of faith — with its attendant rejection of the possibility of inadvertent heresy (*shogeg*) — upon which the idea of principles of faith actually depended.

III. Creation and Messiah

I have repeatedly noted that, with the exception of Crescas and Albo, every single one of the fifteenth-century Iberian figures who contributed to the discussion of the principles of Judaism — Duran, Shalom, Arama, Yavez, Bibago, and even Abravanel — emphasized in one way or another the dogmatic centrality of belief in creation. This unanimity of opinion is all the more surprising when we consider that in the texts available to these thinkers, Maimonides excluded belief in creation from his list of principles.[19]

It does not seem reasonable to surmise that some sort of underground return to Kalam — proving God's existence from the createdness of the world — was operative here. After all, the thinkers surveyed here were aware of Maimonides' devastating criticisms of the Kalam, and were themselves most of them thinkers of a distinctly Aristotelian or even Averroist stripe.

Perhaps the importance of belief in creation can be explained in another way. Maimonides had argued in *Guide*, ii. 25 that belief in creation was an absolute prerequisite for belief in miracles in general and belief in the miracle of revelation in particular. Let us assume that most fifteenth-century Jewish thinkers found this argument compelling; in coming to lay down the principles of the Torah they would feel forced to count among these principles belief in creation, without which the revelation of the Torah would not be possible. Fine and good; but why insist that creation is the single most important principle, underlying all the others? Why not reserve that distinction for belief in God, as Maimonides had done?[20] Well, one does not have to be a *mutakallimun* to see that while belief in creation presupposes belief in God the creator, belief in God in no way necessitates belief in creation. In that sense belief in creation is more fundamental than is belief in the existence of God. We can make this point clearer by contrasting belief in creation with a belief which most of our authors de-emphasized.

Towards the end of the first chapter I noted that Maimonides chose to emphasize the importance of belief in the Messiah *vis-à-vis* his other principles in a variety of subtle but significant ways.[21] It is interesting to note that just as Maimonides emphasized the importance of belief in Messiah it was de-emphasized by most of the other Jewish thinkers who dealt with the principles of Judaism. This is surprising, not only in light of the importance of this belief in the Maimonidean corpus in general and in his principles of belief in particular, but in light of the importance attached to the Messiah by the Bible, Talmud, Midrashim, and, above all, by the one book which captures the essence and flavour of Jewish thinking and feeling better than any other, the *Siddur* or Prayer Book.

Of the many thinkers who dealt with the principles of Judaism after Maimonides only four (Kokhavi, Crescas, Albo, and Shalom) explicitly listed belief in the coming of the Messiah as a principle of the Torah. Of the others, ibn Bilia, Shemariah, Duran, Arama, Yavez, Abravanel, David ben Judah Messer Leon, and Muehlhausen fail to mention it at all while Bibago mentions it as one of the thirteen principles of Maimonides which he accepts wholesale.

Even those thinkers who do affirm belief in the Messiah as a principle of Judaism find one way or another to de-emphasize its importance. Thus, Kokhavi lists it as the sixth of his seven second-tier beliefs. Crescas divides his third-tier beliefs into two groups and counts Messiah as eighth and last of those beliefs taught by the Torah independent of specific commandments. He places Messiah after resurrection, unlike Maimonides, who counted it before resurrection. In this Crescas was followed by Albo, who makes Messiah the last of his six third-tier beliefs, placing it after resurrection as well. Not only does Albo relegate Messiah to the very bottom rung of his dogmatic system, but he explicitly criticizes Maimonides for having counted it as a principle of faith.[22]

Abraham Shalom does not count belief in the Messiah among the four principles which he posits a number of times in the *Neveh Shalom*, but he does mention it once as a 'principle' of the Torah. But even this mention turns out to be less than emphatic. He does not attach any intrinsic dogmatic importance to belief in the

Messiah; rather, he sees it as instrumental to preserving belief in the Torah.[23]

Perhaps the most surprising case of all is that of Isaac Abravanel. Despite his avowed position in the *Rosh Amanah* that the Torah has no principles, we saw above that Abravanel did posit one belief as a 'foundation' of the Torah. One might expect that the author of three emphatically messianic treatises, and an author who repeatedly stressed his own Davidic descent,[24] would, if he were going to choose one belief as a principle of the Torah, choose belief in the Messiah. But such was not the case: as we saw above, Abravanel posited creation, not Messiah, as the one 'foundation' of the Torah.

In sum, even though Maimonides emphasized the dogmatic importance of belief in the coming of the Messiah in his system of principles, not one of his successors followed in his footsteps in so doing. More than that, of the few of his successors who actually counted belief in the Messiah as a principle of faith, every one without exception found some way of de-emphasizing its importance. Given both the importance that the Jewish tradition as a whole attaches to belief in the Messiah, and the importance attached to it by Maimonides, we must ask why Maimonides failed to influence those who came after him to adopt a position similar to his own.

There are, it seems to me, two reasons for this prima facie strange state of affairs. The whole project of creed formulation in medieval Judaism after the beginning of the fifteenth century was part of the general apology for Judaism and polemic against Christianity which characterized so much of the theological writing of the period.[25] We have had occasion to allude to this point above and shall have occasion to do so again. In their actual confrontations with Christian disputants Jewish apologists found the question of the Messiah a dangerous one and often tended to play down its significance. Nahmanides' observation that Judaism does not depend upon belief in the Messiah is perhaps the single most famous example of this tendency.[26] Is it any wonder, then, that Jewish thinkers who propounded their dogmatic systems at least partially in reaction to Christian attacks on Judaism would be willing to de-emphasize or ignore belief in Messiah altogether?

There is more to the story than this, however. Duran had introduced a conception of Judaism as a geometric science into the discussion of the principles of the Torah.[27] Albo followed Duran in this regard while Crescas, typically, was his own man and adopted a distinct, if somewhat similar approach. What they all shared was the belief that a principle of the Torah must be a belief the rejection of which would cause the Torah to collapse. This conception of what a principle of faith is came to dominate subsequent discussions, at least formally.[28] And it cannot be gainsaid that with the notorious statement of R. Hillel well known to everyone[29] there is no compelling reason to assert that without belief in the Messiah belief in the Torah must fall.

This said, we may now revert to the question of creation. Maimonides had affirmed the axiomatic importance of belief in creation. Duran, Crescas, and Albo had contributed to the idea that Judaism was a religion with axioms. Crescas and Albo, under the influence of Rabbenu Nissim, had denied that creation was of axiomatic importance. Other Jewish thinkers, under the sway of Maimonides rather than Rabbenu Nissim, and accepting the axiomatic picture of Judaism, put the two together and affirmed the central axiomatic importance of belief in creation for Judaism.

Thus, the same forces which brought many Jewish thinkers in the late Middle Ages to de-emphasize the importance of a belief central to Jewish thought, Messiah, brought them to emphasize the centrality of a belief, creation, which had played a much less important role in traditional Judaism. This, perhaps better than any other point, sums up the essential character of the whole project of creed formulation in medieval Judaism as an endeavour alien to the spirit of biblical–rabbinic Judaism. That it was accepted — if only for a time — into the very heart of that tradition is an indication of how flexible the tradition is. That it failed to strike permanent roots in the tradition is an indication of how stubborn its basic elements are.

There can be little doubt that the serious, self-conscious study of what we may call 'Jewish dogmatics' failed to strike permanent roots in the tradition. The whole project germinated with Maimonides, flowered in the fifteenth century, and withered shortly after the Expulsion from Spain. We have already discussed why it began with Maimonides[30] and why the fifteenth century provided such fertile soil for it.[31] But the question remains, why did substantial attention to the principles of faith die with the passing of the generation of the Expulsion?

I argued above that extended attention given to the question of the principles of Judaism in the fifteenth century was a function of the fact that a new class had begun to write tracts of Jewish philosophical theology in that period. This was the class of rabbis, Spanish Jewry's communal/halakhic leadership. I argued that before the fifteenth century individuals of this type had no reason to involve themselves seriously in areas essentially independent of and perhaps even foreign to halakhah as they understood it. It was only the needs of the hour which forced them to write on subjects which otherwise would hardly have merited their sustained and serious attention.[32]

Similarly, with the passing of the special theological and conversionary pressures of the fifteenth century due in great measure to the Expulsion, the traditional halakhic leadership no longer had any need to deal with the question of the principles of Judaism and reverted to their customary preoccupations, coupled with ever-increasing attention to Kabbalah.

Furthermore, we argued above that attention to the principles of faith makes sense primarily in a context sufficiently influenced by Greek philosophical categories to understand the content of faith in propositional, not attitudinal terms.[33] The end of the fifteenth century saw the passing of the tradition of sustained philosophical reflection by Jews. When the philosophical perspective lost its sway over the minds of Jewish thinkers the entire project of creed formulation lost its roots; is it any surprise that it dried up? With the end of the important role played by philosophy in medieval Jewish thought there was little possibility for the continued existence of Jewish dogmatics.

Appendix

Texts and Translations of Maimonides' Commentary
on *Perek Ḥelek*

The Arabic text of Maimonides' commentary on *Ḥelek* was first published by Edward Pococke in his *Porta Mosis* (Oxford, 1655), pp. 133–80. It appeared again in J. Holzer, *Zur Geschichte der Dogmenlehre in der jüdischen Religionsphilosophie des Mittelalters: Môse Maimunis Einleitung zu Chelek* (Berlin, M. Poppelauer, 1901). Basing himself on the editions of Pococke and Holzer, Israel Friedlaender published the text in his *Selections from the Arabic Writings of Maimonides* (Leiden, Brill, 1909 and 1951). Rabbi Joseph Kafiḥ published the text in his *Mishnah im Perush Rabbenu Moshe ben Maimon*, iv (*Seder Nezikin*) (Jerusalem, Mossad ha-Rav Kook, 1963), pp. 195–217. Kafiḥ's text is based upon a manuscript published in facsimile by Solomon D. Sassoon in *Maimonidis Commentarius in Mischnam* (Copenhagen, Ejnar, Munksgaard, 1961), ii, plates 290–305. The manuscript itself is held in the Oxford University Library (MS Pococke 295; Neubauer no. 404). Sassoon (i. 33) and Kafiḥ (i. 6) both insist that the manuscript was written by Maimonides himself. This is also the position of S. M. Stern, 'Perush ha-Mishnah bikhtav Yado shel ha-Rambam', *Tarbiẓ*, xxiii (1952), pp. 72–80. In 'Ha-Omnam Yesh be-Yadeinu tofes shel Perush ha-Mishnah be-Eẓem Ketav-Yado shel ha-Rambam?' *Tarbiẓ*, xxvii (1956), pp. 536–43, Joshua Blau questions this claim and raises the possibility that the manuscript is not an autograph but that it was, rather, Maimonides' own working copy. Moshe Lutzky, 'Ve-Katav Mosheh: Ḥamesh Teshuvot Autographiot shel ha-Rambam', *Ha-Tekufah*, xxx–xxxi (1946), pp. 679–704 (esp. p. 683) maintains that Maimonides made some additions and corrections to the manuscript in his own hand. S. M. Stern and S. D. Sassoon respond to the points raised by Blau in their article, 'Al Tofes Perush ha-Mishnah be-Eẓem Ktav Yado shel ha-Rambam', *Tarbiẓ*, xxix (1960), pp. 261–7. In 'Bi-Dvar Kitvei ha-Yad Perush ha-Mishnah la-Rambam, Pock. 295, Hunt. 117, ve-Sassoon 72, 73', *Tarbiẓ*, xxxiii (1964), p. 316, Blau admits that Stern and Sassoon are correct in ascribing the manuscript to

Maimonides' own hand. This position is reiterated in J. Blau and A. Scheiber, *Autograph ha-Rambam Me-Osef Adler u-me-Genizat Leningrad; Teyutat ha-Hakdamah le Seder Toharot* (Jerusalem, Israel Academy of Sciences and Humanities, 1981), p. 5. On the texts of Maimonides' Mishnah commentary in general see A. Ya'ari, 'Perush ha-Mishnah le-ha-Rambam bi-Mekoro', *Kiryat Sefer*, ix (1932–3), pp. 101–9 and 228–35.

There are three known medieval Hebrew translations of the portion of the commentary on *Ḥelek* containing the thirteen principles. That of Solomon ben Joseph ibn Ya'akov of Saragossa is the 'standard' version, published in most editions of the Babylonian Talmud. It was edited by Holzer in his *Zur Geschichte . . .* and by Mordecai Dov Rabinovitch in his *Sefer ha-Ma'or: Ozar ha-Hakdamot* (Tel Aviv, Rishonim, 1948), pp. 105–46. This volume was reissued, in a slightly different format, by Mossad ha-Rav Kook (Jerusalem) in 1961.

Judah al-Ḥarizi also translated the thirteen principles. Portions of his translation were published at the end of the Venice 1517–18 *Mikra'ot Gedolot* Bible and in R. Meir Aldabi's *Shevilei Emunah* (Riva da Trento, 1558–9), p. 10a. The text was published by J. H. Schorr in *He-Ḥaluẓ*, xii (1887), pp. 104–11 and, most recently and most completely, by Moshe Goshen-Gottstein in 'Yod Gimmel ha-Ikkarim le-ha-Rambam be-Targum al-Ḥarizi', *Tarbiẓ*, xxvi (1957), pp. 185–96. See also the discussion between Goshen-Gottstein and Isaiah Sonne in the same volume of *Tarbiẓ*, pp. 335–7.

A third, anonymous translation of the principles appears in the first chapter of Isaac Abravanel's *Rosh Amanah* (Constantinople, 1505), pp. 3a–4a (in my English translation, pp. 56–62).

Joshua Abelson translated the *Ḥelek* commentary into English in 'Maimonides on the Jewish Creed', *JQR*, xix (1907), pp. 24–58. Arnold Jacob Wolf translated the commentary, apparently from the Hebrew of ibn Ya'akov, in *Judaism*, xv (1966), pp 95–101, 211–16, and 337–42. This translation was reprinted by Isadore Twersky in his *A Maimonides Reader* (New York, Behrman House, 1972), pp. 401–23. The principles were translated into English from Rabbi Kafiḥ's edition of the Arabic text by David R. Blumenthal in his *The Commentary of R. Ḥoter ben Shelomoh to the Thirteen Principles of Maimonides* (Leiden, Brill, 1974). This translation is presented above, at the beginning of chapter 1.

Notes

Introduction

1. On Philo's principles see H. A. Wolfson, *Philo* (Cambridge, 1947), i. 164–5.
2. See *Emunot ve-De'ot* by Sa'adia Gaon (882–942).
3. By 'dogma' I mean a belief or teaching explicitly and self-consciously set down as being in some non-trivial sense distinct from and more important than other beliefs. The distinctiveness of these beliefs can be understood (and, as will be shown, was understood) in a wide variety of ways. For example, dogmas may be distinct from other beliefs in that their acceptance defines one as a Jew or is a necessary or even sufficient condition for salvation, or because they are held to be logically distinct from other beliefs (as axioms are distinct from theorems in geometry, for example), or because they are held to present and summarize all the teachings of Judaism in some convenient form.
4. In stating the issue in these terms I reject the thesis which underlies David Neumark's two-volume *Toledot ha-Ikkarim be-Yisrael* (Odessa, 1919 and 1921), to wit: that Judaism has certain immanent principles of faith which may be found in the Bible and which underlay all further developments in Judaism.
5. Compare Rom. 10: 9: 'If thou shalt confess with thy mouth the Lord Jesus, and shalt believe in thy heart that God hath raised him from the dead, thou shalt be saved.' There is no analogue to this in the Torah. It is instructive to compare this verse with the penultimate verse of Ecclesiastes.
6. See Yevamot 47a.
7. It might be suggested that Mishnah Sanhedrin x. 1 (see p. 10 for the text) is a counter-example to my thesis that the Talmud has no systematic theology, let alone principles of faith. Let it be noted, however, that of the six things which cause one to be excluded from the world to come listed in that mishnah, three are actions, not beliefs, and a fourth (*epikoros*) is interpreted in the Gemara in actional terms. Let it be noted further that there is nothing in this mishnah or its accompanying Gemara to indicate that the mishnah was composed in order to summarize or state in dogmatic terms the fundamental beliefs of Judaism.
8. See Daniel Lasker, 'Rabbinism and Karaism: The Contest for Supremacy', in R. Jospe and S. W. Wagner (eds.), *Great Schisms in Jewish History* (New York, 1981), pp. 47–72, for a useful overview of Karaite beliefs.

9. See W. Montgomery Watt, *Muslim Intellectual: A Study of al-Ghazali* (Edinburgh, 1963), pp. 159–61: Muslim interest in Greek philosophy arose in part from the 'need to defend Islamic doctrine against non-Muslims, and in particular against Christian inhabitants of the caliphate who had received philosophical training'. This was associated with a new conception of religious faith: 'It seemed clear that the man who could give reasons for a doctrine he believed was superior to a man who merely held the doctrine but could give no reasons for it.'

10. See David Neumark, *Geschichte der jüdischen Philosophie des Mittelalters*, i (Berlin, 1907), pp. 491–2.

11. Many of the same points are made by Louis Jacobs in the opening chapter of his *Faith* (New York, 1968).

12. On the distinction between 'belief that' and 'belief in' within the context of rabbinic Judaism see, in addition to Jacobs (introduction n. 11 above), E. E. Urbach, *The Sages: Their Concepts and Beliefs* (Jerusalem, 1975), i. 31–6 and Martin Buber's *Two Types of Faith* (New York, 1961), pp. 7–23. The issue has recently been subjected to sophisticated philosophical analysis by Kenneth Seeskin in his 'Judaism and the Linguistic Interpretation of Jewish Faith', *Studies in Jewish Philosophy*, iii (1983), pp. 71–81. Much of my discussion here is indebted to Seeskin, as are some of my formulations.

13. In this connection, examining biblical use of the term *emunah* is instructive. See, for example, Gen. 15: 10, Deut. 32: 4, Prov. 20: 6, and Job 4: 18. For a representative talmudic text see the reduction of the six hundred and thirteen commandments to *emunah* at Makkot 24a.

14. See, for example, Jaroslav Pelikan, *The Growth of Medieval Theology (600–1300)* (Chicago, 1978), p. 4. Compare Adolph Harnack, *History of Dogma* (New York, 1961), i. 17: 'Dogma in its conception and development is a work of the Greek spirit on the soil of the gospel.'

15. See Seeskin, p. 72.

16. If such statements can be so proven what need is there for revelation? The question of reason and revelation only makes sense where religion is construed in propositional terms and thus did not arise in the Talmud.

17. See *Topics* 100a30–100b21. Compare H. A. Wolfson, *Philosophy of the Church Fathers*, 3rd edn., rev. (Cambridge, Mass., 1970), pp. 113 and 115.

18. See Alexander Altmann, 'Translator's Introduction', Sa'adia Gaon, *Book of Doctrines and Beliefs* in *Three Jewish Philosophers* (New York, 1972), pp. 19–20. See also H. A. Wolfson, 'The Double-Faith Theory in Sa'adia, Averroes, and St. Thomas', *Studies in the History*

of Philosophy and Religion, i (Cambridge, Mass., 1973), pp. 583–618, esp. pp. 585, 587–8, and 597. See further, Israel Efros, *Studies in Medieval Jewish Philosophy* (New York, 1974), pp. 27 and 31–2.

19. See Sa'adia Gaon, *Book of Beliefs and Opinions*, introduction, ch. 4; trans. S. Rosenblatt (New Haven, 1948), p. 14.

20. *Guide of the Perplexed*, i. 50. Translated by S. Pines (Chicago, 1963), p. 111. See further H. A. Wolfson, *The Philosophy of Spinoza* (Cambridge, Mass., 1934), ii. 147. See also Wolfson, 'The Aristotelian Predicables and Maimonides' Division of Attributes', *Studies in the History of Philosophy and Religion*, ii (Cambridge, 1977), pp. 163. He there explains our passage from Maimonides in the following way: 'What Maimonides therefore means to say is that belief is that which can be expressed by a logical proposition.'

21. Maimonides opens his commentary on *Ḥelek* (which contains his thirteen principles) with the following words: 'I have seen fit to speak here about many principles concerning very important doctrines [*al-i'tiqādāt*]'. See Rabbi Joseph Kafiḥ (ed. and trans.), *Mishnah im Perush Rambam* (Jerusalem, 1963), iv (*Nezikin*), p. 195. He concludes his discussion with the following statement: 'When all these foundations are perfectly understood and believed in [*i'tiqā-duhū*] by a person he enters the community of Israel . . .' (Kafiḥ, p. 217). See further A. Nuriel, 'Musag ha-Emunah eẓel ha-Rambam', *Da'at*, ii–iii (1979), pp. 43–7. Nuriel shows how Maimonides uses *al-'īmān* in the sense of 'trust' with no reference to cognitive content. The term appears rarely in the writings of Maimonides since he understands the content of faith in terms of specific teachings (*i'tiqādāt*).

22. See Seeskin, p. 72.

23. See A. J. Wensinck, *The Muslim Creed* (Cambridge, 1932), p. 37. Compare Watt (above, introduction n. 9), pp. 97–8 and J. L. Kraemer, 'Heresy vs. the State in Medieval Islam', in S. R. Brunswick (ed.), *Studies in Judaica, Karaitica, and Islamica Presented to Leon Nemoy* (Ramat Gan, 1982), pp. 167–80.

24. Wensinck, p. 49; see also p. 47. See also Majid Fakhry, *A History of Islamic Philosophy* (New York, 1970), pp. 52 and 53 and the sources cited there. See further F. A. Klein, *The Religion of Islam* (London, 1971), pp. 40–1.

25. In addition to Wensinck (see above, introduction n. 23), see also the article by W. Montgomery Watt, ''Akida' in the *Encyclopedia of Islam*, 2nd edn. (Leiden, 1960), ii. 332–6.

26. See G. F. Hourani (ed. and trans.), *Averroes on the Harmony of Religion and Philosophy* (London, 1961), p. 5 and Bernard Lewis, *Islam in History* (London, 1973), p. 232.

27. Ghazzali, for example, is the author of *Al Kitab Qawa'id al-'Aqa'id*

('Book of the Foundations of the Articles of Faith'), trans. N. A. Faris (Lahore, 1963). On this creed see Watt (above, introduction n. 9), p. 152. Averroës composed a (lost) commentary upon the influential creed of ibn Tumart (see Hourani, p. 17).

In connection with this creed of ibn Tumart (who founded the Almohades), it is interesting to note that the Almohade cavalry were wont to chant the creed on their marches. See Aharon Kaminka, *Kitvei Bikkoret Historit* (New York, 1944), p. 145. Given the fact that Maimonides fled Cordoba in the face of the Almohades, this historical sidelight gains further interest.

On Averroës's own dogmatic treatise, *Al-Kashf an Manahij al-Adillah* ('Exposition of the Methods of Proof Concerning the Beliefs of the Community'), see Fakhry (see above, introduction n. 24), pp. 311–16 and Majid Fakhry, 'Philosophy and Scripture in the Philosophy of Averroes', *Mediaeval Studies,* xxx (1968), pp. 78–89, esp. pp. 85–7.

28. *Ḥovot ha-Levavot,* treatise i, introduction; ed. and trans. Rabbi J. Kafiḥ (Jerusalem, 1973), p. 44.

29. *Ḥovot ha-Levavot,* introduction (pp. 32 and 36). Baḥya's book deals with intellectual duties — for the heart as the seat of the intellect see, for example, Berakhot 10a — as noted by M. Mansour, 'Translator's Introduction', Baḥya ben Joseph ibn Paquda, *The Book of Directions to the Duties of the Heart* (London, 1973), p. 5. That Baḥya deplores the fact that none of his predecessors had dealt with such duties (Mansour, p. 88) provides indirect evidence for the thesis adumbrated above concerning the development of theology in medieval Judaism.

30. *Kuzari,* v. 20; ed. H. Hirschfeld (Leipzig, 1887), pp. 347–52. Compare also *Kuzari,* iii. 17 (p. 166), where Halevi speaks of 'the foundations (*al-'aqā'id*) which perfect the Jewish faith (*al-'aqīda al-yahūdiyya*)': God's sovereignty, His eternity, His providential care of the patriarchs, and His revelation of the Torah. See David Kaufmann's note, 'Jehuda ha-Levi on the Dogmas of Judaism', *JQR* (OS), i (1889), pp. 441–2.

31. See C. D. Chavel (ed.), *Perush Rabbenu Ḥananel al ha-Torah* (Jerusalem, 1972), p. 28. Note should also be made of the fact that Joseph ibn Ẓaddik, an older contemporary of Maimonides (and a man whom Maimonides knew personally), called resurrection of the dead 'a great principle [*ikkar*] of the Torah'. See ibn Ẓaddik's *Sefer ha-Olam ha-Katan,* ed. S. Horowitz (Breslau, 1903), p. 76. This text was reprinted by the *Sifriyah le-Maḥshevet Yisrael* in Jerusalem (n.d.); the passage in question occurs on p. 78 of that edition.

32. This distinction will be explained in ch. 3, section ii.

33. On Hadassi see Zvi Ankory, *Karaites in Byzantium* (New York,

1959), p. 200. Elijah ben Moses Basyatchi's 'Ten Principles of Faith' may be found in Leon Nemoy (ed.), *A Karaite Anthology* (New Haven, 1952), p. 250. Basyatchi, an important Karaite thinker, was born around 1420 in Turkey. Further on dogma among the Karaites see A. S. Halkin, 'A Karaite Creed', in S. R. Brunswick (ed.), *Studies in Judaica, Karaitica, and Islamica Presented to Leon Nemoy* (Ramat Gan, 1982), pp 145–53. Extremely valuable in this connection is Daniel J. Lasker, 'Aḥarit ha-Adam ba-Philosophiah ha-Kara'it', *Da'at*, xii (1984), pp. 5–13. See especially p. 11 and the sources cited in n. 38–42.

34. Creedal statements play an important role in Christianity, of course, but there is little reason to suspect that Maimonides had any more than a passing familiarity with Christian thought or doctrine.

Chapter 1

1. In the printed editions of the Babylonian Talmud this is the eleventh, not the tenth chapter. See Hermann L. Strack, *Introduction to the Talmud and Midrash* (Philadelphia, 1931), p. 261 n. 55 and Arthur Hyman, 'Maimonides' "Thirteen Principles"', in Alexander Altmann (ed.), *Jewish Medieval and Renaissance Studies* (Cambridge, Mass., 1967), p. 121 n. 16 (henceforth: Hyman).

2. Classic Jewish eschatology is notoriously vague. The term 'portion in the world to come' means some sort of reward after death. The explanation of Sanhedrin x offered here is given by Maimonides in his Commentary on Sanhedrin x. 2.

3. Maimonides, 'Laws of Repentance', iii. 5, explains this verse in the following terms: '*Land* is a metaphor; that is to say, "the land of the living" which is the world to come.'

4. The standard text of this mishnah reads, 'he who says that resurrection *is not taught in the Torah*'. In Maimonides' text these words are lacking. See Rabbi Joseph Kafiḥ (ed. and trans.), *Mishnah im Perush Rabbenu Moshe ben Maimon* (Jerusalem, 1963), iv (*Nezikin*), p. 195 (henceforth: Kafiḥ).

5. i.e., that it was not divinely revealed.

6. On Maimonides' use of this term in his commentary on *Ḥelek*, see p. 60. For rabbinic use of the term, see Sanhedrin 99b–100a. The word is almost certainly derived from the name Epicurus.

7. See Sanhedrin 100b.

8. i.e., one who uses a verse of the Torah as a charm to heal a wound.

9. i.e., actually pronounces God's name as it is spelled. See Avodah Zarah 19a.

10. The term 'salvation' carries with it a lot of theological baggage. In this book, however, I use it as nothing other than a less cumbersome

version of 'a share in the world to come'. Hyman p. 122, points out that this mishnah need not be interpreted as setting forth a set of dogmas of Judaism. See my comments above, introduction n. 7.

11. The expression 'principles of Judaism' needs much explication. It will be discussed elsewhere in this work.

12. See appendix on the texts and translations of Maimonides' commentary to *Ḥelek*.

13. Hyman, p. 127. In this Hyman was anticipated by R. Isaac Abravanel. See his *Rosh Amanah*, trans. M. M. Kellner as *Principles of Faith* (East Brunswick, NJ, 1982), ch. 6, p. 84. All subsequent references to the *Rosh Amanah* will be to this edition.

14. *'uṣul.* Here and throughout I translate this term as 'principles'.

15. Kafiḥ, p. 195.

16. *qawā'id.* Here and throughout I translate this term as 'foundations'.

17. Kafiḥ, p. 210.

18. *al-bāri.* On this term see p. 296 in Warren Zev Harvey, 'A Third Approach to Maimonides' Cosmogony-Prophetology Puzzle', *Harvard Theological Review*, lxxiv (1981), pp. 287–301, and the sources cited there.

19. On Maimonides' use of the term 'Creator' here, see ch. 1, section vii.

20. Ḥagigah 15a.

21. See Targum to Isa. 11: 14.

22. If God resembled bodies there would be something to which He could be compared.

23. Berakhot 31b. On Maimonides' use of this expression, see Abraham Nuriel, '"Dibrah Torah Ki-lshon Benei Adam" be-*Moreh Nevukhim*', in A. Kasher and M. Ḥallamish (eds.), *Dat ve-Safah* (Tel Aviv, 1981), pp. 97–103.

24. Arabic: *al-kadam*; Hebrew: *kadmon.* This term may denote only ontological, not temporal, precedence.

25. Late in his life Maimonides appended an addition to this principle explicitly importing creation *ex nihilo* into it. See ch. 1, section vii.

26. *yu'taqadu.* On this term see above, introduction, p. 5 and ch. 1, section ix, p. 64 and n. 266.

27. A highly anthropomorphic account of God. See Gershom Scholem, *Major Trends in Jewish Mysticism* (New York, 1941), pp. 63–7. See also Scholem's *Jewish Gnosticism, Merkabah Mysticism and Talmudic Traditions* (New York, 1960), pp. 36–42. Later in his life Maimonides, apparently regretting his reference to the *Shiur Komah* here, erased it from his copy of the commentary. See Kafiḥ, p. 213 n. 42. See further A. Altmann, 'Moses Narboni's Epistle on *Shi'ur Qomah*', in A. Altmann (ed.) *Jewish Medieval and Renaissance Studies* (Cambridge, Mass., 1969), pp. 233–7.

28. See *Sifra* to Lev. 16: 2.

29. *yu'taqadu.*
30. Lit.: 'copyist'.
31. See Ps. 19: 8.
32. Mishnah Sanhedrin x. 1.
33. Sanhedrin 99a.
34. See Kafiḥ, vol. i, pp. 4 ff.
35. *al-'īmān.* See ch. 1, section ix, p. 64 and n. 267.
36. *al-taṣdīq.* See ch. 1, section ix, p. 64 and n. 268.
37. Sanhedrin 99a–b.
38. *yu'taqadu.*
39. Kafiḥ, pp. 210–16. The translation of the principles to this point is that of D. R. Blumenthal; see ch. 1 n. 43.
40. *Kafar bi-ikkar.*
41. *Min.*
42. A reference to Elisha ben Abuyah. See Ḥagigah 15a.
43. See ch. 1, section vii, p. 53. David R. Blumenthal, *The Commentary of R. Ḥoter ben Shelomoh to the Thirteen Principles of Maimonides* (Leiden, 1974), p. 52 n. 2 points out that Maimonides seems to use the terms interchangeably.
44. Maimonides codifies the obligation to love a fellow Jew in 'Laws of Ethics', vi. 3. At 'Laws of the Murderer', xiii. 14 Maimonides strongly implies that it is permissible to hate a Jew who does not believe in *ikkar ha-dat* (the basis or fundament of religion).
45. See 'Laws of Idolatry', ii. 5–6, v. 5, and x. 1. See also *Book of Commandments*, negative commandments 17–21. Note well that at 'Laws of Ethics', vi. 5, Maimonides states that it is forbidden to hate a fellow Israelite.
46. See ch. 1, section iii.
47. *qawā'id al-i'tiqād.*
48. Kafiḥ, p. 217.
49. *qā'ida*; Maimonides explicitly refers to the principles laid down in *Ḥelek* in the previous sentence.
50. Kafiḥ, p. 223. See further Maimonides' commentary on Mishnah Ḥullin i. 2 and his 'Laws of Testimony', xi. 10.
51. *Ikkarei ha-Dat.*
52. From the Hebrew it is evident that Maimonides sees the affirmation of God's unity as equivalent to the prohibition of idolatry; in effect, the two are one principle. This is significant in light of the discussion in ch. 1, section v of the present work.
53. Isadore Twersky, *Introduction to the Code of Maimonides* (New Haven, 1980), pp. 474–5 (henceforth: Twersky) points out that there is no talmudic source for Maimonides' position here. Maimonides codified this as law, it would appear, not on the basis of halakhic

precedents, but on the basis of his definition of what it means to be a Jew.

It is enlightening to compare Maimonides' text here with the talmudic source on which it is apparently based. Yevamot 47a–b (in the Soncino translation) reads as follows:

> Our Rabbis taught: If at the present time a man desires to become a proselyte, he is to be addressed as follows: 'What reason have you for desiring to become a proselyte? Do you not know that Israel at the present time are persecuted and oppressed, despised, harassed and overcome by afflictions?' If he replies, 'I know and yet am unworthy', he is accepted forthwith and is given instruction in some of the minor and some of the major commandments ... He is also told of the punishment for the transgression of the commandments ... And as he is informed of the punishment for the transgression of the commandments, so he is informed of the reward granted for their fulfilment ...

There is no reference here to the 'principles of religion' at all, no demand to 'expatiate on them at length', and no instructions against expatiating at length upon the commandments. These are the issues which have no apparent rabbinic source.

54. The printed editions read *epikorsim*, not 'sectarians', here. That 'sectarians' is the correct reading is attested to by the passage in Maimonides' responsa discussed below. Since 'sectarians' are not Israelites, it is permissible to hate them; see above, ch. 1 n. 45.

55. See Joshua Blau, *et al.* (eds.), Moses b. Maimon, *Responsa* (Jerusalem, 1957), responsum 263 (ii. 495–9).

56. Responsum 264 (ii. 499–501).

57. It is interesting to note that many Karaite discussions of dogma emphasize the fact that animals slaughtered by heretics may not be eaten. See Daniel J. Lasker, 'Hashpa'at ha-Rambam al Maḥshavto ha-Philosophit shel ha-Kara'i Elijah Bashyaẓi', *Jerusalem Studies in Jewish Thought*, iii (1984), p. 408 n. 16.

58. See 'Laws of Rebels', iii. 2, 'Theft', xi. 2, and 'Murderer', xii. 9.

59. See 'Idolatry', ii. 5, 'Testimony', xi. 10, and *Guide*, i. 36 (p. 85). In this last text Maimonides maintains that one who denies God's incorporeality — even if because of faulty education — is an *ukaffir* (denier; Hebrew: *kofer*). Portions of this text are quoted in ch. 1 n. 180. I have no way of accounting for the curious fact that Maimonides fails to extend his condemnation of the *epikoros*, denier, and sectarian as excluded from the community of Israel to issues of personal status (*ishut*) and usury. In this connection mention ought to be made of Gerald Blidstein's interesting discussion, 'Who is not a Jew? — The Medieval Discussion', *Israel Law Review*, xi (1976), pp. 369–90.

60. References to the beliefs embodied in all but the last of the thirteen principles are scattered thoughout the *Book of Knowledge*: principle 1, 'Laws of the Foundations of the Torah', i. 1–6; principle 2, 'Foundations', i. 6–7; principle 3, 'Foundations', i. 7–8; principle 4, 'Foundations', i. 1; principle 5, 'Laws of Idolatry', ii. 1; principle 6, 'Foundations', vii. 1; principle 7, 'Foundations', vii. 6 and viii. 3; principle 8, 'Foundations', vii–ix; principle 9, 'Foundations', ix. 1; principle 10, 'Foundations', ii. 9–10; principle 11, 'Laws of Repentance', viii; principle 12, 'Repentance', ix. 2. Principle 13 is listed with all the others (except the eleventh) in 'Repentance', iii.

61. Abravanel, ch. 5, first objection, p. 74.

62. Nachum L. Rabinovitch, *Yad Peshutah* (Commentary on 'Laws of Repentance') (Jerusalem, 1977), p. 36.

63 *Minim.*

64 *Meshummad.*

65. *Zur.* See ch. 1 n. 220.

66. Moses Hyamson (ed. and trans.), *Maimonides' Book of Knowledge* (New York, 1974), p. 84b. The text quoted here immediately follows a quotation from Isa. 60: 21 ('Thy people are all righteous . . .'), thus connecting this discussion with Mishnah Sanhedrin x. 1.

67. There are actually only twenty-two categories listed; Maimonides, however, divides the 'apostates' and the 'informers' into two groups each, thus reaching the number twenty-four.

68. Were I a disciple of Leo Strauss I would be hard put to resist mentioning that this division parallels his division of the *Guide* into 'Views' and 'Actions'. See Leo Strauss, 'How to Begin to Study the *Guide of the Perplexed*', in Shlomo Pines's translation of the *Guide* (Chicago, 1963), pp. xi–xii. My own view is that this is of no particular importance.

69. These two points were noted by Hyman, p. 132.

70. See ch. 1, section iv.

71. See Rabinovitch, p. 59 and Ya'akov Stieglitz, 'Yod-Gimmel ha-Ikkarim le-ha-Rambam', *Sinai*, lviii (1965), p. 59. (Henceforth: Stieglitz.)

72. The significance of this will become evident in ch. 1, section vii.

73. Stieglitz, p. 60.

74. Ibid.

75. For suggestions about why Maimonides chose to posit thirteen principles precisely, see ch. 1, section iv.

76. On Duran see ch. 3 of the present work.

77. Job 31: 2: 'The portion [*helek*] of God from above . . .'

78. Ch. x, (Venice, 1590), p. 15b, See p. 93f.

79. Isa. 17: 14: 'This is the portion [*helek*] of them that spoil us . . .' i.e., those who deny that the Torah was divinely revealed 'spoil us'.

80. As mentioned above in ch. 1 n. 4, Maimonides' text of the mishnah lacked the phrase, 'is not taught in the Torah'.
81. Jer. 10: 6 and 51: 19: '. . . Jacob's portion [*helek*] . . .'
82. See Ta'anit 5b.
83. Literally, 'the early ones'. I do not know to whom, if anyone, Duran is referring.
84. The last word in the verse, *tesham*, is construed as a *notarikon* (acronym) for the three Hebrew words *torah* (Torah), *sakhar* (reward), and *meziut* (existence).
85. The order is determined by the *notarikon* explained in the previous note.
86. Duran, *Magen Avot* (Leghorn, 1785), p. 2b (bottom).
87. See ch. 5, section i.
88. Hyman, pp. 127–8.
89. See Abravanel, ch. 10, pp. 98–100.
90. See ch. 1, n. 157.
91. Deut. 6: 4.
92. See *Guide*, i. 35, and Lenn Evan Goodman, 'Maimonides' Philosophy of Law', *Jewish Law Annual*, i (1978), pp. 94–5.
93. Lest it be objected that Mosaic prophecy is not a species of the genus 'prophecy' for Maimonides (see *Guide*, ii. 35 , p. 367) let it be noted that Maimonides says there that '. . . to my mind the term *prophet* used with reference to Moses and the others is amphibolous [Arab.: *bi-taškīk*; Heb.: *be-sippuk*]'. In *Millot ha-Higayon*, xiii Maimonides defines amphiboly as follows:

> But the amphibolous term is a term applied to two or more objects because of something which they have in common but which does not constitute the essence of each one of them . . . Hence it resembles a univocal term in so far as it is applied to these objects because they have something in common, and it also resembles the absolute homonym because the essence of one is different from that of the other. It is therefore called amphibolous.

(See Israel Efros, ed. and trans., *Millot ha-Higayon* (New York, 1938), p. 60). Thus, Mosaic prophecy may not be a species of prophecy *simpliciter*, but it is also not entirely unlike it.

This position is strengthened by a comment of Maimonides at *Guide*, iii. 45 (p. 576):

> It is known that the fundamental principle of belief in prophecy precedes the belief in the Torah. For if there is no prophet, there can be no Torah. The prophet receives prophetic revelation only through the intermediary of an angel . . . Even in the case of *Moses our Master*, his prophetic mission is inaugurated through an *angel* . . . Consequently it has been made clear that belief in the existence of angels precedes the belief in prophecy, and the belief in prophecy precedes the belief in the Torah.

94. Gersonides would demur. That Maimonides would not is indicated by his discussion in *Guide*, iii. 18–19.
95. See Joseph Albo, *Sefer Ha-Ikkarim*, ed. and trans. Isaac Husik, 5 vols. (Philadelphia, 1946), i. 4 (vol. i, p. 64).
96. *Ikkarim*, i. 4 (vol. i., p. 69).
97. See ch. 6.
98. *Derekh Emunah* (Constantinople, 1522), p. 99d. For commentary on this, see ch. 7, section ii.
99. Ibid., pp. 101d–102a. For commentary, see ch. 7, section ii.
100. See *Rosh Amanah*, xvi. 147.
101. See *Guide*, i. 51–60 and H. A. Wolfson, 'Maimonides on Negative Attributes', *Studies in the History of Philosophy and Religion*, ii (Cambridge, Mass., 1977), pp. 195–230.
102. See *Guide*, ii. 32 where Maimonides asserts that prophecy is a natural phenomenon (with, of course, one crucial exception).
103. David Neumark, *Toledot ha-Ikkarim be-Yisrael*, ii (Odessa, 1919), p. 151.
104. Meyer Waxman, 'Maimonides as Dogmatist', *CCAR Yearbook*, xlv (1935), p. 404.
105. Stieglitz, p. 59.
106. Rabinovitch, p. 59.
107. Scholom Ben-Chorin, *Jüdische Glaube* (Tübingen, 1975), p. 30.
108. '. . . the greatest of His rewards is the world to come . . .' See above, p. 000.
109. See N. Arieli, 'Torat ha-Ikkarim shel ha-Rambam', MA thesis (Hebrew University, 1971), and 'Mavo li-She'eilat ha-Ikkarim be-Yahadut', *Da'at*, xi (1983), pp. 19–38.
110. See *Guide*, iii. 51.
111. Such worship is idolatry (see 'Laws of Idolatry', i. 1); the second principle comes to forbid idolatry. If principle 5 is 'theological' why isn't principle 2?
112. See especially *Guide*, iii. 18–19.
113. Hyman, pp. 127–8.
114. Hyman, pp. 141–2.
115. Hyman thus disagrees with Arieli on the status of the fifth principle.
116. Hyman, pp. 134–6.
117. Stieglitz, pp. 59–60, notes the difference, but not by way of examining the structure of the thirteen principles.
118. See, for example, Saul Lieberman, *Hilkhot ha-Yerushalmi le-ha Rambam* (New York, 1947), 1 n. 16 and Twersky, p. 339.
119. See ch. 1, section vii.
120. Stieglitz, pp. 60–1.
121. Rabinovitch, pp. 50–9, esp. p. 54.
122. Cited by Hymanson, ad loc.

123. Cited ad loc by Jacob Cohen in his source notes to the Mossad ha-Rav Kook (Jerusalem, 1964) edition of the *Book of Knowledge* under the general editorship of Saul Lieberman. The variations to this text cited ad loc. in *Dikdukei Soferim* make Maimonides' dependence upon it perfectly clear.

124. Hebrew: *Zevul*. Defined as the Temple at Rosh ha-Shanah 17a (see also Rashi, ad loc.). See M. S. Zukermandel, *Tosefta*, 2nd edn. (Jerusalem, 1938), p. 434.

125. Abravanel, *Rosh Amanah*, xxiii, p. 197.

126. See ch. 7.

127. Abravanel, *Rosh Amanah*, xxiii, p. 194.

128. See Maimonides' peroration at the end of the principles (above, p. 16) and above, ch. 1, section ii. On axiomatic vs. dogmatic interpretations of the principles, see ch. 3, section ii and ch. 4, section iii.

129. See ch. 1, section vii.

130. *Studies in Judaism*, 1st series (Philadelphia, 1905), p. 179.

131. Neumark, ii. 130–1. See also Hartwig Hirschfeld, 'Creed (Jewish)', *Encyclopedia of Religion and Ethics* (New York, 1955), iv. 246.

132. Hyman, p. 136. There is, it seems to me, good reason to doubt the correctness of Hyman's last claim. See Shalom Rosenberg, 'Ḥeker ha-Mikra ba-Maḥashavah ha-Yehudit ha-Ḥadashah', in Uriel Simon (ed.), *Ha-Mikra ve-Anaḥnu* (Tel Aviv, 1979), pp. 86–119, esp. p. 90 and Yonah ben-Sasson, '*Mishnato ha-Historit shel ha-Rambam*', in Y. Cohen (ed.), *Ḥevrah ve-Historiah* (Jerusalem, 1980), pp. 543–632, esp. pp. 583–91. See further Daniel Lasker, *Jewish Philosophical Polemics Against Christianity in the Middle Ages* (New York, 1977), pp. 32–3.

133. Hebrew University, 1959. Reprinted by Jacob Twersky (Tel Aviv, n.d.). For similar — but not identical — positions, see Eliezer Schweid, 'Ẓidukan ha-Ḥinukhi ve-ha-Medini shel Miẓvot ha-Emunah le-fi Mishnat ha-Rambam', in *Ta'am ve-Hakashah* (Ramat Gan, 1970), pp. 80–104 and Barry Mesch, 'Principles of Judaism in Maimonides and Joseph ibn Caspi', in J. Reinharz and D. Swetschinski (eds.), *Mystics, Philosophers, and Politicians: Essays in Jewish Intellectual History in Honor of A. Altmann* (Durham, NC, 1982), pp. 85–98.

134. Berman, p. 139.

135. Berman, p. xvii and p. 137.

136. i.e., the masses.

137. Berman, pp. xvii–xviii and pp. 137–8.

138. Hyman, p. 137. To the best of my knowledge, Berman has never publicly disavowed this interpretation of his views.

139. For a very similar position see Shlomo Pines, 'Translator's

Introduction: The Philosophic Sources of *The Guide of the Perplexed*', in his translation of the *Guide*, pp. cxviii–cxix.

140. For an exposition of a position which sees much of Maimonides' writings in this light see Shlomo Pines, 'The Limitations of Human Knowledge According to al-Farabi, ibn Bajja, and Maimonides', in I. Twersky (ed.), *Studies in Medieval Jewish History and Literature* (Cambridge, Mass., 1979), pp. 82–96.

141. See ch. 1, section vii.

142. Hyman, p. 143. Hyman traces the origins of his approach to Julius Guttmann's *Philosophies of Judaism* (New York, 1964), pp. 178–9.

143. David Hartman, *Maimonides: Torah and Philosophic Quest* (Philadelphia, 1976), p. 229 n. 31 (henceforth: Hartman).

144. Hyman, p. 137. For further discussion of Maimonides' opinion on this issue see Z. Harvey, 'R. Ḥasdai Crescas u-Vikorto al ha-Osher ha-Philosophi', *Proceedings of the Sixth World Congress of Jewish Studies*, iii (1977), pp. 143–9.

145. Hyman, pp. 125–6.

146. *Guide*, i. 35 (pp. 79–80 in the Pines translation).

147. i. 35 (p. 81).

148. p. 510.

149. ii. 40 (p. 384).

150. pp. 8–9. See Twersky, pp. 362–3 and Shlomo Pines, 'Translator's Introduction', pp. cxviii–cxvix. See also W. Zev Harvey, 'Bein Philosophiah Medinit le-Halakhah be-Mishnat ha-Rambam', *Iyyun*, xxix (1980), pp. 198–212, for an interpretation of the relationship between halakhah and philosophy in Maimonides which complements the view being urged here.

151. iii. 54 (p. 633). See Twersky, p. 474.

152. See Hartman, pp. 53, 54, and 64. My claim about why Maimonides posited his principles may be clarified by reference to a point emphasized by Leo Strauss in 'The Literary Character of the *Guide of the Perplexed*', in S. W. Baron (ed.), *Essays on Maimonides* (New York, 1941), pp. 37–91. Strauss notes Maimonides' distinction between 'the true science of the law' and the science of the law in its usual sense (*fiqh*) (p. 38). For Strauss, the *Mishneh Torah* is a work of *fiqh* — the legalistic study of the law or the science of the law in its practical aspect — or halakhah purely. The *Guide*, on the other hand, deals not with what man ought to do, but with what man ought to think and believe. It deals, therefore, with the true science of the law, the science of the law in its theoretical aspect. My point here (and in this I follow Twersky and Hartman) — *contra* Strauss — is that for Maimonides proper understanding and observance of *fiqh* demands at least some attention to the the true science of the law.

153. See his statement at the end of the principles (above, p. 16) and Twersky, pp. 337–9 and 346–9.
154. Twersky, p. 361.
155. Kafiḥ, ii. 378.
156. See 'Laws of the Foundations of the Torah', iv. 10 and *Guide*, i, introduction (p. 6).
157. *Guide*, iii. 37 (p. 542); see also, 'Laws of Idolatry', ii. 4 and ii. 5.
158. Maimonides himself alludes to the special character of the principles dealing with God at 'Laws of Forbidden Intercourse', xiv. 2. See above, ch. 1 n. 53.
159. Maimonides was not flogging a dead horse. On the issue of Jewish anthropomorphists in his day see S. Rawidowicz, 'Ba'ayat ha-Hagshamah la-Rasag u-la-Rambam', in his *Iyyunim be-Maḥshevet Yisrael*, edited by B. Ravid, i (Jerusalem, 1969), pp. 171–233, esp. pp. 175–8; Bernard Septimus, *Hispano-Jewish Culture in Transition: The Career and Controversies of Ramah* (Cambridge, Mass., 1982), pp. 78–81 and 119 n. 108; Daniel Jeremy Silver, *Maimonidean Criticism and the Maimonidean Controversy: 1180–1240* (Leiden, 1965), pp. 138–40 and 160–1; and Isaiah Sonne, 'A Scrutiny of the Charges of Forgery Against Maimonides' "Letter on Resurrection"', *PAAJR*, xxi (1952), pp. 101–17, esp, pp. 110–16 and the sources cited there. Rabad's famous gloss to 'Laws of Repentance', iii ought also to be noted (see pp. 209 and 256).
  Attention may also be drawn to Colette Sirat, *Hagut Philosophit biymei ha-Benayim* (Jerusalem, 1975), pp. 13, 31, and 46 and to Isaac Barzilay, *Between Faith and Reason: Anti-Rationalism in Italian-Jewish Thought 1250–1650* (Paris, 1967), p. 139. On Muslim corporealists see A. J. Wensinck, *The Muslim Creed* (Cambridge, 1932), pp. 67–8 and 92–3 and Majid Fakhry, *A History of Islamic Philosophy* (New York, 1970), pp. 231 and 239.
  That Maimonides took the problem of Jewish anthropomorphists seriously is evidenced by the opening lines of *Guide*, i. 2 (p. 21) and by certain of his comments in his *Treatise on Resurrection* (ed. Kafiḥ, p. 71). Note also his attitude towards the *Shiur Komah* (see above, ch. 1 n. 27). H. A. Wolfson, however, rejects the idea that there were serious Jewish anthropomorphists in Maimonides' day. See his 'Jewish Kalam' in *Seventy-fifth Anniversary Volume of the JQR* (Philadelphia, 1967), pp. 544–73.
160. On this issue see Hyman, pp. 133–4 and 140, the editions of Maimonides' *Sefer ha-Mizvot* by Chaim Heller (Jerusalem, 1946), p. 35 n. 1 and J. Kafiḥ (Jerusalem, 1971), p. 53; Shlomo Goren, *Torat ha-Mo'adim* (Tel Aviv, 1963–4), pp. 88–104; Simon Rawidowicz, 'On Maimonides' *Sefer ha-Madda*', in his *Studies in Jewish*

Thought (Philadelphia, 1974), pp. 317–23; and, importantly, Warren Zev Harvey's Ph.D. dissertation, 'Ḥasdai Crescas' Critique of the Theory of the Acquired Intellect' (Columbia University, 1973), pp. 218–9.

161. This point, which needs to be restated from time to time, is emphasized by David Hartman in '"Iggeret ha-Shmad" le-Rabbenu Moshe ben Maimon', *Jerusalem Studies in Jewish Thought*, ii (1982–3), pp. 362–403.

162. See S. Goldman, 'The Halachic Foundation of Maimonides' Thirteen Principles', H. J. Zimmels, *et al.* (eds.), *Essays Presented to Chief Rabbi Brodie on the Occasion of his Seventieth Birthday* (London, 1967), pp. 111–17 and especially Rabinovitch on 'Laws of Repentance', iii *passim*. See also above, ch. 1 nn. 122–4.

163. See Hyman, p. 140.

164. See *Guide*, i. 35.

165. See Hyman, p. 142.

166. Hyman, pp. 134–6.

167. pp. 80–1.

168. It should be noted that I am not claiming that Maimonides himself believed in physical resurrection (although I myself tend to believe that he did); rather, I claim that he accepted the principle of divine retribution and cited resurrection as an example of that retribution which had the sanction of tradition and could be easily appreciated by the masses.

169. This point has been emphasized by H. A. Wolfson, *The Philosophy of the Kalam* (Cambridge, Mass., 1976), p. 47, Hartman, pp. 128–9 and p. 243 n. 58, and Twersky, p. 362 n. 15 and pp. 497–500. Shlomo Pines, however ('Translator's Introduction', p. cxxxiii), dismisses it as a 'convenient fiction'. See also L. V. Berman, 'Maimonides, the Disciple of Alfarabi', *Israel Oriental Studies*, iv (1974), pp. 154–78, esp. p. 167 and Leo Strauss, 'Progress or Return? The Contemporary Crisis in Western Civilization', *Modern Judaism*, i (1981), pp. 17–34, esp. p. 23. It is worthy of note that Samuel ibn Tibbon, at least, believed in the hidden metaphysical tradition. See his *Ma'amar Yikkavu ha-Mayim*, edited by J. Bisseliches (Pressburg, 1837), ch. 22 (p. 173). Compare D. J. Silver, *Maimonidean Criticism and the Maimonidean Controversy: 1180–1240* (Leiden, 1965), pp. 140–1.

170. *Guide*, iii, introduction (p. 415).

171. *Guide*, i. 71 (p. 175).

172. p. 67.

173. The *Commentary on the Mishnah* was Maimonides' first rabbinic work.

174. On 'the masses' see ch. 1 n. 187.

175. See the statement at the end of the principles, above, p. 16.

176. One might ask why Maimonides thought that the adoption of a Muslim model of theological discourse would not stimulate opposition. I suggest that the Jews of Muslim in Maimonides' day were sufficiently assimilated to have adopted a number of Muslim categories of thought; the adoption of one more would hardly cause many raised eyebrows. This idea receives support from the findings of S. D. Goitein, *A Mediterranean Society*, iii: *The Community* (Berkeley, 1971), pp. 273–311, especially pp. 275 and 289–99. See also Goitein's 'Jewish Society and Institutions Under Islam', in H. H. Ben-Sasson and S. Ettinger (eds.), *Jewish Society Through the Ages* (New York, 1971), pp. 170–84. Further in this connection see D. Baneth, 'Sifriyato shel Rofe be-Miẓrayim biymei ha-Rambam', *Tarbiẓ*, xxx (1961), pp. 171–85. That Maimonides felt obligated to warn the readers of his introduction to *Ḥelek* against reading Arabic texts on history, politics, and poetry (Kafiḥ, p. 210) indicates the extensive acculturation of his audience.

177. Note that beyond the fact that the five points adduced in the introduction to summarize Muslim approaches to dogma (p. 7) all apply to Maimonides, he also uses the same terminology adopted by many Muslim authors on the subject, calling his principles *qawaʿīd*.

178. See Maimonides' *Iggeret ha-Shmad* in J. Kafiḥ (ed.), *Iggerot ha-Rambam* (Jerusalem, 1972), pp. 105–20. This text is translated by Leon D. Stitskin in *Letters of Maimonides* (New York, 1977), pp. 34–69. On this text, see Haym Soloveitchik, 'Maimonides' *Iggeret Ha-Shemad*: Law and Rhetoric', in Leo Landman (ed.), *Rabbi J. H. Lookstein Memorial Volume* (New York, 1980), pp. 281–319 and the article by Hartman cited above in ch. 1 n. 161. Maimonides' *Iggeret ha-Shmad* continues what might be called a family tradition. See his father's 'Letter of Consolation' in Franz Kobler, *Letters of the Jews Through the Ages* (London, 1952), i. 166–77.

179. I wish to thank Professor Barry Kogan who suggested this line of thought to me.

180. Support for the claim that Maimonides distinguished between the salvific status of some of his principles may be found in the examination of a number of (admittedly disparate) texts. At the end of *Guide*, i. 36 (p. 85) he writes:

> If, however, it should occur to you that one who believes in the corporeality of God should be excused because of his having been brought up in this doctrine or because of his ignorance and the shortcomings of his apprehension, you ought to hold a similar belief with regard to *an idolator*; for he only worships idols because of his ignorance or because of his upbringing . . . Accordingly there is no excuse for one who does not accept the authority of men who inquire into the truth and are engaged in speculation if he himself is incapable of engaging in such speculation.

In this text Maimonides explicitly denies that inadvertence in general and miseducation in particular is an exculpating factor with regard to heresy concerning God's incorporeality, the third of his thirteen principles. This should be contrasted with the following text from 'Laws of Rebels', iii. 1–3:

> He who repudiates the Oral Law is not to be identified with the rebellious elder spoken of in Scripture but is classed with the *epikorsim* whom any person has a right to put to death . . . This applies only to one who repudiates the Oral Law as a result of his reasoned opinion and conclusion, who walks lightmindedly in the stubbornness of his heart, denying first the Oral Law, as did Zadok and Boethus and all who went astray. But their children and grandchildren, who misguided by their parents, are raised among the Karaites and trained in their views, are like a child taken captive by them and raised in their religion . . .

(trans A. Hershman, *The Book of Judges* (New Haven, 1949), pp. 143–4). In this text (and in his commentary on Mishnah Ḥullin i. 2 (in Rabbi Kafiḥ's edition)) Maimonides explicitly allows miseducation to count as an exculpating factor with respect to heresy concerning the oral Torah, a matter taught explicitly in the eighth of Maimonides' thirteen principles. (My thanks to Rabbi Y. Kellner for drawing my attention to 'Rebels', iii and to Prof. Gerald Blidstein for drawing my attention to the commentary on Ḥullin i. 2.)

181. Maimonides makes reference to a composition on the *uṣul al din* ('principles of religion') in his medical aphorisms. See S. Muntner (ed.), *Pirkei Moshe* (Jerusalem, 1959), p. 381 and J. Kafiḥ (ed.), *Iggerot ha-Rambam* (Jerusalem, 1972), p. 159. Kafiḥ, p. 148 n. and p. 159 n., maintains that this text was written before the *Guide*. If he is correct, this may be a reference to the thirteen principles. L. V. Berman, however, in 'The Structure of Maimonides' *Guide of the Perplexed*', *Proceedings of the Sixth World Congress of Jewish Studies*, iii (Jerusalem, 1977), p. 13 n., takes this to be a reference to the *Guide*.

There is an explicit reference to the thirteen principles in a work attributed to Maimonides, the *Ma'amar ha-Yiḥud* (edited by Moritz Steinschneider and published by him in Berlin, 1847), p. 28. On this text and on the controversy over its authenticity, see Jacob I. Dienstag, 'Moshe Steinschneider Ke-Ḥoker ha-Rambam', *Sinai*, lxvi (1970), pp. 348–50.

182. See the seventh principle (above, p. 12 ff) and the *Guide*, i. 34–5.

183. See *Guide*, iii. 51 (p. 619).

184. i.e., so that the masses would at least know them by tradition if not by demonstration.

185. See I Kgs. 14: 9.

186. J. Kafiḥ (ed. and trans.), *Iggerot ha-Rambam*, pp. 72–3.

187. i.e., individuals having rabbinic erudition but no philosophical training. It is appropriate here, I think, to take note of a question which has hitherto received too little attention: who are the masses according to Maimonides? Maimonides distinguishes, it seems to me, among three groups of people. The lowest category consists of 'children, women [*sic*], stupid ones, and those of a defective natural disposition' (*Guide*, i. 35, p. 81). These, apparently, are those who are cautioned not to read the commentary on *Ḥelek* (Kafiḥ, p. 203), although they ought to be taught the truth concerning God's incorporeality to the extent that they can understand it (*Guide*, i. 35, p. 81). It is evident that the commentary on *Ḥelek* is not addressed to these people, both because Maimonides cautions them not to read it and because it contains a discussion of the service of God from love as opposed to fear, and Maimonides explicitly warns against teaching this doctrine to 'children, women, and the generality of the ignorant [*kelal amei ha-areẓ*]', in 'Laws of Repentance', x. 5.

The second category consists of the rabbinically erudite but philosophically ignorant. This group is described in the 'Parable of the Palace' (*Guide*, iii. 51) and is the primary audience for Maimonides' rabbinic works (including the commentary on *Ḥelek*), as is made evident in the passage from 'Resurrection' cited here.

The members of the third group are individuals like Maimonides' student described in the introduction to the *Guide*: persons having both rabbinic erudition and philosophical sophistication.

The principles, it seems, are addressed to the second group in the expectation that these individuals will not only accept and study them but will, in turn, convey them in some appropriate fashion, to the ignorant masses who comprise the first group.

188. Isaac Abravanel, *Ma'amar Kazer be-Ve'ur Sod ha-Moreh*, published with his answers to the questions of Saul Ashkenazi (Venice, 1574; reprinted in Westmead (England) by Gregg International in 1972 and in Jerusalem by the *Sifriyah le-Maḥshevet Yisrael* in 1967), pp. 21b–26a. (This text also appears at the end of many editions of the *Guide*.)

189. See Simon Rawidowicz's refutation of Abravanel's thesis in his 'She'elat Mivnehu shel *Moreh Nevukhim*', *Hebrew Studies in Jewish Thought* [*Iyyunim be-Maḥshevet Yisrael*] (by S. Rawidowicz), i (Jerusalem, 1969), pp. 288–90. See also David Neumark, *Toledot ha-Ikkarim*, ii. 131 for a position similar in some respects to Abravanel's.

190. See Rawidowicz, pp. 290–1.

191. In addition to Rawidowicz, see Leo Strauss (see above, ch. 1 n. 68), pp. xi–xiii and L. V. Berman (see above, ch. 1 n. 181), pp. 7–13.

192. See *Guide*, ii. 2 (p. 253), where Maimonides says that an analysis of the Separate Intellects is necessary for an understanding of creation.

Creation, as we just noted, is intimately linked to prophecy. See also the seventh of Maimonides' thirteen principles (see above, p. 13) where Maimonides says that an analysis of angels (i.e., Separate Intellects) is a prerequisite for an understanding of Mosaic prophecy. See also ch. 1 n. 93.

193. As Herbert Davidson points out, Maimonides, following Aristotle, held eternity and necessity to imply each other. See his 'Maimonides' Secret Position on Creation', in I. Twersky (ed.), *Studies in Medieval Jewish History and Literature* (Cambridge, Mass., 1979), p. 18. This being so, were the world eternal *a parte ante* it could not have been created by God's free will. In an eternal, necessarily existent world revelation can only be interpreted as a purely natural phenomenon. This reduces it to nothing other than a consequence of Moses' perfection and makes impossible its claim to immutability, for why could not another Moses arise?

194. See above, ch. 1 n. 156.

195. See *Guide*, iii. 27.

196. See Hartman, pp. 65–86, esp. pp. 81–2.

197. One further point should be addressed here. If what I have said here is correct, why then does not Maimonides appeal explicitly to the thirteen principles in the *Guide?* The answer to this question lies in the fact that the *Guide* is, as Maimonides intimated in his introduction and as Leo Strauss forcefully reminded us, an esoteric book. One of the secret teachings of the *Guide*, I suggest, is that the teachings of philosophy, properly understood (i.e., as adumbrated in the *Guide*) do not conflict with the Torah, properly understood (i.e., as adumbrated in the *Guide*). This is a dangerous teaching in the hands of the philosophically unsophisticated: not understanding philosophy properly (e.g., by slavishly following Aristotle even when — as with creation according to Maimonides — he is wrong), they might be led to give up important beliefs of the Torah. Had he openly advertised his claim concerning philosophy and Torah by exoterically structuring the *Guide* on the thirteen principles Maimonides might have led philosophically unsophisticated persons astray. They might have used his authority to justify extensive allegorizations of Scripture in an attempt to make it accord with the 'truth' which they mistakenly understood philosophy to teach.

198. See Duran, *Ohev Mishpat*, viii (ch. 3, section i of the present work) and Abravanel, *Rosh Amanah*, iii (p. 70) for examples of beliefs which medieval authors thought ought to have been included in the thirteen principles.

199. 'Laws of Repentance', v. 3. See also the eighth of Maimonides' 'Eight Chapters', in Kafih's edition of Maimonides' *Commentary on Mishnah Avot* in his *Mishnah im Perush Rabbenu Moshe ben Maimon*

(Jerusalem, 1963), iv. 404. For an English translation see R. L. Weiss and C. E. Butterworth, *Ethical Writings of Maimonides* (New York, 1975), p. 93. See further *Teshuvot ha-Rambam*, ed. J. Blau (Jerusalem, 1957–61), ii. 715.

200. *'uṣul.*

201. *qāwa'id.*

202. i. 71 (p. 182); ii. 13 (p. 282); ii. 23 (p. 321); ii. 29 (p. 346); iii. 50 (p. 613).

203. iii. 17 (p. 469); iii. 20 (p. 482); with explicit reference to human choice, see iii. 32 (p. 529).

204. iii. 24 (p. 500).

205. iii. 24 (pp. 500–1).

206. ii. 2 (p. 253); in support of this interpretation see Rabbi Kafiḥ's note there (p. 170).

207. See Alexander Marx, 'The Correspondence Between the Rabbis of Southern France and Maimonides about Astrology', *HUCA*, iii (1926), pp. 311–58. For creation, see p. 353; for choice, see pp. 354 and 355. This letter was translated from the original Hebrew into English by Ralph Lerner in R. Lerner and M. Mahdi (eds.), *Medieval Political Philosophy* (Ithaca, 1972), pp. 227–36. For creation, see p. 231, and for choice, pp. 233 and 234.

208. I don't think that I can fairly be accused here of trying to eat my cake and have it, too, even though I generally use an anachronistic methodology in this work, treating the corpus of Maimonides' writings as a more or less indivisible whole. I am not suggesting anything more important here, however, than a possible change in terminology on Maimonides' part. This is hardly a major deviation from my assumption that Maimonides is substantially consistent throughout his writings.

209. In his Hebrew translation of the commentary Rabbi Kafiḥ has 'Know that the great foundation of the Torah of Moses . . .' (p. 212). While this translation is also consistent with the Arabic original it is not consistent with Maimonides' stated position in the *Guide* (ii. 13) that creation is *a* foundation of the Torah, second in importance to belief in God's unity. Since Maimonides himself refers us to the *Guide* here it is safe to assume that the translation I offer here is preferable to that of Rabbi Kafiḥ. See also the translation of David Blumenthal (see above, ch. 1 n. 43), p. 91, which agrees with the translation offered here.

210. Kafiḥ, p. 212. Maimonides' statement, 'That you see me circling around the idea of the eternity of the world . . .' refers to his arguments for God's existence, unity, and incorporeality in the *Guide* which he bases on the assumption of the eternity of the world. See his statement in i. 71 (p. 182):

Thus it has become manifest to you that the proofs for the existence and the oneness of the deity and of His not being a Body ought to be procured from the starting point afforded by the supposition of the eternity of the world, for in this way the demonstration will be perfect, both if the world is eternal and if it is created in time. For this reason you will find that whenever, in what I have written in the books of jurisprudence, I happen to mention the foundations and start upon establishing the existence of the deity I establish it by discourses that adopt the way of the doctrine of eternity of the world . . .

(In the beginning of his classic work of 'jurisprudence', the *Mishneh Torah*, Maimonides mentions the 'foundations' — *yesodei ha-Torah* — and does indeed prove God's existence 'by discourses that adopt the way of the doctrine of the eternity of the world'.)

211. There is considerable debate over whether or not the manuscript is actually a Maimonides autograph and over whether or not the marginal notes and additions found in it were actually written by Maimonides. The manuscript is held in Oxford University Library (MS Pococke 295; Neubauer no. 404). A facsimile of it was published by Solomon D. Sassoon in his *Maimonidis Commentarius in Mischnam* (Copenhagen, 1961), ii. (The addition to the fourth foundation is found on plate no. 301). This manuscript, and others allied with it on the other orders of the Mishnah, formed the basis for Kafiḥ's edition. Sassoon (i. 33) and Kafiḥ (i. 6 of his edition) both insist that the manuscript and the additions were written by Maimonides himself. Rabbi Kafiḥ has recently reiterated this position in a letter he wrote to me, dated 12 Kislev 5741 (1980), in which he repeats that the handwriting in which the addition to the fourth principle is made is recognizable as that of Maimonides in his old age. Dr Avraham Nuriel was kind enough to show the addition to Prof. Shlomo Pines and to Dr Malachi Beit-Arié on my behalf, both of whom are of the opinion that it was written by Maimonides. S. M. Stern, in 'Perush ha-Mishnah bikhtav Yado shel ha-Rambam', *Tarbiz*, xxiii (1952), pp. 72–80 takes the position that the manuscript and additions were indeed written by Maimonides. Joshua Blau, 'Ha-Omnam Yesh be-Yadeinu Tofes shel Perush ha-Mishnah be-Ezem Ketav-Yado shel ha-Rambam?' *Tarbiz*, xxvii (1956), pp. 536–43, raises the possibility that the manuscript is not an autograph but that it is, rather, Maimonides' own working copy. Blau does not deny categorically, however, that the marginal notes were written by Maimonides. M. Lutzky, 'Ve-Katav Mosheh: Ḥamesh Teshuvot Autographiot shel ha-Rambam', *Ha-Tekufah*, xxx–xxxi (1946), pp. 679–704, esp. p. 683, maintains that at least some of the additions are in Maimonides' own hand. S. M. Stern and S. D. Sassoon respond to

the points raised by Blau (in his article in *Tarbiz*, xxvii) in 'Al Tofes Perush ha-Mishnah be-Ezem Ktav Yado shel ha-Rambam', *Tarbiz*, xxix (1960), pp. 261–7. Blau admits that Stern and Sassoon are correct in their ascription of the manuscript to Maimonides' own hand in 'Bi-Dvar Kitvei ha-Yad Perush ha-Mishnah la-Rambam, Pock. 295, Hunt. 117, ve-Sassoon 72, 73', *Tarbiz*, xxxiii (1964), p. 316. See further Joshua Blau and Alexander Scheiber, *Autograph ha-Rambam Me-Osef Adler u-me-Genizat Leningrad; Teyutat ha-Hakdamah le-Seder Toharot* (Jerusalem, 1981), p. 5.

212. With the likely exception of Shem Tov Falaquera. See his *Moreh ha-Moreh*, ed. J. Bisseliches (Pressburg, 1837), p. 168. My thanks to Prof. R. Jospe for drawing my attention to this passage.

213. See above, p. 17.

214. i.e., 'Laws of Repentance', iii, *Treatise on Resurrection*, and, if they do refer to the thirteen principles, the two texts described above in ch. 1 n. 181.

215. See above, ch. 1, section iii.

216. Joel Kraemer, 'Alfarabi's *Opinions of the Virtuous City* and Maimonides' *Foundations of the Law*', in Blau, *et al.* (eds.), *Studia Orientalia* (D. H. Baneth Memorial Volume) (Jerusalem, 1979), p. 136 n. 52.

217. 'Laws of Repentance', iii. 7 and *Book of Commandments*, positive commandments 1 and 2, negative commandment 1.

218. i.e., that without God the universe could not exist; but God and the world may have coexisted eternally. So Joseph ibn Kaspi, *Maskiyyot Kesef*, edited by S. Werbluner (Frankfurt, 1848), p. 100, interprets Maimonides. Kaspi's work was reproduced in *Sheloshah Kadmonei Mefarshei ha-Moreh* (Jerusalem, 1961).

219. See also Abraham Nuriel, 'Hiddush ha-Olam o Kadmuto al pi ha-Rambam', *Tarbiz*, xxxiii (1964), pp. 372–87. Nuriel argues that the term *al-bari* — at least in the *Guide* — does not refer to creation *ex nihilo*. See further Sara Klein-Braslavy, *Perush ha-Rambam le-Sippur Ma'aseh Bereshit* (Jerusalem, 1978), pp. 114–31, and, importantly, W. Z. Harvey, 'A Third Approach to Maimonides' Cosmogony-Prophetology Puzzle', *Harvard Theological Review*, lxxiv (1981), pp. 287–301, esp. p.296.

220. 'Laws of Repentance', iii. 7: '. . . he who denies that He alone is the First Cause and Rock [*zur*] of the Universe . . .' Rabad, in his gloss to this statement, was obviously troubled by Maimonides' terminology. By playing on the similarity between the words *zur* (rock), *zayyar* (artisan), and *yozer* (creator), he uses Genesis Rabbah i. 9 to show that Maimonides used *zur* in the sense of *yozer* and not in the sense of *zayyar*. See Isadore Twersky, *Rabad of Posquières*, rev. edn. (Philadelphia, 1980), p. 280 n. 41. Compare Albo, i. 12 (p. 120).

221. I would like to thank Dr Avraham Nuriel for suggesting this line of reasoning to me.
222. See S. D. Goitein, 'Moses Maimonides, Man of Action: A Revision of the Master's Biography in the Light of the Genizah Documents', in G. Nahon and C. Touati (eds.), *Hommage A Georges Vajda* (Louvain, 1980), pp. 155–67.
223. The view that Maimonides ultimately denied creation *ex nihilo* is held by, among others, Avraham Nuriel and W. Z. Harvey, (see above, ch. 1 n. 219), Colette Sirat, *Hagut Philosophit biymei ha-Benayim* (Jerusalem, 1975), p. 253, and L. V. Berman, 'Ibn Bajjah ve-ha-Rambam', p. xxv. See also Y. Glicker, 'Ha-Ba'ayah ha-Modalit ba-Philosophiah shel ha-Rambam', *Iyyun*, x (1969), pp. 190–1 and H. A. Davidson (see above, ch. 1 n. 180). In the Middle Ages this position was held by Joseph ibn Kaspi. See *Maskiyyot Kesef*, p. 100 (see above, ch. 1 n. 218) and Basil Herring, *Joseph ibn Caspi's Gevia Kesef* (New York, 1982), p. 108.
224. Among the medieval Jewish writers who dealt with the question of the principles of Judaism, Maimonides was one of the few who did not list creation as a principle in his (original) list; indeed, almost all the other authors insisted that it was the most important principle. See ch. 10.
225. See above, ch. 1 n. 220.
226. See above, ch. 1 n. 212.
227. See Blumenthal's edition (see above, ch. 1 n. 43), p. 91.
228. In the beginning of his polemic *Even Boḥan* ibn Shaprut paraphrases Maimonides' principles, introducing creation into the list. The work is preserved in many manuscripts. I am grateful to Dr Daniel Lasker for drawing my attention to it.
229. 'He preceded all that was created . . .' See Philip Birnbaum, *Daily Prayer Book* (New York, 1949), p. 12.
230. See *Derekh Emunah*, p. 101b.
231. See Abravanel, *Rosh Amanah*, xvi. 146, and his *Ma'amar Kazer* . . . (see above, ch. 1 n. 188), p. 24a.
232. See Neumark, ii. 132.
233. See Louis Jacobs, *Principles of the Jewish Faith* (New York, 1964), pp. 135–6.
234. See Shlomo Pines, *Toledot ha-Philosophiah ha-Yehudit me-ha-Rambam ad Spinoza* (Jerusalem, 1976–7), p. 17.
235. See Rabbi Kafiḥ's translation of the *Guide* (Jerusalem, 1972), ii. 21 n. 4. My thanks to Dr Daniel Lasker for this reference.
236. See Sirat (see above, ch. 1 n. 223), p. 227.
237. This, it turns out is not ibn Bilia's *Yesodot ha-Maskil*. See ch. 2.
238. *Ohev Mishpat*, viii (p. 13b). See p. 84.
239. Ibid.

240. pp. 13b–14a. See ch. 3, section i, p. 85.
241. p. 14a.
242. *Neveh Shalom* (Venice, 1575), i. 3 (p. 3b). For a similar position, see Bibago, *Derekh Emunah*, iii. 1 (p. 78d) and ch. 7 n. 16 of the present work.
243. See above, ch. 1, section ii.
244. Hyman, pp. 138–9; emphasis Hyman's.
245. *i'tiqād.*
246. Kafiḥ, p. 209.
247. Maimonides uses the term *epikoros* in a variety of ways in the *Mishneh Torah* but they are all related to one or another of the thirteen principles. See David Assaf, *Oẓar Leshon ha-Rambam* (Haifa, 1968), ii. 164–6, and above, ch. 1, section ii.
248. *Rosh Amanah*, xxiii. See ch. 8, p. 187 of the present work.
249. *Rosh Amanah*, xxiii, p. 197.
250. Isadore Twersky, *Introduction to the Code of Maimonides* (New Haven, 1980), p. 362 n.
251. Ibid., p. 361.
252. Ibid., p. 360.
253. Ibid.
254. Ibid.
255. See above, ch. 1 n. 53.
256. See above, ch. 1, section vii.
257. See above, ch. 1, section iii.
258. 'Laws of the Foundations of the Torah', i. 6.
259. See, for example, Steven S. Schwarzschild, 'A Note on the Nature of Ideal Society — A Rabbinic Study', in H. A. Strauss and H. G. Reissner (eds.), *Jubilee Volume Dedicated to Curt C. Silberman* (New York, 1969), pp. 86–105; Gershom Scholem, 'Towards an Understanding of the Messianic Idea in Judaism', in his *The Messianic Idea in Judaism* (New York, 1971), pp. 1–36; Amos Funkenstein, 'Maimonides: Political Theory and Realistic Messianism', *Miscellanea Mediaevalia*, xi (1977), pp. 81–103; and David Hartman, 'Sinai and Messianism' in his *Joy and Responsibility* (Jerusalem, 1978), pp. 232–58.
260. See Kafiḥ, pp. 207–9; 'Laws of Repentance', ix and 'Laws of Kings', xi–xii; and Kafiḥ's *Iggerot ha-Rambam* (see above, ch. 1 n. 178), pp. 16–60.
261. See Aviezer Ravitzky, 'Kefi Ko'aḥ ha-Adam — Yemot ha-Mashiaḥ be-Mishnat ha-Rambam', *Meshiḥiut ve-Eschatalogiah* (Jerusalem, 1983), p. 191 n. 1.
262. See Solomon Zeitlin, 'Maimonides', *American Jewish Yearbook*, xxxvii (1935), pp. 78–80.
263. See above, p. 16.

264. See above, p. 16.
265. See Neumark, ii. 151, Hyman, p. 129, and Abraham Nuriel, 'Musag ha-Emuhah ezel ha-Rambam', *Da'at*, ii–iii (1979), p. 44. According to Neumark, Maimonides uses cognitive terms in principles 7, 8, 12, and 13. I find Neumark's remarks concerning the thirteenth principle entirely unconvincing. Hyman cites Neumark without comment. According to Nuriel, Maimonides uses cognitive terms in principle 5, 7, and 12. In point of fact such terms appear only in principles 7, 8, and 12.
266. On the meaning of this term see Nuriel, p. 44.
267. On the meaning of this term see Nuriel, p. 44, and Fazlur Rahman, 'Some Key Ethical Concepts of the *Qur'an*', *Journal of Religious Ethics*, xi (1983), pp. 170–85.
268. On the meaning of this term see Shalom Rosenberg, 'Emunah ve-Kategoriot Epistimiot ba-Hagut ha-Yehudit ha-Beinaimit', in *Derakhim le-Emunah be-Yahadut* (Jerusalem, 1980), p. 87 and the sources cited there. See also Harry A. Wolfson, 'The Terms *Taṣawwur* and *Taṣdiq* in Arabic Philosophy and their Greek, Latin, and Hebrew Equivalents', *Studies in the History and Philosophy of Religion*, i (Cambridge, Mass., 1973), pp. 478–92.
269. See above, p. 26.
270. See ch. 10, section iii.

Chapter Two

1. Hoter's commentary was edited and translated by David R. Blumenthal in *The Commentary of R. Hoter ben Shelomoh to the Thirteen Principles of Maimonides* (Leiden, E. J. Brill, 1974).
2. Particularly striking in this regard is the fact that while many dozens of poems based on Maimonides' thirteen principles were composed, very few date from the thirteenth and fourteenth centuries. See Alexander Marx, 'A List of Poems on the Articles of the Creed', *JQR*, ix (1919), pp. 305–36. Of the eighty poems with which Marx deals, he dates one to the thirteenth century and four to the fourteenth; see poems 26, 40, 56, 62, and 70. There are a number of poems which Marx was not able to date, but even taking these into account the vast majority date from after 1400.
3. There are brief, informal, and passing references to principles or foundations in the writings of Nahmanides (1194–1270), Bahya ben Asher (thirteenth century), Joseph ibn Kaspi (*c*.1280–1340), Rabbenu Nissim ben Reuben Gerondi (*c*.1310–75), and R. Isaac ben Sheshet Perfet (1326–1408).
    In his *Commentary on Job* Nahmanides refers to belief in God's knowledge of particulars and belief in divine providence as

'corner-stones of the Torah of Moses'. See C. D. Chavel (ed.), *Kitvei Ramban* (Jerusalem, 1963), i. 17. In his sermon, 'The Law of the Eternal is Perfect', Naḥmanides calls creation, divine knowledge, and divine providence 'foundations of the Torah'. See C. D. Chavel (trans.), *Ramban: Writings and Discourses* (New York, 1978), i. 59 and 68–9 (Hebrew text in *Kitvei Ramban*, i. 153). For an unconvincing attempt to read a systematic account of the principles of Judaism into Naḥmanides' remarks see Chayim Henoch, *Ha-Ramban ke-Ḥoker u-ke-Mekubbal* (Jerusalem, 1978), pp. 159–79.

In his commentary on Lev. 1: 1 Rabbenu Baḥya speaks of three issues which are 'roots of the Torah and corner-stones of faith': creation, revelation, and resurrection. See C. D. Chavel (ed.), *Rabbenu Baḥya al ha-Torah* (Jerusalem, 1982), ii. 390–1. In his *Kad ha-Kemaḥ* Rabbenu Baḥya writes:

> The principle of the *Torah and commandment* [2 Chr. 14: 3] is faith [*emunah*] for he who lacks faith would have been better off had he not been created. It is a commandment dependent upon the heart. It consists of believing that the world has a creator, existent and one, and that he extends providence over the sublunar world with respect to the human species, both generally and particularly . . .

See C. D. Chavel (ed.), *Kitvei Rabbenu Bayḥa* (Jerusalem, 1969), p. 21. My thanks to Avinoam Kellner for drawing my attention to these texts.

In a number of places Joseph ibn Kaspi (*c.*1280–1340) relates to the opening paragraphs of Maimonides' 'Laws of the Foundations of the Torah' as an independent system of principles. See Barry Mesch, *Studies in Joseph ibn Caspi* (Leiden, 1975), pp. 105–6 and 'Principles of Judaism in Maimonides and Joseph ibn Caspi', in J. Reinharz and D. Swetschinski (eds.), *Mystics, Philosophers, and Politicians: Essays in Jewish Intellectual History in Honor of Alexander Altmann* (Durham, 1982), pp. 85–98, esp. pp. 91–2.

On Rabbenu Nissim see Sara Klein-Braslavy's two articles, 'Ma'amad Har Sinai be-Mishnato shel R. Nissim ben Reuven Gerondi', *Sinai*, lxxx (1977), pp. 26–37 and 'Terumato shel R. Nissim Gerondi le-Iẓuvan shel Torot ha-Ikkarim shel Ḥasdai Crescas ve-shel Yosef Albo', *Eshel Beer Sheva*, ii (1980), pp. 177–97.

Perfet refers to creation and divine providence over individuals as 'principles of our holy Torah' and as 'the supporting pillars' upon which the Torah rests. See his forty-fifth responsum, translated in M. M. Kellner, 'R. Isaac bar Sheshet's Responsum Concerning the Study of Greek Philosophy', *Tradition*, xv, no. 3 (1975), pp. 110–18 and *Tradition*, xv, no. 4 (1976), p. 134.

4. Daniel Jeremy Silver, *Maimonidean Criticism and the Maimonidean*

Controversy: 1180–1240 (Leiden, 1965), p. 32, points out that the text of the thirteen principles was not translated into Hebrew by Solomon ibn Ya'akov of Saragossa till 1290 or thereabouts and that the principles were therefore unknown to the controversialists in the thirteenth century. Were this correct we would have a possible explanation for why the principles do not figure in thirteenth-century Jewish literature at least.

Silver, however, was apparently unaware of the fact that Judah al-Ḥarizi (1170–1235) had translated the principles into Hebrew; they were available in that language, therefore, from early in the thirteenth century. Furthermore, many thirteenth-century Jewish philosophers knew Arabic and did not need translations in order to become familiar with the thirteen principles. On al-Ḥarizi's translation see the appendix.

5. Even Gersonides (1288–1344) is no exception to this generalization. His halakhic writings include a lost commentary on tractate Berakhot and two responsa. But this represents a small fraction of his overall output; moreover we have no evidence that Gersonides served in any sort of communal or rabbinic capacity. For details of his rabbinic writings see M. M. Kellner, 'R. Levi ben Gerson: A Bibliographical Essay', *Studies in Bibliography and Booklore*, xii (1979), pp. 13–23, esp. p. 22.

6. See Isadore Twersky, 'Aspects of the Social and Cultural History of Provençal Jewry', in H. H. Ben-Sasson and S. Ettinger (eds.), *Jewish Society Through the Ages* (New York, 1971), pp. 185–207, esp. pp. 190 and 204.

7. Ibid., p. 205.

8. It is interesting to contrast the position of a representative fifteenth-century figure such as Abraham Bibago in this regard. Bibago accepts the philosophical position that human felicity depends upon intellectual perfection but couples this with the claim that one can reach such felicity as well by the *Path of Faith* (the title of his major work). See ch. 7, section i.

9. My thanks to Dr Aviezer Ravitsky for starting me thinking along these lines. For a valuable treatment of many of the themes discussed here see his dissertation, 'Mishnato shel R. Zeraḥiah ben Shealtiel Ḥen ve-he-Hagut ha-Maimonit-Tibbonit ba-Me'ah ha-Yod-Gim-mel', (Hebrew University, 1977). See esp. pp. 2 and 58–9 and, in the English summary, p. ii.

10. This is not to say that thirteenth and fourteenth-century rabbinic figures were ignorant of philosophical issues. The example of Rabbenu Nissim refutes this supposition. See the articles by Klein-Braslavy cited above in ch. 2 n. 3.

11. See D. J. Silver, *Maimonidean Criticism . . .*, pp. 136 and 197. In this

regard it is interesting to compare W. Montgomery Watt, *Muslim Intellectual: A Study of al-Ghazali* (Edinburgh, 1963), p. 32: 'What stands out clearly from this list is that the bearers of the Greek sciences and the new Islamic philosophy were quite different from the bearers of Islamic religious learning.' See also p. 172.

12. On Abba Mari, see Daniel J. Silver, *Maimonidean Criticism . . .*, pp. 42–3; Joseph Sarachek, *Faith and Reason: the Conflict over the Rationalism of Maimonides* (New York, 1970), pp. 195–205; J. Gross, 'Notice sur Abba Mari de Lunel', *REJ*, iv (1882), pp. 192–207; Yizhak Baer, *A History of the Jews in Christian Spain* (Philadelphia, 1966), i. 289–305; Israel Zinberg, *A History of Jewish Literature*, iii (Philadelphia, 1973), pp. 66–73.

13. Published by M. J. Bisseliches in Pressburg, 1838 (photo-edition, New York, 1958).

14. *Avot*. Duran (see ch. 3, p. 86) uses the same term.

15. *Yesod Olam*. Perhaps, 'foundation of the world'.

16. On these 'contemporary preachers' see Zinberg (see above, ch. 2 n. 12), ii. 103–31.

17. On the question of whether or not Exod. 20: 2 constitutes a commandment, see ch. 4, p. 109ff.

18. Abba Mari is here positing God's incorporeality, simplicity, and unity as derivatives of God's existence. This may anticipate Duran's conception of fundamental and derived principles. See ch. 3, section ii.

19. Compare Maimonides, *Guide of the Perplexed*, ii. 25 and *Treatise on Resurrection* (ed. and trans. by Rabbi J. Kafih, *Iggerot ha-Rambam* [Jerusalem, 1972]), p. 94.

20. On belief in creation as a central principle see M. M. Kellner, 'Jewish Dogmatics After the Spanish Expulsion: Rabbis Isaac Abravanel and Joseph Ya'bes on Belief in Creation as an Article of Faith', *JQR*, lxxii (1982), pp. 178–87 and the present work, ch. 10, section iii.

21. Compare Maimonides, *Guide*, ii. 31.

22. On the connection between creation and the revelation of the Torah, compare Maimonides, *Guide*, ii. 25.

23. See Makkot 24a.

24. See Avodah Zarah 3b.

25. See Avot i. 4–15.

26. Abba Mari is referring to the first-century Aramaic paraphrase (*Targum*) of the prophets attributed to Jonathan ben Uzziel, a student of Hillel's. See Megillah 3a.

27. See Eccles. 8: 1 and Ta'anit 7b.

28. *Makhtir*.

29. See Eruvin 53b and Berakhot 4a. By using this expression Abba Mari

means that he consulted with rabbinic leaders before embarking upon his book.

30. See *Kuzari* i: 1.
31. See Eruvin 13a.
32. See Avot v. 17.
33. Chs. 4 and 5.
34. Ch. 18.
35. Ch. 5.
36. Ch. 4.
37. Chs. 4, 10, 15, and 18.
38. Chs. 12 and 18.
39. Chs. 4, 15, and 18.
40. Chs. 4 and 18.
41. See especially ch. 18.
42. i.e., by the hand of the prophet.
43. Ed. A. Jellinek (Vienna, 1875 (Jerusalem: Mekorot, 1970)), p. 65.
44. *Iggeret ha-Ḥalom*, edited by H. Malter in his article, 'Shem Tob ben Joseph Palquera', *JQR*, i (1910–11), pp. 151–81, 451–501. Our text appears on p. 489.
45. On Kokhavi see Henri Gross, *Gallia Judaica* (Amsterdam: 1969), pp. 53–4 and the sources cited there; and Adolf Neubauer, 'Documents inédits XIV: David Kokhabi', *REJ*, ix (1884), pp. 214–30 and the sources cited there. Kokhavi is the author of an important halakhic work, patterned on the *Mishneh Torah* of Maimonides, called variously *Sefer ha-Batim* (which name reflects the architectural motifs which dominate the structure of this book as they do the structure of *Migdal David*) and *Kiryat Sefer*. Portions of this text were published by Moshe Hershler in '*Sha'arei Bet ha-Mikdash* le-Rabbenu David ben Shmuel me-Estella (ha-Kokhavi)', *Sinai*, lxii (1968), pp. 199–228. The book was edited by M. J. Blau (New York, 1968). Further on Kokhavi, see Blau's introduction, pp. 8–10, and the references in Isadore Twersky, *Rabad of Posquières*, rev. edn. (Philadelphia, 1980), pp. xvii, 18, and 350. A portion of a chronicle which Kokhavi composed was published by Neubauer in the second volume of his *Medieval Jewish Chronicles* (Oxford, 1895), pp. 230–3.
46. Moritz Steinschneider collated a kind of analytical table of contents of the book from passages scattered through it. This he published in *Hebraeische Bibliographie* (*Ha-Mazkir*), viii (Berlin, 1865), pp. 63 and 100–3. The Institute of Microfilmed Hebrew Manuscripts at the Jewish National and University Library (JNUL) in Jerusalem has microfilms of two manuscripts of *Migdal David*. One is from the Günzberg Collection (Moscow), n. 234 (JNUL 16874); it has 382 pages and was copied in Avignon in 1396. The second manuscript dates from the fourteenth century and is held in the Palatina Library

in Parma, Italy (no. 3541; JNUL 14048). I used the Moscow manuscript. Moshe Hershler edited the complete text of the *Migdal David* (Jerusalem, Institute Schalem Sefunot Kadmonim, 1982). Unfortunately, this work, which contains a lengthy introduction, appeared too late for me to be able to use it in preparing this study; I provide page references to it in parentheses.

47. Throughout the introduction to *Migdal David* Kokhavi stresses his indebtedness to Maimonides.
48. pp. 1a–8b (pp. 12–24).
49. pp. 8b–9b (p. 25).
50. pp. 29a (p. 39).
51. pp. 29b (p. 40).
52. Ibid.
53. Kokhavi devotes considerable space to the elucidation of these principles. Principle 1: pp. 30b–49a (pp. 43–72); principle 2: pp. 49b–65b (pp. 73–101); principle 3: pp. 65b–86b (pp. 102–37); principle 4: pp. 86b–98a (pp. 138–58); principle 5: pp. 98a–105b (pp. 159–72); principle 6: pp. 105b–16b (pp. 173–94); principle 7: pp. 116b–20b (pp. 195–8).
54. Crescas patterned his proposed work, *Ner Elohim*, in the same way. See ch. 4, section i.
55. See Nehemiah Allony, 'David ibn Bilia vi-Yẓirotav', *Areshet* (1944), pp. 277–86. This article was reprinted in Allony's *Mi-Sifrut Yemei ha-Benayim* (Jerusalem, 1945), pp. 13–22.
56. This work was published, with a French translation, by Eliezer Askenasi in his *Divrei Ḥakhamim* (Metz, 1849). I compared Askenasi's text with Paris MS Heb. 661 and found no significant differences.
57. *Ha-hasagah ha-iyyunit.*
58. *Sevarot.*
59. i.e., that they are philosophically as well as rabbinically erudite.
60. *Ha-datot ha-nimusiot.*
61. *Ha-ḥasidim anshei ma'aseh.*
62. The numerical equivalent of the Tetragrammaton is twenty-six.
63. p. 56 in *Divrei Ḥakhamim.*
64. See, for example, his 'Parable of the Palace' in *Guide*, iii. 51.
65. Ibn Bilia, then noted Maimonides' failure to include belief in creation in the 'first edition' of his thirteen principles. See above, p. 54.
66. Ibn Bilia is here adopting the theory of the acquired intellect.
67. i.e., the Torah has esoteric and exoteric senses.
68. See Avot iv. 2.
69. i.e., they do not by themselves lead to human perfection.
70. See, for example, Zinberg (see above, ch. 2 n. 12), ii. 103–31.

71. This oblivion may have been well deserved, but it may not have been total. It is possible that Albo referred to him obliquely in *Sefer ha-Ikkarim*, i (pp. 36 and 61 in Husik's edition).

72. On Shemariah generally see the text published by Abraham Geiger in *He-Ḥaluz*, ii (1853), pp. 25–7 and 158–60 and in *Oẓar Neḥmad*, ii (1857), pp. 90–4. See also A. Z. Aescoly, *Ha-Tenuot ha-Meshiḥiot be-Yisrael* (Jerusalem, 1956), pp. 218–22. See further Colette Sirat, 'Mikhtav al Beriat ha-Olam li-Shemariah ben Eliah Ikriti', *Eshel Beer Sheva*, ii (1980), pp. 199–228.

   Steinschneider described the manuscript of Shemariah's *Sefer Amaziah* in *Die Hebraeischen Handschriften der K. Hof-und Staats-bibliothek in Muenchen* (Munich, 1895), p. 93. This is MS Munich Cod. Hebr. 210/7a (JNUL 1119).

73. It was not entirely unknown. As Neumark (*Toledot ha-Ikkarim*, ii. 163) points out, the book was cited by Johanan Alemanno (fifteenth century), in his *Likkutim*, p. 133. See M. D. Cassuto, *Ha-Yehudim be-Firenze bi-Tekufat ha-Renaissance* (Jerusalem, 1967), pp. 243–4.

74. See generally, Yiẓhak Baer, *A History of the Jews in Christian Spain* (Philadelphia, 1966), ii. 95–243.

75. Jeremy Cohen traces the origins of this development to the rise of the mendicant brotherhoods. See *The Friars and the Jews: the Evolution of Medieval Anti-Judaism* (Ithaca, 1982).

76. On the conversos see ch. 3 n. 153.

77. See the discussions on Duran, Crescas, Albo, Bibago, and Abravanel in Daniel J. Lasker, *Jewish Philosophical Polemics Against Christianity in the Middle Ages* (New York, 1977). On Arama, see S. Heller-Wilensky, *R. Yiẓhak Arama u-Mishnato* (Jerusalem, 1956), p. 27.

Chapter 3

1. He is the author of an important collection of responsa, *Tashbeẓ* (*Teshuvot Shimon ben Ẓemaḥ*) (Amsterdam, 1738–41). Isidore Epstein described Duran's halakhic work in *The Responsa of R. Simon ben Zemach Duran as a Source of the History of the Jews of North Africa* (London, 1930).

2. On Duran as a philosopher see Heinrich Jaulus, 'Simon ben Zemach Duran', *MGWJ*, xxiii (1874), pp. 241–59, 308–17, 355–66, 398–412, 447–63, and 499–514; Jakob Guttmann, 'Die Stellung des Simeon ben Zemah Duran in der jüdischen Religionsphilosophie', *MGWJ*, lii (1908), pp. 641–72 and liii (1909), pp. 46–79 and 199–228; and Naḥum Arieli, 'Mishnato ha-Philosophit shel R. Shimon ben Ẓemaḥ Duran', Ph.D. diss. (Hebrew University, 1976).

3. See Solomon Schechter, 'The Dogmas of Judaism', in the first series of his *Studies in Judaism* (Philadelphia, 1905), pp. 170–1; David

Neumark, *Toledot ha-Ikkarim be-Yisrael*, ii (Odessa, 1919), pp. 175–6; Mayer Waxman, 'Shitato shel R. Yosef Albo be-Ikkarei ha-Dat ve-Yihusah le-Torot Bnei Doro, R. Hasdai Crescas ve-R. Shimon ben Zemah Duran', *Ha-Tekufah*, xxx–xxxi (1946), pp. 712–46; repr. in Waxman's *Bi-Shvilei ha-Sifrut ve-ha-Mahashavah ha-Ivrit* (Tel Aviv, 1956), pp. 135–65; Louis Jacobs, *Principles of the Jewish Faith* (New York, 1964), pp. 19–20; Eliezer Schweid, 'Bein Mishnat ha-Ikkarim shel R. Yosef Albo le-Mishnat ha-Ikkarim shel ha-Rambam', *Tarbiz*, xxxiii (1963–4), pp. 74–84; and Alexander Altmann, 'Articles of Faith', *Encyclopaedia Judaica* (Jerusalem, 1971), iii, cols. 654–60.

On the question of Duran's influence on Albo see the article by Jaulus cited above in ch. 3 n. 2 and Julius Guttmann, 'Le-Heker ha-Mekorot shel Sefer ha-Ikkarim', in *Dat u–Madda* (Jerusalem, 1955), pp. 169–91, n. 2 (p. 169). See further Warren Zev Harvey, 'Albo's Discussion of Time', *JQR*, lxx (1979–80), pp. 210–30 n. 4 (pp. 210–11). Although the bulk of scholarly opinion holds that Duran influenced Albo, not the other way round, there is no conclusive proof to that effect. Although Albo's dates are not known, he was clearly already a mature man in 1413, the year he participated in the notorious disputation at Tortosa. It is certainly possible that he had already composed at least book i of the *Sefer ha-Ikkarim* by that date and it is even possible that he was chosen as one of the representatives of the Jews in the disputation precisely because he had already written a work the polemical nature of which is quite evident (although it is ordinarily supposed that he wrote the *Ikkarim* because of his participation in the disputation and not vice versa; see, for example, Baer's *History of the Jews in Christian Spain*, ii. 173 and 210 and Waxman, p. 731). Abraham ben Samuel Zacuto (1452–*c.*1515), in *Sefer ha-Yuhasin ha-Shalem* (ed. Z. H. Filipowski in London, 1857, and re-issued by A. Freimann in Frankfurt, 1924 (Jerusalem, 1963)), p. 226, states that Albo wrote the *Ikkarim* in 1425. But even if Zacuto is correct that only proves that the book was completed by 1425; the first treatise may have been written much earlier. Thus, on the basis of the facts available it is not really possible to prove that Albo borrowed from Duran as opposed to the other way round.

There are a number of points, however, which seem to have been overlooked by scholars who have taken up the subject and which add weight to the claim that Duran published his account of the principles before Albo and may properly be taken as the source and not as the borrower. In the first place, the points that the two of them both make are scattered over much of the *Ikkarim* but concentrated in three contiguous chapters in Duran's *Ohev Mishpat* and in the introduction to the *Magen Avot*. It seems more reasonable to me to assume that Albo used ideas of Duran's in various places in his book than to assume that Duran gathered a variety of ideas from Albo which were scattered over the *Ikkarim* and worked them together into a fairly consistent whole in the *Ohev Mishpat*. The second point relates to Albo's relationship to his teacher, Ḥasdai Crescas. Albo cites Crescas on a number of occasions and uses his work without citing his source on an even greater number of occasions. He does this in book i of the *Ikkarim*, which was written some time before books ii, iii, and iv. (On this, see Isaac Husik's introduction to the first volume of his Philadelphia, 1946 translation of the *Ikkarim*, p. xxii and I. Joel, *Torat ha-Philosophiah ha-Datit shel R. Ḥasdai Crescas* (Tel Aviv, 1927), pp. 100–3). Crescas finished his *Or Adonai* in 1410, after having worked on it for a number of years. Now it is possible that Albo was familiar with Crescas's work as it progressed, and that his borrowings really reflect things he had learned from Crescas in his capacity as student, and do not prove that he had a finished copy of the *Or Adonai* before him when he composed the first treatise of the *Ikkarim*. But the fact that he makes free use of Crescas's thoughts without crediting their author (so much so that he was accused of plagiarism by his contemporaries; see Husik) seems to prove that Crescas was already dead when Albo composed the *Ikkarim*. It does not seem credible that Albo would borrow so freely from Crescas during the latter's lifetime. This being so, we have persuasive evidence to the effect that the *Ikkarim* was written after Crescas's death. Crescas died after 1410. The *Ohev Mishpat* was written in 1405 and the *Magen Avot* may have been written before it (see ch. 3 n. 8). This being the case, there can be little doubt that it was Duran who influenced Albo, not the other way round. (For a contrary view see Arnold Taenzer, *Die Religionsphilosophie des Joseph Albo* (Pressburg, 1896), cited by Emil G. Hirsch in his article on Joseph Albo in the *Jewish Encyclopedia* (New York, 1901), i. 324–7.)

4. See Guttmann's article, cited in the previous note, and my refutation of this thesis in 'R. Shimon ben Ẓemaḥ Duran on the Principles of Judaism', *PAAJR*, xlviii (1981), pp. 231–65 and ch. 5, section iii of the present work. Guttmann is followed by Naḥum Arieli (see above, ch. 3 n. 2), p. 16, by Colette Sirat, *Hagut Philosophit biymei ha-Benayim* (Jerusalem, 1975), pp. 432–3, and by Alexander Altmann in his article on Joseph Albo in *Encyclopaedia Judaica* (Jerusalem, 1971), ii, col. 536. Guttmann repeats his thesis in *Philosophies of Judaism* (New York, 1964), pp. 278–82. See further, S. Pines, 'Shi'ite Terms and Conceptions in Judah Halevy's *Kuzari*', *Jerusalem Studies in Arabic and Islam*, ii (1980), pp. 165–219. At p. 181 n.

116 Pines notes that Averroës's three dogmas were anticipated by Abū Ya'qūb al-Sijistani (d. 942).

5. See Jaulus (see above, ch. 3 n. 2), p. 453 and Harvey (see above, ch. 3 n. 3), p. 14.

6. The book was first published in Venice in 1590 together with the *Mishpat Zedek* of Obadiah ben Jacob Sforno (*c*.1470–*c*.1550). The Venice edition was photographically reproduced in Tel Aviv in 1970. The commentary, without the introductory treatise, was published a second time in Moses Frankfurt's *Kehillot Moshe* (Amsterdam, 1724–7). The text of that edition is based upon the *editio princeps*. The Institute of Microfilmed Hebrew Manuscripts at the Jewish National and University Library in Jerusalem has microfilm copies of three manuscripts of the *Ohev Mishpat*. These are: (*1*) Bodleian 347 (Laud. Or. 84), JNUL catalogue number 17266; the manuscript was copied in 1485. (*2*) Bodleian 127, JNUL catalogue number 16191; the manuscript dates from the fifteenth century. (*3*) Paris Heb. 240, JNUL catalogue number 27837; the manuscript dates from the fifteenth–sixteenth centuries. The first manuscript has many mistakes, some caught and corrected by the scribe, some corrected in another hand, and some not corrected at all. The second manuscript appears to have been much more carefully written while the third is damaged and hard to read. In establishing the text for the present translation I have used the printed edition and the first two manuscripts. I have generally followed the reading of the manuscripts (which largely agree with each other) except in the few instances where the reading of the printed edition clearly makes more sense. Page numbers in square brackets refer to the *editio princeps*.

7. The *Magen Avot* was published in Livorno in 1785 (reproduced in Jerusalem, n.d.). The JNUL has microfilms of nine manuscripts, complete and partial, of this text. I compared the printed text with the microfilm copy of MS 738/1 of the Bibliothèque Nationale, Paris (JNUL no. 11663) and found no significant differences in the passage translated here. Arieli's dissertation (see above, ch. 3 n. 2) is largely based on the *Magen Avot* and analyses it in detail.

8. Harvey (see above, ch. 3 n. 2), p. 211, deals with the issue of which book preceded the other. He surmises that the *Magen Avot* was written before the *Ohev Mishpat* because the former is cited in the latter (on p. 12a; it is also cited on p. 29b) even though in his own listing of his writings (at the end of *Tashbez*, ii), Duran places the *Ohev Mishpat* before the *Magen Avot*. Duran, however, cites the *Ohev Mishpat* in the *Magen Avot*! See p. 2b and p. 94 of the present work. That fact would seem to cancel out the citations of the *Magen Avot* in the *Ohev Mishpat*, leaving as our only evidence Duran's own

list. We may conclude, therefore, with very little confidence, that the *Ohev Mishpat* preceded the *Magen Avot*.

9. Duran seems to be distinguishing between 'foundations' on the one hand (creation and providence) and the 'principle' of the Torah (that we believe it to be divine and believe in its promises) on the other hand. Compare, *Ohev Mishpat*, ix p. 88.

10. Were the world eternal *a parte ante* (*kadmon*) it would be impossible for things to deviate from their natures, for it was a given of the Aristotelian world view that eternity and necessity implied each other. See above, ch. 1 n. 193.

11. This passage is taken from the introduction to the *Ohev Mishpat* (p. 3b). Duran discusses the dependence of providence upon creation in *Ohev Mishpat*, i (p. 7a).

12. Literally: 'compared it with'.

13. i.e., portion of the world to come.

14. The plausible inference, that this refers to ibn Bilia's *Yesodot ha-Maskil* ('Foundations of the Intellectual'), discussed above in ch. 2 (pp. 77–79), is incorrect. Ibn Bilia does not make this claim in his treatise. I do not know to whom Duran refers.

15. See Exod. 34: 6. Jakob Guttmann (see above, ch. 3 n. 2), p. 58 n, points this out as the source of Albo, *Ikkarim*, i. 3, p. 60.

16. *Nitparsem be-ummatenu*. In a number of places in these chapters Duran emphasizes the importance of a belief's having been generally accepted by the Jewish people. There may be an echo of the Muslim concept of *ijma* here. See G. F. Hourani (ed. and trans.), *Averroes on the Harmony of Religion and Philosophy* (London, 1961), pp. 19 and 29–32, and G. Cohen (ed. and trans.), Abraham ibn Daud, *Sefer ha-Qabbalah* (Philadelphia, 1967), pp. xxxi, xliv, and lx. This supposition is strengthened by Duran's terminology; the usual Hebrew translation of *ijma* is *mefursamot*. This issue might also be related to the idea that a rabbinic enactment (*takkanah*) which was not widely accepted by the Jewish people could be nullified. See Maimonides, 'Laws of Rebellious Elders', ii. 7, and the introduction to the *Mishneh Torah*, shortly before the list of positive commandments.

17. *Nizhi*.

18. This is the criticism of the 'intellectual'.

19. *Toladot*. I also translate this term as 'derivative principles', as the context requires.

20. i.e., the 'intellectual'.

21. 'Laws of Repentance', v. 1–5.

22. See the eighth of Maimonides' 'Eight Chapters' (above, ch. 1 n. 199).

23. *Guide*, iii. 32 (p. 529). As Jakob Guttmann points out (see above, ch. 3 n. 2), we find this in Albo, *Ikkarim*, i. 3 (p. 59).

24. *Toladot*. i.e., the beliefs which are logically dependent upon them.

25. Compare *Guide of the Perplexed*, ii. 25 (pp. 327–30).
26. The bracketed material is found in the printed text but not in the manuscripts. That is of no importance, however, since Duran includes incorporeality in the first principle in *Magen Avot*. See p. 94.
27. *Min*. Printed text has *epikoros*. See 'Laws of Repentance', iii. 7 where Maimonides has *min*.
28. *Teluyim be-emunah*. My translation is not literal, but makes the best possible sense of the sentence.
29. See Shabbat 49b.
30. *Avot*. Compare Albo, *Ikkarim*, i. 4, p. 70.
31. *Toladot*. Compare Albo, *Ikkarim*, table of contents, p. 6.
32. *Tikannu*.
33. On these 'independent proofs' see H. A. Wolfson, *Crescas' Critique of Aristotle* (Cambridge, Mass., 1929), p. 324 n. 10.
34. Compare Crescas, *Or Adonai*, III, introduction (p. 61a).
35. *Po'al*. Compare Crescas, II, introduction (p. 28a). See p. 113.
36. Compare Albo, *Ikkarim*, i. 4, p. 69.
37. It is possible that this phrase should be translated as 'adherent of *a* Torah' (my emphasis). That reading emphasizes the connection between Duran and Albo.
38. i.e., the remaining ten principles.
39. His 'subject' is providence; disquisitions on its dogmatic status are digressions.
40. Duran's translation here is that of al-Ḥarizi. See appendix i.
41. Kaspi interprets Maimonides in this fashion; see above, ch. 1 n. 218. For the source of the expression 'heart . . . aches' see Berakhot 7b and compare Naḥmanides, *Sha'ar ha-Gemul* in C. D. Chavel (ed.), *Kitvei Ramban* (Jerusalem, 1963), ii. 291. The Hebrew word which I translate in this sentence as 'precedence' is *kadmut*.
42. *Kadmon*.
43. i.e., the world. On the issue here see also ch. 1 nn. 24 and 219.
44. *Guide*, ii. 25.
45. As Jaulus (see above, ch. 3 n. 2), p. 458, points out, we find this idea in Albo at *Ikkarim*, i. 2, p. 49.
46. We find an echo of this idea in Abravanel's *Rosh Amanah*, xxiii. See ch. 8, p. 187.
47. Makkot 23b–24a.
48. i.e., all the commandments and teachings of the Torah.
49. *Se'ifim*. (Albo, i. 13 calls his secondary principles *ha-shorashim ha-mista'afim*, using the same root.)
50. As Jaulus (see above, ch. 3 n. 2), p. 458, points out, we find a similar statement in Albo, i. 2, p. 49.
51. Genesis Rabbah iii. 7. Compare Albo, i. 2, p. 50.

52. Genesis Rabbah iii. 9.
53. *Guide*, ii. 26. Rabbi Eliezer's dictum is found in Pirkei de'Rabbi Eliezer, iii. As Jaulus, p. 459, points out, we find a similar statement in Albo, i. 2, p. 50.
54. Rabbi Hillel at Sanhedrin 99a.
55. Ḥagigah 14b.
56. R. Abraham ben David of Posquières. See I. Twersky, *Rabad of Posquières*, rev. edn. (Philadelphia, 1980), pp. 282–6.
57. 'Laws of Repentance', iii. 7.
58. i.e., that God is incorporeal.
59. This version of Rabad's gloss is considerably more polite than that found in the standard printed texts:

> Why has he called such a person a heretic [*min*]? There are many people greater than and superior to him who adhere to such a belief on the basis of what they have seen in verses of Scripture and even more in the words of those *aggadot* which corrupt right opinion about religious matters.

(I cite the translation of Isadore Twersky in his *Rabad of Posquières*, p. 282.) Albo, i. 2, p. 53 quoted Duran's version almost word for word. In this he was followed by Abraham Bibago, *Derekh Emunah*, iii. 5 (Constantinople, 1522, p. 102c) and Isaac Abravanel, *Rosh Amanah*, xii (p. 112). Joseph Karo, in his commentary to 'Laws of Repentance', iii. 3 suggests that Albo's version (i.e., Duran's version) is the correct text. As Jaulus, p. 459, points out, the two preceding paragraphs in Duran's text find their echo in Albo, i. 2, pp. 52–3.

In Duran's version Rabad writes *ikkar ha-emunah ken hu* ('the essence of the belief is like this'). It might be supposed that Rabad here is actually referring to principles of faith (*ikkarei ha-emunah*). I do not think that this is correct. The simple sense of the passage supports the first rendition. Moreover, Rabad was not familiar with Maimonides' *Commentary on the Mishnah* (see Twersky, *Rabad*, p. 107) in which Maimonides introduced the concept of principles of faith into medieval Judaism. It strains belief to suppose that Rabad would have independently and apparently casually arrived at a similar position.

It is possible that both versions of Rabad's gloss are authentic. It is known that he worked on his glosses for many years and revised them continually. In his article 'Hassagot ha-Rabad bi-Defusim u-ve-Kitvei Yad', *Kiryat Sefer*, xxxiii (1959), pp. 360–75, E. E. Urbach even goes so far as to talk of two 'editions' of the glosses. For an interesting study see Jerome Gellman, 'The Philosophical *Hassagot* of Rabad on Maimonides' *Mishneh Torah*', *The New Scholasticism*, lviii (1984), pp. 145–69.
60. *Guide*, ii. 42, p. 389.

61. See Sanhedrin 105a–106b.
62. Gersonides maintained that the world was created out of a pre-existing, formless matter. See *Milḥamot Adonai*, VI, i. 17 and Jacob J. Staub, *The Creation of the World According to Gersonides* (Chico, Calif., 1982), pp. 45–72.
63. It is entirely possible that Duran was reacting here to the critique of Maimonides and Gersonides found in R. Isaac bar Sheshet's forty-fifth responsum. See M. M. Kellner, 'Rabbi Isaac bar Sheshet's Responsum Concerning the Study of Greek Philosophy', *Tradition*, xv, no. 3 (1975), pp. 110–18 and xv, no. 4 (1976), p. 134 and ch. 3 n. 127 of the present work.
64. *Le-karvam ha-devarim el ha-muskal.* i.e., to explain the Torah rationally.
65. As Jaulus, pp. 459–60, points out, we find a similar statement in Albo, i. 2, pp. 51–2. See also Gersonides, *Milḥamot*, introduction, pp. 6–7 and especially VI, ii, 1, p. 419.
66. Compare *Guide*, ii. 25, p. 328.
67. First-century translator of the prophetic books of the Bible into Aramaic.
68. Second-century translator of the Bible into Aramaic.
69. Onkelos and Jonathan are cited with approval by Maimonides for their non-anthropomorphic interpretations of Scripture. See *Guide*, i. 28 (p. 60) and i. 37 (p. 85). See also Albo, i. 2, p. 52.
70. Compare *Guide*, ii. 25 (p. 328), where Maimonides says that proof that the world is eternal *a parte ante* would destroy the Torah. For Duran, however, mistaken belief even on so crucial a point as this, is not heresy.
71. Compare Gersonides, *Milḥamot*, VI, ii, 1, p. 418 and VI, ii, 10, p. 450.
72. Exod. 4: 3–4. Compare Gersonides, *Milḥamot*, VI, ii, 1, p. 418.
73. Exod. 16: 4–36.
74. Compare Maimonides, *Guide*, ii. 25, pp. 328–9.
75. Note here that Duran, like Maimonides, is interested in the question, what beliefs must a person hold in order to be counted as a Jew (and, by implication, in order to merit a share in the world to come).
76. The point here is that belief in providence is neither a commandment *d'oraita* (on Torah authority) nor *d'rabbanan* (on rabbinic authority).
77. Compare Albo, *Ikkarim*, i. 14, p. 123.
78. Compare Crescas, *Or Adonai*, II, introduction, pp. 27b–28a and ch. 4, section ii of the present work.
79. i.e., any principle.
80. See *Yalkut Shim'oni* to Exod. 12: 2, *Tanḥuma*, Genesis, section 11 (ed. S. Buber (Vilna, 1885), p. 7), and Rashi on Gen. 1: 1.
81. Duran's point is that according to R. Isaac there was no point in the

Torah opening with the creation account, even though belief in creation is a principle of the Torah.

82. Compare Albo, *Ikkarim*, i. 3 (pp. 55–6).

83. i.e., the eternity of the Torah.

84. Maimonides counts God's existence as a commandment in *Book of Commandments*, positive commandment 1, and in 'Laws of the Foundations of the Torah', i. 6. He counts God's unity as a positive commandment in the second positive commandment of the *Book of Commandments* and in 'Foundations of the Torah', i. 7. That God alone may be worshipped is counted as commandment in *Book of Commandments*, negative commandment 10. Maimonides counts the eternity of the Torah as a commandment in 'Foundations', x. 1.

85. *Se'if*. See above, ch. 3, n. 49.

86. See Sanhedrin 26a.

87. Compare Isaac ben Joseph of Corbeil, *Sefer Mizvot Kazar* (or *Katan*) [*Ammudei Golah*] (Jerusalem, 1960), pp. 1–2; Crescas, *Or Adonai, haza'ah*, p. 3a, and Albo, *Ikkarim*, i. 14 (p. 128) and iii. 8 (p. 163). See further Abravanel's *Rosh Amanah*, ch. 7.

88. *Dibbur*; one of the ten elements of the Decalogue.

89. Possibly a reference to the *Halakhot Gedolot* attributed to the Gaon Simeon Kayyara. Compare Crescas, *Or Adonai*, preface (ch. 4, section ii of the present work).

90. Deut. 6: 4 ('Hear O Israel . . .').

91. A reference to Elisha ben Abuyah. See above, ch. 1, section i, p. 16.

92. i.e., one who affirms that God is corporeal without, however, intending thereby to commit heresy.

93. Maimonides cites this verse at 'Laws of Kings', xi. 4. That, however, is not a context in which Maimonides discusses God's incorporeality. I do not understand, therefore, Duran's point here.

94. I have not succeeded in locating the source of this reference.

95. i.e., in Sanhedrin x. 1.

96. See Avot iii. 12, Baba Mezia 59a, Megillah 28a, and TJ Hagigah ii. 1. See further Maimonides' commentary on *Helek* (Kafih, p. 210). The point here is that if the Sages mentioned many different things which cost one his share in the world to come, why did they not mention failure to accept the thirteen principles?

97. See above, *Ohev Mishpat*, viii, p. 86.

98. Avot ii. 19.

99. Sanhedrin 96b–100a.

100. Pesahim 22b.

101. Tosefta Sanhedrin xiii (ed. Zuckermandel (Jerusalem, 1934) p. 434); see also Rosh ha-Shanah 17a.

102. See Avodah Zarah 26b.

103. i.e., the *epikorsim* (pl. of *epikoros*).

104. 'Laws of Repentance', iii. 8.
105. i.e., the *epikorsim*.
106. The source of this reference eludes me.
107. 'Laws of Repentance', iii. 8.
108. As Duran notes below, it is customary to begin the study of Avot by quoting from Mishnah Sanhedrin x. 1. That is why he opens his commentary on Avot with an analysis of that mishnah. It is that mishnah also which laid down the tripartite structure of his long philosophical introduction to Avot, each part of the introduction corresponding to a term in the mishnah, and thereby to one of the groups into which he holds Maimonides' principles to fall.
109. Job 31: 2, 'The portion [*helek*] of God from above . . .'
110. Ch. x, p. 15b. See above, p. 92.
111. Isa. 17: 14, 'This is the portion [*helek*] of them that spoil us . . .' i.e., those who deny that the Torah was divinely revealed 'spoil us'.
112. Jer. 10: 6 and 51: 19, '. . . . Jacob's portion [*helek*] . . .'
113. See Ta'anit 5b.
114. The last word in this verse, *tesham*, is interpreted by Duran as a *notarikon* (acronym) for the three Hebrew words *Torah*, *sakhar* (reward), and *meziut* (existence). I do not know to which 'earlier scholars' Duran is referring in this sentence, but I suspect that he is guilty of 'false modesty' here and originated the acronym himself. Attributing it to earlier figures can only enhance its authority and acceptability.
115. The order is determined by the *notarikon* explained in the previous note.
116. Deut. 32: 9, 'For the portion [*helek*] of the Lord is His people.'
117. This is only a sentence fragment; it is not clear to me how Duran meant it to be related to the preceding and succeeding sentences.
118. *Magen Avot*, introduction, p. 2b (bottom).
119. This seems to be the question which underlies Albo's discussion. See especially *Ikkarim*, i. 3. Compare *Ohev Mishpat*, xvii.
120. See above, introduction, p. 7.
121. See Aristotle's *Posterior Analytics*, especially book i, chs. 10 and 13. This source is cited by Husik in a note to Albo, i. 17 (in memory of Leo Strauss I cannot forbear noting that in chapter 17 of *Ohev Mishpat* Duran says that the teachings of the Torah ought to be accepted as axiomatic). See further W. D. Ross, *Aristotle's Prior and Posterior Analytics* (Oxford, 1965), pp. 51–75.
122. book i, question 1, article 2. In the Cambridge, 1964 translation of Thomas Gilby, pp. 11–13. See further Gilby's 'Appendix 6: Theology as Science', pp. 67–87. See also the essays by H. A. Wolfson, 'The Classification of Sciences in Medieval Jewish Philosophy' and 'Additional Notes to the Article on the Classifica-

tion of Sciences in Medieval Jewish Philosophy' in his *Studies in the History of Philosophy and Religion* (Cambridge, Mass., 1973), i. 493–545 and 546–50. As is evident from Wolfson, it was not Duran's definition of theology as a science which was revolutionary so much as his application of that definition to the question of dogma.

123. This work was actually part of the *Magen Avot*. It was published in Livorno in 1762. See Daniel Lasker, *Jewish Philosophical Polemics Against Christianity* (New York, 1977), p. 18 and index, s.v. 'Duran, Simon ben Zemaḥ'.

124. For a discussion of Duran's views on providence see J. David Bleich, 'Duran's View of the Nature of Providence', *JQR*, lxix (1978–9), pp. 208–25.

125. Thus, human freedom is called a 'principle' (*ikkar*) and a 'root' (*shoresh*) at *Ohev Mishpat*, pp. 11a and 11b.

126. We have found this distinction already in Abba Mari. See above, ch. 2, section ii, p. 74.

127. Compare, for example, the attitude of Duran's elder contemporary and sometime colleague, sometime antagonist, R. Isaac bar Sheshet Perfet (1326–1408). Perfet condemned Maimonides and Gersonides for their alleged divergences from strict orthodoxy as he defined it. See above, ch. 3 n. 63. Duran's position here was criticized by Abraham Bibago and by Isaac Abravanel, although neither author mentions Duran by name. See above, ch. 3 n. 59, ch. 7, p. 174 and ch. 8, p. 183f.

128. See above, ch. 3 n. 77.

129. See Abravanel's *Rosh Amanah*, xi, and the present work, ch. 8, p. 182.

130. See above, pp. 84, 87f, and 91f.

131. Although I suppose Duran would count as a heretic one who, although not intending heresy, denied God's existence.

132. Guttmann '*le-Ḥeker . . .*' (see above, ch. 3 n. 3; henceforth I will refer to this essay as 'Guttmann'), p. 171.

133. Guttmann, p. 173, The text of Averroës with which Guttmann is dealing, *Kitāb faṣl al-maqāl*, was translated by George F. Hourani as *On the Harmony of Religion and Philosophy* (London, 1961).

134. Guttmann, p. 170.

135. Averroës (see above, ch. 3 n. 133), p. 58.

136. Albo, *Ikkarim*, i. 4, p. 64.

137. Albo, *Ikkarim*, i. table of contents, p. 2.

138. Albo, *Ikkarim*, i. 1, pp. 43–4 and i. 10, p. 98. Actually, Albo is ambivalent on this issue. See the present work, ch. 5, section iv.

139. Albo cites him often. See the index to Husik's edition of the *Ikkarim*, s.v., 'Averroes'.

140. See above, ch. 3 n. 114.

141. See above, *Ohev Mishpat*, ix, p. 86.

142. See above, ch. 1, section iv.

143. See M. M. Kellner, 'R. Isaac Abravanel on Maimonides' Principles of Faith', *Tradition*, xviii (1980), pp. 343–56. For further textual evidence supporting the position urged in this section, see my article cited above in ch. 3 n. 4.

144. See *Ikkarim*, i. 3 and the present work, ch. 3, section iii.

145. See *Ikkarim*, i. 4, p. 69 and p. 141.

146. See his 'Maimonides' "Thirteen Principles"', in Alexander Altmann (ed.), *Jewish Medieval and Renaissance Studies* (Cambridge, Mass., 1967), p. 138.

147. See ch. 3 n. 49.

148. See ch. 3 n. 77.

149. See above, p. 85 and *Ikkarim*, i. 15 (pp. 129–30).

150. See ch. 10, section iii.

151. See above, p. 84 and p. 113.

152. Albo was ambiguous on the issue and Crescas may very well have adopted a position similar to Duran's; neither of them, however, made their positions explicit. See ch. 4, section vi and ch. 5, section iv.

153. It is possible that Duran's position was motivated in part by the desire not to alienate the conversos by making it possible for them — despite their outward acceptance of Christianity and violation of many halakhic norms — still to be considered as Jews. If this is the case, then it is reasonable to expect that in halakhic contexts Duran would evidence a relatively lenient attitude towards the conversos. And this is precisely what we find, at least towards the beginning of Duran's career. See Isidore Epstein, *The Responsa of R. Simon ben Zemach Duran* (see above, ch. 3 n. 1), p. 30 and Benzion Netanyahu, *The Marranos of Spain* (New York, 1966), p. 33. Later he adopted a much harsher stance (see Epstein, p. 30 and Netanyahu, pp. 35–8). This hardening of judgement, however, is not truly inconsistent with a generally lenient attitude towards the conversos since harsh judgements concerning the non-Jewish character of conversos in effect meant leniency towards their relatives who remained Jews or who escaped from the lands of persecution. See Y. H. Yerushalmi, *From Spanish Court to Italian Ghetto* (New York, 1971), pp. 24–31. On this subject generally, see H. J. Zimmels, *Die Marranen in der rabbinischen Literatur* (Berlin, 1932); Simḥa Assaf, 'Anusei Sefarad u-Portugal be-Safrut ha-Teshuvot', in *Be-Oholei Ya'akov* (Jerusalem, 1943), pp. 145–80; and G. D. Cohen's review of Netanyahu's *Marranos of Spain* in *Jewish Social Studies*, xxix (1967), pp. 178–84.

154. See item 12 in Duran's own list of his writings appended to *Tashbez*, ii.

Chapter 4

1. For Crescas's biography and influence, see Yiẓhak Baer, *A History of the Jews in Christian Spain* (Philadelphia, 1966), ii. 110–30 and the sources there cited; Abraham M. Hershman, *Rabbi Isaac ben Sheshet Perfet and his Times* (New York, 1943), index, s.v. 'Crescas, Ḥasdai'; and Leon A. Feldman (ed.), *Perush ha-Ran al ha-Torah* (Jerusalem, 1968), pp. 19–21.

2. See Feldman, pp. 19–21.

3. See Hershman, pp. 171–2.

4. See Isidore Epstein, *The Responsa of R. Simon ben Zemach Duran as a Source of the History of the Jews of North Africa* (London, 1930), p. 5 and Leon A. Feldman (ed.), *Derashot ha-Ran* (Jerusalem, 1973), p. 45.

5. Portions of this chronicle were translated by Franz Kobler in vol. i of his *Letters of the Jews Through the Ages* (London, 1952), pp. 272–5 and by Warren Zev Harvey in his dissertation, 'Ḥasdai Crescas' Critique of the Theory of the Acquired Intellect' (Columbia University, 1973 (Xerox University Microfilms Order no. 74-101488)), pp. 15–17 (henceforth: Harvey).

6. Aviezer Ravitzky is preparing an edition of this sermon for the Israel Academy of Sciences. He describes it in 'Ketav Nishkaḥ le-R. Ḥasdai Crescas', *Kiryat Sefer*, li (1975), pp. 705–11. See further Ravitzky's two articles, 'Zehuto ve-Gilgulav shel Ḥibbur Philosophi she Yuḥas le-R. Michael ben Shabbtai Balbo', *Kiryat Sefer*, lvi (1980), pp. 153–63 and 'Hitpatḥut Hashkafotav shel R. Ḥasdai Crescas bi-She'elat Ḥofesh ha-Raẓon', *Tarbiz*, li (1982), pp. 445–69.

7. This work was published in Kearny, NJ, by Ephraim Deinard in 1904 under its Hebrew title, *Bittul Ikkarei ha-Noẓrim*. See Daniel J. Lasker, *Jewish Philosophical Polemics Against Christianity in the Middle Ages* (New York, 1977), p. 19 and index, s.v. 'Crescas, Ḥasdai'.

8. This book is preserved in many manuscripts and has been published several times. It first appeared in Ferrara (1555); this edition was reproduced photographically in London (1969) and in Jerusalem (1972). The book appeared a second time in Vienna (1859/60) (reproduced in Tel Aviv in 1963). It was published most recently in Johannisburg, Germany (1861). Portions of the first treatise were edited, translated and extensively analysed by Harry A. Wolfson in his *Crescas' Critique of Aristotle* (Cambridge, Mass., 1929); further portions of the text were edited, translated, and analysed by Harvey (see above, ch. 4 n. 5). Wolfson discusses the extant manuscripts on pp. 703–5 and Harvey does so on pp. 230–2. Yehudah Eisenberg has edited and briefly commented on treatise III, part i, section 1 in

Torat ha-Beriah shel R. Ḥasdai Crescas (Jerusalem, 1981) and treatise II, parts i and vi in *Ha-Reshut Netunah* (Jerusalem, 1983). In establishing the texts translated in ch. 4, section ii I relied most heavily on the manuscript considered by Harvey to be the most reliable, MS Florence: Biblioteca Medicea Laurenziana, Conventi Soppressi 417. I also consulted MS Vienna Hebr. 150/1 (JNUL no. 1323) and MS Adler held at the Jewish Theological Seminary in New York (ENA 1802; Seminary Microfilm no. 2428) as well as the printed editions.

On the *Or Adonai* see further Symcha Bunim Urbach, *Mishnato ha-Philosophit shel R. Ḥasdai Crescas* (Jerusalem, 1961) and Eliezer Schweid, *Ha-Philosophiah ha-Datit shel R. Ḥasdai Crescas* (Jerusalem, 1970).

9. This introduction was edited by Harvey. His translation of it may be found on pp. 342–67 of his dissertation.

10. See Wolfson, p. 17.

11. Sara Klein-Braslavy, 'Terumato shal R. Nissim Gerondi le-Iẓuvan shel Torot ha-Ikkarim shel Ḥasdai Crescas ve-shel Yosef Albo', *Eshel Beer Sheva*, ii (1980), pp. 177–97, esp. pp. 188–9, 190, and 191, shows that Crescas derived this idea from Rabbenu Nissim. This article will be cited henceforth as *EBS*. Klein-Braslavy also discusses Crescas' dependence upon Rabbenu Nissim in a second article, 'Ma'amad Har Sinai be-Mishnato shel R. Nissim ben Reuven Gerondi (ha-Ran)', *Sinai*, lxxx (1977), pp. 26–37. This essay will be cited henceforth as *Sinai*.

12. In his article on Crescas in the *Encyclopaedia Judaica* (Jerusalem, 1971), vol. v, cols. 1080–5 and in his dissertation, pp. 24–5.

13. Harvey, dissertation, p. 25.

14. In doing this, of course, he also establishes the autonomy of science and philosophy from religion. His influence in this regard on certain Renaissance thinkers was not inconsiderable. See Wolfson, pp. 32–8 and Harvey, dissertation, pp. 4–5.

15. i.e., belief in God is a prerequisite for 'knowledge of truth concerning the corner-stones of the divine Torah'.

16. i.e., this part of the *Ner Elohim*, the *Or Adonai*.

17. Crescas here presents the *Or Adonai* as being primarily a work of systematic dogmatics.

18. As we shall see again, Crescas typically divides his discussions into two parts: the issue itself, and how we come to know it. Certain things can be known philosophically, but others can only be known on the basis of religious tradition.

19. Starting from the assumption, in other words, that there exists a divine Torah, what beliefs are thereby presupposed? The answer is, belief in God.

20. Isaac Abravanel (*Rosh Amanah*, ch. iv, p. 72) takes this, correctly in my view, to be a reference to Maimonides. I. Joel, *Torat ha-Philosophiah ha-Datit shel R. Ḥasdai Crescas* (Tel Aviv, 1927), p. 32, however, understands Crescas to be referring to some other unknown author. See also Klein-Braslavy, *EBS*, p. 188 and *Sinai*, p. 35 for Crescas's dependence on Rabbenu Nissim in this matter.

21. This is Crescas's first argument against Maimonides' claim that one ought to count belief in God as a commandment. See p. 117, and Harvey, dissertation, pp. 222–6.

22. See *Or Adonai*, treatise II, section 5, ch. 5 (Vienna, p. 49b). This is Crescas's second argument against Maimonides; see p. 117.

23. See p. 118.

24. Makkot, 23b–24a.

25. This is the view of Naḥmanides, as expressed in his commentary on Exod. 20: 2. Crescas was strongly influenced by Naḥmanides in his understanding of this verse. The point here is that Makkot 23b–24a does not teach that the existence of God is a commandment, but that the God of the Exodus and the God of the Decalogue are one and the same.

26. *Sefer ha-Mizvot* (*Book of Commandments*) positive commandment 1. I follow here the translation of Charles B. Chavel (London, 1967), i. 1, with some minor emendations.

27. In *Rosh Amanah*, ch. vii, p. 88, Abravanel analyses this passage of Crescas and concludes that Crescas held that Maimonides contradicted himself. Abravanel writes:

> This scholar thus thought that Maimonides' statements in these two places, i.e., the *Book of Knowledge* and the *Book of Commandments* were not in agreement. He thought that in the *Book of Knowledge* [Maimonides held] that the first commandment is simply that God exists, while he thought that in the Book of Commandments [Maimonides held] that the first commandment is belief that God is the efficient cause and creator of the world.

Abravanel appears to be correct. We may add that Crescas maintains that in the *Book of Commandments* Maimonides construes Exod. 20: 2 as a commandment. Crescas cannot accept that. But at least in this context Maimonides does not construe the verse as a commandment to believe in God's existence simply, as he does in the *Book of Knowledge*; rather — on Crescas's interpretation — Maimonides construes it as a commandment to believe that God is the Creator of the world, capable of working the miracle of the Exodus.

28. Crescas cannot accept this approach either, even though it is less objectionable than the approach found in the *Book of Knowledge*, since he holds that the Torah, while it teaches beliefs, cannot command them, because beliefs, not being subject to will and choice, cannot be commanded. See above, p. 110f and ch. 4, section v.

29. i.e., in the passage from *Makkot*.
30. I have no idea why this verse, which is not in the Decalogue, appears here.
31. Poems listing the commandments. See A. Z. Idelson, *Jewish Liturgy and its Development* (New York, 1972), pp. 42 and 197.
32. Namely, not to make a graven image (v. 4), not to bow down to such an image (v. 5), and to believe in God (v. 2).
33. On the assumption that Moses taught six hundred and eleven commandments but none of those contained in the portion of the Decalogue (vv. 2–6) in which God is presented as speaking in the first person.
34. Maimonides, *Book of Commandments*, negative commandment 1 (Chavel translation, ii. 1).
35. Adding this admonition to the three listed in ch. 4 n. 32 above.
36. Those who count the *Azharot*, and of course Crescas himself.
37. Crescas's argument here may be explicated as follows: commandments are not a matter of belief (because one cannot will or choose to believe something); if 'Thou shalt have no other gods before Me' is a commandment, it must be given an actional interpretation, such as forbidding the worship of other gods. In such a case, 'Thou shalt have no other gods before Me' becomes equivalent to 'Thou shalt not bow down unto them'.
38. Sanhedrin 56b.
39. By way of summarizing the issue, it may be helpful to point out that both Crescas and Maimonides agree that Exod. 20: 2–6 constitutes the first two utterances of the Decalogue. According to Crescas, these utterances contain two commandments: the commandment prohibiting the worship of idols and the one prohibiting the bowing down to idols. According to Maimonides, the two utterances contain five commandments: (*a*) to believe (or know) that God exists (v. 2); (*b*) not to have other gods (v. 3); (*c*) not to make images for the purpose of worship (v. 4); (*d*) not to bow down before, or serve, idols (v. 5); and (*e*) not to worship idols (v. 5). These are, in Maimonides' *Book of Commandments*, positive commandment 1 and negative commandments 1, 2, 5, and 6.
40. These six beliefs (*pinnot*) are the subject matter of treatise II.
41. These true doctrines (*de'ot amitiot*) are the subject matter of parts i and ii of treatise III.
42. It is evident from this passage that Crescas did not posit his principles in order to define heresy, since the principles themselves (the corner-stones of treatise II) are not distinguished in this regard from the true doctrines (of treatise III). Maimonides posited his principles to answer one sort of question; Crescas posited his to answer another sort of question altogether. See p. 135.

43. These theories form the subject matter of treatise IV.

44. This passage, the *haza'ah* (preface) to the *Or Adonai*, is found on pp. 3a–b of the Vienna edition.

45. This is Crescas's definition of a principle of religion: any belief the denial of which would necessarily involve the 'collapse' of the Torah. By 'collapse' Crescas seems to mean the impossibility of holding belief in Torah from heaven without self-contradiction.

46. On Crescas's discussion of free will vs. determinism see W. Zev Harvey, 'Le-Zihuiy Meḥabran shel Histaiguyot min ha-Determinism be-Sefer *Or Ha-Shem* le-R. Ḥasdai Crescas — Edut Ketav Yad Firenze', *Kiryat Sefer*, lv (1980), pp. 794–801 and Seymour Feldman, 'Crescas' Theological Determinism', *Da'at*, ix (1982), pp. 3–28. See further Yiẓhak Julius Guttmann, 'Ba'ayat ha-Beḥirah ha-Ḥofshit be-Mishnatam shel Ḥasdai Crescas ve-ha-Aristotelaim ha-Muslamim', in *Dat u-Madda* (Jerusalem, 1979), pp. 149–68, Phillip Bloch, *Die Willensfreiheit von Chasdai Kreskas* (Munich, 1879) and Ravitzky's article in *Tarbiz* cited above in ch. 4 n. 6, from which references to the text will be cited.

47. By 'purpose' Crescas means the purpose or end of the Torah. See ch. 4 n. 118.

48. Vienna, pp. 27b–28a.

49. These beliefs are hierarchically less fundamental than the preceding group, but their religious value is no less: one is just as much a sectarian for denying these as for denying the 'corner-stones of the Torah'.

50. i.e., one 'root' (God's existence), six 'corner-stones', and eight 'true doctrines' independent of specific commandments make up fifteen. There are 'more than fifteen', since we have not yet included the three beliefs found in treatise III, part ii (not yet introduced by Crescas and therefore not mentioned here) or the belief in Torah from heaven.

51. i.e., one 'root' and six 'corner-stones'.

52. i.e., one 'root', and six 'corner-stones', and belief in the divinity of the Torah.

53. Most likely Maimonides and Naḥmanides. On Maimonides see above, ch. 1, p. 53. For Naḥmanides, see his commentary on Gen. 1: 1, in the translation of Charles B. Chavel (New York, 1971), i. 17.

54. As Herbert A. Davidson has pointed out, for Aristotle, eternity and necessity 'are mutually implicative'. See Aristotle, *De Generatione et Corruptione*, ii. 11, 337b, 35 ff; *Metaphysics*, vi. 2, 1026b, 27, and Herbert A. Davidson, 'Maimonides' Secret Position on Creation', in I. Twersky (ed.), *Studies in Medieval Jewish History and Literature* (Cambridge, Mass., 1979), p. 18.

55. i.e., since belief in creation *ex nihilo* in time is not absolutely

necessary for belief in Torah from heaven it ought not to be counted as a 'corner-stone of the Torah'. This is not to say that Crescas rejects belief in creation *ex nihilo* in time; quite the contrary — it is affirmed by the Torah and must be held by every Jew on pain of becoming a sectarian. But that of itself does not cause it to have the status of a 'corner-stone'. It is this logical point which Crescas claims was missed by his predecessors. Sara Klein-Braslavy shows how Crescas derived this idea, and through it his entire idea of a hierarchical system of dogmas, from Rabbenu Nissim. See Klein-Braslavy, *EBS*, p. 186. Crescas reiterates this point at the end of his discussion of creation. There he writes: 'The necessity of God's power to make a body out of nothing has also been established — the opposite of what has been thought — even according to those who believe in eternity. It is for this reason that we did not place belief in creation as a corner-stone without which the existence of the Torah could not be conceived.' Crescas goes on to cite Rabbenu Nissim in this regard. See Vienna, p. 70b and Eisenberg (see above, ch. 4 n. 8), p. 47.

56. Vienna, p. 61a and p. 61b. Israel Zinberg, *A History of Jewish Literature*, iii (Philadelphia, 1973), p. 205, was apparently the first author to note that the printed editions are all corrupt here, containing in the middle of the passage just translated a passage belonging to the last chapter of the preceding treatise.

57. See above, ch. 4 n. 55.

58. i.e., the subject matter of treatise III, part ii.

59. Compare Duran, *Ohev Mishpat*, x, p. 15b (see above, p. 91) and Rabbenu Nissim's commentary on the Torah (see above, ch. 4 n. 1), p. 4.

60. Once again I call attention to the fact that from the perspective of the question of heresy and salvation there is no difference between the beliefs discussed in treatise II and those discussed in treatise III. Crescas emphasizes the point here by calling them all 'roots'.

61. Vienna, p. 82b.

62. Crescas defines the belief implied by prayer and the priestly blessing as the belief that God answers those who address Him in prayer and blesses the people of Israel when they are blessed by the priests. See treatise III, part ii, section 1 (Vienna, pp. 82b–83b).

63. Crescas defines this belief as belief that God accepts the repentance of the sinner. See treatise III, part ii, section 2 (Vienna, pp. 83b–84a).

64. With respect to the four divisions (*Perakim*) of the year, we find in Mishnah Rosh ha-Shanah, i. 2: 'The World is judged at four divisions in the year: on Passover, for grain; on Shavuot, for the fruits of trees; on Rosh ha-Shanah, all the inhabitants of the world

pass before Him, like flocks of sheep . . . and on Sukkot, they are judged for water.' These four divisions of the year and the Day of Atonement are all times of judgement, and hence of repentance. At II. iii. 2 Crescas maintains that certain seasons of the year, such as the time around the Day of Atonement, are particularly propitious for receiving God's providence. See also II, ii. 6.

65. See Num. 5: 11–31. Why the *Sotah* is any more of a 'particular commandment' than the matters included in the three beliefs included by Crescas is not clear. Urbach (see above, ch. 4 n 8), p. 344, opines that the three beliefs are all expressions of God's love for the Jewish people and are all included for that reason: God's willingness to answer prayer and accept repentance are signs of special love, over and above the love expressed in all the commandments.

66. Vienna, p. 82b.

67. According to Wolfson, pp. 17–18, some of these discussions were written by Crescas as preliminary studies for portions of the book which appear earlier.

68. Vienna, p. 85a.

69. See Harvey's discussion of the arguments here on pp. 218–29 of his dissertation.

70. This argument is analysed in greater detail on p. 127ff.

71. On Crescas's determinism, see above, ch. 4 n. 46 and ch. 4, section vi.

72. *Hathalah*; see Wolfson, p. 465, who traces the concept to the Greek *arché*. See also Wolfson's *Philosophy of Spinoza* (Cambridge, Mass., 1934), ii. 118–19.

73. If I may use the term!

74. Each letter of the Hebrew alphabet has a numerical equivalent. The sum of the numerical equivalents of the letters in the word 'Torah' is 611.

75. On the *Halakhot Gedolot* see the article by Yehoshua Horowitz in the *Encyclopaedia Judaica* (Jerusalem, 1971), vol. vii, cols. 1167–70.

76. *Book of Commandments*, i. 1.

77. 'Laws of the Foundations of the Torah', i. 1 and i. 6.

78. p. 364.

79. Crescas rejects this position. For his possible dependence upon Rabbenu Nissim in this matter see Klein-Braslavy, *EBS*, p. 188 and *Sinai*, p. 35.

80. Introduction to treatise II, section iii (p. 40a).

81. See treatise II, section vi, chapter 1 (p. 56b) and W. Zev Harvey, 'R. Hasdai Crescas u-vikorto al ha-Osher ha-Philosophi', *Proceedings of the Sixth World Congress of Jewish Studies* (Jerusalem, 1977), iii. 143–9.

82. See above, p. 115.

83. See above, ch. 4 n. 53.

84. See above, ch. 4 n. 55.
85. See above, ch. 1, section ii.
86. i.e., axioms.
87. Deut. 12: 30; the context of the verse, dealing as it does with idolatry, is instructive.
88. Rosh Amanah, xxiii. 194–5.
89. Vienna, p. 27b; see above, p. 113.
90. It would be interesting, in this context, if we knew what the original Catalan title of Crescas's *Bittul Ikkarei ha-Nozrim* was: was he refuting the *hakdamot* (axioms) or *pinnot* (corner-stones) of Christianity?
91. See above, p. 113. Compare Duran; see above, ch. 3, p. 87. I am grateful to Dr W. Zev Harvey for drawing my attention to this point.
92. In his *Encyclopaedia Judaica* article on Crescas, col. 1083.
93. See Shalom Rosenberg, 'Hitgalut ve-Torah min ha-Shamayim', *Hagut u-Mikra* (Jerusalem, 1977), p. 22.
94. See above, p. 110. Crescas, of course, denies that there is such a commandment.
95. Eliezer Schweid (see above, ch. 4 n. 8), p. 18 raises the same question; he bases his answer, however, on the assumption that Crescas held that certain beliefs were indeed commanded; I do not think that assumption is correct.
96. Compare Duran, *Ohev Mishpat*, ch. x. See above, ch. 3, p. 91.
97. Compare Duran's reduction of all the principles of Judaism to one: the belief that the Torah was revealed from heaven. See above, ch. 3, p. 88.
98. In this, as in so many other points, Crescas was most distinctly *not* followed by Albo. See ch. 5, section i.
99. See above, ch. 3, p. 99f.
100. Crescas, *Or Adonai*, III, introduction (Vienna, p. 61a), See above, p. 113f.
101. In the first of his thirteen principles. See above, p. 11.
102. 'Laws of the Foundations of the Torah', i. 1.
103. See *Or Adonai*, preface (p. 3a). See above, p. 110.
104. Ibid.
105. *Or Adonai*, II. v. 5; Ravitzky (ch. 4 n. 6), p. 450.
106. Ibid.
107. As Crescas proves to his own satisfaction in II. v. 5.
108. This, at least, is the way Crescas is interpreted by Isaac Abravanel. See *Rosh Amanah*, ch. xi (pp. 108–9) and ch. xvii (pp. 154–5).
109. At II. v. 3 (p. 48a) Crescas argues that punishment is a consequence of sin in the same way that burning is a consequence of approaching too closely to a fire. See above, ch. 4 n. 70.
110. See *Or Adonai*, II. v. 5 (Ravitzky, p. 452).

111. *Or Adonai*, introduction (p. 2b). I quote from the translation provided in Harvey's dissertation, p. 361–2.
112. *Or Adonai*, introduction (Vienna, p. 2b); Harvey dissertation, pp. 362–3.
113. Ibid.
114. Ravitzky, p. 452.
115. At II. v. 5 (Ravitzky, p. 450) Crescas notes that the Sages exclude heretics from the world to come. This is the only reference to such exclusion that I have encountered in Crescas.
116. Compare Crescas's comments at the end of II. v. 5.
117. See above, pp. 4–7.
118. See, in addition to Harvey's dissertation, his Hebrew article, cited above in ch. 4 n. 81.
119. See nn. 11, 20, 55, and 79 to this chapter.
120. In the two articles cited above in ch. 4 n. 11.
121. See Klein-Braslavy, *EBS*, p. 178.
122. See Klein-Braslavy, *Sinai*, pp. 26 and 30.
123. *EBS*, pp. 188–9, 190, and 191.
124. Rabbenu Nissim, *Perush al ha-Torah* (see above, ch. 4 n. 1), pp. 1–4.
125. *Sinai*, p. 32. See above, ch. 4 n. 97.
126. *EBS*, p. 100; *Sinai*, p. 35.
127. See above, ch. 4 n. 97.
128. See above, ch. 4 n. 91.
129. See above, p. 91 and p. 113.
130. See above, ch. 4 n. 96.

Chapter 5

1. First published in 1485 (by Gershon Soncino), the *Sefer ha-Ikkarim* was critically edited by Isaac Husik in five volumes (Philadelphia, 1929). Husik translated the book in his edition, obviating the necessity of my providing the text here. All references will be to his edition. Although there is a considerable body of literature on Albo's contributions to Jewish philosophy, little has been written specifically on his system of the principles of Judaism. See Meyer Waxman, 'Shitato shel R. Yoseph Albo be-Ikkarei ha-Dat . . .', *Ha-Tekufah*, xxx–xxxi (1946), pp. 712–46; reprinted in Waxman's *Bi-Shvilei ha-Sifrut ve-ha-Maḥashavah ha-Ivrit* (Tel Aviv, 1956), pp. 135–65. See also Eliezer Schweid, 'Bein Mishnat ha-Ikkarim shel R. Yoseph Albo le-Mishnat ha-Ikkarim shel ha-Rambam', *Tarbiz*, xxxiii (1963–4), pp. 74–84. See also above, ch. 3 n. 3.
2. *Ikkarim*, i. 26 (p. 200) and iii. 15 (p. 148).
3. See *Rosh Amanah*, introduction (p. 9 in the Tel Aviv, 1956, edition).

4. See Abraham Zacuto, *Sefer ha-Yuḥasin ha-Shalem* (ed. Z. H. Filipowski (1857 (Frankfurt, 1924)), p. 226.
5. See Y. Baer, *A History of the Jews in Christian Spain* (Philadelphia, 1966), ii. 173. On the disputation see Hyam Maccoby, *Judaism on Trial* (East Brunswick, NJ, 1982), pp. 89–94 and 168–215 and Baer, pp. 170–243.
6. See *Ikkarim*, i, p. 37. For further biographical details see Baer, index., s.v. 'Joseph Albo'.
7. See *Ikkarim*, i, p. 1.
8. Ibid. See also i. 8 and iii. 7.
9. On Albo's use of this term see Ralph Lerner, 'Natural Law in Albo's *Book of Roots*', in J. Cropsey (ed.), *Ancients and Moderns* (New York, 1964), pp. 132–47.
10. See *Ikkarim*, i, p. 36. Cf. Crescas's formulation, above, p. 113.
11. See i. 11, p. 100.
12. pp. 37–8.
13. This is the order of the principles as presented on p. 38; it is also the order of treatises ii, iii, and iv of the *Ikkarim*. But see i. 4, (p. 64) for another ordering. Cf. Duran, above, ch. 3, p. 86.
14. See i. 4.
15. See i. 10, p. 98. Cf. Duran, above, p. 94.
16. i. 4, p. 64; emphasis added.
17. Cf. Crescas, above, ch. 4, p. 113.
18. i. 10, p. 97.
19. See above, p. 88 and p. 128.
20. Albo holds that a succession of divine laws — those of Adam, Noah, and Abraham — preceded that of Moses.
21. i. 13, p. 121.
22. See above, ch. 3, p. 9.
23. i. 14, p. 123.
24. Ibid. Cf. Maimonides in his statement after the thirteenth principle, above, ch. 1, section i, end.
25. Again following Duran. See *Ikkarim*, i. 14, p. 127 and *Ohev Mishpat*, x, above, p. 91.
26. Albo's criticisms of Maimonides (see i. 1, pp. 44–7; i. 3, pp. 56 f; i. 4, pp. 64–70; i. 14, pp. 124 and 125; i. 15, pp. 132 and 136; and iii. 16, p. 148) and Crescas (i. 3, p. 62; i. 15, p. 136; and i. 23, p. 186) are largely — though not exclusively — based upon his own understanding of the term *ikkar* and thus generally miss the mark. It is curious that most of these thinkers who dealt with the principles were unaware of, or chose to ignore, the fact that each of them defined the term in his own fashion.
27. i. 13, p. 121.
28. Compare A. S. Halkin, 'A Karaite Creed', in S. R. Brunswick (ed.),

Studies in Judaica, Karaitica, and Islamica Presented to Leon Nemoy (Ramat Gan, 1982), p. 149 n: 'In view of the large field of agreement between Judaism and Islam on matters such as God, His attributes, revelation, reward and punishment, the need to emphasize the uniqueness of the messenger and the eternity of the revealed book was felt to be most imperative.' See Albo, i. 18. Albo's idea here is that even if one accepts that prophecy occurs one is not automatically committed to the belief that God sends specific messengers to ordain laws. On the expression 'messenger' (*shaliaḥ*) see Jose Fauer, *Iyyunim ba-Mishneh Torah le-ha-Rambam* (Jerusalem, 1978), p. 13 n. 2. To the sources adduced by Fauer there may be added Baḥya ibn Pakuda, *Ḥovot ha-Levavot*, ed. J. Kafiḥ (Jerusalem, 1973), p. 15 n. 36. Compare further Sa'adia, *Emunot ve-De'ot*, iii. 4.

29. i. 15, pp. 129–30, 131, and 133.
30. i. 15, p. 130.
31. See above, ch. 1, section i.
32. i. 15, p. 135.
33. i. 15, p. 131.
34. See i. 15, p. 133.
35. i. 23, p. 181. Albo calls these beliefs *anafim* ('branches').
36. Duran also emphasizes the importance of a belief's being 'generally accepted'. See above, ch. 3 n. 16.
37. i. 23, p. 187. It ought to be noted that Albo's apologetic intent is particularly clear in the case of at least three of these six beliefs. Beliefs 2, 3, and 4 are specifically anti-Christian in their intent.
38. Cf. Duran, *Ohev Mishpat*, x (above, ch. 4, section i).
39. i. 23, p. 186.
40. i. 13, pp. 120–1.
41. Gersonides to the contrary notwithstanding.
42. Albo himself admits this at i. 15, p. 133.
43. pp. 130 and 131.
44. Cf. Duran, *Ohev Mishpat*, x (above, ch. 4, section i) and Crescas, *Or Adonai*, ii, introduction (above, ch. 4, section ii).
45. p. 132.
46. i. 26, p. 199.
47. iii. 12, p. 109
48. iii.12, p. 110.
49. Ibid.
50. Ibid.
51. Abravanel certainly did not. See *Rosh Amanah*, xxii, p. 191.
52. But see i. 15, p. 133.
53. p. 35.
54. Gen. 1: 1–5: 8.
55. i.e., Albo's three fundamental principles.

56. pp. 100–1.
57. i. 10 and 13.
58. pp. 145–6. See p. 76 of Eliezer Schweid's article cited in ch. 5 n. 1 above. Schweid sees Albo's attempt to make religion a science with its own axioms as part of an attempt to make religion independent of philosophy.
59. See above, ch. 4, section ii.
60. See above, ch. 5 n. 26.
61. See i. 4, p. 69. Schweid, in his article cited in ch. 5 n. 1 above, draws attention to Albo's attitude towards Maimonides, but from a somewhat different perspective.
62. See, for example, i. 15, p. 135.
63. See, for example, i. 26, p. 202.
64. p. 43.
65. Sanhedrin 99a; *Ikkarim* i. 1, p. 44.
66. i. 1, p. 47.
67. p. 48.
68. Albo does not really make this explicit; but his whole discussion in i. 1 makes no sense unless he adopts this position. See also i. 13, p. 121 and i. 14, p. 123.
69. i.e., the subject of the principles of the Torah.
70. e.g., Maimonides' treatment of resurrection. See *Ikkarim*, i. 2, p. 54.
71. e.g., Maimonides' treatment of creation. See *Ikkarim*, i. 2, p. 51.
72. Albo hints at the example of Gersonides. See *Ikkarim*, i. 2, p. 52.
73. i. 2, pp. 49–50. Cf. Duran above, p. 88.
74. Avot iii. 15.
75. i. 2, p. 52. Albo goes on immediately to support his position by citing Rabad's famous gloss on 'Laws of Repentance', iii. 7. See above, ch. 3 n. 59.
76. i. 2, p. 54.
77. pp. 55.
78. On this basis, we must question, then, whether Guttmann's claim that Albo was decisively influenced by Averroës in the formulation of his principles is in fact true. See above, ch. 3, section iii. Indeed, Albo may be rejecting a position adopted by Averroës. The latter (*Harmony* (see above, ch. 3 n. 133) pp. 57–8) exculpates scholars who commit errors in regard to religious belief but condemns as 'sheer sin' error 'proceeding from any other class of people'. In contrast, Albo seems to defend not only scholars but simple individuals as well.
79. p. 43, emphasis added.
80. See i. 13, pp. 120–1; i. 14, p. 123; and i. 23. p. 187.
81. See above, introduction, p. 4f.

Chapter 6

1. On Shalom's life and writings, see Herbert A. Davidson, *The Philosophy of Abraham Shalom: A Fifteenth Century Exposition and Defense of Maimonides* (Los Angeles, 1964). *Neveh Shalom* does not cover the entire Talmud, but only its first tractate, *Berakhot*, providing a philosophic exposition of the *midrashim* found there.

2. On Shalom's discussion of the principles of Judaism, see Davidson, p. 8 n. 74.

3. *Neveh Shalom* (Venice, 1575; Westmead, England, 1969), treatise ii, ch. 1, p. 29a; ii. 9, p. 37a; and vii. 2, p. 149b.

4. i. 3, p. 3b–4a.

5. i. 3, p. 3b.

6. See above, ch. 1, sections ii and vi.

7. See above, ch. 1, section vi.

8. ii. 1, p. 29b; emphasis added.

9. On Arama and his writings, see Sara Heller-Wilensky, *Rabbi Yiẓḥak Arama u-Mishnato* (Jerusalem, 1956) and Chaim Pearl, *The Medieval Jewish Mind: The Religious Philosophy of Isaac Arama* (London, 1971).

10. On Arama as a preacher, see Israel Bettan, *Studies in Jewish Preaching* (New York, 1939) which includes his 'The Sermons of Isaac Arama', originally published in *HUCA*, xii–xiii (1937–8), pp. 583–634.

11. On Arama's discussion of the principles of Judaism, see Heller-Wilensky, pp. 78–96.

12. *Akedat Yiẓḥak* (Pressburg, 1849) sermon 67, p. 103a.

13. This seems to be a conscious rejection of Crescas's position; compare above, p. 113.

14. Compare Albo, *Ikkarim*, i. 9.

15. i.e., to the Torah.

16. *Mofetim muḥlati'im.*

17. Sermon 67, pp. 103a–b.

18. In making acceptance of the principles a defining characteristic of being a Jew, Arama comes close to the position enunciated by Maimonides after the statement of his own principles. See above, ch. 1, section i.

19. See sermon 31, pp. 261a–b, Heller-Wilensky, pp. 191–4, and Pearl, pp. 104–8.

20. Sermon 67, p. 99b.

21. i.e., the Torah.

22. Sermon 67, p. 103b. On the centrality of creation, see further 4, p. 38b; 55, p. 199a; and 67, p. 103b.

23. Sermon 55, pp. 199a–201b. See Heller-Wilensky, p. 83 n. 25.

24. On Yaveẓ see G. Nigal, 'De'otav shel R. Yosef Yaveẓ al ha-Philosophiah ve-ha-Mitpalsephim, Torah, u-Miẓvot', *Eshel Beer Sheva*, i (1976), pp. 258–87 and the literature cited there.

25. On Yaveẓ's statements concerning the principles of Judaism, see Isaac Barzilay, *Between Faith and Reason* (Paris, 1967), pp. 138–9 and G. Nigal's 1960 Hebrew University master's thesis, 'Rabbi Yosef Yaveẓ: Perakim be-Mishnato', pp. 74–92.

26. *Shem Havayah*; i.e., the Tetragrammaton which appears to be derived from the verb 'to be'.

27. i.e., source of providence.

28. *Ma'amar ha-Aḥdut* (n.p., but probably Piotrków, 1862), p. 2a.

29. This list is repeated in *Yesod ha-Emunah*, (n.p., but probably Piotrków, 1862), p. 2a.

30. *Yesod ha-Emunah*, pp. 2a and 2b.

31. See Yaveẓ's commentary on Ps. 36:11. This commentary was edited by J. Heilprin (London, 1952); see pp. 216–7. In his thesis on Yaveẓ (see above, ch. 6 n. 25), Nigal, p. 88, construes the third principle as referring to the messianic era.

32. *Yesod ha-Emunah*, p. 2b.

33. Ibid. p. 2a.

34. *Or ha-Ḥayyim* (n.p., but probably Piotrków, 1862), p. 2a.

35. See above, p. 84 and pp. 213–217.

36. *Or ha-Ḥayyim*, p. 2a.

37. *Ma'amar ha-Aḥdut*, p. 3a.

38. Ibid, p. 2a.

39. *Or ha-Ḥayyim*, p. 7a.

40. *Yesod Ha-Emunah*, p. 6b.

Chapter 7

1. There is some controversy concerning Bibago's name. See Allan Lazaroff, *The Theology of Abraham Bibago* (University, Alabama, 1981), p. 1.

2. On Bibago's life see, in addition to Lazaroff, pp. 1–2, Abraham Nuriel, 'Mishnato ha-Philosophit shel R. Abraham ben Shem Tov Bibago', Ph.D diss. (Hebrew University, 1975), pp. 1–3, and Chava Fraenkel-Goldschmidt's introduction to her edition of selections from Bibago's *Derekh Emunah* (Jerusalem, 1978), pp. 7–10.

3. On Bibago's works see Lazaroff, pp. 2 and 4–6 and Nuriel, pp. 3–36.

4. See Lazaroff, pp. 6–7, Nuriel, pp. 139–47, and Ḥava Tirosh-Rothschild, 'Mishnato ha-Philosophit shel R. David ben Yehudah Messer Leon', Ph.D. diss. (Hebrew University, 1978), pp. 227–9.

5. See Lazaroff, p. 1. The book was printed once (Constantinople, 1522). Portions of it were critically edited by Chava Fraenkel-

Goldschmidt (see ch. 7 n. 2 above). The only complete extant manuscript of the book is Paris Hebr. 747 (JNUL 14680). The *editio princeps* was reproduced photographically twice (Farnborough, England, 1970 and Jerusalem, 1970). The Jerusalem reprint is missing pp. 98–101.

6. See Fraenkel-Goldschmidt, p. 25, and Lazaroff, p. 8. See also Baer, *A History of the Jews in Christian Spain* (Philadelphia, 1966), ii. 296.

7. *Derekh Emunah*, p. 94, col. b (in Fraenkel-Goldschmidt's edition — henceforth FG — p. 284). We see here that Bibago adopts the 'propositional' understanding of 'faith'. See above, introduction and below, ch. 7 at n. 71. I have compared the printed text with MS Paris Hebr. 747; there are no significant differences between the manuscript and the printed text in the passages discussed below. Tirosh-Rothschild (see above, ch. 7 n. 4), p. 230, points out that Bibago is the first Jewish thinker to undertake a thoroughgoing examination of the concept 'faith' and to tackle the question of the principles of Judaism from that perspective. In this he was followed by R. David ben Judah Messer Leon (see ch. 9, section iii of the present work). Tirosh-Rothschild traces Bibago's approach to the influence of Aquinas.

8. See above on Duran, p. 96 and on Albo, p. 149ff.

9. See FG, p. 35.

10. I translate this term differently above; see ch. 4 n. 72.

11. p. 73a (FG, p. 263). Compare Aristotle, *Posterior Analytics*, i. 10, Albo's *Ikkarim*, i. 17, and Abravanel's Rosh Amanah, xxiii (p. 190).

12. Bibago uses this term not only to mean faith (as a disposition) and belief (in terms of propositions held), but also in the way in which Albo uses the term *dat elohit* (see above, p. 141). This latter usage is translated here as 'religion'.

13. p. 73a (FG, p. 263).

14. p. 73b (FG, p. 265); see also p. 90a (FG, p. 270).

15. p. 74b (FG, p. 266); compare Sa'adia Gaon, *Emunot ve-De'ot*, introduction, ch. 5.

16. p. 78d.

17. Ibid. Bibago is a bit careless here with respect to the question of which of his axioms is first.

18. p. 86b.

19. See above, ch. 1 n. 193 and ch. 3 n. 10.

20. p. 89c.

21. p. 90a (FG, p. 271).

22. Ibid.

23. p. 90b (FG, p. 272).

24. Ibid.

25. p. 90c.

26. pp. 94d–95a (FG, p. 289).
27. See p. 188.
28. p. 95a (FG, p. 290).
29. See above, ch. 5, section iii.
30. Bava Mezia 85b.
31. p. 99d–100a.
32. *Guide*, i. 51–60.
33. Literally: 'absolutely invisible to us'.
34. p. 99c; this passage is copied by Abravanel at *Rosh Amanah*, x (p. 102).
35. i.e., some men — not all — are prophets.
36. Moses was part (an individual) of part (the prophets).
37. p. 99d.
38. pp. 100b–c.
39. pp. 100c–101a.
40. pp. 101a–101b.
41. p. 101b; see above, on Duran, p. 84.
42. p. 101b; Abravanel cites the same texts, Ta'anit 25a and Sanhedrin 97b, at *Rosh Amanah*, x (pp. 104–5).
43. p. 101c; compare Albo, *Ikkarim*, i. 1, p. 44 and iv. 42, p. 413, and Abravanel, *Rosh Amanah*, iii, fifth objection (p. 69).
44. Bibago cities Rabad as the source of this objection. See above, ch. 3 n. 59 and ch. 10, section ii.
45. Compare Abravanel, *Rosh Amanah*, iii, eighth objection (pp. 69–70).
46. Compare Albo, *Ikkarim*, i. 3, p. 59 and Abravanel, Rosh Amanah, iii, eleventh objection (p. 70).
47. *Ma'amad har Sinai.*
48. Compare Abravanel, *Rosh Amanah*, iii, twelfth objection (p. 70).
49. Compare Albo, *Ikkarim*, i. 14 (pp. 124–5) and Abravanel, *Rosh Amanah*, iii, second objection (pp. 66–7). See also on Duran, above at p. 91.
50. p. 101d. Compare Albo, i. 3 (p. 58) and Abravanel's third objection (p. 67).
51. *Emuna ḥelkit.*
52. p. 102a.
53. See above, p. 167.
54. See above, p. 172.
55. Compare Albo's *Ikkarim*, i. 9 (p. 94) and Abravanel, *Rosh Amanah*, xvi, response to the twelfth objection (pp. 148–50).
56. See Sanhedrin 99a.
57. 102c.
58. See above, ch. 3, section ii.
59. See *Rosh Amanah*, xii (p. 112) and below, p. 183f.
60. See above, ch. 1, section ii.

61. p. 102c. This portion of the *Derekh Emunah* was published by A. S. Halkin in *Be-Ikvot Rambam* (Jerusalem, 1979), pp. 196–9. Compare Abravanel's seventh objection (p. 69).
62. Compare Abravanel's solution to his seventh objection in *Rosh Amanah*, xvi (p. 144).
63. See Maimonides' twelfth principle; above, ch. 1, section i.
64. Compare Abravanel's thirteenth objection (p. 70). His solution however, differs from Bibago's. See *Rosh Amanah*, xvi, response to the thirteenth objection (p. 150).
65. Compare the similar solution proposed by Abraham Shalom. See above, ch. 6, section i.
66. p. 90a (FG, p. 271); quoted above, p. 168.
67. See above, ch. 4, p. 113.
68. p. 101d; see above, p. 173.
69. 94d–95a; see above, p. 169.
70. See above, ch. 1, section ii.
71. See ch. 10, section ii.
72. p. 95a (FG, p. 290); see above, p. 169.
73. p. 28.
74. See Lazaroff, p. 64 n. In addition to the borrowings listed there the following correspondences ought to be noted:
    i. *Derekh Emunah* (DE), iii. 5, pp. 95d–96a and
       Rosh Amanah (RA), xii, pp. 116–18;
    ii. DE, iii. 5, p. 102a and RA, xvi, pp. 148–9;
    iii. DE, iii. 5, p. 102c and RA, iii, p. 69 and RA, xvi, p. 144.
75. Especially since it was congenial to Abravanel's own predilections as a commentator. See p. 180f.
76. At *Rosh Amanah*, iii, thirteenth objection (p. 70), Abravanel refers to a 'recent scholar', There is little doubt that he has Bibago in mind. That is the closest he comes to mentioning Bibago in any of his extant writings.

Chapter 8

1. For Abravanel's life and thought see Benzion Netanyahu, *Don Isaac Abravanel*, 3rd edn. (Philadelphia. 1972).
2. The book was published by Abravanel in Constantinople in 1505 (photographically reproduced in Don Isaac Abravanel, *Opera Minora* (Westmead, 1972)). It has appeared in at least nine subsequent editions, the latest being Tel Aviv, 1958. The *Rosh Amanah* was translated into Latin by Guilielmus Vorstium, as *Liber de Capite Fidei*. This work was published twice in Amsterdam, in 1638 and in 1684. B. Mossé translated the book into French (Avignon, 1884; microfiche repr. by InterDocumentation Company

of Zug, Switzerland, n.d.) under the title *Le Principe de la foi*. The first five chapters of the book were loosely translated into English by Isaac Mayer Wise as *The Book on the Cardinal Points of Religion*. This translation appeared in instalments in vol. viii of Wise's newspaper, *The Israelite* (Cincinnati, 1862), pp. 212, 220–1, 228–9, 236–7, and 244–5. My own translation of the book with introduction and notes, is called *Principles of Faith* (East Brunswick, NJ, 1982).

On Abravanel's position in the *Rosh Amanah* see, in addition to my translation, my 'R. Isaac Abravanel on the Principles of Judaism', *Journal of the American Academy of Religion*, xliv (supplement) (1977), pp. 1183–200 and Eugene Mihaly, 'Abravanel on the Principles of Faith', *HUCA*, xxvi (1955), pp. 481–502.

3. On the translation, see the appendix.
4. As was noted above, ch. 7 n. 74, he borrowed several passages from Bibago's *Derekh Emunah* in the *Rosh Amanah*.
5. Indeed, Arama's son Meir accused Abravanel of plagiarizing his father's works. On this whole issue see p. 219 of my translation of the *Rosh Amanah* and the sources cited there.
6. Abravanel, however, never mentions Duran. See Jakob Guttmann, *Die Religionsphilosophischen Lehren des Isaak Abravanel* (Breslau, 1916), pp. 23–40. Guttmann presents an exhaustive list of all Jewish authors mentioned by Abravanel; Duran's name does not appear.
7. See above, p. 91 and p. 142.
8. These seventeen objections may be summarized as follows:
   (*1*) If we define 'principle' as 'a term applied to a thing upon which the existence and duration of another thing depends and without which it cannot endure', then many of Maimonides' principles ought not to be called principles.
   (*2*) The fifth of Maimonides' principles, that God ought to be worshipped, is a particular commandment and as such ought not to be counted as a principle.
   (*3*) How would praying to an intermediary cause the Torah to collapse?
   (*4*) Contrary to the ninth principle (eternity of the Torah), why should not the Torah change if those who are guided by it change?
   (*5*) Given that R. Hillel denied the coming of the Messiah (Sanhedrin 99a), how could belief in his coming be construed as a principle of faith?
   (*6*) Why would denying belief in resurrection cause the Torah to collapse?
   (*7*) How can we count belief in the Messiah and the resurrection of the dead as principles since, after they occur, there will be no need to believe in them?

(*8*) Why did not Maimonides count as a principle the belief that the *Shekhinah* dwells in Israel through the medium of the Torah?

(*9*) Why did Maimonides fail to count belief in creation as a principle?

(*10*) Why did Maimonides fail to count as a principle that we ought to believe in the miracles of the Torah in their literal sense?

(*11*) Why did Maimonides fail to count as a principle that we ought to accept ancestral tradition?

(*12*) Why did Maimonides fail to count as a principle that we ought to believe in human choice?

(*13*) Why did Maimonides fail to count as a principle that we ought to believe that God acts by will?

(*14*) Why did Maimonides fail to count belief in more of God's attributes as principles? Why were his principles thirteen in number?

(*15*) Why did Maimonides fail to count as principles belief in the end of man and survival of the soul after death?

(*16*) Why did Maimonides fail to count as a principle belief in the oracular character of the *Urim* and *Tummim*?

(*17*) Why did Maimonides fail to count as principles prayer and the other beliefs counted by Crescas?

9. The three objections drawn from Crescas may be summarized in the following way (continuing the numbering from the objections listed in ch. 3):

(*18*) Maimonides ought not to have counted belief in God as a commandment.

(*19*) Beliefs cannot be commanded, yet two of Maimonides' principles are commandments.

(*20*) Critique of Maimonides' proof from Makkot 23a–b that Exod. 20: 2 is a commandment.

On the question of the commandment of beliefs, see above, ch. 4, section v.

10. Abravanel's own objections (again continuing the numbering from the objections listed in ch. 3 and 4) may be summarized as follows:

(*21*) Why did Maimonides fail to include all of his principles in 'Laws of the Foundations of the Torah'?

(*22*) Why did Maimonides include beliefs which are not principles of Judaism in 'Laws of the Foundations of the Torah'?

(*23*) Why did Maimonides only count the first two principles, God's existence and unity, as commandments?

(*24*) Why in the *Book of Knowledge* did Maimonides call the first principle 'the foundation of all foundations and the pillar of the sciences' instead of calling it '*one* of the foundations'? Further, of what interest is it to us if this belief is the pillar of Gentile sciences? Further still, why does Maimonides make the unnecessary claim, '(God's) truth is not like the truth of any one of them' and why does he support this contention with an irrelevant verse?

(*25*) Maimonides' statement in 'Laws of the Foundations of the Torah' that God moves the highest sphere is either unnecessary or heterodox.

(*26*) Maimonides' discussion of God's unity in 'Laws of the Foundations of the Torah' raises many problems.

(*27*) Ought not principles 2, 3, and 4 be included in principle 1?

(*28*) Why does Maimonides present the thirteenth principle as belief in the resurrection of the dead simply, as opposed to belief that the Torah teaches resurrection?

11. The teachings are as follows:

Principle 1: God's existence is the most perfect possible (the second teaching is missing in the text).

Principle 2: God has no partner or second in divinity; God has no composition or multiplicity at all.

Principle 3: God is not a body, neither complex nor simple; God is not the power of a body.

Principle 4: God is eternal, *a parte ante*; all other things are created.

Principle 5: We ought to worship God; one may not posit intermediaries between man and his Creator.

Principle 6: Prophecy cannot occur without natural and speculative preparation; prophecy will not occur if the divine will withholds it.

Principle 7: Moses was more perfect in his temperament and intellect than any other member of the human race; in the degree of his prophecy, Moses was exalted above all the other prophets.

Principle 8: Both the written and oral Torahs come from Sinai.

Principle 9: The Jews will never exchange nor uproot the Torah; God will never give another Torah, whether in whole or in part.

Principle 10: God knows all the actions of men; God extends His providence over human beings.

Principle 11: God will reward the righteous and punish the wicked; the greatest reward is life in the world to come and the greatest punishment is the cutting off of the soul.

Principle 12: The Messiah will come; he will be a descendant of David and Solomon.

Principle 13: The dead will live again in body and soul; resurrection will be for the righteous only.

12. p. 98 (all page references to the *Rosh Amanah* are to my translation, cited above in ch. 8 n. 2).

13. See above, ch. 1, section iv, where the three 'lessons' and their sources are discussed.

14. This may represent an echo of Arama's position. See above, ch. 6, section ii.

15. See above, ch. 3 n. 59.

16. See above, ch. 1, section ii, and ch. 10, section ii.

17. iii. 5 (p. 102c).

18. See above, ch. 3, p. 98.

19. See ch. 10, section ii.

20. Ch. xii, pp. 112–13. Compare Bibago, *Derekh Emunah*, iii. 5 (p. 102c top) and above, ch. 7, at n. 57.

21. Ch. xxii, p. 192.

22. See below, ch. 10, section iii.

23. *Shamayim Ḥadashim* (Roedelheim, 1892), p. 2b.

24. *Mifalot Elohim* (Venice, 1592), 6a, col. 1.

25. The partial verse is Deut. 12: 30. The context of this verse, dealing as it does with idol worship, is instructive.

26. See Pesaḥim 15a; the phrase means that the cases are dissimilar.

27. pp. 196–7.

28. See David Neumark, *Toledot ha-Ikkarim be-Yisrael* ii (Odessa, 1919), p. 179; Eugene Mihaly, 'Isaac Abravanel on the Principles of Faith', *HUCA*, xxvi (1955), p. 484; Benzion Netanyahu, *Don Isaac Abravanel*, 3rd edn. (Philadelphia, 1972), p. 291; Joseph Sarachek, *Don Isaac Abravanel* (New York, 1938), p. 151; and M. M. Kellner, 'R. Isaac Abravanel on the Principles of Judaism', *Journal of the American Academy of Religion*, xliv (supplement) (1977), p. 1187.

29. Ch. xxiv, p. 205.

30. p. 112.

31. Albo, *Ikkarim*, i. 2 (p. 55). Compare Leo Strauss, 'On Abravanel's Philosophical Tendency and Political Teaching', in J. B. Trend and H. Loewe (eds.) *Isaac Abravanel: Six Lectures* (Cambridge, 1937), pp. 95–129, esp. p. 104.

32. p. 195.

33. p. 200.

34. See Netanyahu (see above, ch. 8 n. 28), p. 73 and the introduction to the *Rosh Amanah* (not included in my translation).

35. p. 80.

36. p. 82; see also pp. 96–7 and 142.

37. p. 97.

38. p. 187.

39. pp. 197–8. See *Kuzari*, i. 2.

40. p. 198.

41. p. 198.
42. p. 198.
43. p. 80.
44. p. 201.
45. Albo also emphasizes the importance of this claim; see *Ikkarim*, i. 23, pp. 183–4. Albo's position seems to be motivated by anti-Christian polemical considerations. Abravanel's position, on the other hand, would seem to be motivated by anti-philosophical considerations; he insists with Arama and Yavez that it is perfection through commandments and not through the intellect which is of crucial importance for earning a share in the world to come.
46. pp. 208–9.
47. Abravanel's discussion in *Rosh Amanah*, ch. xii (see above, p. 183f) proves that he was aware of the type of position adopted by Duran.
48. Reflected here also may be Abravanel's fundamentally negative attitude towards the conversos and his insistence on a sharp break between them and faithful Jews. See Benzion Netanyahu, *The Marranos of Spain* (New York, 1966), p. 203.

Chapter 9

1. Printed in Altdorf, Switzerland in 1644 (photoreproduction, New York, 1979).
2. Professor Frank Talmage provides the manuscript evidence in an introduction he wrote for the *Sefer Ha-Nizzahon* (Jerusalem, 1984) which he was kind enough to show me before its publication. I wish to thank him for sharing the results of his research with me. See Bodleian MS Opp. 145, pp. 7b–8a. See also Yehudah Kaufman (Even Shmuel), *R. Yom Tov Lippman Muelhausen* (New York, 1927), p. 34.
3. On Delmedigo see David Geffen, 'Insights into the Life and Thought of Elijah del Medigo Based on his Published and Unpublished Works', *PAAJR*, xli–xlii (1975), pp. 69–86.
4. The *Behinat ha-Dat* was published in Vienna in 1833. An English translation may be found in David Geffen, 'Faith and Reason in Elijah del Medigo's *Behinat ha-Dat* and the Philosophic Background of the Work', Ph.D. diss. (Columbia University, 1970 (Xerox University Microfilms no. 71–0675)).
5. The principles appear on pp. 21–8 of *Behinat ha-Dat*. On Delmedigo's reasons for including them in his work see Geffen's dissertation, p. 259.
6. On David ben Judah Messer Leon see Hava Tirosh-Rothschild, 'Mishnato ha-Philosophit shel R. David ben Yehudah Leon', Ph.D. diss. (Hebrew University, 1978).

7. See, for example, Reuven Bonfil, *Ha-Rabbanut be-Italiah bi-Tekufat ha-Ranaissance* (Jerusalem, 1979), index, s.v. 'David ben Judah (Messer Leon)'.

8. Montefiore 290; JNUL 7328. Solomon Schechter published the introduction to this work in 'Notes sur Messer David Leon', *REJ*, xxiv (1892), pp. 118–38.

9. See Tirosh-Rothschilds' dissertation, pp. 226–31.

10. On David ben Judah Messer Leon and Halevi see Ḥava Tirosh-Rothschild, 'Hashpa'at Mishnato shel R. Yehudah Halevi al Haguto shel R. David Messer Leon', *Proceedings of the Eighth World Congress of Jewish Studies, Division C* (Jerusalem, 1982), pp. 79–84.

11. *Magen David*, pp. 157b–158a.

12. I present here a summary of David ben Judah Messer Leon's fifteen objections to Maimonides' principles:

    (*1*) Why are there exactly 13?

    (*2*) Why are there commandments among them?

    (*3*) God's unity and incorporeality ought not to be counted as foundations.

    (*4*) How can God's incorporeality be a foundation if it is contradicted by the plain sense of Scripture?

    (*5*) Why did Maimonides count God's ontic priority as a principle and not that God lives, is wise, is powerful, and wills?

    (*6*) Why is the fifth principle — a commandment — included?

    (*7*) Why is creation not included in the list?

    (*8*) Why is free choice not included in the list?

    (*9*) Why is ancestral tradition not included in the list?

    (*10*) Why did Maimonides divide prophecy, Mosaic prophecy, and Torah from heaven into three distinct principles?

    (*11*) Why is Torah from heaven a principle — it thus becomes a principle of itself!

    (*12*) The verse, 'Thou shalt not add,' does not prove that the Torah will never be abolished in its entirety.

    (*13*) Messiah and resurrection are examples of reward and punishment. Why are they counted separately?

    (*14*) Principles never cease to obtain; but after the Messiah comes and the resurrection occurs we will no longer have to believe in them and they will cease to be principles.

    (*15*) How can Messiah be a principle if it was denied by R. Hillel (Sanhedrin 99a)? Further, why can we not conceive of a divine Torah without belief in the Messiah?

    With the exception of the fourth, all of these objections are drawn either from Abravanel (see above, ch. 8 nn. 8–10) or Bibago (see above, p. 172).

13. See above, ch. 7, pp. 170–171.

14. See p. 36a. For creation, see i. 9 (p. 40a); for prophecy, see ii. 32 (p. 51a); and for miracles see ii. 51 (p. 61a).
15. Trani's *Bet Elohim* was published in Venice in 1576 and in Warsaw in 1872. His discussion of Maimonides' principles is analysed by Mordecai Pachter in 'Safrut ha-Derush ve-ha-Musar bi-Zefat ba-Me'ah ha-Shesh-Esreh', Ph.D. diss. (Hebrew University, 1976), pp. 330–42.

Chapter 10

1. For general surveys of contemporary developments in Christianity see M. D. Lambert, *Medieval Heresy* (London, 1977) and Gordon Leff, *Heresy in the Later Middle Ages* (Manchester, 1967). With specific reference to the connection between dogma and heresy see Jaroslav Pelikan, *The Growth of Medieval Theology 600–1300* (Chicago, 1978), pp. 17–18 and 229, and W. L. Wakefield and A. P. Evans (eds.), *Heresies of the High Middle Ages* (New York, 1969), p. 2.
2. See above, ch. 1, section i.
3. 'Laws of Repentance', iii. See above, ch. 1, section iii.
4. I am referring here to the two categories *zadon* ('intentional sinning') and *shegagah* ('unintentional sinning').
5. I cite the gloss as translated by Isadore Twersky in his *Rabad of Posquières*, rev. edn. (Philadelphia, 1980), p. 282. See above, ch. 3 n. 59.
6. See Twersky, pp. 282–6.
7. See Abravanel's *Rosh Amanah*, xxiv (p. 205).
8. *Rosh Amanah*, xii (p. 122).
9. Ibid. See above, ch. 8, p. 184.
10. See above, ch. 3, p. 91.
11. On Rabad's gloss in Duran's version see above, ch. 3 n. 59.
12. *Ohev Mishpat*, p. 15a. See above, p. 88.
13. Ibid.
14. This, at least, is Duran's expressed position. Whether he would be willing to stick to it if confronted by a figure like Mordecai Kaplan is another question altogether.
15. See Bibago, *Derekh Emunah* (Constantinople, 1522), iii. 5 (p. 102c). See above, p. 174.
16. See above, ch. 10 n. 8.
17. See Albo's *Sefer ha-Ikkarim*, i. 1–2 and above, ch. 5, section iv.
18. Bibago, on the other hand, appears to belong to the Maimonides-Abravanel camp. See above, ch. 10 n. 15.
19. See above, ch. 1, section vii.
20. See 'Laws of the Foundations of the Torah', i. 1.

21. See above, ch. 1, section ix.
22. See *Ikkarim*, i. 1 (pp. 44–7).
23. See above, p. 157f.
24. See B. Netanyahu, *Don Isaac Abravanel*, pp. 3–4 and 266.
25. See Meyer Waxman, 'Shitato shel R. Yosef Albo be-Ikkarei ha-Dat. . . ', *Ha-Tekufah*, xxx–xxxi (1946), pp. 712–46.
26. See C. D. Chavel (ed.), *Kitvei Ramban* (Jerusalem, 1963), i. 310. Compare, on Albo, Y. Baer, *A History of the Jews in Christian Spain* (Philadelphia, 1966), ii. 178. See also Gershom Scholem, *The Messianic Idea in Judaism* (New York, 1971), p. 33.
27. See above, p. 96.
28. See Duran, *Ohev Mishpat*, x (above, p. 91); Crescas, *Or Adonai*, treatise II, introduction (above, p. 113); Arama, *Akedat Yizhak*, sermon 67 (above, p. 159); Bibago, *Derekh Emunah*, iii. 4 (p. 95a) (above, p. 169); and David ben Judah Messer Leon, *Tehillah le-David*, p. 11b (above, p. 198).
29. Sanhedrin 99a.
30. See above, introduction.
31. See above, ch. 2, section vii.
32. Ibid.
33. See above, introduction.

Bibliography

Abba Mari Astruc of Lunel, *Minḥat Kena'ot*, ed. M. J. Bisseliches (Pressburg, 1838; photo-edition, New York, 1958).

Abelson, Joshua, 'Maimonides on the Jewish Creed', *JQR*, xix (1907), pp. 24–58.

Abraham ben David of Posquières, *Hasagot* [*al ha-Mishneh Torah*].

Abravanel, Isaac, *Ma'amar Kazer be-Ve'ur Sod ha-Moreh* (Venice, 1574). Repr. in Don Isaac Abravanel, *Opera Minora* (Westmead, Gregg International, 1972; Jerusalem, Sifriyah le-Maḥshevet Yisrael, 1967).

—— *Mifalot Elohim* (Venice, 1592). Repr. in Don Isaac Abravanel, *Opera Minora* (Westmead, Gregg International, 1972).

—— *Rosh Amanah* (Tel Aviv, 1958).

—— [*Rosh Amanah*] *The Book on the Cardinal Points of Religion*, trans. Isaac Mayer Wise, *The Israelite*, vol. viii (Cincinnati, 1862), pp. 212, 220–1, 228–9, 236–7, and 244–5.

—— [*Rosh Amanah*] *Le Principe de la foi*, trans. B. Mossé (Avignon, 1884; microfiche repr. Zug, Switzerland, InterDocumentation Co., n.d.).

—— [*Rosh Amanah*] *Liber de Capite Fidei*, trans. Guilielmus Vorstium (Amsterdam, 1638 and 1684).

—— [*Rosh Amanah*] *Principles of Faith*, trans. M. M. Kellner (East Brunswick, NJ, Associated University Presses for the Littman Library of Jewish Civilization, 1982).

—— *Shamayim Ḥadashim* (Roedelheim, 1892). Repr. in Don Isaac Abravanel, *Opera Minora* (Westmead, Gregg International, 1972).

Aescoly, A. Z., *Ha-Tenuot ha-Meshiḥiot be-Yisrael* (Jerusalem, Mossad Bialik, 1956).

Albo, Joseph, *Sefer Ha-Ikkarim*, ed. and trans. I. Husik, 5 vols. (Philadelphia, Jewish Publication Society, 1929).

Aldabi, Meir, *Shevilei Emunah* (Riva da Trento, 1558–9).

Allony, Nehemiah, 'David ibn Bilia vi-Yzirotav', *Areshet* (1944), pp. 277–86. Repr. in *Mi-Sifrut Yemei ha-Benayim* (Jerusalem, Mossad ha-Rav Kook, 1945), pp. 13–22.

Altmann, Alexander, 'Albo Joseph', *Encyclopaedia Judaica* (Jerusalem, 1971), ii, col. 536.

—— 'Articles of Faith', *Encyclopaedia Judaica* (Jerusalem, Keter, 1971), iii, cols. 654–60.

—— 'Moses Narboni's Epistle on *Shi'ur Qomah*', *Jewish Medieval and Renaissance Studies*, ed. A. Altmann (Cambridge, Mass., Harvard University Press, 1969), pp. 225–89.

—— 'Translator's Introduction [to Sa'adia's *Doctrines and Beliefs*]', *Three Jewish Philosophers* (New York, Atheneum, 1972).

Ankory, Zvi, *Karaites in Byzantium* (New York, Columbia University Press, 1959).

Arama, Isaac, *Akedat Yizḥak* (Pressburg, 1849).

Arieli, Nahum, 'Mavo li-She'eilat ha-Ikkarim be-Yahadut', *Da'at*, xi (1983), pp. 19–38.

—— 'Mishnato ha-Philosophit shel R. Shimon ben Zemaḥ Duran', Ph.D. diss. (Hebrew University, 1976).

—— 'Torat ha-Ikkarim shel ha-Rambam', MA thesis (Hebrew University, 1971).

Aristotle. *De Generatione et Corruptione.*

—— *Metaphysics.*

—— *Prior and Posterior Analytics*, trans. W. D. Ross (Oxford, Clarendon Press, 1965).

—— *Topics.*

Assaf, David, *Oẓar Leshon ha-Rambam* (Haifa, Maimonides Research Institute, 1968).

Assaf, Simḥa, 'Anusei Sefarad u-Portugal be-Safrut ha-Teshuvot', *Be-Oholei Ya'akov* (Jerusalem, Mossad ha-Rav Kook, 1943), pp. 145–80.

Averroës, *Al Kashf an Manahij al-Adillah.*

—— *On the Harmony of Religion and Philosophy*, ed. and trans. G. F. Hourani (London, Luzac, 1961).

Baer, Yizḥak, *A History of the Jews in Christian Spain* (Philadelphia, Jewish Publication Society, 1966).

Baḥya ben Asher, *Kitvei Rabbenu Baḥya*, ed. C. D. Chavel (Jerusalem, Mossad ha-Rav Kook, 1969).

—— *Rabbenu Baḥya al ha-Torah*, ed. C. D. Chavel (Jerusalem, Mossad ha-Rav Kook, 1982).

Baḥya ibn Pakuda, *Ḥovot ha-Levavot*, ed. and trans. J. Kafiḥ (Jerusalem, 1973).

Baneth, David, 'Sifriyato shel Rofe be-Miẓrayim biymei ha-Rambam', *Tarbiẓ*, xxx (1961), pp. 171–85.

Barzilay, Isaac, *Between Faith and Reason* (Paris, Mouton, 1967).

Basyatchi, Elijah ben Moses, 'Ten Principles of Faith', *A Karaite Anthology*, ed. L. Nemoy (New Haven, Yale University Press, 1952), p. 250.

Ben-Chorin, Scholom, *Jüdische Glaube* (Tübingen, J. C. B. Mohr, 1975).

Ben-Sasson, Yonah, 'Mishnato ha-Historit shel ha-Rambam', *Ḥevrah ve-Historiah*, ed. Y. Cohen (Jerusalem, Ministry of Education and Culture, 1980), pp. 543–632.

Berman, Lawrence V, 'Ibn Bajjah ve-ha-Rambam', Ph.D. diss. (Hebrew University, Jerusalem, 1959).

—— 'Maimonides, the Disciple of Alfarabi', *Israel Oriental Studies*, iv (1974), pp. 154–78.

—— 'The Structure of Maimonides' *Guide of the Perplexed'*, *Proceedings of the Sixth World Congress of Jewish Studies*, iii (Jerusalem, World Union of Jewish Studies, 1977), pp. 7–17.

Bettan, Israel, 'The Sermons of Isaac Arama', *HUCA*, xii–xiii (1937–8), pp. 583–634.

—— *Studies in Jewish Preaching* (New York, 1939).

Bibago, Abraham, *Derekh Emunah* (Constantinople, 1522; repr. editions: London, Gregg International, 1969 and Jerusalem, Makor, 1970). Selections, edited with introductions and notes by Chava Fraenkel-Goldschmidt (Jerusalem, Mossad Bialik, 1978).

Birnbaum, Philip, *Daily Prayer Book* (New York, Hebrew Publishing Company, 1949).

Blau, Joshua, 'Bi-Dvar Kitvei ha-Yad Perush ha-Mishnah la-Rambam Pock. 295, Hunt. 117, ve-Sassoon 72, 73', *Tarbiz*, xxxiii (1964), p. 316.

—— 'Ha-Omnam yesh be-Yadeinu Tofes shel Perush ha-Mishnah be-Ezem Ketav-Yado shel ha-Rambam?' *Tarbiz*, xxvii (1956), pp. 536–43.

—— and Alexander Scheiber, *Autograph ha-Rambam Me-Osef Adler u-me-Genizat Leningrad; Teyutat ha-Hakdamah le-Seder Toharot* (Jerusalem, Israel Academy of Sciences and Humanities, 1981).

Bleich, J. David, 'Duran's View of the Nature of Providence', *JQR*, lxix (1978–9), pp. 208–25.

Blidstein, Gerald, 'Who is not a Jew? — The Medieval Discussion', *Israel Law Review*, xi (1976), pp. 369–90.

Bloch, Phillip, *Die Willensfreiheit von Chasdai Kreskas* (Munich, 1879).

Blumenthal, David R., *The Commentary of R. Hoter ben Shelomoh to the Thirteen Principles of Maimonides* (Leiden, E. J. Brill, 1974).

Bonfil, Reuven, *Ha-Rabbanut be-Italiah bi-Tekufat ha-Renaissance* (Jerusalem, Magnes Press, 1979).

Buber, Martin, *Two Types of Faith* (New York, Harper and Row, 1961).

Cassuto, M. D., *Ha-Yehudim be-Firenze bi-Tekufat ha-Renaissance* (Jerusalem, Makhon Ben-Zvi, 1967).

Cohen, Gerson D., 'Introduction' to Abraham ibn Daud, *Sefer ha-Qabbalah* (Philadelphia, Jewish Publication Society, 1967).

—— Rev. of *Marranos of Spain*, by B. Netanyahu, *Jewish Social Studies*, xxix (1967), pp. 178–84.

Cohen, Jeremy, *The Friars and the Jews: The Evolution of Medieval Anti-Judaism* (Ithaca, Cornell University Press, 1982).

Crescas, Hasdai, *Bittul Ikkarei ha-Nozrim*, ed. Ephraim Deinard (Kearny, NJ, 1904).

—— *Or Adonai* (Vienna, 1859; repr. Tel Aviv, Offset Esther, 1963).

—— [Untitled Chronicle], in Franz Kobler, *Letters of Jews Through the Ages*, vol. i (New York, East and West Library, 1978), pp. 272–5.

Davidson, Herbert A., 'Maimonides' Secret Position on Creation', *Studies in Medieval Jewish History and Literature*, ed. I. Twersky (Cambridge, Mass., Harvard University Press, 1979), pp. 16–40.

—— *The Philosophy of Abraham Shalom: A Fifteenth Century Exposition and Defense of Maimonides* (Los Angeles, University of California Press, 1964).

Delmedigo, Elijah, *Behinat ha-Dat* (Vienna, 1833).

Dienstag, Jacob I., 'Mosheh Steinschneider Ke-Hoker ha-Rambam', *Sinai*, lxvi (1970), pp. 347–66.

Duran, Shimon ben Zemah, *Magen Avot* (Leghorn (Livorno), 1785; repr. Jerusalem, Makor, n.d.).

—— *Ohev Mishpat* (Venice, 1590; repr. Tel Aviv, Zion, 1971).

—— *Tashbez* [Teshuvot Shimon ben Zemah] (Amsterdam, 1738–41).

Efros, Israel, *Studies in Medieval Jewish Philosophy* (New York, Columbia University Press, 1974).

Eisenberg, Yehudah, *Ha-Reshut Netunah* (Jerusalem, Haskel, 1983).

—— *Torat ha-Beriah shel R. Hasdai Crescas* (Jerusalem, Haskel, 1981).

Epstein, Isidore, *The Responsa of R. Simon ben Zemach Duran as a Source of the History of the Jews of North Africa* (London, 1930).

Fakhry, Majid, *A History of Islamic Philosophy* (New York, Columbia University Press, 1970).

—— 'Philosophy and Scripture in the Philosophy of Averroes', *Mediaeval Studies*, xxx (1968), pp. 78–89.

Falaquera, Shem Tov ben Joseph, *Iggeret ha-Halom*, in H. Malter, 'Shem Tob ben Joseph Palquera', *JQR*, i (1910–11), pp. 151–81, 451–501.

—— *Moreh ha-Moreh*, ed. J. Bisseliches (Pressburg, 1837).

Fauer, Jose, *Iyyunim ba-Mishneh Torah le-ha-Rambam* (Jerusalem, Mossad ha-Rav Kook, 1978).

Feldman, Seymour, 'Crescas' Theological Determinism', *Da'at*, ix (1982), pp. 3–28.

Fraenkel-Goldschmidt, Chava, 'Introduction', in Abraham Bibago, *Derekh Emunah*, ed. Chava Fraenkel-Goldschmidt (Jerusalem, Mossad Bialik, 1978).

Funkenstein, Amos, 'Maimonides: Political Theory and Realistic Messianism', *Miscellanea Mediaevalia*, xi (1977), pp. 81–103.

Geffen, David, 'Faith and Reason in Elimah del Medigo's *Behinat ha-Dat* and the Philosophic Background of the Work', Ph.D. diss. (Columbia University, 1970 (Xerox University Microfilms no. 71–0675)).

—— 'Insights into the Life and Thought of Elijah del Medigo Based on his Published and Unpublished Works', *PAAJR*, xli–xlii (1975), pp. 69–86.

Geiger, Abraham, 'Iggeret R. Shemariah mi-Negroponto el ha-Yehudim me-Romah', *Ozar Nehmad*, ii (1857), pp. 90–4.

—— 'Nosafot al Devar R. Shemariah ha-Ikriti', *He-Haluz*, ii (1853), pp. 25–7, 158–60.

Gellman, Jerome, 'The Philosophical *Hassagot* of Rabad on Maimonides' *Mishneh Torah*', *The New Scholasticism*, lviii (1984), pp. 145–69.

Gersonides, Levi, *Milḥamot Adonai* (Leipzig, 1866).

Ghazzali, Abu Hamid, *Al Kitab Qawa'id al-'Aqa'id*, trans. N. A. Faris (Lahore, Ashraf, 1963).

Glicker, Y., 'Ha-Ba'ayah ha-Modalit ba-Philosophiah shel ha-Rambam', *Iyyun*, x (1969), pp. 177–91.

Goitein, S. D., 'Jewish Society and Institutions Under Islam', *Jewish Society Through the Ages*, ed. H. H. Ben Sasson and S. Ettinger (New York, Schocken, 1971), pp. 170–84.

—— *A Mediterranean Society* iii: *The Community* (Berkeley, University of California Press, 1971).

—— 'Moses Maimonides, Man of Action: A Revision of the Master's Biography in the Light of the Genizah Documents', *Hommage A Georges Vajda*, ed. G. Nahon and C. Touati (Louvain, Deeters, 1980), pp. 155–67.

Goldman, S., 'The Halachic Foundation of Maimonides' Thirteen Principles', *Essays Presented to Chief Rabbi Brodie on the Occasion of his Seventieth Birthday*, ed. H. J. Zimmels, *et al.* (London, Soncino Press and Jews College, 1967), pp. 111–17.

Goodman, Lenn Evan, 'Maimonides' Philosophy of Law, *Jewish Law Annual*, i (1978), pp. 72–107.

Goren, Shlomo, *Torat ha-Mo'adim* (Tel Aviv, Zioni, 1963–4).

Goshen-Gottstein, M., 'Yod Gimmel ha-Ikkarim le-ha-Rambam be-Targum al-Ḥarizi', *Tarbiz*, xxvi (1957), pp. 185–96.

Gross, Henri, *Gallia Judaica* (Amsterdam, Philo Press, 1969).

Gross, J., 'Notice sur Abba Mari de Lunel', *REJ*, iv (1882), pp. 192–207.

Guttmann, Jakob, *Die Religionsphilosophischen Lehren des Isaak Abravanel* (Breslau, 1916).

—— 'Die Stellung des Simeon ben Zemah Duran in der jüdischen Religionsphilosophie', *MGWJ*, lii (1908), pp. 641–72 and liii (1909), pp. 46–79 and 199–228.

Guttmann, Yiẓhak Julius, 'Ba'ayat ha-Beḥirah ha-Ḥofshit be-Mishnatam shel Ḥasdai Crescas ve-ha-Aristotelaim ha-Muslamim', *Dat u-Madda* (Jerusalem, Magnes Press, 1979), pp. 149–68.

—— 'Le-Ḥeker ha-Mekorot shel Sefer ha-Ikkarim', *Dat u-Madda* (Jerusalem, Magnes Press, 1955), pp. 169–91.

—— *Philosophies of Judaism* (New York, Anchor Books, 1964).

Halevi, Judah, *Kuzari*, ed. H. Hirschfeld (Leipzig, 1887).

Halkin, A. S., *Be-Ikvot Rambam* (Jerusalem, Merkaz Zalman Shazar, 1979).

—— 'A Karaite Creed', *Studies in Judaica, Karaitica, and Islamica Presented to Leon Nemoy*, ed. S. R. Brunswick (Ramat Gan, Bar Ilan University Press, 1982), pp. 145–53.

Hananel ben Hushiel, *Perush Rabbenu Hananel al ha-Torah*, ed. C. D. Chavel (Jerusalem, Mossad ha-Rav Kook, 1972).

Harnack, Adolph, *History of Dogma* (New York, Dover, 1961).

Hartman, David, '"Iggeret ha-Shmad" le-Rabbenu Moshe ben Maimon', *Jerusalem Studies in Jewish Thought*, ii (1982–3), pp. 362–403.

—— *Maimonides: Torah and Philosophic Quest* (Philadelphia, Jewish Publication Society, 1976).

—— 'Sinai and Messianism', *Joy and Responsibility* (Jerusalem, Posner, 1978), pp. 232–58.

Harvey, Warren Zev, 'Albo's Discussion of Time', *JQR*, lxx (1979–80), pp. 210–30.

—— 'Bein Philosophiah Medinit le-Halakhah be-Mishnat ha-Rambam', *Iyyun*, xxix (1980), pp. 198–212.

—— 'Crescas, Hasdai', *Encyclopaedia Judaica* (Jerusalem, Keter, 1971), vol. v, cols. 1080–85.

—— 'Hasdai Crescas' Critique of the Theory of the Acquired Intellect', Ph.D. diss. (Columbia University, 1973).

—— 'Le-Zihuiy Mehabran shel Histaiguyot min ha-Determinism be-Sefer Or Ha-Shem le-R. Hasdai Crescas — Edut Ketav Yad Firenze', *Kiryat Sefer*, lv (1980), pp. 794–801.

—— 'R. Hasdai Crescas u-Vikorto al ha-Osher ha-Philosophi', *Proceedings of the Sixth World Congress of Jewish Studies* (Jerusalem, World Congress of Jewish Studies, 1977), iii. 143–9.

—— 'A Third Approach to Maimonides' Cosmogony-Prophetology Puzzle', *Harvard Theological Review*, lxxiv (1981), pp. 287–301.

Heller-Wilensky, Sara, *Rabbi Yizhak Arama u-Mishnato* (Jerusalem, Mossad Bialik, 1956).

Henoch, Chayim, *Ha-Ramban ke-Hoker u-ke-Mekubbal* (Jerusalem, Makhon Harry Fischel, 1978).

Herring, Basil, *Joseph ibn Caspi's Gevia Kesef* (New York, Ktav, 1982).

Hershler, Moshe, 'Sha'arei Bet ha-Mikdash le-Rabbenu David ben Shmuel me-Estella (ha-Kokhavi)', *Sinai*, lxii (1968), pp. 199–228.

Hershman, Abraham M., *Rabbi Isaac ben Sheshet Perfet and his Times* (New York, Jewish Theological Seminary, 1943).

Hirsch, Emil G., 'Albo, Joseph', *Jewish Encyclopedia* (New York, 1901), i. 324–7.

Hirschfeld, Hartwig, 'Creed (Jewish)', *Encyclopedia of Religion and Ethics*, vol. iv (New York, Scribners, 1955), pp. 244–6.

Holzer, J., *Zur Geschichte der Dogmenlehre in der jüdischen Religionsphilosophie des Mittelalters: Môse Maimunis Einleitung zu Chelek* (Berlin, M. Poppelauer, 1901).

Horowitz, Yehoshua, 'Halakhot Gedolot', *Encyclopaedia Judaica* (Jerusalem, Keter, 1971), vii, cols. 1167–70.

Hyman, Arthur, 'Maimonides' "Thirteen Principles"', *Jewish Medieval and Renaissance Studies*, ed. A. Altmann (Cambridge, Mass., Harvard University Press, 1967), pp. 119–44.

Ibn Bilia, David, *Yesodot ha-Maskil*, in *Divrei Ḥakhamim*, ed. Eliezer Askenasi (Metz, 1849).

Ibn Kaspi, Joseph, *Maskiyyot Kesef*, ed. S. Werbluner (Frankfurt, 1848). Repr. in *Sheloshah Kadmonei Mefarshei ha-Moreh* (Jerusalem, 1961).

Ign Shaprut, Shem Tov ben Yizhak, *Even Bohan*.

Ibn Tibbon, Samuel, *Ma'amar Yikkavu ha-Mayim*, ed. J. Bisseliches (Pressburg, 1837).

Ibn Zaddik, Joseph, *Sefer ha-Olam ha-Katan*, ed. S. Horowitz (Breslau, 1903; repr. Jerusalem, n.d.).

Idelson, A. Z., *Jewish Liturgy and its Development* (New York, Shocken, 1972).

Isaac ben Joseph of Corbeil, *Sefer Mizvot Kazer* [*Ammudei Golah*] (Jerusalem, 1960).

Jacobs, Louis, *Faith* (New York, Basic Books, 1968).

—— *Principles of the Jewish Faith* (New York, Basic Books, 1964).

Jaulus, Heinrich, 'Simon ben Zemach Duran', *MGWJ*, xxiii (1874), pp. 241–59, 308–17, 355–66, 398–412, 447–63, and 499–514.

Joel, I., *Torat ha-Philosophiah ha-Datit shel R. Ḥasdai Crescas* (Tel Aviv, 1927).

Kaminka, Aharon, *Kitvei Bikkoret Historit* (New York, Sefarim, 1944).

Karo, Joseph, *Kesef Mishnah*.

Kaufman [Even Shmuel], Yehudah, *R. Yom Tov Lippman Muelhausen* (New York, 1927).

Kaufmann, David, 'Jehuda ha-Levi on the Dogmas of Judaism', *JQR* (OS), i (1889), pp. 441–2.

[?] Kayyara, Simeon, *Halakhot Gedolot*.

Kellner, M. M., 'Dogma in Medieval Jewish Thought: A Bibliographical Survey', *Studies in Bibliography and Booklore*, xv (1984), pp. 5–21.

—— 'Jewish Dogmatics After the Spanish Expulsion: Rabbis Isaac Abravanel and Joseph Ya'beṣ on Belief in Creation as an Article of Faith', *JQR*, lxxii (1982), pp. 178–87.

—— 'Kefirah be-Shogeg be-Hagut Yehudit biymei ha-Benayim: ha-Rambam ve-Abravanel Mul Rashbaz ve-Raḥak?' *Jerusalem Studies in Jewish Thought*, iii (1984), pp. 393–403.

—— 'Maimonides "Thirteen Principles" and the Structure of the *Guide of the Perplexed*', *Journal of the History of Philosophy*, xx, no. 1 (Jan. 1982), pp. 76–84.

—— 'R. Isaac Abravanel on Maimonides' Principles of Faith', *Tradition*, xviii (1980), pp. 343–56.

—— 'R. Isaac Abravanel on the Principles of Judaism', *Journal of the American Academy of Religion*, xliv (supplement) (1977), pp. 1183–200.

—— 'R. Isaac bar Sheshet's Responsum Concerning the Study of Greek

Philosophy', *Tradition*, xv, no. 3 (1975), pp. 110–18 and *Tradition*, xv, no. 4 (1976), pp. 134.

—— 'R. Levi ben Gerson: A Bibliographical Essay', *Studies in Bibliography and Booklore*, xii (1979), pp. 13–23.

—— 'R. Shimon ben Ẓemaḥ Duran on the Principles of Judaism', *PAAJR*, xlviii (1981), pp. 231–65.

—— 'What is Heresy?' *Studies in Jewish Philosophy*, iii (1983), pp. 55–70.

Klein, F. A., *The Religion of Islam* (London, Curzon, 1971).

Klein-Braslavy, Sara, 'Ma'amad Har Sinai be-Mishnato shel R. Nissim ben Reuven Gerondi (ha-Ran)', *Sinai*, lxxx (1977), pp. 26–37.

—— *Perush ha-Rambam le-Sippur Ma'aseh Bereshit* (Jerusalem, Israel Bible Society, 1978).

—— 'Terumato shel R. Nissim Gerondi le-Iẓuvan shel Torot ha-Ikkarim shel Ḥasdai Crescas ve-shel Yosef Albo', *Eshel Beer Sheva*, ii (1980), pp. 177–97.

Kobler, Franz, *Letters of the Jews Through the Ages* (London, East and West Library, 1952).

Kokhavi, David, *Kiryat Sefer*, ed. M. J. Blau (New York, 1968).

—— *Migdal David*, ed. Moshe Hershler (Jerusalem, Schalem, 1982).

—— [Untitled Chronicle], in *Medieval Jewish Chronicles*, ed. A. Neubauer (Oxford, Oxford University Press, 1895), pp. 230–3.

Kraemer, Joel L., 'Alfarabi's *Opinions of the Virtuous City* and Maimonides' *Foundations of the Law*', *Studia Orientalia* (D. H. Baneth Memorial Volume), ed. J. Blau, *et al.* (Jerusalem, Magnes Press, 1979), pp. 107–52.

—— 'Heresy vs. the State in Medieval Islam', *Studies in Judaica, Karaitica, and Islamica Presented to Leon Nemoy*, ed. S. R. Brunswick (Ramat Gan, Bar Ilan University Press, 1982), pp. 167–80.

Lambert, M. D., *Medieval Heresy* (London, Edward Arnold, 1977).

Lasker, Daniel, J., 'Aḥarit ha-Adam ba-Philosophiah ha-Kara'it', *Da'at*, xii (1984), pp. 5–13.

—— 'Hashpa'at ha-Rambam al Maḥshavto ha-Philosophit shel ha-Kara'i Elijah Bashyaẓi', *Jerusalem Studies in Jewish Thought*, iii (1984), pp. 405–25.

—— *Jewish Philosophical Polemics Against Christianity in the Middle Ages* (New York, Ktav, 1977).

—— 'Rabbinism and Karaism: The Contest for Supremacy', *Great Schisms in Jewish History*, ed. R. Jospe and S. W. Wagner (New York, Ktav, 1981), pp. 47–72.

Lazaroff, Allan, *The Theology of Abraham Bibago* (University of Alabama Press, 1981).

Leff, Gordon, *Heresy in the Later Middle Ages* (Manchester, Manchester University Press, 1967).

Lerner, Ralph, 'Natural Law in Albo's *Book of Roots*', *Ancients and Moderns*, ed. J. Cropsey (New York, Basic Books, 1964), pp. 132–47.

Lewis, Bernard, *Islam in History* (London, Alcove Press, 1973).

Lieberman, Saul, *Hilkhot ha-Yerushalmi le-ha-Rambam* (New York, Jewish Theological Seminary, 1947).

Lutzky, M., 'Ve-Katav Mosheh: Ḥamesh Teshuvot Autographiot shel ha-Rambam', *Ha-Tekufah*, xxx–xxxi (1946), pp. 679–704.

Maccoby, Hyam, *Judaism on Trial* (East Brunswick, NJ, Associated University Presses for the Littman Library of Jewish Civilization, 1982).

Maimonides, Moses, *Book of Commandments*, trans. Charles B. Chavel (London, Soncino, 1967).

—— *The Book of Judges*, trans. A. Hershman (New Haven, 1949).

—— *Book of Knowledge*, ed. and trans. Moses Hyamson (New York, Feldheim, 1974).

—— [*Book of Knowledge*] *Sefer ha-Madda*, ed. S. Lieberman (Jerusalem, Mossad ha-Rav Kook, 1964).

—— *Maimonidis Commentarius in Mischnam*, ed. Solomon D. Sassoon (Copenhagen, Ejnar, Munksgaard, 1961).

—— 'Eight Chapters', *A Maimonides Reader*, ed. I. Twersky (New York, Behrman House, 1972), pp. 361–86.

—— *Ethical Writings of Maimonides*, trans. R. L. Weiss and C. E. Butterworth (New York, New York University Press, 1975).

—— *The Guide of the Perplexed*, trans. S. Pines (Chicago, University of Chicago Press, 1963).

—— *Iggerot ha-Rambam*, ed. and trans. J. Kafiḥ (Jerusalem, Mossad ha-Rav Kook, 1972).

—— 'Letter on Astrology', trans. Ralph Lerner, *Medieval Political Philosophy*, ed. Ralph Lerner and Muhsin Mahdi (Ithaca, Cornell University Press, 1972), pp. 227–36.

—— *Letters of Maimonides*, trans. Leon D. Stitskin (New York, Yeshiva University Press, 1977).

—— *Ma'amar ha-Yiḥud*, ed. Moritz Steinschneider (Berlin, 1847).

—— *Millot ha-Higayon*, ed. and trans. Israel Efros (New York, American Academy for Jewish Research, 1938).

—— *Mishnah im Perush Rabbenu Moshe ben Maimon*, ed. and trans. J. Kafiḥ (Jerusalem, Mossad ha-Rav Kook, 1963).

—— *Mishneh Torah.*

—— *Moreh Nevukhim*, trans. J. Kafiḥ (Jerusalem, Mossad ha-Rav Kook, 1972).

—— *Pirkei Moshe*, ed. S. Muntner (Jerusalem, Mossad ha-Rav Kook, 1959).

—— *Porta Mosis*, ed. Edward Pococke (Oxford, 1655).

—— *Responsa*, ed. Joshua Blau, *et al.* (Jerusalem, 1957).

—— *Sefer ha-Ma'or: Ozar ha-Hakdamot*, ed. Mordecai Dov Rabinovitch (Tel Aviv, Rishonim, 1948; reissued Jerusalem, Mossad ha-Rav Kook, 1961).

—— *Sefer ha-Mizvot*, ed. and trans. J. Kafih (Jerusalem, Mossad ha-Rav Kook, 1971).

—— *Sefer ha-Mizvot*, ed. Chaim Heller (Jerusalem, Mossad ha-Rav Kook, 1946).

—— *Selections from the Arabic Writings of Maimonides*, ed. Israel Friedlaender (Leiden, Brill, 1909 and 1951).

—— *Teshuvot ha-Rambam*, ed. Joshua Blau, 3 vols. (Jerusalem, Mekize Nirdamim, 1957–61).

Mansour, Menachem, 'Translator's Introduction', in Bahya ben Joseph ibn Paquda, *The Book of Directions to the Duties of the Heart* (London, Routledge and Kegan Paul for the Littman Library of Jewish Civilization, 1973).

Marx, Alexander, 'The Correspondence Between the Rabbis of Southern France and Maimonides about Astrology', *HUCA*, iii (1926), pp. 311–58.

—— 'A List of Poems on the Articles of the Creed', *JQR*, ix (1919), pp. 305–36.

Mesch, Barry, 'Principles of Judaism in Maimonides and Joseph ibn Caspi', *Mystics, Philosophers, and Politicians: Essays in Jewish Intellectual History in Honor of Alexander Altmann*, ed. J. Reinharz and D. Swetschinski (Durham, NC, Duke University Press, 1982), pp. 85–98.

—— *Studies in Joseph ibn Caspi* (Leiden, 1975).

Messer Leon, David ben Judah, *Magen David*. MS Montefiore 290 (Jews College, London).

—— *Tehillah le-David* (Constantinople, 1576).

Mihaly, Eugene, 'Isaac Abravanel on the Principles of Faith', *HUCA*, xxvi (1955), pp. 481–502.

Muelhausen, Yom Tov Lippmann, *Sefer ha-Nizzahon* (Altdorf, 1644; photo-edition, New York, MP Press, 1979; second photo-edition with introduction by Frank Talmage, Jerusalem, Merkaz Dinur, 1984).

Nahmanides, Moses, *Commentary on the Torah*, trans. C. D. Chavel (New York, Shilo, 1971).

—— *Kitvei Ramban*, ed. C. D. Chavel (Jerusalem, Mossad ha-Rav Kook, 1963).

—— *Ramban: Writings and Discourses*, trans. C. D. Chavel (New York, Shilo, 1978).

Netanyahu, Benzion, *Don Isaac Abravanel*, 3rd edn (Philadelphia, Jewish Publication Society, 1972).

—— *The Marranos of Spain* (New York, American Academy for Jewish Research, 1966).

Neubauer, Adolf, 'Documents inédits XIV: David Kokhabi', *REJ*, ix (1884), pp. 214–30.

Neumark, David, *Geschichte der jüdischen Philosophie des Mittelalters*, vol. i (Berlin, 1907).

—— *Toledot ha-Ikkarim be-Yisrael* (Odessa, Moriah, 1919 and 1921).

Nigal, G., De'otav shel R. Yosef Yavez al ha-Philosophiah ve-ha-Mitpalsephim, Torah, u-Mizvot', *Eshel Beer Sheva*, i (1976), pp. 258–87.

—— 'Rabbi Yosef Yavez: Perakim be-Mishnato', MA thesis (Hebrew University, 1960).

Nissim ben Reuben Gerondi, *Derashot ha-Ran*, ed. Leon A. Feldman (Jerusalem, Shalem, 1973).

—— *Perush ha-Ran al ha-Torah*, ed. Leon A. Feldman (Jerusalem, Shalem, 1968).

Nuriel, Abraham, '"Dibrah Torah Ki-lshon Benei Adam" be-*Moreh Nevukhim*', *Dat ve-Safah*, ed. A. Kasher and M. Hallamish (Tel Aviv, University Publications, 1981), pp. 97–103.

—— 'Hiddush ha-Olam o Kadmuto al pi ha-Rambam', *Tarbiz*, xxxiii (1964), pp. 372–87.

—— 'Mishnato ha-Philosophit shel R. Abraham ben Shem Tov Bibago', Ph.D. diss. (Hebrew University, 1975).

—— 'Musag ha-Emunah ezel ha-Rambam', *Da'at*, ii–iii (1979), pp. 43–7.

Pachter, Mordecai, 'Safrut ha-Derush ve-ha-Musar bi-Zefat ba-Me'ah ha-Shesh-Esreh', Ph.D. diss. (Hebrew University, 1976).

Pearl, Chaim, *The Medieval Jewish Mind: The Religious Philosophy of Isaac Arama* (London, Vallentine, Mitchell, 1971).

Pelikan, Jaroslav, *The Growth of Medieval Theology (600–1300)* (Chicago, University of Chicago Press, 1978).

Pines, Shlomo, 'The Limitations of Human Knowledge According to al-Farabi, ibn Bajja, and Maimonides', *Studies in Medieval Jewish History and Literature*, ed. I. Twersky (Cambridge, Mass., Harvard University Press, 1979), pp. 82–96.

—— 'Shi'ite Terms and Conceptions in Judah Halevy's *Kuzari*', *Jerusalem Studies in Arabic and Islam*, ii (1980), pp. 165–219.

—— *Toledot ha-Philosophiah ha-Yehudit me-ha-Rambam ad Spinoza* (Jerusalem, Akadamon, 1976–7).

—— 'Translator's Introduction: The Philosophic Sources of *The Guide of the Perplexed*', *The Guide of the Perplexed*, trans. S. Pines (Chicago, University of Chicago Press, 1963).

Rabinovitch, Nachum L., *Yad Peshutah* (Jerusalem, Feldheim, 1977).

Rahman, Fazlur, 'Some Key Ethical Concepts of the *Qu'ran*', *Journal of Religious Ethics*, xi (1983), pp. 170–85.

Ravitzky, Aviezer, 'Hitpathut Hashkafotav shel R. Hasdai Crescas bi-She'elat Hofesh ha-Razon', *Tarbiz*, li (1982), pp. 445–69.

—— 'Kefi Ko'aḥ ha-Adam — Yemot ha-Mashiaḥ be-Mishnat ha-Rambam', *Meshiḥiut ve-Eschatalogiah*, ed. Zvi Baras (Jerusalem, Merkaz Zalman Shazar, 1983), pp. 191–220.

—— 'Ketav Nishkaḥ le-R. Ḥasdai Crescas', *Kiryat Sefer*, li (1975), pp. 705–11.

—— 'Mishnato shel R. Zeraḥiah ben Shealtiel Ḥen ve-he-Hagut ha-Maimonit-Tibbonit ba-Me'ah ha-Yod Gimmel', Ph.D. diss. (Hebrew University, 1977).

—— 'Zehuto ve-Gilgulav shel Ḥibbur Philosophi she-Yuḥas le-R. Michael ben Shabbtai Balbo', *Kiryat Sefer*, lvi (1980), pp. 153–63.

Rawidowicz, Simon, 'Ba'ayat ha-Hagshamah la-Rasag u-la-Rambam', *Iyyunim be-Maḥshevet Yisrael*, i, ed. B. Ravid (Jerusalem, Rubin Mass, 1969), pp. 171–233.

—— 'On Maimonides' *Sefer ha-Madda*', in his *Studies in Jewish Thought* (Philadelphia, Jewish Publication Society, 1974), pp. 317–23.

—— 'She'elat Mivnehu shel *Moreh Nevukhim*', *Iyyunim be-Maḥshevet Yisrael*, i, ed. B. Ravid (Jerusalem, Rubin Mass, 1969), pp. 237–96.

Rosenberg, Shalom, 'Emunah ve-Kategoriot Epistimiot ba-Hagut ha-Yehudit ha-Beinaimit', *Derakhim le-Emunah be-Yahadut* (Jerusalem, Ministry of Education, 1980), pp. 85–101.

—— 'Ḥeker ha-Mikra ba-Maḥashavah ha-Yehudit ha-Ḥadashah', *Ha-Mikra ve-Anaḥnu*, ed. Uriel Simon (Tel Aviv, Dvir, 1979), pp. 86–119.

—— 'Hitgalut ve-Torah min ha-Shamayim', *Hagut u-Mikra* (Jerusalem, Ministry of Education and Culture, 1977), pp. 13–25.

Sa'adia Gaon, *Book of Beliefs and Opinions*, trans. S. Rosenblatt (New Haven, 1948).

Sarachek, Joseph, *Don Isaac Abravanel* (New York, Bloch, 1938).

—— *Faith and Reason: The Conflict over the Rationalism of Maimonides* (New York, Hermon Press, 1970).

Schechter, Solomon, 'The Dogmas of Judaism', *Studies in Judaism* (Philadelphia, Jewish Publication Society, 1905), pp. 147–81.

—— 'Notes sur Messer David Leon', *REJ*, xxiv (1892), pp. 118–38.

Scholem, Gershom, *Jewish Gnosticism, Merkabah Mysticism and Talmudic Traditions* (New York, Jewish Theological Seminary, 1960).

—— *Major Trends in Jewish Mysticism* (New York, 1941).

—— 'Towards an Understanding of the Messianic Idea in Judaism', *The Messianic Idea in Judaism* (New York, Schocken, 1971).

Schorr, J. H., 'Mavo le-Perek Ḥelek', *He-Ḥaluz*, xii (1887), pp. 104–11.

Schwarzschild, Steven S., 'A Note on the Nature of Ideal Society . . . A Rabbinic Study', *Jubilee Volume Dedicated to Curt C. Silberman*, ed. H. A. Strauss and H. G. Reissner (New York, American Federation of Jews from Central Europe, 1969), pp. 86–105.

Schweid, Eliezer, 'Bein Mishnat ha-Ikkarim shel R. Yosef Albo le-

Mishnat ha-Ikkarim shel ha-Rambam', *Tarbiz*, xxxiii (1963–4), pp. 74–84.

—— *Ha-Philosophiah ha-Datit shel R. Ḥasdai Crescas* (Jerusalem, Makor, 1970).

—— 'Ẓidukan ha-Ḥinukhi ve-ha-Medini shel Miẓvot ha-Emunah le-fi Mishnat ha-Rambam', *Ta'am ve-Hakashah* (Ramat Gan, Massada, 1970), pp. 80–104.

Seeskin, Kenneth, 'Judaism and the Linguistic Interpretation of Jewish Faith', *Studies in Jewish Philosophy*, iii (1983), pp. 71–81.

Septimus, Bernard, *Hispano-Jewish Culture in Transition: The Career and Controversies of Ramah* (Cambridge, Mass., Harvard University Press, 1982).

Shalom, Abraham, *Neveh Shalom* (Venice, 1575; repr. Westmead, England, 1969).

Silver, Daniel J., *Maimonidean Criticism and the Maimonidean Controversy: 1180–1240* (Leiden, E. J. Brill, 1965).

Sirat, Colette, *Hagut Philosophit biymei ha-Benayim* (Jerusalem, Keter, 1975).

—— 'Mikhtav al Beriat ha-Olam li-Shemariah ben Elia Ikriti', *Eshel Beer Sheva*, ii (1980), pp. 199–228.

Soloveitchik, Haym, 'Maimonides' *Iggeret ha-Shemad*: Law and Rhetoric', *Rabbi J. H. Lookstein Memorial Volume*, ed. Leo Landman (New York, Ktav, 1980), pp. 281–319.

Sonne, Isaiah, 'A Scrutiny of the Charges of Forgery Against Maimonides' "Letter on Resurrection"', *PAAJR*, xxi (1952), pp. 101–17.

Staub, Jacob, *The Creation of the World According to Gersonides* (Chico, Calif., Scholars Press, 1982).

Steinschneider, Moritz, *Hebraeische Bibliographie* (*Ha-Mazkir*), vol. viii (Berlin, 1865).

—— *Die Hebraeischen Handschriften der K. Hof-und Staatsbibliothek in Muenchen* (Munich, 1895).

Stern, S. M., 'Perush ha-Mishnah bikhtav Yado shel ha-Rambam', *Tarbiz*, xxiii (1952), pp. 72–80.

—— and S. D. Sassoon, 'Al Tofes Perush ha-Mishnah be-Eẓem Ktav Yado shel ha-Rambam', *Tarbiz*, xxix (1960), pp. 261–7.

Stieglitz, Ya'akov, 'Yod-Gimmel ha-Ikkarim le-ha-Rambam', *Sinai*, lviii (1965), pp. 58–61.

Strack, Hermann L., *Introduction to the Talmud and Midrash* (Philadelphia; Jewish Publication Society, 1931).

Strauss, Leo, 'How to Begin to Study the *Guide of the Perplexed*', *The Guide of the Perplexed*, trans. S. Pines (Chicago, University of Chicago Press, 1963), pp. xi–lvi.

—— 'The Literary Character of the *Guide of the Perplexed*', *Essays on*

Maimonides, ed. S. W. Baron (New York, Columbia University Press, 1941), pp. 37–91.

—— 'On Abravanel's Philosophical Tendency and Political Teachings', *Isaac Abravanel: Six Lectures*, ed. J. B. Trend and H. Loewe (Cambridge, Cambridge University Press, 1937), pp. 95–129.

—— 'Progress or Return? The Contemporary Crisis in Western Civilization', *Modern Judaism*, i (1981), pp. 17–34.

Taenzer, Arnold, *Die Religionsphilosophie des Joseph Albo* (Pressburg, 1896).

Thomas Aquinas, *Summa Theologiae*, trans. Thomas Gilbey (Cambridge, Cambridge University Press, 1964).

Tirosh-Rothschild, Ḥava, 'Hashpa'at Mishnato shel R. Yehudah Halevy al Haguto shel R. David Messer Leon', *Proceedings of the Eighth World Congress of Jewish Studies, Division C* (Jerusalem, World Union of Jewish Studies, 1982), pp. 79–84.

—— 'Mishnato ha-Philosophit shel R. David ben Yehudah Messer Leon', Ph.D. diss. (Hebrew University, 1978).

Tosefta, ed. M. S. Zukermandel, 2nd edn. (Jerusalem, Bamberger and Wahrman, 1938).

Trani, Moses ben Joseph, *Bet Elohim* (Venice, 1576; Warsaw, 1872).

Twersky, Isadore, 'Aspects of the Social and Cultural History of Provençal Jewry', *Jewish Society Through the Ages*, ed. H. H. Ben-Sasson and S. Ettinger (New York, Schocken, 1971), pp. 185–207.

—— *Introduction to the Code of Maimonides* (New Haven; Yale University Press, 1980).

—— *A Maimonides Reader* (New York, Behrman House, 1972).

—— *Rabad of Posquières*, rev. edn. (Philadelphia, Jewish Publication Society, 1980).

Urbach, E. E., 'Hassagot ha-Rabad bi-Defusim u-ve-Kitvei Yad', *Kiryat Sefer*, xxxiii (1959), pp. 360–75.

—— *The Sages: Their Concepts and Beliefs* (Jerusalem, Magnes Press, 1975).

Urbach, Symcha Bunim, *Mishnato ha-Philosophit shel R. Ḥasdai Crescas* (Jerusalem, World Zionist Organization, 1961).

Wakefield, W. L., and A. P. Evans (eds.), *Heresies of the High Middle Ages* (New York, Columbia University Press, 1969).

Watt, W. Montgomery, '"Akida', *Encyclopedia of Islam*, 2nd edn. (Leiden, Brill, 1960), vol. ii.

—— *Muslim Intellectual: A Study of al-Ghazali* (Edinburgh, Edinburgh University Press, 1963).

Waxman, Meyer, 'Maimonides as Dogmatist', *CCAR Yearbook*, xlv (1935), pp. 397–418.

—— 'Shitato shel R. Yosef Albo be-Ikkarei ha-Dat ve-yiḥusah le-Torot Bnei Doro, R. Ḥasdai Crescas ve-R. Shimon ben Ẓemaḥ Duran', *Ha-*

Tekufah, xxx–xxxi (1946), pp. 712–46. Repr. M. Waxman, *Bi-Shvilei ha-Sifrut ve-ha-Maḥashavah ha-Ivrit* (Tel Aviv, Yavneh, 1956), pp. 135–65.

Wensinck, A. J., *The Muslim Creed* (Cambridge, Cambridge University Press, 1932).

Wolf, Arnold Jacob, 'Maimonides on Human Immortality', *Judaism*, xv (1966), pp. 95–101, 211–16, and 337–42. Repr. in *A Maimonides Reader*, ed. Isadore Twersky (New York, Behrman House, 1972), pp. 401–23.

Wolfson, H. A., 'Additional Notes to the Article on the Classification of Sciences in Medieval Jewish Philosophy', *Studies in the History of Philosophy and Religion*, i (Cambridge, Mass., Harvard University Press, 1973), pp. 546–50.

—— 'The Aristotelian Predicables and Maimonides' Division of Attributes', *Studies in the History of Philosophy and Religion*, ii (Cambridge, Mass., Harvard University Press, 1977), pp. 161–94.

—— 'The Classification of Sciences in Medieval Jewish Philosophy', *Studies in the History of Philosophy and Religion*, i (Cambridge, Mass., Harvard University Press, 1973), pp. 493–545.

—— *Crescas' Critique of Aristotle* (Cambridge, Mass., Harvard University Press, 1929).

—— 'The Double-Faith Theory in Sa'adia, Averroes, and St. Thomas', *Studies in the History of Philosophy and Religion*, i (Cambridge, Mass., Harvard University Press, 1973), pp. 583–618.

—— 'The Jewish Kalam', *Seventy-fifth Anniversary Volume of the JQR* (Philadelphia, Dropsie University, 1967), pp. 544–73.

—— 'Maimonides on Negative Attributes', *Studies in the History and Philosophy of Religion*, ii (Cambridge, Mass., Harvard University Press, 1977), pp. 195–230.

—— *Philo* (Cambridge, Mass., Harvard University Press, 1947).

—— *Philosophy of the Church Fathers*, 3rd edn., rev. (Cambridge, Mass., 1970).

—— *The Philosophy of the Kalam* (Cambridge, Mass., Harvard University Press, 1976).

—— *The Philosophy of Spinoza* (Cambridge, Mass., Harvard University Press, 1934).

—— 'The Terms *Taṣawwur* and *Taṣdiq* in Arabic Philosophy and their Greek, Latin, and Hebrew Equivalents', *Studies in the History and Philosophy of Religion*, i (Cambridge, Mass., Harvard University Press, 1973), pp. 478–92.

Ya'ari, Abraham, 'Perush ha-Mishnah le-ha-Rambam bi-Mekoro', *Kiryat Sefer*, ix (1932–3), pp. 101–9 and 228–35.

Yavez, Joseph, *Ma'amar ha-Aḥdut* ([?] Piotrków, 1862).

—— *Or ha-Ḥayyim* ([?] Piotrków, 1862).

—— *Perush Tehillim*, ed. J. Heilprin (London, Hamadfis, 1952).

—— *Yesod ha-Emunah* ([?] Piotrków, 1862).

Yerushalmi, Yosef H., *From Spanish Court to Italian Ghetto* (New York, Columbia University Press, 1971).

Zacuto, Abraham, *Yuḥasin ha-Shalem*, ed. Z. H. Filipowski (London, 1857), reissued with introduction by A. H. Freimann (Frankfurt, Wahrman, 1924, Jerusalem, 1963).

Zeitlin, Solomon, 'Maimonides', *American Jewish Yearbook*, xxxvii (1935), pp. 61–97.

Zimmels, H. J., *Die Marranen in der rabbinischen Literatur* (Berlin, Rubin Mass, 1932).

Zinberg, Israel, *A History of Jewish Literature*, trans. Bernard Martin, vol. ii (Cleveland, Case Western Reserve University Press, 1973); vol. iii (Philadelphia, Jewish Publication Society, 1973).

General Index

Abba Mari Astruc of Lunel, 66, 69–74, 76, 82, 201; and Duran, 105, 260; and Maimonides, 73, 74; on creation, 70–1, 73, 74; on providence, 70–3, 201; why he posited his principles, 70–3, 201.

Abraham ben David of Posquieres. *See* Rabad

Abravanel, Isaac, 179–95, 206; and Albo, 184, 186–7, 188; and Arama, 282, 283; and Bibago, 176–8, 181; and Crescas, 184, 186–7; and Duran, 107, 186–7, 195, 211–12; and Maimonides, 179, 186–8, 190–1; and Yavez, 283; on commandments and principles, 182; on creation, 29, 184–5, 186, 192, 280; on definition of principles of faith, 181, 186–7, 190, 215; on division of Maimonides' principles, 26, 29–30; on God, incorporeality of, 30, 83; on heresy, 183–4, 195, 209–10, 212; on the masses, 187, 189–90; on Maimonides' principles and other Torah beliefs, 61–2; on the Messiah, 30, 192–3, 214–5, 279, 281; on Mosaic prophecy, 29, 281; on objections to Maimonides' principles, 178–81, 279–81; on prophecy, 30, 184, 281; on resurrection, 30, 194, 279, 281; on reward and punishment, 30, 184, 281; on sectarians, 184, 186, 188, 194, 210; on Torah and philosophy, 187–9, 194–5

Albo, Joseph, 67, 140–56, 207; and Abravanel, 184, 186–7, 188; and Averroës, 103–4, 273; and Bibago, 166, 170, 176; and Crescas, 140, 142, 145–6, 155; and Duran, 142, 143–4, 152–3, 155, 251–2; and Maimonides, 143, 144, 151, 155, 156; on commandments and principles, 142–3, 155; on creation, 145; on definition of principles of faith, 141, 146–9, 150–1; on division of Maimonides' principles, 25, 27; on the eternity of the Torah, 145, 204, 272; on God, incorporeality of, 27, 143, 147, 204; on heresy, 151–5; on the Messiah, 145, 151, 154, 214; on objections to Maimonides' principles, 143, 271; on

prophecy, 27, 144, 147, 148–9, 204, 272; on providence, 27, 143, 144, 147, 148, 203; on resurrection, 27, 214, 273; on revelation, 27, 141, 144, 146, 147, 177, 204, 272; on reward and punishment, 27, 142, 143, 144, 146, 148, 203; on sectarians, 145, 153; on Torah as a science, 149–51

Alexander of Aphrodisias, 44

al-Farabi, 36, 232, 241

al-Harizi, Judah, 219, 246.

am ha-arez. See Masses

anafim, 141, 146–49, 204

angels, 11, 12, 13, 38, 53, 229, 238

anthropomorphists, 233

Aquinas, Thomas, 96, 101, 276

Arama, Isaac, 159–61, 164, 205, 207, 212, 214, 274; and Abravanel, 180, 279, 282, 283; on creation, 160–1, 213; on definition of principles of faith, 159–60; on God, incorporeality of, 159

Arama, Meir, 279

Arieli, Nahum, 31

Aristotle, 4, 29, 71, 72, 73, 96, 108, 140, 238, 259, 266. *See also Posterior Analytics*

Attributes, 12, 24, 27, 30, 32, 43, 50, 57, 84, 170, 176, 182, 272, 280

Averroës, 223, 260; and Albo, 103–4, 273; and Duran, 83, 103–5; 252–3

avot, in Abba Mari, 74, 201, 247; in Duran, 86, 255

Azharot, 112, 118, 265

Bahya ben Asher, 244–5

Bahya ben Joseph ibn Paquda, 7–8, 67, 68, 223, 272

Basyatchi, Elijah ben Moses, 224

Behinat ha-Dat, 197, 283

Ben-Chorin, Scholom, 30

Berman, Lawrence V. 231, 236; on why Maimonides posited his principles, 36–7, 39, 48

Bet Elohim, 198, 285

Bibago, Abraham, 67, 165–78, 205–6; and

Bibago, Abraham (*cont.*)
    Abravanel, 176-8, 181; and Albo, 166,
    170, 176; and Crescas, 175-6; and David
    ben Judah Messer Leon, 197; and Mai-
    monides, 170-5, 176; on creation, 167,
    168; on definition of 'belief', 165; on the
    definition of principles of faith, 169, 175-
    6; on the division of Maimonides' prin-
    ciples, 27-8, 30, 171; on eternity of the
    Torah, 171; on God, incorporeality of, 28,
    171; on heresy, 174; on Messiah, 28, 171,
    172, 173-5; on objections to Maimonides'
    principles, 172; on resurrection, 28, 144,
    171, 173, 174-5; on reward and punish-
    ment, 28, 171, 173; on sectarians, 174,
    184; on Torah as a science, 165, 166-8,
    205
Bittul Ikkarei ha-Nozrim, 262, 269
Book of Commandments, 111, 119, 258, 264
Book of Knowledge, 21, 76, 85, 86, 181, 228,
    264

choice, in Abba Mari, 71, 74; Abravanel,
    280; in Bibago, 172, 173; in Crescas, 110,
    113, 117, 121, 127-9, 130-5, 201, 264,
    266; in David ben Judah Messer Leon,
    284; in Duran, 85, 97; in Kokhavi, 76,
    201; in Maimonides, 35, 53, 57, 58, 60,
    239
Christian(s), Christianity, 2, 4, 35, 80-2, 96,
    101, 108, 161, 174, 175, 193, 196, 215,
    224, 251, 261, 269, 272, 283, 285
commandments and principles, in Abrava-
    nel, 182; in Albo, 142-3, 155; in Crescas,
    128, 138; in Duran, 91-4, 100, 155
community of Israel, in Albo, 152-3; in
    Crescas, 212; in Duran, 88, 91, 212; in
    Maimonides, 16, 17, 20, 46, 208, 222, 227
creation, in Abba Mari, 70-1, 73, 74; in
    Abravanel, 29, 184-5, 186, 192, 280; in
    Albo, 145, 204; in Arama, 160-1, 205,
    213; in Bibago, 167, 168, 205; in Crescas,
    114, 121, 123-4, 127, 137, 203, 266-7; in
    David ben Judah Messer Leon, 198, 206,
    284, 285; in Duran, 57-9, 84, 85, 87-8,
    90-1, 95-6, 97, 203, 254, 258; in Fala-
    quera, 74, 201; in ibn Bilia, 77, 78, 202; in
    Kokhavi, 76, 201; in Maimonides, 29, 32,
    54-61, 225, 237-8, 239, 241; in Muehl-
    hausen, 196, 206; in Shalom, 59, 157, 205;
    in Shemariah, 80, 202; in Yavez, 163. *See
    also* creation, centrality of; creation and
    miracles

creation, centrality of, 206, 213-7, 247; in
    Abravanel 184-5; in Arama, 160-1, 164,
    274; in Bibago, 167-8; in Duran, 95-6; in
    David ben Judah Messer Leon, 198; in
    Shalom, 59, 158, 164; in Yavez, 163, 164
creation and miracles, 51, 90, 193, 238, 267
Crescas, Hasdai, 108-39; and Abravanel,
    184, 186-7; and Albo, 140, 142, 145-6,
    155; and Duran, 108, 137-9; and Maimo-
    nides, 114, 116-21, 124, 125, 132-6, 265;
    and Rabbenu Nissim, 108, 137; on choice,
    110, 113, 117, 121, 127-9, 130-5, 203,
    264, 266; on commandments and princi-
    ples, 127-9, 138; on creation, 114, 121,
    123-4, 127, 137, 203, 266-7; on definition
    of principles of faith, 122-3, 125-7; on
    eternity of Torah, 114, 115, 121, 123, 204;
    on God, incorporeality of, 108, 120, 121,
    203; on heresy, 129-36, 211-2; on Mes-
    siah, 114, 115, 121, 123, 214; on Mosaic
    prophecy, 114, 115, 121, 123, 203; objec-
    tions to Maimonides' principles, 114, 124,
    280; prophecy, 113, 121; providence, 113,
    121, 123, 203, 268; resurrection, 114, 115,
    123, 204, 214; revelation, 121, 122, 126-7,
    128, 138, 155, 203; reward and punish-
    ment, 114, 115, 121, 123, 131, 134, 203;
    sectarian(s), 113, 114, 115, 129, 266, 267

dat, 140, 276
David ben Judah Messer Leon, 67, 197-8,
    206, 212, 214, 276; objections to Maimo-
    nides' principles, 284;
Davidson, Herbert, 238, 266
Delmedigo, Elijah, 67, 197, 206, 283
Derekh Emunah, 27, 66, 165, 166, 167, 168,
    175, 176, 177, 178, 197, 206, 230, 256, 274
dogma, 220; in Islam, 7, 46, 65, 96, 222-3;
    235; in Judaism, 4-6; in religion, 2-4. *See
    also* dogma, defined; dogma, definitions of
dogma, defined, by Abravanel, 181, 186-7,
    190, 215; by Albo, 141, 146-9, 150-1; by
    Arama, 159-60; by Bibago, 169, 175-6;
    by Crescas, 122-3, 125-7; by Duran, 95-
    103; by Maimonides, 17-21, 34, 96
dogma, definitions of: analytic, 125-7; axio-
    matic, 35, 61, 96, 97, 101, 105, 125-6, 138,
    149-51, 176, 186, 215-6; dogmatic, 17-
    21, 35, 62, 65, 96, 102, 186, 187; halakhic,
    38-49; heuristic/pedagogical, 21, 34, 48,
    189, 191; metaphysical, 37-8, 48; politi-
    cal, 36-7, 48
denier, 20, 22-3, 33, 74, 88, 154, 211, 227

d'Estella. *See* Kokhavi
Duran, Shimon ben Ẓemaḥ, 67, 83–107, 202–3; and Abba Mari, 105, 260; and Abravanel, 107, 186–7, 195, 211–12; and Albo, 142, 143–4, 152–4, 155, 251–2; and Averroës, 103–5; and Crescas, 108, 137–9; and Maimonides, 24–7, 49, 53, 57–9, 64, 84–8, 94–5, 97, 98, 102; and Rabbenu Nissim, 108; influence of, 105–7; on commandments and principles, 91–4, 100, 155; on creation, 57–9, 84, 85, 87–8, 90–1, 95–6, 97, 254, 258; on the definition of principles of faith, 95–103; on *epikoros*, 93–4; on eternity of the Torah, 28, 94, 258; on God, incorporeality of, 24, 25, 85, 86, 87, 90, 92, 94, 255, 258; on heresy, 98–100, 102, 104, 106–7, 210–12; on Messiah, 25, 87, 94; on prophecy, 87, 94, 144; on providence, 24, 84, 85, 87, 91, 95, 97, 100, 203, 254, 255, 260; on resurrection, 25, 58–9, 85, 87, 88, 93, 94, 95, 98; on revelation, 24, 84, 86–7, 93–4, 155, 203; on reward and punishment, 25, 58, 85, 87, 93, 94, 95, 97, 102, 144; on sectarians, 88, 89, 92, 93, 255; on Torah as a science, 96, 259–60

Elisha ben Abuyah (Aḥer), 16, 89, 99, 107, 153, 226, 258
Emunah Ramah, 8
Epicurus, 92, 93, 224
epikoros, epikorsim, 10, 16, 220, 227, 255, 258; in Abravanel, 186, 188, 194; in Duran, 24, 25, 93–4, 94–5; in Maimonides, 35–7, 60, 236; in *Mishneh Torah*, 20–1, 22, 33, 34, 243
Eshkol ha-Kofer, 9
eternity of Torah, 15, 24, 25, 28, 94, 279; in Albo, 145, 204, 272; in Bibago, 171; in Crescas, 114, 115, 121, 123, 204; in Duran, 28, 94, 258; in Maimonides, 15, 24, 25, 200; in Shalom, 157

faith, propositional understanding of, 4, 5–6, 18, 207, 213, 217; rabbinic understanding of, 4, 207–8
Falaquera, Shem Tov ben Joseph, 54, 57, 66, 67, 74–5, 201
Ferrer, Vincente, 81
free will. *See* choice

Gersonides, 67, 89, 99, 107, 157, 230, 246, 257, 260, 272, 273

God, corporeality, naive belief in, 92, 183, 209, 256, 258
God, existence, belief in, commanded, 110, 116–20, 127–9
God, incorporeality of, in Abba Mari, 70, 74, 201, 243; in Abravanel, 30, 83; in Albo, 27, 143, 147, 204; in Arama, 159; in Bibago, 28, 171; in Crescas, 108, 120, 121, 203; in Duran, 24, 25, 85, 86, 87, 90, 92, 94, 255, 258; in Maimonides, 11, 26, 38, 40, 41, 43, 45, 47, 50, 200, 227, 236, 237, 239; in Muehlhausen, 196, 206; in Shemariah, 80, 202; in Yavez, 163
Guide of the Perplexed, 17, 18, 27, 30, 31, 32, 38, 39, 44, 47, 53, 54, 56, 57, 61, 63, 65, 85, 88, 89, 98, 109, 120, 133, 190, 235, 236, 237, 239, 240, 241; and Maimonides' thirteen principles, 27, 49–53, 198, 238; part one, chapter thirty-five, 32, 38, 41, 43, 232, 234, 237; part two, chapter twenty-five, 50, 88, 98, 168, 191, 23, 247, 255, 257
Guttmann, Julius (Yizḥak), 103–5, 232, 252, 260, 273

Hadassi, Yehudah, 9, 223
Halakhot Gedolot, 118, 258, 268
Halevi, Judah, 8, 197, 223. *See also Kuzari*
Harvey, Warren Zev, 109, 127, 232, 242, 253, 262–3
Hartman, David, 37, 38
Ḥelek. See Perek Ḥelek
heresy, in Abravanel, 183–4, 195, 209–10, 212; in Albo, 151–2; in Bibago, 174; in Crescas, 129–36, 211–12; in Duran, 98–100, 102, 104, 106–7, 210–12; in Maimonides, 18, 19–21, 208–9, 212; in Rabad, 89, 99, 129, 174, 183, 209, 210–11, 212, 259
Hillel II (R. Hillel), 151, 172, 173, 216, 256, 279, 284
Ḥoter ben Shlomo, 57, 66
Hyman, Arthur, 10, 25, 30, 31, 32, 35, 36, 37, 38, 41, 43, 48, 59, 60, 105, 225, 231, 244

ibn Bilia, David ben Yom Tov, 77–9, 82, 202, 207, 212, 214, 242, 254
ibn David, Abraham, 8, 67
ibn Falaquera. *See* Falaquera
ibn Kaspi, Joseph, 67, 241, 242, 244, 245, 255
ibn Shaprut, Shem Tov ben Yizḥak, 57, 242

ibn Ya'akov, Solomon ben Joseph, 57, 219, 246
ibn Ẓaddik, Joseph, 67, 223
idolatry, 12, 19, 26, 40, 41
Iggeret ha-Ḥalom, 248
ijma, 254
ikkar, ikkarim, 8, 40, 59, 63, 74, 84, 141, 146–8, 150, 152, 157, 158, 166, 181, 189, 191, 205, 223, 226, 256, 260, 271
Islam, 1, 2, 4, 6, 7, 8, 9, 35, 45, 46, 49, 65, 96, 221, 222–3, 235, 272

Jacobs, Louis, 57
Jonathan ben Uzziel, 247
Jew. *See* community of Israel

Kafiḥ, Joseph, 57, 236, 239, 240
Kalam, 4, 213
Karaism, 1, 3, 6, 7, 8, 9, 23, 223–4, 227, 236
Karo, Joseph, 256
kefirah. See heresy
Keshet u-Magen, 96
Klein-Braslavy, Sara, 137, 138, 263
kofer. See denier
Kokhavi, David ben Samuel, 75–6, 82, 201–2, 212, 248–9
Kraemer, Joel, 55
Kuzari, 8, 233, 248, 282

Lasker, Daniel J., 242
'Laws of Repentance' and Maimonides' thirteen principles, 21–4, 32–4, 42, 46, 55, 56, 60, 181, 228, 241, 256
'Letter on Astrology', 239

Ma'amar ha-Aḥdut, 162
Ma'aseh Bereshit, 40, 116
Ma'aseh Merkavah, 50, 51, 116
Ma'ayanei Yeshuah, 193
Mabit, 198–9, 206, 285
Magen Avot, 24, 83, 94–5, 97, 98, 101, 251, 252, 253–4, 255, 260
Magen David, 197, 206
Maimonides, and Abba Mari, 73, 74; and Abravanel, 179, 186–8, 190–1; and Albo, 143, 144, 151, 155, 156; and Bibago, 170–5, 176; and Crescas, 114, 116–21, 124, 125, 132–6, 265; and Duran, 24–7, 49, 53, 57–9, 64, 84–8, 94–5, 97, 98, 102; and Rabad, 89, 92, 99, 174, 209, 256; and Shalom, 158, 164; and Yavez, 162–3, 164; interpretation of, vii, 69; on choice, 35, 53, 57, 58, 60, 239; on community of Israel, 16, 17, 20, 46, 208, 222, 227; on creation, 29, 32, 54–61, 225, 237–8, 239,

241; on deniers, 20, 22–3, 33, 227; on *epikoros*, 35–7, 60, 236; on eternity of the Torah, 15, 24, 25, 200; on God, incorporeality of, 11, 26, 38, 40, 41, 43, 45, 47, 50, 200, 222, 236, 237, 239; on heresy, 18, 19–21, 208–9, 212; on the masses, 32, 36–49, *passim*, 53, 56, 61, 234, 237; on Messiah, 16, 20, 23, 24, 33, 34, 52, 60, 63–5, 243; on Mosaic prophecy, 12–14, 20, 26, 49, 200, 229, 238; on principles of faith, *see* Maimonides' principles of faith; on prophecy, 12, 20, 22, 26, 32, 43, 49, 120, 200, 229, 238; on providence, 15–16, 43, 50, 51–2, 200; on resurrection, 16, 20, 22, 23, 26, 33, 34, 52, 55, 57, 59, 64, 200, 234; on revelation, 14–15, 26, 32, 49, 64, 200, 247; on reward and punishment, 15–16, 23, 26, 32, 48, 50, 52, 60, 64, 200, 234; on sectarians, 22, 40, 86, 89, 92, 209, 227, 255
Maimonides' principles of faith, definition of, 17–21, 34, 96; division of, 24–34, 42–3; in *Guide of the Perplexed*, 49–53; in *Mishneh Torah*, 21–4; missing, 53–61; objections to, in Abravanel, 178–81, 279–81; in Albo, 143, 271; in Bibago, 143, 271; in Crescas, 114, 124, 280; in David ben Judah Messer Leon, 284. *See also, Book of Commandments; Book of Knowledge; Guide of the Perplexed;* 'Laws of Repentance' and the thirteen principles; 'Letter on Astrology'; *Millot ha-Higayon; Mishneh Torah; Perek Ḥelek; Treatise on Resurrection*
masses, in Abravanel, 187, 189–90; in Delmedigo, 197; in ibn Bilia, 78; in Maimonides, 32, 36–49, *passim*, 53, 56, 61, 234, 237
Messiah, 79, 213–17; in Abravanel, 30, 192–3, 214–15, 279, 281; in Albo, 145, 151, 154, 214; in Bibago, 28, 171, 172, 173–5; in Crescas, 114, 115, 121, 123, 214; in Duran, 25, 87, 94; in Maimonides, 16, 20, 23, 24, 33, 34, 52, 60, 63–5, 243; in Rabbenu Ḥananel, 8; in Shemariah, 157, 214; in Yavez, 163. *See* Hillel II
Migdal David, 75, 201, 248–9
Milḥamot Adonai, 89
Millot ha-Higayon, 229
min. See sectarian(s)
Minḥat Kena'ot, 70, 200
Mishneh Torah, 18, 19, 21, 23, 39, 47, 62, 63, 76, 108, 208, 232, 240, 243, 248; Maimonides' principles in, 21–4

Mosaic prophecy, in Abravanel, 29, 281; in
  Albo, 27, 144, 204; in Bibago, 28, 171; in
  Crescas, 114, 115, 121, 123, 204; in David
  ben Judah Messer Leon, 284; in Duran,
  24, 87, 94, 144; in Maimonides, 12–14, 20,
  26, 49, 200, 229, 238; in Yavez, 163
Muehlhausen, Yom Tov Lippmann, 196,
  206, 207, 212
Muslim. *See* Islam

Naḥlat Avot, 193
Naḥmanides, 123, 137, 215, 244–5, 255, 264,
  266
Neumark, David, 30, 35, 46, 48, 57, 220
Ner Elohim, 108, 249, 263
Ner Mizvah, 108
Neveh Shalom, 157
Nissim Gerondi. *See* Rabbenu Nissim
Nuriel, Abraham, 222, 240, 241, 242, 244

Ohev Mishpat, 24, 57, 83, 84, 94, 95, 97, 98,
  101, 203, 211, 251–2
Onkelos, 90, 257
Or Adonai, 108, 109, 110, 116, 122, 123, 129,
  140, 203, 252
Or ha-Ḥayyim, 162

Perek Ḥelek, 10, 19, 22, 23, 33, 37, 47, 48, 54,
  59, 60, 63, 114, 181, 194, 222, 224, 225,
  226, 235, 237, 258
Perfet, Isaac bar Sheshet, 108, 244–5, 260
Philo, 1, 220
Pines, Shlomo, 38, 57, 231–2, 234, 240
pinnot, 109, 121, 126, 175, 203, 265, 269
Plato, 4
poems of the Creed, 244
Posterior Analytics, 96, 150, 259, 276
principles of faith. *See* dogma
prophecy, in Abravanel, 30, 184, 281; in
  Albo, 27, 144, 147, 148–9, 204, 272; in
  Arama, 160, 161, 205; in Bibago, 28, 171;
  in Crescas, 113, 121, 203; in David ben
  Judah Messer Leon, 198, 206, 284; in
  Duran, 87, 94, 144; in Falaquera, 74, 201;
  in ibn Bilia, 77; in Kokhavi, 76, 202; in
  Maimonides, 12, 20, 22, 26, 32, 43, 49,
  120, 200, 229, 238; in Shalom, 157, 205; in
  Yavez, 163
providence, in Abba Mari, 70–73, 201; in
  Albo, 27, 143, 144, 147, 148, 204; in
  Arama, 160, 205; in Bibago, 28, 168, 171,
  173; in Crescas, 113, 121, 123, 203, 268; in

David ben Judah Messer Leon, 197, 206;
  in Duran, 25, 84, 85, 87, 91, 95, 97, 100,
  203, 254, 255, 260; in Falaquera, 75, 201;
  in ibn Bilia, 77; in Kokhavi, 76, 201; in
  Maimonides, 15–16, 43, 50, 51–2, 200; in
  Shalom, 157, 158, 205; in Yavez, 162, 163

Rabad, 57, 89, 92, 129, 132, 174, 183, 209,
  210–11, 212, 233, 241, 256, 273, 277; and
  Maimonides, 89, 92, 99, 174, 209, 256
Rabbenu Ḥananel, 8, 223
Rabbenu Nissim ben Reuben Gerondi, 108,
  137–8, 216, 244–5
Rabinovitch, Nachum, 23, 31, 33
Ravitzky, Aviezer, 246
resurrection, 10, 94, 223, 224; in Abravanel,
  30, 194, 279, 281; in Albo, 27, 194, 273; in
  Bibago, 28, 144, 171, 173, 174–5; in
  Crescas, 114, 115, 123, 204, 214; in David
  ben Judah Messer Leon, 284; in Duran,
  25, 58–9, 85, 87, 88, 93, 94, 95, 98; in
  Kokhavi, 76, 202; in Maimonides, 16, 20,
  22, 23, 26, 33, 34, 52, 55, 57, 64, 200, 234;
  in Shalom, 156, 205; in Yavez, 163
retribution. *See* reward and punishment
revelation, 213, 221, 238; in Albo, 27, 141,
  144, 146, 147, 155, 204, 272; in Arama,
  159, 160, 205; in Bibago, 28, 171; in
  Crescas, 121, 122, 126–7, 128, 138, 155,
  203; in Duran, 24, 84, 86–7, 93–4, 155,
  203; in Kokhavi, 76, 201; in Maimonides,
  14–15, 26, 32, 49, 59, 64, 200, 247; in
  Shalom, 157, 205. *See also* Mosaic prophecy
reward and punishment, in Abravanel, 30,
  184, 281; in Albo, 27, 142, 143, 144, 146,
  148, 203; in Bibago, 28, 171, 173; in
  Crescas, 114, 115, 121, 123, 131, 134, 203;
  in Duran, 25, 58, 85, 87, 93, 94, 95, 97,
  102, 144; in Falaquera, 75, 201; in Kokhavi, 76, 201; in Maimonides, 15–16, 23,
  26, 32, 48, 50, 52, 60, 64, 200, 234; in
  Shalom, 157, 205
Rosenberg, Shalom, 127
Rosh Amanah, 29, 34, 107, 177, 179–95,
  passim, 225, 278, 219

Sa'adia Gaon, 1, 3, 5, 7, 8, 67, 68, 103
Schechter, Solomon, 35, 46, 48
sectarian(s), 207, 212, 256; in Abravanel,
  184, 186, 188, 194, 210; in Albo, 145, 153;
  in Bibago, 174, 184; in Crescas, 113, 114,
  115, 129, 266, 267; in Duran, 88, 89, 92,

sectarian(s) (*cont.*)
  93, 255; in Maimonides, 22, 40, 86, 89, 92,
  209, 227, 255
Seeskin, Kenneth, 6
Sefer Amaziah, 79, 80, 250
Sefer ha-Ikkarim, 105, 140, 141, 148, 149,
  151, 154, 162, 180, 251–2, 270
Sefer ha-Madda. *See* Book of Knowledge
Sefer ha-Mevakkesh, 74
Sefer ha-Mizvot. *See* Book of Command-
  ments
Sefer ha-Nizzahon, 196
Separate Intellects, 51, 78, 86, 202, 238
Shalom, Abraham, 59, 60, 66, 67, 157–8,
  164, 205, 206, 207, 212, 213, 214, 274, 278
Shamayim Hadashim, 185, 192, 193
Shiur Komah, 13, 225, 233
Strauss, Leo, 228, 232, 238, 254

Tehillah le-David, 197, 206
Torah, abrogation of, 15; and philosophy,

43–4, 62–3, 75, 109–110, 187–9, 194–5; as
  a science, 96, 149–51, 166–7, 194
Torah from Heaven. *See* revelation
Tortosa, Disputation of, 80, 140, 251
Trani, Moses ben Joseph. *See* Mabit
Treatise on Resurrection, 47, 48, 55, 57, 233,
  241
Twersky, Isadore, 38, 40, 62–3

Yavez, Joseph, 66, 67, 161–4, 205, 207, 212,
  213, 214
Yeshu'ot Meshiho 193
yesod(ot), 59, 84, 157, 158, 184, 185, 189,
  191, 192, 205
Yesod ha-Emunah 162
Yesodot ha-Maskil, 77, 79, 202, 242, 254

Waxman, Meyer, 30–1

Zacuto, Abraham, 251
Zedek Olamin, 193
Zevah Pesah, 193

Index of Biblical Citations

Genesis
1: 1   91, 167
6: 15   15
10: 6   14
18: 20   15
19: 4   189
20: 3   13
28: 12   13
36: 39   14
47: 19   25, 29

Exodus
12: 2   91
15: 26   10
16: 2   14
20: 2   11, 14, 70, 92, 111, 112, 118, 119, 127
20: 3   111, 112, 118
20: 4   112
20: 5   111, 112
20: 6   111
20: 7   111
20: 11   111
21: 11   71
25: 22   13
31: 17   13
32: 32   16
32: 33   16
33: 11   14

Leviticus
16: 2   14
23: 3   160

Numbers
9: 8   14
12: 6   14
12: 7   14
12: 8   13, 14
15: 31   15
16: 28   15
21: 18   14

Deuteronomy
4: 15   12

4: 35   120
6: 4   11, 15, 89
6: 13   93
32: 9   259
13: 1   15
33: 4   111, 118, 119
33: 27   12
34: 11   167

II Kings
3: 15   14

Isaiah
2: 5   110
2: 6   72
11: 14   11
17: 14   259, 40: 25, 11
40: 26   72
40: 28   72
44: 5   168
60: 21   10, 94

Jeremiah
10: 6   259
18: 6   111, 114
32: 19   15

Ezekiel
8: 3   13
8: 12   15

Habakkuk
2: 3   16
2: 4   88

Zephaniah
3: 9   92

Zachariah
14: 9   77, 92

Malachi
3: 6   71

Psalms
19: 11   77

25: 14   72
119: 18   15
134: 21   16

Proverbs
19: 21   73

Job
8: 19   168
11: 9   15
31: 2   259
33: 15   13
34: 14   184

Lamentations
3: 21   188

Ecclesiastes
5: 11   170

Esther
1: 3   189
10: 8   14

Daniel
10: 16   14

Nehemiah
9: 5   115

II Chronicles
14: 3   245